Malaysia
a country study

Foreign Area Studies
The American University
Edited by
Frederica M. Bunge
Research completed
January 1984

On the cover: Decorative trees and shrubs enhance the architectural style of the Sultan Abdul Samad building, one of the noteworthy edifices in Kuala Lumpur.

Fourth Edition, 1984; First Printing, 1985

Library of Congress Cataloging in Publication Data

Main entry under title:

Malaysia, a country study.

(Area handbook series)
Rev. ed. of: Area handbook for Malaysia/coauthors, Nena Vreeland ... [et al.]. 3rd ed. 1977.
Bibliography: p.
Includes index.
"DA pam 550-45."
1. Malaysia. I. Bunge, Frederica M. II. Vreeland, Nena, 1934- . Area handbook for Malaysia. III. American University (Washington D.C.). Foreign Area Studies. IV. Series.

DS592.M345 1984 959.5'053 84-16790

Headquarters, Department of the Army
DA Pam 550-45

For sale by the Superintendent of Documents, U.S. Government Printing Office
Washington, D.C. 20402

Foreword

This volume is one of a continuing series of books prepared by Foreign Area Studies, The American University, under the Country Studies/Area Handbook Program. The last page of this book provides a listing of other published studies. Each book in the series deals with a particular foreign country, describing and analyzing its economic, national security, political, and social systems and institutions and examining the interrelationships of those systems and institutions and the ways that they are shaped by cultural factors. Each study is written by a multidisciplinary team of social scientists. The authors seek to provide a basic insight and understanding of the society under observation, striving for a dynamic rather than a static portrayal of it. The study focuses on historical antecedents and on the cultural, political and socioeconomic characteristics that contribute to cohesion and cleavage within the society. Particular attention is given to the origins and traditions of the people who make up the society, their dominant beliefs and values, their community of interests and the issues on which they are divided, the nature and extent of their involvement with the national institutions, and their attitudes toward each other and toward the social system and political order within which they live.

The contents of the book represent the views, opinions, and findings of Foreign Area Studies and should not be construed as an official Department of the Army position, policy, or decision, unless so designated by other official documentation. The authors have sought to adhere to accepted standards of scholarly objectivity. Such corrections, additions, and suggestions for factual or other changes that readers may have will be welcomed for use in future new editions.

William Evans-Smith
Director, Foreign Area Studies
The American University
Washington, D.C. 20016

Acknowledgments

The authors are grateful to numerous individuals in the international community, in various agencies of the United States government, and in private organizations in Washingtion, D.C., who gave of their time, research materials, and special knowledge to provide data and perspective for this study. In particular, they wish to thank Dr. Llewellyn D. Howell of the School of International Service of the College of Public and International Affairs at The American University for sharing valuable insights and knowledge, as well as the contents of his personal library and the resources of the university's Center for Asian Studies.

The authors also thank members of the Foreign Area Studies staff who contributed directly to the preparation of the manuscript. These include Dorothy M. Lohmann, Andrea T. Merrill, and Denise Ryan, who edited the manuscript and the accompanying figures and tables; Harriett R. Blood, who prepared the graphics; and Gilda V. Nimer, librarian. The team appreciates as well the assistance provided by Ernest A. Will, publications manager, and Eloise W. Brandt and Wayne W. Olsen, administrative assistants. Margaret Quinn typed the manuscript, with the help of Charlotte B. Pochel, and gave valuable help in various phases of production. Special thanks are owed to Farah Ahannavard, who designed the illustrations for the cover of this volume and for the title pages of the chapters.

The inclusion of photographs in this study was made possible by the generosity of various individuals and private and public agencies. The authors acknowledge their indebtedness to those who offered original work not previously published.

Contents

List of Figures

Preface

Earlier editions of this study were completed in times of considerable ferment in Malaysia. Research for the 1970 edition was conducted in the wake of the violent communal riots of May 1969. The 1976 edition was completed five months after the unexpected death in office of the prime minister, Tun Abdul Razak, and in the aftermath of a series of international events that had radically altered Malaysia's foreign policy environment. As the 1984 edition was undertaken, the situation was relatively settled, although the country's political, economic, and social conditions were undeniably undergoing change. The year 1984, marked by significant constitutional and economic developments, made an appropriate point for reconsidering the course of the country and the aspirations of its people.

Spellings of place-names used in the study conform generally to those in *Gazetteer No. 10: Malaysia, Singapore, and Brunei Official Standard Names* (2d ed.), prepared in the Geographic Names Division of the United States Army Topographic Command and dated November 1970. Certain exceptions include the use of Penang and Malacca instead of Pinang and Melaka. This study has followed the official Malaysian convention of using the term *Malay* to describe the indigenous ethnic group and its language; when referring to citizens without regard to ethnic designation, the text uses the term *Malaysian*. The plural form for most communal groups other than Malay(s) and for Malaysian words has been given without an *s* ending. Unless otherwise noted, weights are presented in metric tons. The reader may refer to the Glossary for United States dollar-Malaysian ringgit equivalents and for definitions of other frequently used terms.

The bewildering array of Malaysian honorific words and titles presented an especially ticklish problem for the authors, who apologize for any inadvertent error in their use of personal names. In determining the order of elements in personal names in both the Bibliography and the Index, the authors have generally followed principles set forth in *Anglo-American Cataloguing Rules* (2d ed.) as well as authoritative alphabetic lists from the country.

Table A. Historical Political Evolution

Date	Event
1786	British acquire island of Penang from sultan of Kedah
1800	Kedah cedes coastal region of Perai (Province Wellesley) to British
1819	Singapore established by Thomas Stamford Raffles
1824	Anglo-Dutch Treaty of 1824 defines British and Dutch spheres of influence; Malacca ceded to British
1826	Straits Settlements established under British East India Company government in India; consists of Singapore (made the capital in 1832), Malacca, Penang, Province Wellesley, and Dindings
1841	James Brooke made raja of Sarawak by sultan of Brunei
1844	Labuan Island off coast of Brunei made part of Straits Settlements
1867	Straits Settlements made crown colony, separate from British India
1874	Treaty of Pangkor establishes British resident in Perak; residents also in Sungai Ujung (in Negeri Sembilan) and Selangor
1881	British North Borneo Company chartered
1888	British resident established in Pahang
1895	Nine states of Negeri Sembilan confederation constituted as single unit under a resident
1896	Federated Malay States, with capital at Kuala Lumpur, organized, consisting of Perak, Negeri Sembilan, Selangor, and Pahang
1909	British treaty with Siam brings states of Terengganu, Kedah, Perlis, and Kelantan into British sphere of influence as Unfederated Malay States
1914	Unfederated Malay State of Johore receives British adviser having extensive powers
1946	Malayan Union proposal; Sarawak and North Borneo (called Sabah as of 1963) made crown colonies
1948	Federation of Malaya established; Singapore a separte crown colony
1957	Federation of Malaya becomes independent state with own constitution
1963	Federation of Malaysia (Malaya, Sarawak, Sabah, and Singapore) established; constitution of Federation of Malaya amended to accomplish merger
1965	Singapore becomes separate state

Source: Based on information from Barbara Watson Andaya and Leonard Y. Andaya, *A History of Malaysia*, New York, 1982; John M. Gullick, *Malaysia: Economic Expansion and National Unity*, Boulder, 1981; and D.G.E. Hall, *A History of South-East Asia*, London, 1964.

Country Profile

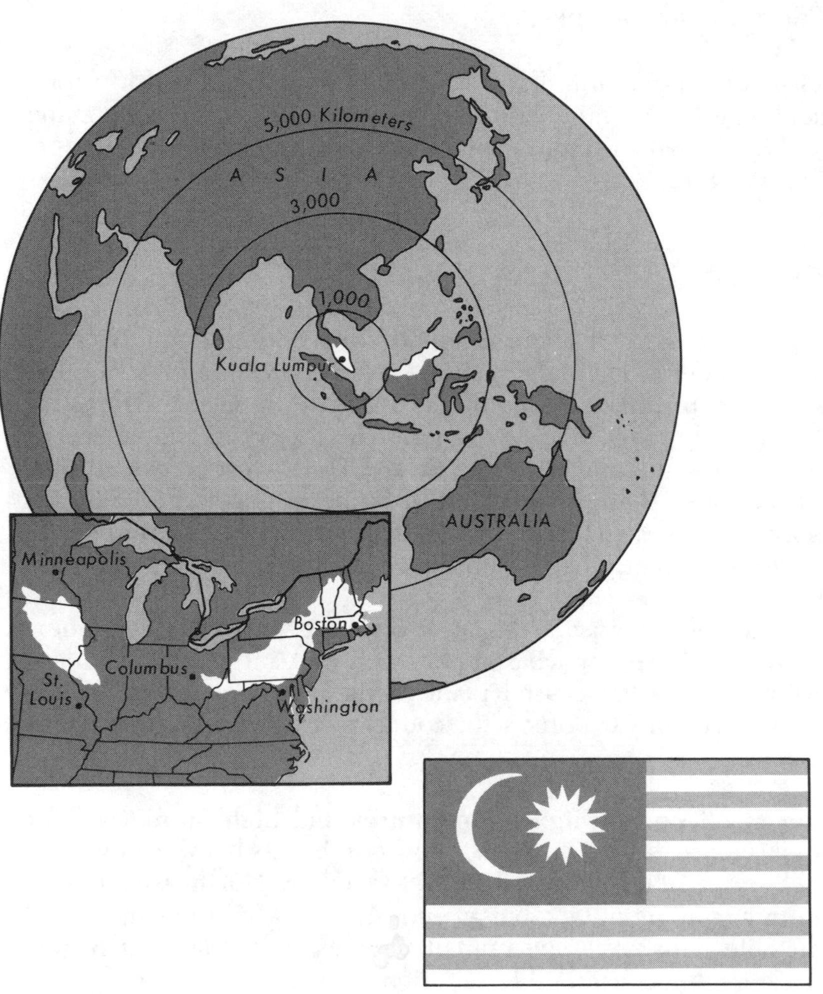

Country

Formal Name: Malaysia.

Term for Citizens: Malaysians.

Preindependence Political Status: British colonies and protectorates. Peninsular Malaysia attained independence as Federation of Malaya on August 31, 1957; states on island of Borneo—Sabah and Sarawak—joined federation to form Malaysia on September 16, 1963.

Capital: Kuala Lumpur.

Flag: 14 horizontal red and white stripes of equal width, representing equal membership in federation of 13 component states and federal government. Yellow crescent and star in blue upper left quadrant.

Geography

Size: Land area of about 330,000 square kilometers. Two regions—Peninsular Malaysia and states of Sabah and Sarawak—separated by some 650 kilometers of South China Sea. Peninsular Malaysia borders Thailand on north; linked to Singapore by causeway south across Johore Strait. To its west across Strait of Malacca lies Indonesian island of Sumatra. Sabah and Sarawak border Indonesian territory of Kalimantan on island of Borneo. To northeast of Sabah lies Philippines.

Topography: Peninsular Malaysia has long, narrow, steep mountain range in center, coastal plains on east and west; Sabah and Sarawak have flat coastal plain rising to mountainous mass in center. About 70 percent of country covered by tropical rain forest.

Climate: Tropical; high temperatures and high humidity. Two monsoon seasons. Southwest monsoon brings heavy, unpredictable rains from mid-April to mid-October. Northeast monsoon from beginning of October to end of February brings more predictable rains. Average rainfall between 2,000 and 2,540 millimeters, but considerable variation according to location.

Society

Population: 1980 census reported 13,137,000. Of total population 956,000 in Sabah, 1,236,000 in Sarawak, and remainder in Peninsular Malaysia. Average annual growth rate in Peninsular

Malaysia during 1970-80 period 2.2 percent. Urban percentage of population 34 percent for country as a whole; 37 percent in Peninsular Malaysia, 21 percent in Sabah, and 18 percent in Sarawak.

Ethnic Composition and Language: 1980 census reported 6,132,000 Malays, 3,651,000 Chinese, 1,093,000 Indians, and 69,000 others for Peninsular Malaysia. Majority of populations of Sarawak and Sabah made up of indigenous people. Malay (Bahasa Malaysia) official language. Numerous Chinese languges and dialects and Tamil, respectively, used by Chinese and Indian communities. English widely used in government and business.

Religion: Malays are Muslims; official religion is Islam. Buddhism, Confucianism, and Taoism of major importance in Chinese community. Hinduism the faith of most Indians; Christianity embraced by small number of adherents.

Education: Educational ladder follows British system with six-year primary level (Standards 1-6), five-year secondary level (lower secondary; Forms 1-3), and middle secondary (Forms 4 and 5). Students may go on to teaching, technical, or agricultural colleges or enter two-year preuniversity preparatory course (Form 6; upper and lower divisions). Malay, Chinese, and Tamil mediums of instruction in primary schools. Malay main medium of instruction in all secondary schools up to Form 6. English retained as compulsory second language in all schools. Five universities and other higher level institutions are increasing enrollments.

Health: Marked improvement during 1960s and 1970s. Mortality rates declining as result of increasing availability of medical treatment in hospitals, dispensaries, and clinics using up-to-date techniques, drugs, and equipment. Major public health problems, such as malaria, dengue fever, cholera, and filariasis, being effectively attacked. Nutrition, family health, and environmental sanitation also subject of government programs.

Economy

Gross National Product (GNP): Equivalent to US$1,792 per person in 1982 and estimated US$1,877 in 1983. Per capita GNP net of inflation grew by more than 5 percent per year during 1970-81 but by only 3 percent in 1982. Revived in 1983 but highly dependent on international trends. Private individuals and corporations contributed three-fourths of GNP in 1982; rapidly expanding public sector accounted for 43 percent of GNP growth after 1975. Investment constituted 36.4 percent of GNP in 1982, about equally divided between public and private sectors. Some 13 percent of gross domestic product (GDP—see Glossary), however, left country to cover current account deficit in 1982.

Agriculture, Forestry, and Fishing: Produced 24 percent of GDP and 38 percent of employment in 1982 but created only 19 percent of GDP growth and 3 percent of new employment after 1975. Smallholder farms predominate; large estates growing commercial crops important but decreasing in size. Major products: rice, rubber, palm oil, coconuts, pepper, and tropical hardwood.

Industry: Manufacturing, mining, construction, and utilities made up 30 percent of GDP and 23 percent of employment in 1982 but contributed about 37 percent of growth of GDP and employment after 1975. Mining employment actually declining, except in capital-intensive offshore petroleum and gas industry, replacing tin mining as most valuable. Textiles, electronic equipment, and assembled machinery important manufactures. Construction and building materials industries generally booming, responding to both public and private investment.

Services: Urban transportation, communications, business, professional, finance, real estate, government, and other services made up bulk of economic activity and growth. Government services especially important, generating 28 percent of new employment during 1975-82.

Imports: Equivalent to US$12 billion in 1982. Intermediate materials and components accounted for 49 percent of total, capital goods and equipment for 32 percent, nonfood consumer goods for 13 percent, and food for remaining 6 percent. Major suppliers: Japan (25 percent), United States (16 percent), Singapore (13 percent), and Britain, Federal Republic of Germany (West Germany), Australia, and Saudi Arabia (5 percent each).

Exports: Equivalent to US$12.6 billion in 1982. Petroleum contributed 27 percent; timber, 16 percent; equipment (including electronic components), 15 percent; palm oil, 11 percent; rubber, 9 percent; tin, 5 percent; other agricultural and crude materials, 6 percent; other processed minerals, 5 percent; and chemicals and other manufactures the remainder. Major buyers: Singapore (22 percent), Japan (21 percent), United States (14 percent) and Netherlands (6 percent).

Balance of Payments: Positive trade balances until 1981 and 1982, when export prices fell. Current account balance likewise turned sharply into deficit in early 1980s to a maximum of 13.3 percent of GDP in 1982. Inflow of investment capital and foreign loans enough to offset negative balance, but debt-service ratio low by international standards at about 6 percent of export receipts in 1983.

Railroads: Some 1,666 kilometers of chiefly meter-gauge track in Peninsular Malaysia and 155 kilometers of similar track in Sabah in 1982. Total track length, according to official statistics, 2,215 kilometers in 1981, including minor branches. About 1.7 million passenger-kilometers and 1.1 million ton-kilometers of traffic in 1981; passenger volume up 6 percent per year and freight volume down 2 percent per year since 1977.

Roads: Peninsular Malaysia: some 17,770 kilometers of national roads (15,700 kilometers hard surface) and more than 6,000 kilometers state roads in 1982; about 25 motor vehicles per 100 population. Sabah: about 2,700 kilometers hard surface and 2,300 kilometers other roads; approximately 15 motor vehicles per 100 people. Sarawak: some 1,600 kilometers hard surface and 1,600 kilometers other surface; about 12 motor vehicles per 100 people.

Ports: Kelang (the largest), Penang, Johore Baharu, Kuching, Kota Kinabalu, and Sandakan major ports; about 25 minor ports. National shipping line about 1.1 million deadweight tons of vessels in 1982 but hauled less than one-fifth of international freight.

Civil Airports: Kuala Lumpur (largest), Penang Island, Johore Baharu, Kuching, and Kota Kinabalu major airports; 23 other permanent surface and 110 minor airfields. National airlines fleet of 19 jet (five wide-body) and 15 other aircraft in 1982.

Telecommunications: Peninsular Malaysia: good intercity and international microwave networks serving 5.1 telephones per 100 population in 1982; 20 AM, one FM, and 20 television stations reaching 1.4 licensed radios and 9.4 licensed televisions per 100 people in 1981. Sabah: fair intercity network serving 3.9 telephones per 100 people in 1982; 14 AM, one FM, and seven television stations for six radios and 6.4 televisions per 100 people in

1981. Sarawak: fair intercity network and 4.7 telephones per 100 population in 1982; five AM and six television stations for 2.4 radios and 4.3 television sets per 100 people in 1981.

Government and Politics

Government: Parliamentary democracy under constitutional monarch, known as supreme head of the federation, or paramount ruler, elected for five-year term from among and by hereditary rulers; prime minister appointed from majority party in parliament of 68-member Senate and 154-member House of Representatives. Universal adult suffrage.

Politics: National Front and its predecessor, Alliance Party, both multiethnic coalitions, have controlled government since 1957. National Front dominated by United Malays National Organization and embraced Malayan Chinese Association, Malayan Indian Congress, and six other parties representing other ethnic groups. Opposition parties active but small; include Pan-Malaysia Islamic Party and Democratic Action Party.

Administrative Divisions: Federal government with 13 states and Federal Territory of Kuala Lumpur. In Peninsular Malaysia each state divided into districts and subdistricts *(mukim)* ; Sabah has residencies and districts; Sarawak has divisions and districts.

Legal System: Judicial and legal practices reflect British influence. Court system consists of lower courts at principal urban and rural centers, two high courts having original and appellate jurisdiction, and Supreme Court (formerly called Federal Court), highest court of nation. Certain civil and domestic matters under jurisdiction of Islamic courts.

Major International Memberships: United Nations and many of its specialized agencies, including World Bank (see Glossary), International Monetary Fund, and General Agreement on Tariffs and Trade; Asian Development Bank; Five-Power Defense Arrangement; Commonwealth of Nations; Movement of Nonaligned Nations; Organization of the Islamic Conference; and Association of Southeast Asian Nations.

National Security

Armed Forces: In 1984 army—80,000; navy—8,700; air force—11,000; paramilitary police—19,000; reserves estimated at 35,000 as of mid-1982.

Major Tactical Units: In 1984 army—12 infantry brigades, 37 infantry battalions, three cavalry regiments, four field artillery regiments, one armored personnel carrier regiment, two antiaircraft batteries, five engineer regiments, five signals regiments, and one special forces (conmando) regiment. Navy—one regional command for Peninsular Malaysia and one for Sabah and Sarawak. Air force—two fighter squadrons, two counterinsurgency/training squadrons, one maritime reconnaissance squadron, three transport squadrons, one liaison squadron, two transport helicopter squadrons, two liaison helicopter squadrons, two training squadrons. Paramilitary police—21 battalions.

Major Weapons Systems: In 1984 army—light tanks, armored and scout cars, armored personnel carriers, howitzers and field guns, antitank guided wire missiles, and antiaircraft guns. Navy—frigates, missile fast attack craft, large patrol craft, landing ships (tank), coastal minesweepers, and support ships. Air force—F-5E/F Tiger IIs, M.B. 339As, numerous transport and reconnaissance aircraft and helicopters, and Sidewinder air-to-air missiles. Paramilitary police—armored cars and personnel carriers.

Security Expenditures: In 1984 armed forces—about M$3 billion (for value of the ringgit--see Glossary) representing 11.3 percent of total central government expenditures. Development expenditures 31 percent, operating expenditures 69 percent. Defense budgets declining since 1982. Internal security expenditures (mainly for police) M$1.4 billion.

Internal Security: In 1984 communist insurgents in Peninsular Malaysia; two parties, Communist Party of Malay and Malaysian Communist Party, together totaling 1,800 to 2,300, mostly located in southern Thailand. In Sarawak one party, North Kalimantan Communist Party, about 100 to 120 strong. Government also identifies interethnic group tension, Islamic religious extremists, Vietnamese refugees, and drug addiction as potential threats to internal order.

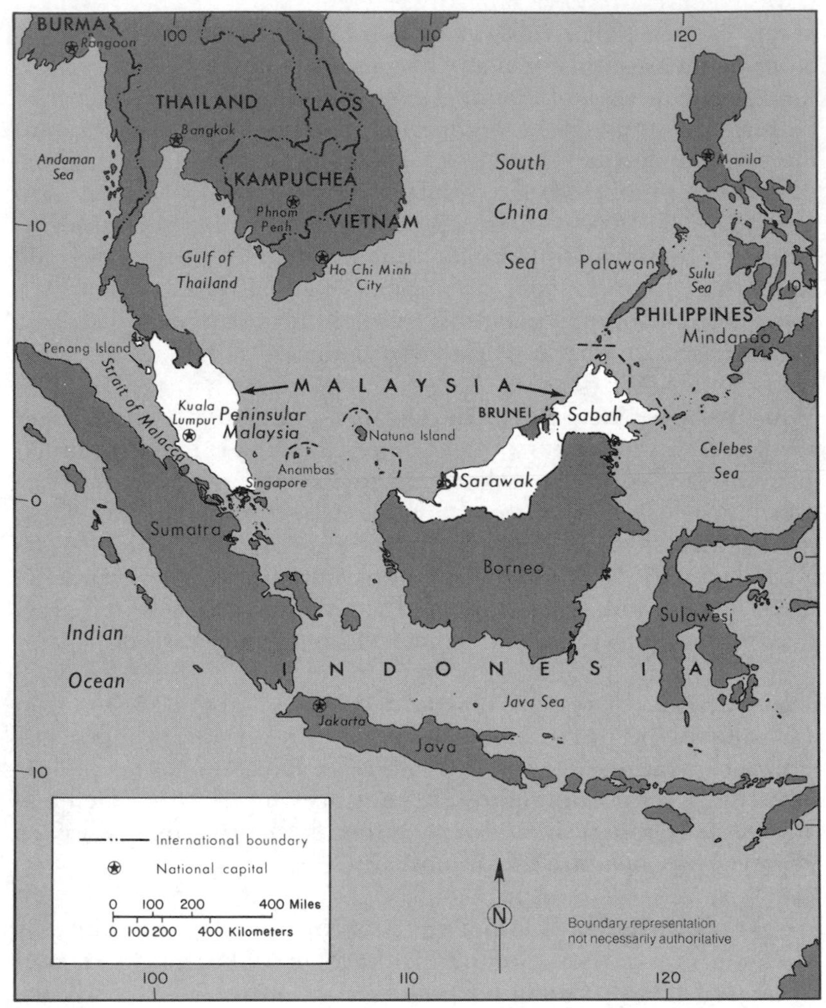

Figure 1. Malaysia, Position in Southeast Asia, 1984

Introduction

IN AUGUST 1957 future prime minister Tengku Abdul Rahman, scion of a long line of Malay sultans, stood before a colorful gathering in Kuala Lumpur to proclaim the independence of the Federation of Malaya. Dignitaries of the Commonwealth of Nations watched in approval as officials lowered the Union Jack and raised a new banner bearing 11 stripes—one for each of the states of the federation—and a star and crescent, signifying the Islamic faith of Malays, who formed the country's largest ethnic community. Relations between Malay aristocrats and their former mentors remained warm and close. Nonetheless, the moment of independence invoked a mood of pride and jubilation in many of the participants.

Optimism among Malays reflected the prospective political arrangements. At long last they had achieved not only independence but also British backing for a governmental system that guaranteed Malay rulers continued sovereignty in their own states under a framework of constitutional monarchy and parliamentary democracy. The arrangement, born of strenuous negotiation and compromise, struck a delicate balance between the interests and influence of the Malay community and those of the other segments of the population. Yet Malay nationalists could be satisfied that the structure of the system deliberately gave heaviest weighting to the needs of Malays, allaying their deeply held fears of encroachment by non-Malays upon traditional Malay prerogatives.

The constitutional arrangements, nonetheless, left room for optimism among the country's large Chinese and Indian ethnic communities and numerous smaller ones as well. Wealthy Chinese had become a powerful force in the commercial affairs of the Malay Peninsula in the preindependence period and had foreseen a rewarding role for their community in an independent Malaya. Given this presumption, in the early 1950s a number of leading Chinese intellectuals and businessmen had joined Malays in forming the interethnic ruling Alliance coalition (later joined by Indians as well) that the British had deemed a necessary step toward self-rule. On Merdeka (Independence) Day, therefore, many Chinese had shared with Malays the vision of a free and economically strong country in which stability would be preserved in delicate balance through compromise and consensus, reflecting the political strength of one community, the economic strength of the other.

Less than a dozen years later, on May 13, 1969, the prospect was shattered by interracial violence in Kuala Lumpur. To a large extent unanticipated, the rioting had evidently grown out of socioeconomic frustration among poor Malays and their resentment of gains at the polls by Chinese opposition parties. Between 1969 and 1971 all communal groups in the ruling coalition undertook a painful reassessment of the country's approach to development. The period marked the end of an era. Abdul Rahman resigned, and power was gradually relinquished to a new generation of nationbuilders, generally more Malay-oriented than their predeccessors. During the 1970s this ruling elite formulated and implemented a radically new approach to the country's endemic problems, growing out of the realization on all sides that interethnic harmony must be fostered and poverty, as a source of tension and disaffection, must be eliminated.

The endemic problems stemmed not from an unfavorable ratio of land and resources to population as in neighboring Indonesia—Malaysia is relatively well endowed—but from disparities in the level of their enjoyment among different groups. Poor Chinese are to be found, but relative to the predominantly rural Malay majority, the Chinese in general are urbanized, modernized, and well-off. As for the Indian community, except for a prosperous few, most are little better off than the improverished Malays. Language, culture, and regional distinctions between and within communal groups also give impetus to conflicting aspirations and political competition in the multiethnic society.

The origins of the economic imbalances in this plural society could be traced to the previous century, at which time a predominantly immigrant Chinese population had consolidated a strong economic base in a country Malays regarded as essentially their own and in which they had gradually become an impoverished minority as others thrived. The amassing of Chinese wealth stemmed from entrepreneurial activities and, after the eighteenth century, from exploitation of tin deposits concentrated on the western coast of the peninsula. This was further augmented after 1900 by large-scale rubber cultivation. Labor was provided not by Malays but by large numbers of immigrant Chinese and Indian contract laborers. Thus, under the British there developed a dichotomy between an alien economy, overwhelmingly under Chinese and foreign control, and an indigenous, traditional one providing a marginal livelihood for Malays. While the traditional ecomony languished, the export economy made giant strides. Between 1881 and 1931 the monetary value of exports from the peninsula increased thirtyfold. Small numbers of

Indians found a place in expanding urban commercial enterprise, but most remained on the rubber plantations.

Initially, traditional Malay society was little affected by the economic and social changes that were transforming many parts of the peninsula, particularly the western coast. Most Malay villagers continued as in the past to earn their livelihood in rice cultivation or fishing—although eventually some became rubber smallholders. The Malay sultans—on whom most villagers focused political and religious loyalities—had been permitted by the British to retain sovereignty over their Muslim subjects in their respective domains.

Perhaps the most dynamic force for change was the spread of secular education within a society whose heritage was almost exclusively one of religious learning, consisting for most Malays of the memorization of passages from the Quran in Arabic. British administrators and private groups introduced the Malay peasantry to primary-level education in its own language. Prospective village schoolmasters went for further training to the Sultan Idris Training College, where Malay nationalist ideas first emerged. Sons of the ruling elite, however, and future Malay administrators were educated in English, many of them in England or at Malay College, an institution modeled on the British public school.

Educational expansion and the spreading use of English were simultaneously creating, or solidifying, lines of cleavage within the Chinese community as well. Differences in dialect, culture, level of prosperity, and political orientation became more apparent as the community grew and stabilized. Chinese immigration continued in the early twentieth century on a scale so rapid that by 1941 in the Malay states and Singapore combined, Chinese outnumbered Malays—even though some immigrants continued to return to China after some years' residence. Among Chinese, attitudes toward the homeland in China and its significance for them varied. On the one side were conservative Chinese to whom communal solidarity and institutional strength were all-important; they spoke Chinese in the home, educated their children through the Chinese medium, and preserved their ethnic and cultural ties in every way possible. On the other side were Chinese seeking collaboration with the politically dominant Malays. This latter attitude was mainly represented among the long-settled Chinese of the Straits Settlements (see Glossary), who in accordance with their convictions educated their children through the medium of English.

These varying perspectives bore an important relation to the issues of nationality, citizenship, and loyalty that assumed great importance in the struggle for power on the Malay Peninsula at the close of World War II and during the traumatic Japanese occupation. In the postwar political arrangements for the peninsula, the British government had hoped to put Malays and Chinese on an equal footing. The 1946 Malayan Union, bringing together all its territories except Singapore, proposed accordingly to give citizenship status to all Chinese who could demonstrate that they had made their home in one of the various Malay states and territories that were to be unified. To the outrage of Malays, it further proposed to relieve the sultans of their right to sovereignty, which all had signed away obligingly, if in some cases reluctantly. Wasting no time, Malays organized politically even though communal political activity and awareness had heretofore been at low levels. So effectively did they lay the foundation for a political organization dedicated to the preservation of traditional Malay rights and prerogatives—the United Malays National Organization (UMNO)—that more than 35 years later it remained the dominant political organization in the country. British administrators quickly developed a proposal more to Malay liking, and in February 1948 the union plan was scuttled and replaced by the Federation of Malaya. The new constitutional framework called for continued sovereignty of Malay rulers in their separate states and the preservation of what came to be known as the "special position" of Malays. In the intervening months, Chinese had tried but failed to unite opposition against the federation.

The pattern of communal politics was in place well before Merdeka Day. After the setback in opposing the federation, revealing the polarization and disunity within the Chinese community, the Malayan Chinese Association (MCA) had been organized, mainly to protect Chinese interests. Moving into the political sphere in 1952, the MCA formed a limited alliance with UMNO to participate in a local election. Victory consolidated the arrangement; the coalition (which came to be called the Alliance) was joined in 1955 by the Malayan Indian Congress (MIC) and endured for more than two decades. In these years, attempts to persuade UMNO's leadership to accept non-Malays into that organization had failed, as had attempts to organize support for a multicommunal party.

The promulgation of the new federation in 1948 coincided with the start of an armed insurrection—later referred to as the Emergency—mounted by the Communist Party of Malaya (CPM). Insurgents initially harassed British-led security forces with considerable effect by conducting raids from jungle hideaways, disrupting the economy, and terrorizing the countryside, although they never brought fixed areas under their authority. The situation was gradually stabilized only with intervention by the British government, however, and officially the Emergency was not ended until 1960, although its main impact had waned well before that. The insurgents were isolated from the people and deprived of their sources of supply and intelligence through a system of so-called New Villages into which rural Chinese—thought to include a number of CPM sympathizers—had been forcibly removed. The sources of support for the insurgency were in fact far from clear; its origins were complex, to say the least, given the domestic and external milieu of the time. Chinese sympathy for the movement—to the extent that it did exist among poor Chinese—was probably in part a carry-over from the experience of World War II during which time the Japanese had tended to be least hard on Malays while the Chinese became the core of the resistance.

In the Federation of Malaya the political primacy of Malays was symbolically evidenced in the person of the *yang di-pertuan agong*, or paramount ruler, elected for a five-year term by the hereditary Malay rulers. On February 9, 1984, Tunku Mahmood Iskandar Ibni Al-Marhum Sultan Ismail—Sultan Mahmood Iskandar of Johore—was elected as new paramount ruler to succeed Sultan Ahmad Shah of Pahang (1979-84). The *yang di-pertuan agong* was the highest ranking political figure, and the law required that he be Malay. On a day-to -day basis, however, policy was controlled by the prime minister, concurrently leader of UMNO. A Malay-led multiethnic ruling coalition chosen from members of parliament worked out the concessions and compromises that became the standard mode of operation in communal politics.

Other constitutional features, carefully negotiated through interethnic collaboration and subsequently passed into law by the government of the federation, included the declaration of Islam as the state religion. Freedom of worship, however, was guaranteed to all creeds. A preindependence controversy on language was also resolved by agreement that Malay would be the national language, but for the next 10 years (after 1957) English would be a second official language. Citizenship was extended to all persons born in the federation after independence. Additionally, the paramount ruler was to "safeguard the special position of the Malays" (seen as the indigenous community) and to protect the "legitimate interests of other communities" as well.

At independence in 1957 the Federation of Malaya had highly

favorable economic prospects. A number of observers viewed it as being better off than any Southeast Asian country or territory except Hong Kong. Although a high rate of population growth could eventually offset the favorable ratio of land to people, its resource base was rich, and the energy, skill, and enterprise of the Chinese entrepreneurial group—given free rein under liberal economic policies—was a definite asset. As in the past, the export economy was owned and managed almost entirely by local Chinese and some foreign interests, and it was marked by a lopsided dependency on Britain both as a source of capital and technological know-how and as a trade partner. Malays participated only negligibly in the export economy, and productivity in traditional agriculture was low. Nonetheless, the prevailing view among many in the ruling elite was that in time economic growth would substantially ameliorate the relative improverishment of the rural Malays. Moreover, programs were planned and developed specifically to address problems in rural areas.

Developments up to May 1969, when voters went to the polls in the third postindependence general elections, appeared in many respects to justify optimistic expectations. The growth of the gross national product (GNP—see Glossary) for Malaya (after 1963, for Peninsular Malaysia) grew by more than 5 percent per annum. The economy had shown remarkable resilience in the face of a military threat from Indonesia and of fluctuating prices for export commodities. Palm oil and timber were added to the list of traditional exports, and the manufacturing sector showed modest growth.

Contribution to and benefits from this growth were not in balance, however. Rubber and palm oil continued to be most profitable on Indian-worked plantations. Smallholder agriculture was faring badly. Rice cultivators, small-scale rubber growers, and fishermen, using techniques that produced modest or low yields, remained poor, their condition all the more frustrating as they saw the gap widening between themselves and other population segments. In particular, awareness that 95 percent of all corporate assets in Peninsular Malaysia were in the hands of Europeans and non-Malay Asians contributed to growing resentment. The government was by no means unmindful of this situation and gave considerable attention to drainage and irrigation, land development, and rice price support programs.

More pressing developments in the political and international arena were demanding its attention, however. Particularly significant in this context was the formation in 1963 of Malaysia as successor to the Federation of Malaya, adding three new states to the political arrangement: Sabah and Sarawak on the northern coast of the island of Borneo, and Singapore, the great trading seaport off the southern tip of the Malay Peninsula—one of the former Straits Settlements. Singapore's participation in the federation was short-lived, however. Malay leaders, apparently concerned about economic competition from and political turbulence in that neighboring state, had supported its incorporation, especially because the Malay-speaking peoples in Sabah and Sarawak would soften the impact of Singapore's overwhelmingly Chinese population on Malaysia's ethnic balance. Singapore withdrew from Malaysia in 1965, however, at a time when Malays had become apprehensive over growing Chinese advocacy of a more "Malaysian Malaysia".

The establishment of Malaysia had stirred up a hornet's nest of regional antagonism. Indonesian president Sukarno vilified the move as one of a "neocolonialist" regime, calling for all-out "Confrontation" in opposition to the merger. The Philippines was drawn into the conflict on the basis of its claim to Sabah that the territory had once been part of the sultanate of Sulu in the southern Philippine Islands. Sukarno's crusade ended after a military coup in his own country forced him to step down from power in September 1965, but not before Indonesia and Malaysia had engaged in sporadic armed conflict.

The disaster of May 13, 1969, leaving several hundred Chinese dead in the wake of violent communal rioting, struck without critical forewarning. When the short-lived outburst was over, nonetheless, the ruling coalition read the danger signals in the environment and reacted accordingly. Parliamentary rule was suspended, an emergency was proclaimed, and the National Operations Council ruled by decree. Discussion of matters that might incite communal resentment was banned under amendments to the 1948 Sedition Act, making it an offense to question such matters as the "special position of the Malays and other indigenous groups." This provision was later added to the Constitution as an amendment. A government-led multiethnic council examined the sensitive problem of communal tension; a new national ideology emphasizing the unity of all peoples was promulgated; and, under a changing of the guard, a new economic strategy was devised.

With the return to parliamentary government in February 1971, Malaysia was prepared to lay the groundwork for implementation of the New Economic Policy (NEP). The power and resources of the government were to be set in motion to counteract economic imbalances perceived by many to be the root cause of intercommunal tension. The overarching objective of the NEP was national unity, which was to be attained through the dual means of erdicating poverty and restructuring society so that the identification of particular groups with economic function and geographical location would be eventually eliminated.

Performance of the economy during the first decade of NEP guidelines was highly satisfactory. Growth during the 1970s substantially exceeded that of the 1960s. Throughout the period the country experienced an increase in exports of primary commodities, both traditional and new, such as palm oil, timber, and petroleum. A credible expansion of growth in manufacturing was registered. Official statistics showed that the proportion of households living in poverty had been reduced by one-fifth, from 49 to 29 percent. Observers cautioned, however, that the real effect of the strong economic performance of the 1970s on long-standing forms of inequality and poverty was yet uncertain.

During the 1970s the government permitted a broad latitude of freedom in the political process, albeit constraints on discussion of sensitive political issues remained in effect. No one wanted to see a return to confrontation. In 1974 the Alliance Party and most former opposition parties were absorbed under the umbrella of a new ruling coalition, the National Front. This was believed to be essential as a manifestation of intercommunal solidarity; the usual searches for compromise and consensus continued to be conducted behind closed doors within the framework of the coalition. By the late 1970s the two major opposition groups remaining outside the National Front were the Democratic Action Party (DAP), drawing its support chiefly from non-Malay voters (mainly Chinese), and the Pan-Malaysia Islamic Party, better known by its Malaysian acronym, PAS (see Glossary). Founded some 30 years earlier by Islamic clergy, theologians, and ultranationalist Malays, PAS was supported by the more conservative elements of the Malay rural electorate.

Changes in eduction since the 1970-71 reassessment have given rise to particularly vehement intercommunal controversy. The usual discreet search for compromise within the ruling coalition has failed to alleviate concern among Chinese over the educational prospects of the youth of their community, particularly with respect to access to higher education. One of the government's early actions was a progressive phasing-out of the use of English as a medium of instruction in government-aided schools, satisfying the long-held grievance of many Malays against the continued dominance of English secondary education. This was seen as appropriate, given that Malay is the national language. But

Chinese and Indians, a majority of whom had opted for an English-language education, now had no alternative and perceived themselves to be at a disadvantage in competition with Malays. More troublesome perhaps was the area of university admissions, where policies reflected the overall national goal of restructuring society and preparing qualified Malays for an expanded role in business and administration. Chinese efforts to establish their own university were blocked on the grounds that a center of Chinese nationalism in Malaysia was not in the national interest.

In July 1981 Deputy Prime Minister Dato' Seri Dr. Mahathir Mohamad succeeded to the prime ministership. He had become the dominant political figure in the country little more than a decade after his ouster from UMNO following an outspoken attack on its leaders in the wake of the 1969 riots. The unprecedented scale of the UMNO-led victory in elections in April 1982 suggested that Mahathir had been quick to consolidate popular support behind his new administration. His co-optation of Anwar Ibrahim, former leader of the Islam-based Muslim Youth Movement of Malaysia, into the cabinet was generally conceded as an astute maneuver in a milieu of Islamic resurgence. Mahathir has rendered himself less vulnerable to extremist demands for social justice accentuated by the resurgence. Further evidence of his political skills was his successful handling of a crisis between himself and the Conference of Rulers over proposed amendments to the 1957 Constitution. Mahathir and Anwar headed a vanguard of new Malay leaders, reform-minded and cast in a nonroyal mold. Many of Mahathir's popular supporters welcomed his firm approach, seen as giving impetus to Malaysia's search for independence, self-reliance, and a strong national identity.

An increasing emphasis on self-reliance and regional cooperation characterized Malaysian foreign relations in the 1970s. Consistent with a firmly established pragmatic approach, the trend stemmed from security concerns raised by British and United States decisions to reduce military commitments in Southeast Asia, continued Chinese covert aid to communist guerrillas in the region, and the expansion of the Soviet naval presence in the Indian Ocean and the Pacific Ocean.

Active interest in regionalism had already become evident through Malaysian participation in the Association of Southeast Asian Nations (ASEAN), formed in 1967 by Indonesia, Malaysia, the Philippines, Singapore, and Thailand as a forum for consultation and nomilitary cooperation. (Brunei joined in January 1984.) In September 1970 Malaysian leaders carried the concept of regional cooperation still further, publicly proposing for the first time that the five nations support as a common goal the neutralization of Southeast Asia. Malaysia's quest for a scheme that would ensure peace and security in the region was rewarded shortly thereafter with the endorsement of ASEAN members for a "Zone of Peace, Freedom, and Neutrality" in Southeast Asia.

The pragmatic approach to foreign policy had been dictated by economic considerations as well. Once dependent on Britain and the West for trade and assistance, Malaysia shifted in the 1970s to a policy of broadened trade and diplomatic links, cultivating additional ties to communist nations and Third World countries. The emergence of China as a new center of power and the economic growth and strength of Japan and the Republic of Korea (South Korea) influenced foreign policy development as well. The declaration of the Mahathir administration of what it called a "Look East" policy indicated a trend toward reduced economic ties with Britain and increased ties with Japan and South Korea. The latter two countries were singled out as examples for Malaysia to follow.

In the mid-1980s the pattern of ethnic cleavage remained as persistent as ever. Nonetheless, the Malay-led, multiethnic national leadership could find cause for muted celebration, for it was successful in moving toward its goals while maintaining intercommunal harmony through consensus and compromise.

March 1984

Frederica M. Bunge

Chapter 1. Historical Setting

Bronze figure of a Brahman sage, discovered in Jalong, Perak, probably dating from the ninth century to the eleventh

BECAUSE OF THEIR strategic position and natural resources, the territories that make up Malaysia—the states of the Malay Peninsula, Sabah, and Sarawak—attracted sailors and traders from other parts of Asia from at least the first centuries of the Christian Era onward. The coastal peoples of the peninsula and the Malay Archipelago were themselves skilled navigators. Their control of the Strait of Malacca, through which ships carrying goods from the countries on the Indian Ocean littoral to China had to pass, made it possible for them to establish prosperous entrepôt states where the products of East and West, as well as those native to the region, were traded. The most important of these entrepôt states were Srivijaya, which arose in the late seventh century on Sumatra and lasted until the fourteenth century, and Malacca, which flourished during the fifteenth century. During Malacca's brief golden age, Malay became the principal language of commerce of the entire region. This state's most significant contribution to Malay history, however, was its role as the center for the propagation of the Islamic religion throughout insular Southeast Asia and the Malay Peninsula. The descendants of the Malaccan royal family established kingdoms on the peninsula that were the forebears of many of Malaysia's present-day states.

In the sixteenth century the Portuguese occupied Malacca, forcing its ruler to flee and establish another state in the Johore and Riau Archipelago region at the southern tip of the peninsula. From the sixteenth through the nineteenth centuries, the Malay world grew increasingly fragmented owing to European rivalries (the Dutch captured Malacca from the Portuguese in 1641); the intervention of regional powers, such as Aceh in western Sumatra; the migration of Minangkabau peoples from central Sumatra into the peninsula; and the growing power of Buginese chiefs, from central Sulawesi in the eastern Malay Archipelago, who gained tremendous political influence in many of the Malay states.

For commercial and strategic reasons, the British East India Company established a port on the island of Penang across from the Malay state of Kedah in 1786. This was the first decisive step in the development of the region as a British sphere of influence through the nineteenth and early twentieth centuries. Impetus to greater British involvement in the internal affairs of the Malay states was provided by the growth of commercial interests in Singapore, which had been founded in 1819, and by demand for its products, particularly tin, in the industrialized countries of Europe and North America. The residency system, first set up in the Malay state of Perak in 1874, ensured effective but indirect colonial rule. By 1909 the peninsula had been divided into the Straits Settlements, which were British colonies, the Federated Malay States, where residents exercised indirect rule, and the Unfederated Malay States, where the Malay rulers retained a greater measure of autonomy but were still within the British sphere of influence. On Borneo, "White Raja" Sir James Brooke had established his own state of Sarawak in 1841, and the British North Borneo Company, which had gained control over what is now Sabah, was chartered by the Crown in 1881.

The Borneo territories remained tranquil and largely undeveloped, but the peninsula, particularly its west coast where the Federated Malay States were located, was transformed during the nineteenth and twentieth centuries as a result of the growth of an export economy based first on tin and then on rubber. The indigenous population, including Malays, was small, and there was a great demand for labor. Malay rulers, moreover, were unwilling or unable to exploit new economic opportunities; as a consequence foreigners gained control of the modern sectors of the economy. Large numbers of Chinese and Indian immigrants came to the penisula to work in the mines and on the plantations; more successful set up their own commercial and industrial enterprises.

In the plural society of British Malaya (and on a smaller scale in the Borneo territories), the indigenous peoples were excluded from the modern economy. There was, however, little assertive Malay nationalism before World War II. Malays regarded the British as protectors of their special status, symbolized by the retention of the rulers in the Federated and Unfederated Malay States and by the opportunities that existed for elite Malays in the colonial administration. The Japanese occupation of 1942–45, however, disturbed the equilibrium of colonial society and shattered the illusion that the British would remain indefinitely to mediate between the different ethnic communities. Antagonisms sharpened, moreover, as the Japanese sought to enlist Malay support for their war effort and treated the Chinese with extreme harshness; the latter formed a communist-led guerrilla resistance movement, the Malayan People's Anti-Japanese Army. Interethnic hostilities deepened during the emergency of 1948–60 as this armed movement, with bases of support almost exclusively within Chinese settlements, attempted to overthrow the government.

Independence for Malaya came in 1957 after the Alliance, a coalition of elite Malay, Chinese, and Indian community leaders, proved its popularity in local and federal elections and worked out a compromise, embodied in the Constitution of 1957, that extended citizenship to all persons born on the peninsula but also reaffirmed the status of the Malay rulers and certain Malay special privileges. In September 1963 the Federation of Malaysia, including the Malay states of the peninsula, Singapore, Sarawak, and Sabah, was proclaimed. During its stormy first few years Malaysia faced the hostility of Indonesia and the Philippines and a direct challenge to its constitutional basis by the leaders of Singapore, who demanded equal political rights for all Malaysians in place of Malay special privileges. This led to the separation of Singapore from the federation in 1965. Through the 1960s and 1970s Malaysian leaders—first in the Alliance and then in the National Front after 1974—undertook the delicate task of fostering racial harmony within the framework of a Malay polity. The communal riots that occurred in Kuala Lumpur in May 1969, however, convinced them that basic economic and political readjustments were necessary. By the early 1980s a sense of national unity and purpose had developed, but communal jealousies and tensions were still a major factor in the country's social, economic, and political life.

Early History of the Malay World

Historical sources on the Malay Peninsula and northern Borneo before the sixteenth century are extremely sketchy. The most reliable are Chinese records that include not only the official histories of the ruling imperial dynasties but also the journals of the Buddhist pilgrims Fa Hsien, who lived in the fifth century A.D., and I Tsing, who lived in the seventh century A.D. Both had traveled by sea between China and India. There are also compendiums on foreign countries, such as the ninth-century *Man Shu* (History of the Southern Barbarians) and Chao Ju-kua's thirteenth-century *Chu Fan Chih* (Record of Foreign Nations). Indian writings, such as the Hindu *Ramayana* and the Buddhist *Jatakas* (Birth Tales) allude to the lands of Southeast Asia but are too vague and fanciful to be helpful.

One thing is evident from the available historical sources—the Malay Peninsula and even remote Borneo were integrated into a larger economic and cultural system from as early as the first few centuries after the birth of Christ. The sea was more of a highway than a barrier to the exchange of peoples, goods, and ideas. The Strait of Malacca, described by one historian as a "gullet...through which the foreigners' sea and land traffic in either direction must pass," linked the trade routes of China and India. Control of the strait was a preoccupation of indigenous rulers who established states on the western Malayan and northern Sumatran coasts and on the Riau and Lingga islands that cluster at the southern end of the strait.

The early development of the Malay Peninsula illustrates the workings of an international economic system a millennium and a half before the Industrial Revolution and the invention of modern modes of transportation and communications. Early Indian texts refer to the peninsula (and, more broadly, to Southeast Asia as a whole—preciseness was not a virtue of Indian writers) as Suvarnabhumi, the Land of Gold. This mineral was not found in significant amounts on the subcontinent and had customarily been obtained from goldfields in Siberia. By the first century A.D., however, the aggressive expansion of those nomadic peoples known as the Hsiung-nu by the Chinese and Huns by Westerners cut off the overland gold trade. An edict of the Emperor Vespasian (A.D. 69–79) prohibiting gold exports from the Roman Empire deprived the Indians of supplies from the West. Thus, the Indians turned to the East, and most particularly the peninsula, for their needs. Trade was facilitated by their development of large and seaworthy ships, carrying as many as 700 persons. By the fifth century, tin, which was to have a much more significant role in the history of Malaysia, began to be exported to India; in the "land of ten million deities" there was perennial demand for tin alloys to make religious images.

Between the fourth and sixth centuries A.D., the growth of a far-flung trade network linking the Middle East, India, the Malay Peninsula, the islands of the western Indonesian archipelago, and China was stimulated by the further deterioration of conditions in Central Asia and the closing of overland trade routes. Starting in the early fourth century, the Hsiung-nu repeatedly invaded the North China Plain, their devastation turning it into a vast cemetery; but native Chinese dynasties were established south of the Yangtze River, and the southern region experienced unprecedented development and prosperity. Such dynasties were obliged to trade by sea for luxury goods that had formerly come to China overland. Among the most important were resins, particularly pine resins, camphor, and aromatic woods, used for incense and medicinal purposes. Frankincense and myrrh were originally obtained from the Arabian Peninsula and then shipped along the Indian Ocean littoral and through the Strait of Malacca to Canton and other southern Chinese ports. Much of this trade in "Persian goods," as the Chinese called them, was carried in Malay ships manned by Malay sailors. Gradually, demand for the exotic goods of Arabia was supplanted by that for substitutes obtained from trees on the Malay Peninsula, Sumatra, and western Java. The forested interior of the peninsula was at that time the exclusive habitat of the Orang Asli (see Glossary), and these peoples gathered the rare wood products and brought them to the coast. Chinese and Indian records give spare accounts of a succession of a small kingdoms clustered around the Strait of Malacca and along the west and east coasts of the peninsula as far north as what is now southern Thailand. These kingdoms served as entrepôts for the transshipment of "Persian goods" and as collection centers for local goods, which were then carried by sea to China.

Among the most important entrepôts were Tan-Tan (as the Chinese referred to it), possibly located on the coast of the modern state of Terengganu; Chih-T'u, in what is now the state of Kelantan; and Lo Yueh, which may have been located in Johore (see fig. 2). Langkasuka was in southern Thailand, and Kataha, described by a contemporary Indian writer as an "abode of all felicities," was located on the Malay Peninsula in the area of the modern state of Kedah. By the late seventh century the powerful kingdom of Srivijaya was established with its center at Palembang in southeast Sumatra, part of modern Indonesia. This kingdom controlled passage through the strait and dominated Malay-Indonesian trade until its disintegration in the fourteenth century.

Although the markets of southern China were of primary importance for the entrepôt states of the region of the Strait of Malacca, it was India, rather than China, that provided the main impetus for religious, cultural, and political developments. The thesis, proposed by several historians, that the "Indianization" of the peninsula and other Southeast Asian regions was the result of massive migrations from the subcontinent, has been largely discredited. Instead, it appears that Indian merchants settled along the coasts, marrying the daughters of local rulers. Indian and indigenous Malay rulers found Hindu concepts of kingship useful for the establishment of stable regimes. They adopted the concept of the *devaraja* (god-king), which depicted the ruler as the incarnation of a Hindu god, particularly Shiva, and the royal court was permeated by an elaborate system of ritual and ceremony presided over by Brahman priests. The fusion of the temporal and

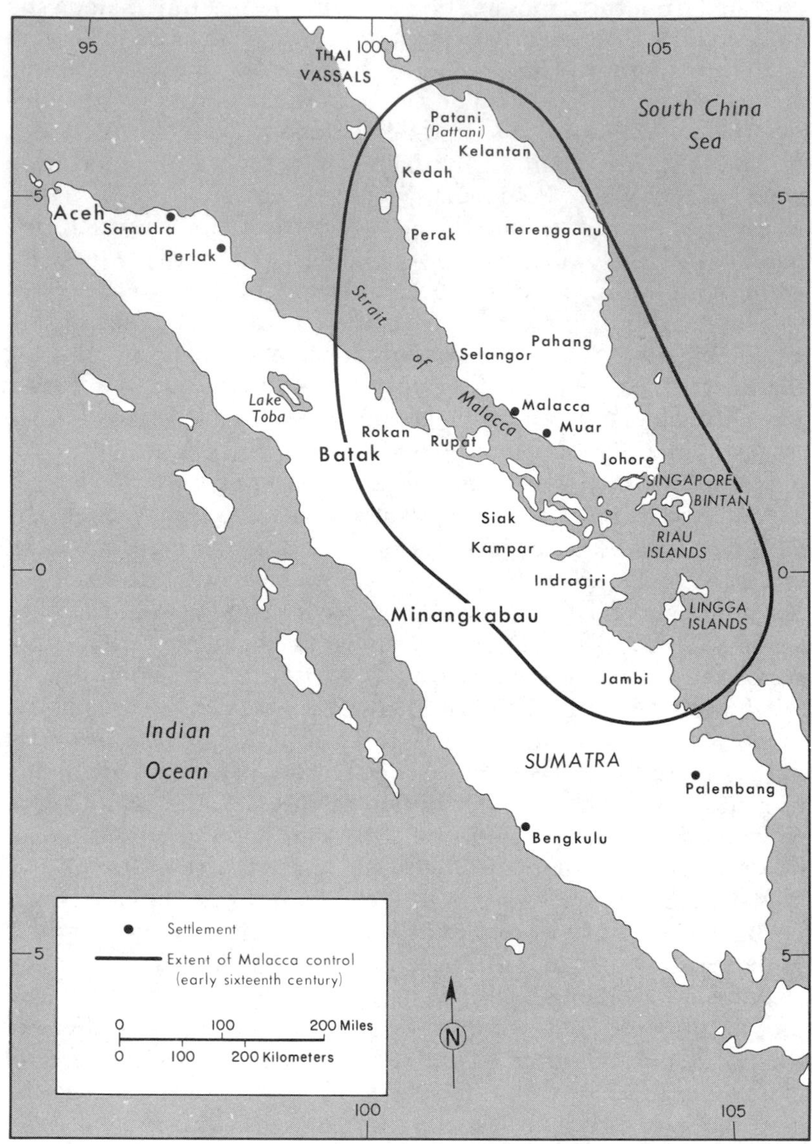

Source: Based on information from M. C. Ricklefs, *A History of Modern Indonesia: c. 1300 to the Present*, Bloomington, 1981, 311; and Kernial Singh Sandhu, *Early Malaysia*, Singapore, 1973, 57.

Figure 2. Historical Map of the Malay World

the divine gave a more stable foundation to the creation of larger and more potent political units. Especially significant was the transition from the indigenous concept of the ruler as a "first among equals" chosen by his contemporaries for his superior prowess to the imported notion of hereditary dynasties in which the throne was transmitted from father to son.

Archaeological evidence of Indian influence on the peninsula includes Sanskrit inscriptions found in Perai, opposite the island of Penang, which have been dated to the fourth century, and a Buddhist inscription in slate found in Kedah. The most interesting archaeological site on the peninsula comes, however, from a later era—the tenth-century Candi Sungai Batu Pahat in Kedah, a temple dedicated to a deceased ruler, which combines Hindu and Buddhist motifs in its design.

Srivijaya to the Fourteenth Century

The rise of Srivijaya on the island of Sumatra in the late seventh century was stimulated in large measure by the renewed strength and prosperity of China, unified under T'ang Dynasty since A.D. 618. The Chinese emperor prohibited his subjects from engaging in foreign trade, and thus it fell under the control of foreigners, who came to China on what were ostensibly "tribute missions." Srivijaya is described as having started as a commercial outpost at Palembang, connected by river to the northern coast of southeastern Sumatra, and evolving into a *negara* (royal capital city) ruled by an Indian-style maharaja. It gradually extended its influence to the Malay Peninsula and the Strait of Malacca, thus dominating the trade between China and the Indian Ocean and that of insular Southeast Asia. The maharaja's status as tributary of the Chinese emperor assured him a monopoly of lucrative Chinese markets, while his naval power in the Strait of Malacca and the Indonesian archipelago ensured a steady flow of exotic goods through Srivijayan ports.

According to the *Hsin T'ang Shu* (New History of the T'ang Dynasty), Srivijaya ruled over 14 cities; Kataha in present-day Kedah State was apparently its northern outpost. It was not a centralized state but, in the words of one scholar, "a sort of federation of trading ports on the fringe of a large area of forest," the interior of the Malay Peninsula and Sumatra remaining virtually uninhabited save for small numbers of the Orang Asli. Royal revenues were derived from trade. The most important of the maharaja's subjects were Malay seafarers, the Orang Laut (men of the sea), who had a reputation as able sailors and fierce fighters. In Chao Ju-kua's words, they "have not their equal among other nations" in "facing the enemy and braving death." Their loyalty was essential, for without their war fleets the maharaja could not maintain comtrol of the strait; the islands along the north Sumatran coast and just south of the peninsula were the natural habitat of pirates. The Orang Laut, like their nineteenth- and twentieth-century successors in the more remote parts of Malaysia, lived on rafts or in houses built on stilts just offshore.

Chao, writing in the thirteenth century, gives a long list of Srivijaya's products, which included not only resins, camphor, sandalwood, and *gharu* wood but also cloves, cardamom, elephant tusks, and pearls. The Arabs knew of Srivijaya as Zabag, a country of legendary wealth, and an inscription of 1079 records the maharaja's largess—the donation of 600,000 pieces of gold for the maintenance of a Taoist temple in the Chinese port of Kuangchou.

Although masters of a commercial empire, Srivijaya's maharajas apparently did not neglect spiritual matters, and Palembang was a center of Buddhist studies for several centuries. The Chinese pilgrim I Tsing studied Buddhist texts there for a number of years and wrote that there was a flourishing community of 1,000 Buddhist monks. The city's renown as a center of Buddhist learning and its international connections are underlined by the fact that the Indian scholar Atisa, later famous for his reformation of the Buddhist church in the distant country of Tibet, studied at Palembang under Dharmakirti, a master of the Tantric School, in the early eleventh century. There are, however, no great Buddhist monuments on the Malay Peninsula or Sumatra comparable to Borobudur in central Java or the temples of Pagan in Burma.

The maharaja's trading monopoly could be maintained only through the ruthless suppression of his rivals. Wars with both neighboring and distant states, envious of this monopoly, contributed to Srivijaya's gradual decline. In the late tenth century a costly war was fought with a king of eastern Java. Chinese records indicate that by the eleventh century the state of Jambi on Sumatra had become a strong rival of Palembang. The most damaging blow, however, was struck by the Cholas of South India, whose king sent a large fleet to lay waste to Srivijayan port cities on the Malay Peninsula and Sumatra in 1025. Srivijaya's demise was slow but sure. Aggressive expansion of Chinese shipping into the region beginning in the twelfth century—the tribute system and the prohibition of Chinese private trade having fallen into abeyance—undercut Srivijaya's commercial monopoly. Thai incursions into the Malay Peninsula weakened it still further, as did the imperial ambitions of the Singosari and Majapahit dynasties on the island of Java. Although the historical records are unclear, Srivijaya had apparently ceased to exist by the end of the fourteenth century, absorbed by Majapahit.

Borneo

Although located at some distance from the Strait of Malacca, the island of Borneo was not untouched by Indian influence. A Sanskrit inscription, dated as early as A.D. 400 and recording the exploits of native rulers, has been discovered at Kutei on the east coast of the island (most of which is now part of the Republic of Indonesia). A Hindu statue of the sixth or seventh century has been found at Limbang and a Buddhist statue of the eighth or ninth century at Santubong, both in Sarawak. Borneo was never a dominion of Srivijaya, however, and remained outside the mainstream of cultural, political, and commercial development. Chinese records mention that, beginning in the seventh century, gold and iron were exported from the Sarawak region, and the ninth-century *Man Shu* mentions P'o-ni, which with some confidence can be identified with the kingdom of Brunei on the island's northern coast. Brunei was an important power on Borneo until the nineteenth-century British colonization.

Writing in 1225, Chao Ju-kua described P'o-ni as a settlement of 10,000 people in 14 districts. A rustic place, its walls were built of wood, and the king's palace was thatched with nipa palm. Chao mentions, however, that many of the household pots and pans were made of gold. P'o-ni carried out a lively trade with China, exporting four varieties of camphor, wax, *laka* (tropical wood), and tortoiseshell. A temple was maintained in which were enshrined two sacred pearls that worshipers claimed had gradually grown in size to the dimensions of thumbnails. It is an intriguing coincidence that Antonio Pigafetta, the chronicler of Ferdinand Magellan's circumnavigation of the world, mentions that when the expedition reached Brunei in 1521 the sultan had in his possession two miraculous pearls the size of hens' eggs, which the European voyagers sought in vain to see. According to Javanese accounts, Brunei was conquered by Majapahit forces in 1365; its vassalage—if it occurred at all—was brief.

The Malacca Sultanate and the Evolution of Malay Identity

Although patterns of culture, statecraft, and commerce in the Malay world are very old, it can be argued that Malay history properly begins with the establishment of Malacca (Melaka) on the west coast of the peninsula in the opening years of the fifteenth century. Malacca's significance was twofold: as a center of trade and master of the strait, it was the successor to Srivijaya and brought a new and stronger unity to the Malay people; more significantly, it served as the outpost of the Islamic religion in peninsular and insular Southeast Asia through the fifteenth century. Malacca's court life and culture were a blend of the older Hindu-Buddhist heritage and newer Islamic elements. Much as Europeans sought to emulate and recapture the glory of classical Greece and Rome, Malay rulers through the succeeding centuries sought to reflect and restore the magnificence of Malacca in its golden age. Peninsular Malay ties to Malacca were particularly close given the hereditary links between the rulers of later states and the Malaccan royal family. The extinction of the most important branch of the royal family in Johore in 1699, seemingly only another minor chapter in a long history of assassinations and succession struggles, was a great loss to subsequent generations of Malays who perceived the eighteenth and nineteenth centuries as a period of fragmentation and irrevocably departed glory.

The principal sources available on the foundation of Malacca are the *Suma Oriental*, composed by the Portuguese explorer Tomé Pires as a guide to the countries of Asia in 1515, and the *Malay Chronicles* (Sejarah Melayu), the first Malay literary work of significance, written in the seventeenth century. According to Pires, Sri Paramesvara, a Malay prince of Palembang, fled that city to escape the domination of the Majapahit rulers and, more specifically, the wrath of his Javanese father-in-law. He sought refuge on the island of Singapore, killing the local ruler, who was a vassal of the Thai kingdom of Ayutthaya. There, he probably made an alliance with the ruler of Bintan, the largest of islands in the Riau Archipelago; this proved decisive for the future prosperity of Malacca, for Bintan was the home of the Orang Laut, whose support was necessary for effective control of the strait. Around 1403, however, the errant prince was driven out of Singapore by another Thai vassal, perhaps the raja of Pahang or Patani (present-day Pattani). The *Malay Chronicles* gives a colorful account of his flight north along the coast. At Muar his party was attacked by a huge number of monitor lizards, and, at what would become the site of Malacca, Paramesvara saw a white mouse deer kick one of his hunting dogs into the water. This was an unusual feat of courage for such a small animal, and the prince took it as a good omen for the establishment of a permanent settlement (*melaka* is the name of the tree he stood under while witnessing the event). Although Paramesvara is credited in the *Malay Chronicles* with establishing a system of court usages and etiquette that would be the model for later Malay rulers, Malacca in its earliest years was little more than a pirates' lair and a fishing village.

Two factors that made Srivijaya great ensured the paramountcy of its successor, Malacca. The first was the support of the Orang Laut. Their swift *perahu*, powered by oars or sail, were the match of any ships in the region until the coming of tall European craft armed with cannon. The second was the reestablishment of the tribute system by the Chinese, following the establishment of the Ming Dynasty in 1367. The dynasty's founder, Hung Wu, reimposed the prohibition of Chinese private trade overseas. His successor, the Yung-lo emperor (1403–24), initiated a series of maritime expeditions in 1405, lasting until 1433, in which fleets containing as many as 30,000 men sailed as far west as Hormuz, on the Persian Gulf, and East Africa. Undertaken to consolidate the tribute system, the expeditions made China the foremost sea power in Southeast Asian and Indian waters several decades before the European Age of Discovery. Paramesvara was fortunate in gaining the attention of the commander of the expeditions, the eunuch Cheng Ho, and sent a delegation to the imperial court at Nanking in 1405.

The emperor, whose sublime conceit it was to bestow titles of legitimacy on all the rulers of the world, "raised [Malacca] to the status of a city, since when it has been known as the Kingdom of Malacca" (according to a fifteenth-century Chinese account). Paramesvara, a mere local chieftain in the eyes of the Chinese, was made a king; the appropriate regalia, including seals and an inscribed "stone of state," were brought to the city by Cheng Ho in 1409. Two years later, Paramesvara himself visited China on a tribute mission. For the new king the most immediate benefit of the relationship was to bring the weight of China to bear against his old nemesis, the Thai kingdom of Ayutthaya. The Chinese needed Malacca as a naval base for future maritime expeditions and as an emporium "at the end of the monsoons" (as they referred to the Strait of Malacca), where the products of Southeast Asia and the West could be obtained.

Malacca's reputation as a port favored by China drew merchants from all parts of coastal Asia. The city became, like

Srivijaya's capital of Palembang, an entrepôt for the trade of goods from East and West—better situated than Palembang, given its dominant position on the strait. The harbor was sheltered from storms and in its heyday was excellently equipped with underground warehouses that were safe from fire. Weights and measures were standardized, and by the late fifteen century an extensive code of maritime laws was drawn up to cover all aspects of commercial and ship life. Malacca's great prosperity inspired Pires to claim in the early sixteenth century that "no trading port as large as Malacca is known, nor any where they deal in such fine and highly prized merchandise. Goods from all over the East are sold here. Goods from all over the West are sold here. It is at the end of the monsoons, where you find what you want, and sometimes more than you are looking for." In Pires' time Malacca might have had a population of as many as 100,000 persons, remarkable given its lack of an agricultural hinterland (rice had to be imported from Java) and the fact that a settlement of 20,000 was regarded as a big city in contemporary Europe. Owing to Malacca's influence Malay became the principal language of commerce in insular Southeast Asia.

Four *shahbandar* (harbor masters) were in charge of the entrepôt trade: one for ships from the Gujarat area on the west coast of India (the largest trading group); a second for those from other parts of India, Sumatra, and Pegu in Lower Burma; a third for ships from the Indonesian archipelago; and fourth for the Chinese, Annamese, and other nationalities. Ships took advantage of the easterly tradewinds each December and January to bring spices—cloves, nutmeg, mace, cinnamon, and peppers—from Java and the eastern Indonesian archipelago and silks, brocades, and ceramics from China. In May the prevailing westerly winds brought the merchants from India, Pegu, Persia, and the Arabian Peninsula and sped the eastern merchants home with products such as Indian textiles. The Malay Peninsula itself contributed resins, tropical woods, and tin, which was mined in the hills nearby and served as the city's currency. During the fifteenth century Malacca was the linchpin of the world spice trade, the main collecting and purchasing point for those substances that commanded princely sums by the time they reached Europe after shipment through the the Indian Ocean, the Levantine ports of the eastern Mediterranean, and Venice.

Malacca and Islam

In his last years Paramesvara converted to Islam, signified by his assumption of the name Iskandar Shah (1407–36). His motivation was apparently more political than spiritual, for he was concluding a marriage alliance with the northern Sumatran state of Pasai, whose ruler had recently become a Muslim. His conversion promoted closer ties with Malacca's Indian and Arab trading partners. At the time of his death in 1424, however, the prospects for the religion in Southeast Asia were somewhat unclear. The neighboring states, with the exception of Pasai and others on the Sumatra coast, were Buddhist or Hindu-Buddhist, and Iskandar Shah's successor, who took the old Srivijayan title of "Sri Maharaja," remained faithful to the old Indian religions. Upon his death in 1444 there was a succession struggle, which ended with the accession of Muzaffar Shah, a zealous Muslim. He proclaimed Malacca a Muslim state (though many old Hindu-Buddhist usages were retained), and thereafter its prosperity and expansion were linked with the propagation of the religion throughout the region.

Islam gained a firm foothold in Southeast Asia at a relatively late date, despite cosmopolitan trade ties. The religion had been founded by the Prophet Muhammad in western Arabia in the seventh century A.D., and by the eighth century there were Arabs as far east as the southern Chinese port of Kuang-chou and, most likely, also in Southeast Asia. Yet the first certain evidence of an indigenous Muslim community is provided by Marco Polo. Polo landed in northern Sumatra in 1292, on his way back to Venice from China, and relates in his book of travels that Perlak's inhabitants, having been converted by traders, followed the law of Muhammad, while those of neighboring states did not. The fourteenth-century Arab traveler Ibn Batuta related that the ruler of Samudra on Sumatra was a Muslim of the Shafi'i School (see Glossary). Early evidence of Islam on the Malay Peninsula, a boundary stone dated between 1303 and 1387 defining the limits of the "country of Islam" and the "country of war," has been found in the state of Terengganu. Apparently, Muslim Arab communities in the region were neither numerous nor influential enough in the early centuries to challenge the state Hindu-Buddhist cults or the animistic beliefs of the common people. In fact, it was not Arabs, but Indians, particularly those from the port city of Cambay on the Gujarat coast, who provided the dynamic for Islamization.

As Polo's record indicates, Islam came with trade, apparently in a manner similar to that of the propagation of the Indian religions. Although religious conflict was an issue in many locaL succession struggles, such as that which brought Muzaffar Shah to the throne, conversion was accomplished relatively peacefully, with little of the large-scale bloodshed that accompanied its expansion in the Middle East. Merchants from Cambay had long sailed to ports in Southeast Asia. In 1298 that city was captured by Muslims and its ruling class converted. Converts included the traders who began to propagate the new religion in their ports of call, including those of the northern Sumatran coast and the Malay Peninsula.

Scholars have speculated that Sufism, a mystical movement in Islam whose practitioners seek to achieve union with God, may have played an important role in Islamization. The austere, legalistic nature of orthodox Islam may have had less appeal for Malay rulers and their subjects—with their Hindu-Buddhist and animist heritages—than Sufism, which was well established in India. There is, however, no concrete evidence that there were Sufi orders in the region in the thirteenth or fourteenth centuries, so the thesis of Sufi proselytization remains speculative.

During the latter half of the fifteenth century, a golden age both commercially and politically for Malacca, the city took the lead in bringing about conversions on the Malay Peninsula and in the kingdoms of the Indonesian archipelago. The new religion gave its rulers confidence to pursue aggressive policies of expansion. Soon after coming to the throne in 1446, Muzaffar Shah refused to continue paying tribute to the Buddhist Ayutthaya kingdom, provoking a war that resulted in a defeat for the Thai forces and those of their vassals on the peninsula. Instrumental in this victory was the leadership of Tun Perak, whom the Malaccan ruler made prime minister. Described by one historian as "the brain of Malacca's imperialist policy in Malaya and Sumatra for more than three reigns," Tun Perak led an expedition against Pahang, a Thai vassal, which at the time controlled most of the southern part of the Malay Peninsula. The capital was seized, the Thai governor was deposed, and a prince of the Malaccan royal family was placed on the throne as the Muslim sultan of Pahang. By the time of Tun Perak's death in 1498, he had expanded the borders of the kingdom to include both sides of the strait—all of the Malay Peninsula south of what are now the states of Kelantan and Kedah, the Riau and Lingga archipelagos, the island of Singapore, and states along the northern Sumatran coast, such as Rokan, Siak, Kampar, and Indragiri. During the reign of Mahmud Shah (1488–1511), the last of Malacca's seven rulers, the territory was extended further to include all of what is now Peninsular Malaysia and the state of Patani (now in Thailand) as well. As tributaries of Malacca, the rulers of all these states became Muslim, and Islam provided Malacca's dominions with considerable internal cohesion.

Malacca's influence extended well beyond the peninsula and the north coast of Sumatra. The Brunei sultanate, the first Islamic state on the island of Borneo, was established as a consequence of the earlier Brunei kingdom's close trade and political relations with Malacca; the religion's propagation on the island of Java was promoted by Malaccan merchants, who traded at the north coast ports of Tuban and Gresik.

European Intrusion and the Fall of Malacca

The Portuguese initiated the European Age of Discovery in the late fifteenth century. Their motivations were both spiritual and commercial. Zealous Christians who had been charged by the pope with spreading the faith throughout the world, the Portuguese carried out a crusade against the forces of Islam and sought to break Muslim control of the sea-lanes over which the rich spice trade was carried. In 1510 the royal governor of Portugal's overseas enterprises, Alfonso de Albuquerque, captured Goa, on the Indian coast north of Calicut, and it soon became the most important Portuguese base on the Indian Ocean. Malacca, however, was essential to their spiritual and temporal ambitions, given its status as Southeast Asia's most important entrepôt and the point of convergence for Muslim shipping bringing spices westward. A trading expedition had been dispatched there in 1509, and in May 1511 Albuquerque himself led an armada of 18 ships to capture the city. It fell in August, after a bloody, month-long onslaught in which the city was gutted by fire and sacked. The *Malay Chronicles* depicts Malacca's last sultan Mahmud Shah, as personally leading a brave resistance: the Portuguese "fired their cannon from their ships so that the cannon balls came like rain, and the noise of the cannon was as the noise of thunder in the heavens and the flashes of fire of their guns were like flashes of lightning in the sky; and the noise of their matchlocks was like that of groundnuts popping in the frying pan. ... The King went forth on the bridge and stood there amid a hail of bullets." He was forced to flee to Pahang, across the peninsula, where a kinsman of the Malay royal family was ruler.

Although the Portuguese now had a commanding position on the strait and Malacca continued to flourish, the trading monopoly that they sought eluded them. Within a few years of his flight from Malacca, Mahmud Shah had left his refuge at Pahang and set up a new kingdom on the island of Bintan in the Riau Archipelago. Most of the peninsula remained loyal to him, and the Portuguese were perched precariously on the coast. Commanding the allegiance of the Orang Laut, Mahmud Shah orderd them to attack Malacca in 1516 and 1519. He never gave up his hope of regaining it, although the Portuguese captured at Bintan in 1526, and he was forced to flee on foot through the jungle, dying two years later at Kampar on the northern Sumatran coast. Muzaffar, his heir apparent, was made sultan of Perak, while a second son, who ruled as Alaedin Riayat Shah II, established the kingdom of Johore on the river of that name in the southern peninsula. At this time there were three Malay states on the peninsula that claimed royal connections with Malacca. One of them, Johore—because of its strategic position at the southern end of the strait, its Orang Laut war fleets, and its ruler's claim to represent the senior branch of the Malaccan royal family—was the most important.

An equal, if not greater, threat to the Portugese was Aceh, a Muslim state that had been established at the western end of the island of Sumatra and that sought for itself the entrepôt monopoly formerly enjoyed by Malacca. Through the sixteenth century Portugal, Johore, and Aceh fought each other on land and sea. Fortunately for the Portugese, their fortress at Malacca, A Famosa (The Famous One), its walls almost three meters thick and seven meters high and access to the sea at high tide, was strong enough to withstand repeated sieges, including one launched by Aceh in 1558 in which that state mustered a force of 300 warships, 15,000 soldiers, and some 400 artillerymen with cannon brought from Ottoman Turkey. Between 1570 and 1575, A Famosa was hammered by three separate Acehnese attacks and by one undertaken by the state of Japara on the north coast of Java. Yet the Muslim powers soon developed a strong mutual antagonism. In 1575 the Acehnese fleet, fresh from an attack on Malacca, sailed north and captured Perak; its ruler, a relative of the sultan of Johore, was killed; and the surviving royal family was deported to Aceh. Although a political marriage was set up between Perak (a vassal of Aceh) and Johore in order to smooth over relations, Aceh attacked Johore in 1582. The attack was repulsed with the aid of the Portugese, and the sultan came to Malacca to proffer his thanks. Five years later, however, Johorese forces attacked Malacca, and in a counterattack the Portuguese seized and pillaged the sultan's capital of Johore Lama, driving out the ruler and receiving the warm congratulations of the sultan of Aceh.

By the end of the century it had become clear that as long as the Portugese maintained naval superiority, they could inflict punishing blows on their enemies in Malay and Indonesian waters and not be budged from Malacca. Their fortunes, however, were on the wane. The Dutch, who had declared their independence from the Spanish Empire in 1579, were rapidly becoming a significant maritime power, building faster and better ships than their Iberian rivals. The first decades of the seventeenth century witnessed their concerted pressure and attack on practically the entire global network of Portuguese outposts, stretching from Brazil and coastal Africa eastward to Malacca, Macau, and the trading port of Nagasaki in southern Japan. As early as 1595 Dutch ships had reached Malay waters to gain a portion of the rich spice trade. The establishment in 1602 of the Dutch United East India Company (Vereenigde Oostindische Campagnie—VOC) coordinated and strengthened their efforts. Although primarily a commercial institution chartered by the Dutch parliament, the VOC had the authority to raise armies and navies, conclude treaties with indigenous rulers, and build fortresses. The Dutch made alliances with Johore and Aceh, pushed the Portuguese out of the so-called Spice Islands of the eastern Indonesian archipelago, and established in 1619 a permanent base at Batavia on the north coast of Java (the present-day Indonesian capital of Jakarta) from which to control the sea-lanes.

For a short time, however, the most powerful militaty force in the region was Aceh. Its ruler, Iskandar Shah, gained control over the states of Pahang and Kedah and reasserted Acehnese power in Perak, which because of its tin deposits, was deemed a rich prize. The capital of Johore was ravaged twice. The depredations of the Acehnese led the Johorese, the Portguese, and the northern Malay state of Patani to form a united front in 1629 defeating the Acehnese war fleet. Although this marked the end of Acehnese ascendancy in the region, they retained influence in Perak.

The Dutch were not slow to fish in troubled waters. The death of Iskandar Shah of Aceh in 1636 gave Johore greater freedom of action, and the following year the Johorese sultan made a treaty with the Dutch, promising to aid them in the reduction of Malacca. A siege was initiatied in July 1640; it lasted until January 1641 when the Dutch-Johorese forces succeeded in breaking into A Famosa. A Dutch blockade of the harbor of Goa had prevented the Portuguese from sending reinforcements by sea, and their garrison at Malacca, which had withstood innumerable earlier sieges, was worn down by disease and starvation.

The Portuguese contribution to Malay history was—in contrast to that of the earlier Hindu-Buddhist and Islamic merchants and seamen—largely negative. Their seizure of Malacca in 1511 shattered the unity of the Malay world and made it more vulnerable to outside depredations. Part of their mission in the East was to convert native peoples to Christianity, but their harsh treatment of local populations probably spurred the propagation of Islam in insular Southeast Asia as local rulers and their subjects rejected the Portuguese blend of piracy and proselytization. The Protestant Dutch were more tolerant in religious matters but also more thoroughgoing in the mechanics of exploitation and extraction. In the words of Isabella Bird, a nineteenth-century traveler who visited Malacca: "If the Portuguese were little better than buccaneers, the Dutch who drove them out were little better than hucksters—mean, mercenary traders, without redeeming qualities, content to suck the blood of their provinces and give nothing in return." This harsh judgement, however, is better applied to the Indonesian archipelago than to the peninsula. Although the Dutch had great hopes for Malacca as a key to effective, monopolistic control of the trade in spices and other tropical products, Batavia would surpass it as the center of their emerging East Indian empire, and it was—from the seventeenth to the nineteenth centuries—the unfortunate Javanese and inhabitants of the eastern Indonesian archipelago who felt the brunt of their heavy regime.

The Malay States to the End of the Eighteenth Century

The eclipse of Aceh following the death of Iskandar Shah in 1636 and the Dutch capture of Malacca in 1641 heralded a period of relative good fortune for Johore, whose ruler, Abdul Jalil Shah (1623–77), was able to reassert control over the coastal states of Rokan, Kampar, Indragiri, Siak, and Bengkalis on Sumatra. Johore's capital of Batu Sawar grew into a prosperous center of trade, and it seemed for a while that the glory of old Malacca was to a large extent restored. In 1673, however, the eastern Sumatran state of Jambi seized and pillaged Batu Sawar, and Abdul Jalil Shah was forced to flee to Pahang. Although the state was restored by his successor in the Riau Archipelago and then at Kota Tinggi on the Johore River, its power and prestige were much diminished. A misfortune of great ideological as well as political significance occurred in 1699. The ruler, Mahmud Shah, described in Malay and European records alike as a madman and sadist (according to the British trader Alexander Hamilton, he once tried out a pair of new pistols on an unfortunate passerby to test their effectiveness), was assassinated by court nobles, who made the prime minister the new ruler. Mahmud was the last of the senior branch of the royal family of Malacca. In the Malay political world, treason was the greatest of offenses, whatever the provocation (its being up to God to punish tyrants), and the violent end to the royal line seemed to Malays to mark a permanent decline in their fortunes.

The eighteenth century was a period of even greater fragmentation in the Malay world than the sixteenth and seventeenth centuries. Dutch monopolistic policies, the resultant thriving black market in tropical goods, and the desire of well-born but idle *anak raja* (sons of rulers) to find suitable income and recreation stimulated piracy on a grand scale, making Malay waters among the most dangerous in the world. Another factor was the influx of non-Malay peoples into the peninsula. The most important were the Buginese—tough, able traders and fighters whose homeland was in the southeastern portion of the island of Sulawesi. After 1667, when the Dutch cut them off from their traditional control of the Sulawesi-to-Java spice trade, a good number sought their fortunes in the peninsula.

The Minangkabau, from central Sumatra, were another important group of outsiders who over the centuries had established a number of settlements in the peninsula. In 1717 the Minangkabau ruler of the Sumatran state of Siak seized the Johorese throne, and the deposed sultan, in turn, sought Buginese aid to drive him out. Although this was accomplished, it was much easier for the Malays to invite in the Buginese chieftains and their followers than to get them to leave. The latter placed their own nominee on the Johorese throne, while real power was in the hands of a Buginese regent. Buginese control over the Johorese kingdom was strengthened through the marriage of their chiefs to the sultan's female relations, and in fact they boasted that the relation of Johorese royalty to them was like that of a wife to a traditional husband. Conflict between the Buginese and the Minangkabau broke out in Kedah when they intervened on opposite sides in a royal succession struggle in 1724; the former prevailed. The Buginese fought the Minangkabau again in Perak and in 1740 established a Buginese ruling house in the peninsular west coast state of Selangor. Pahang was under the Minangkabau, who also ruled a number of small states on or near the west coast. These states formed a confederation in 1775, which was the basis of what later became the Negeri Sembilan, or Nine States.

Dutch interests in the peninsula centered on tin. The Dutch grew concerned over increasing Buginese power and especially over their attempts in Perak and elsewhere to evade the Dutch efforts to maintain a monopoly in the tin trade. In 1755 the sultan of Johore offered the Dutch trade and tin monopolies if they would rid him of the Buginese. The Dutch and Buginese fought each other intermittently until 1784, when Buginese rulers were overthrown by the Dutch in Johore, Riau, and Selangor. The Dutch established a garrison at the Buginese stronghold in the Riau Archipelago in 1785. The consequence of this was that the sultan of Johore now had a Dutch, rather than a Buginese, "husband."

Another factor in the distress of the Malay world was Siam

(modern Thailand). By the sixteenth century the Thai had established a power base at Ligor (present-day Nakhon Sithammarat) and held the Malay states of Pahang, Terengganu, and Patani as vassals. These states were obliged to send tribute to Ayutthaya. When Patani asserted its independence in the early seventeenth century, it was invaded and devastated by a Thai army. Wars between the Thai and the Burmese in the seventeenth and eighteenth centuries gave the northern Malay states some respite, but the establishment of the Chakri Dynasty at Bangkok in 1782 initiated a new period of Thai expansionism. King Rama I (1782–1809) demanded that the rulers of the northern Malay states come to his capital to make personal obeisance. Most sent polite refusals, but the ruler of Patani—on the front line of Thai expansionism—refused defiantly; his kingdom was invaded, its inhabitants put to the sword, and divided into seven districts under the control of a Thai governor.

Brunei and the Northern Borneo Coast

There seems to have been a significant Chinese presence on the northern coast of Borneo by the late fourteenth century, which is not remarkable given its position on the southern rim of the South China Sea. There are accounts of a Chinese dignitary, Wang Sen-ping, who established a settlement around 1375 on the Kinabatangan River, in what is now the state of Sabah, and was designated governor of the region. Wang married his daughter to the ruler of Brunei, and his granddaughter married an Arab who ascended the Brunei throne. Local tradition maintains that the first ruler of Sulu, a state centered in the Sulu Archipelago (now part of the Republic of the Philippines), which developed into Brunei's strongest rival in the region, was a Chinese with the surname Ch'en. The name of Malaysia's tallest mountain, Kinabalu (the Chinese Widow), reflects this early Chinese presence, as does the traditionally high regard the Iban people of Sarawak have for Chinese jars, some dating back to the Sung Dynasty (960–1279), which were believed to have magic powers and were exchanged as pledges between two chiefs or as dowries. Possession of these jars remains today a significant mark of status.

In the early fifteenth century the ruler of Brunei, like the ruler of Malacca, was recognized as a king by the Chinese emperor and traveled to the imperial capital to pay his respects. As in the case of Malacca, however, the formative influence on that state's development was Islam. Trade, diplomatic, and marriage connections with Malacca facilitated the conversion of this kingdom, originally based on a Hindu-Buddhist cult, into an Islamic state, and thus it became part of the larger Malay world. Muslim chiefs, speaking Malay and maintaining close ties with the peninsula, established themselves along the coast and came to owe allegiance to the sultan of Brunei. This ruler's prestige and fortunes grew after the fall of Malacca in 1511; Muslim merchants, wishing to shun the Christian-dominated entrepôt, flocked to his port. Brunei's influence as an Islamic power gradually extended into the Philippines, and settlements as far north as Manila had Muslim rulers by the time the Spanish established their colony in 1571. Only in the southern portions of the Philippine archipelago, however—on the island of Mindanao and the Sulu Archipelago—were Muslim rulers successful in resisting Spanish dominance and Christianization.

The northern Borneo coast itself was affected more by Spanish than by Portuguese intrusions in the sixteenth century. Ships of Magellan's expedition reached Brunei in 1521. According to its chronicler, Pigafetta, the city had as many as 25,000 families and an elegant court given to displays of wealth. Never as powerful as Malacca, it had only one *shahbandar* but was described by Pigafetta as indubitably the greatest state on the island of Borneo. In 1578 the Spanish became involved in Brunei politics and succeeded in placing their own candidate on the sultan's throne, although his lack of cooperation forced a second expedition two years later.

This left Brunei significantly weakened and allowed the Sulu sultanate, which had been established in the mid-fifteenth century, to assert its independence. At the end of the seventeenth century the rivalry of two heirs to the Brunei throne brought on a civil war; one of the pretenders asked the sultan of Sulu for military aid in return for a portion of what is now Sabah. Although Sulu's ally won the war, it later became unclear whether the promised cession actually took place or whether the sultan of Sulu unilaterally claimed the territory as his reward. This question of overlapping claims was to become important in the late nineteenth century when some enterprising Western businessmen sought to obtain a grant of the disputed territory north and east of Brunei. Some of the ramifications of this dispute also carried over into the twentieth-century controversy between Malaysia and the Philippines over title to Sabah (see External Threats: "Confrontation" and the Philippine Claim to Sabah, this ch.).

Until the nineteenth century, Dutch interest in the island of Borneo was minimal, although they attempted to set up factories on the south and west coasts at Sambas, Sukadana, and Banjermasin. The growth of trade between southern China and British India in the eighteenth century, however, spurred British East India Company interest in the northern coast and the Sulu Archipelago. A base was needed for ships on the India-China trade route to free them from dependence on Dutch facilities at Batavia and provide them with a strategic edge in their struggles at that time with the French. In January 1761 British East India Company representative Alexander Dalrymple concluded a commercial treaty with the sultan of Sulu and the following year negotiated cession of the island of Balambangan, just north of Sabah, as a company trading post. It was not until 1773, however, that a settlement was actually established on the island. It came rapidly to an ignominious end, being destroyed by pirates in 1775. Its survivors fled to Brunei, where they were able to gain from the sultan the cession to the island of Labuan, although that was abandoned the following year.

Sulu, in fact, was a center for piracy, particularly in the eighteenth and early nineteenth centuries; the sultan and his notables commissioned bands of Ilanun seamen, originally from the island of Mindanao in the Philippines, to carry out slave raids along the Borneo coast and as far west as the Malay Peninsula and Sumatra. According to contemporary records, the yearly "season of the Ilanun" was a time of terror beside which the depredations of the Buginese and the Orang Laut paled.

The British Colonial Presence

The British role in developments in the Malay world was minimal before the late eighteenth century when the British East India Company sought to establish a naval base at the eastern rim of the Indian Ocean. A number of different locations were investigated, but in 1785 Francis Light, a former naval officer and private trader, negotiated on his own an agreement with the sultan of Kedah. This provided for the grant of the island of Penang to the British, on the understanding that they would provide the sultan with armed protection and an annual payment. The company, however, was reluctant to agree to anything that might resemble a defensive alliance. The sultan, becoming aware of this, tried twice to expel the British from Penang but was unsuccessful. In March 1791 he was obliged to sign an official agreement providing him with only a small annual payment. In 1800 the sultan ceded an additional small strip of land, Perai, on the mainland opposite

Penang, guaranteeing that the British would have complete control of Penang's harbor and a supply of food.

Even without a defensive alliance, the cession of Penang disturbed the Dutch, ever jealous of their monopoly, and the Thai, who considered Kedah a vassal. Yet the settlement of George Town, which Light established on Penang's shore in July 1786, soon flourished. Penang's policy was initially one of free trade, and the island became an entrepôt where the products of India and the West were exchanged for local commodities, such as tin, spices, ebony, rattan, and pepper. Soon it eclipsed Malacca, which under the Dutch had attained an advanced state of decrepitude; in 1795 Malacca had a population of only 1,500, compared with Penang's 20,000. In a significant sense, Penang was in miniature an image of the Malaysia to come. Light and his successors encouraged pepper and spice plantations, and a cosmoplitan community of Malays, Chinese, Indians, other Asians, and Europeans assembled, each group observing its own laws and customs. Officially a dependency of British Bengal, Penang's administrative development was haphazard; only in 1807 were law courts and a code of law firmly established. Plans to make Penang a naval base commanding the eastern Indian Ocean never came to fruition.

Events in Europe, however, ensured that the British would become more deeply involved in the Malay world. In 1795 Holland was occupied by the forces of revolutionary France, and the Dutch government in exile in London made an agreement that the British would occupy Dutch overseas territories in order to prevent them from being taken over by the French. British troops and administrators entered Malacca, as well as several points in the Indonesian archipelago. Although the old port was to be returned to the Dutch in 1802, the allied struggle against Napoleon in Europe prolonged the British stay until 1818.

The central figure in a more active British role in the region was Thomas Stamford Raffles, a British East India Company man who had been stationed at Penang. He gained an extensive knowledge of Malay affairs and customs and served as lieutenant governor of Java after the British wrested control of that island from a pro-French regime in 1811. Raffles was a man of scholarly attainments despite a limited formal education, and his *History of Java* was one of the earliest and best studies on that subject. His knowledge of indigenous languages and customs reflected a deeper sympathy for the people than was common among Europeans in the region. While in control of Java, he had promoted reforms aimed at the abolition of slavery and forced labor. Yet he was also, in the words of an unsympathetic observer, "full of tricks and not so full of truth as was desirable, and he was the most nervous man I ever knew." His aspirations to establish permanent British rule in the Indonesian archipelago were frustrated by the ultimate decision in London to return the East Indies possessions to Holland. Raffles was given command of the remote settlement of Bengkulu on Sumatra, an exile that did not prevent him from continuing his efforts to challenge Dutch control of the region.

Raffles had gotten permission from the British governor general of India, Warren Hastings, to locate and establish a new British naval station in the Johore and Riau Archipelago region. Penang, despite its early prosperity, had limitations both as a commercial center and as a naval base, being located north of the Strait of Malacca; Malacca had been returned to the Dutch, although shorn of that fine old fort, A Famosa, which the British blew up with great difficulty, fearing that in the future they might have to seize it by force. The fluid and unconsolidated state of Johorese politics at this time afforded Raffles an opportunity to make an agreement with the Tunku Hussain, elder brother of the man the Dutch recognized as ruler, in which the British would recognize him as sultan. In return, Tunku Hussain agreed in 1819 to grant the British the right to establish a settlement on the island of Singapore, which at that time was largely swamp, inhabited only by a handful of fisherfolk.

Despite Dutch indignation and British skepticism, the new port proved an extraordinary success, owing largely to its commanding position at the southern end of the strait and Raffles' free-trade policies. Unlike many, if not most, colonial enterprises at the time, Singapore paid for itself—in fact, within a year of its foundation. Its history, according to colonial official and historian Sir Richard Winstedt, "is written mainly in statistics." By 1825 its trade had already surpassed that of Penang and Malacca combined, totaling £2.6 million; by 1850 this had increased to £5.6 million, more than doubling to £13.3 million in 1864.

Singapore was in a very significant sense the successor to Srivijaya and Malacca—a link between China and India as well as a center for the commercial life of Southeast Asia and for the diffusion of new ideas and techniques into the region. The great difference was that Malays were no longer the principal actors but bystanders in the development of the new entrepôt. Singapore had a British administration and what would rapidly evolve into a Chinese-controlled economy (see Colonial Economy and Society, this ch.).

Singapore's international position was secured by the Anglo-

Dutch Treaty of 1824, which defined the Malay Peninsula and the island as being within the British sphere of influence, while Sumatra and the Riau and Lingga archipelagos would be within the Dutch sphere. This removed a constant irritant between the two countries, but the Malay world, which had maintained a considerable sense of cultural and ideological, if not political, unity through centuries of fragmentation and foreign intervention, was split between the two European powers, and the basis for the two separate nations of Malaysia and Indonesia was established.

The treaty returned Malacca to the British, and in 1826 the five territories of Malacca, Penang, Perai (known at that time as Province Wellesley), Dindings, and Singapore were joined under a single administration with the capital first at Penang and, after 1832, in Singapore. These "Straits Settlements" were under the jurisdiction of the British Indian government (until 1857 the British East India Company government) at Calcutta. The India connection, however, was seen as something of an impediment, particularly by commercial interests, and in 1867 the Straits Settlements were made a separate crown colony under the British Colonial Office.

Federated and Unfederated Malay States, 1826–1909

British colonial rule and institutions on the Malay Peninsula evolved at a slow and uncertain pace, in large part because of the British government's reluctance to acquire additional territory and commitments in the region. Nevertheless, from the vantage point of the Straits Settlements, the British could not be totally uninvolved in developments in the Malay states. Siam's brutal invasion of Kedah in 1821 led to the ruler's and thousands of his subjects' seeking asylum in Penang. The British needed Siam as an ally against Burma (war between British India and that country broke out in 1824) but could not tolerate the disruption and instability that resulted from the continued push southward by the rulers of Siam. When a Thai fleet threatened the Malay state of Perak in 1825, the British sent gunboats to the scene to discourage an invasion. In the following year a treaty was concluded with Bangkok in which the independence of Perak and Selangor was guaranteed in exchange for recognition of Siamese suzerainty over Kedah. Although a clause guaranteeing the freedom of British merchants to conduct business in the Malay east coast states of Kelantan and Terengganu was included, dependence of these states on Siam was recognized de facto. Kedah, Kelantan, Terengganu, and the much abused state of Patani were expected to send tribute to Bangkok every three years. Continued Thai threats against Perak led to an agreement in October 1826 between the sultan and the British in which the latter guaranteed assistance in case Perak was threatened. Although the British East India Company was very reluctant to recognize the agreement as a binding treaty, it marked a significant departure from the policy of nonintervention. North of Perak and on the east coast, the Thai continued to dominate. When a Malay prince led a revolt against them in Kedah in 1838, a British blockade of the coast helped Bangkok to reassert its authority.

In 1861 Siam stirred the troubled waters of succession politics in the east coast state of Pahang by supporting one claimant, Mahmud, and bringing him to neighboring Terengganu in a Thai ship. To forestall Siamese designs, the governor of the Straits Settlements, Orfeur Cavenagh, ordered gunboats to shell the Terengganu capital of Kuala Terengganu in November 1862, forcing Mahmud to return to Bangkok. The following year one of Mahmud's rivals, Ahmad, gained the throne with the support of local Pahang chiefs. The British action effectively blocked the expansion of Thai influence south of Terengganu, but the status of the northern Malay states would not be fully resolved until the Anglo-Siamese Treaty of 1909. Siam's King Mongkut (1851–68) and his successor, King Chulalongkorn (1868–1910), were enlightened rulers whose policies toward the northern Malay states were less heavy-handed than those of their predecessors; the rulers were allowed virtually complete internal autonomy in exchange for the traditional gestures of tribute and submission.

Piracy was a factor in British intervention in the peninsula. Although the most dreaded pirates were the Ilanun hirelings of the Sulu sultanate, local Orang Laut bands conducted piracy on a troublesome scale, regarding the plundering of passing ships more as a seasonal occupation than a life of crime. Malay rulers often got a portion of the booty, and thus the British had some difficulty persuading them to cooperate in an antipiracy campaign. Yet by 1870 the threat of piracy had been largely removed in peninsular waters. One result of this was the decline of the Orang Laut as an identifiable group; their ancient way of life—a combination of commerce and piracy—was undercut. British patrol boats and the forces of cooperative Malay rulers made piracy increasingly risky, and the competition of foreign shippers—Chinese, European, and Indian—employing steamships drove them out of commerce.

Singapore's rapid progress through the nineteenth century made it increasingly difficult for colonial authorities to maintain the favored policy of nonintervention. By 1867, when the Straits

Settlements were made a crown colony, Singapore had a population of 100,000. Sixty percent of the total was Chinese. In the early years Singapore's most important commerce was with China, the city serving as the collecting point for the products that the Chinese had sought for centuries from the South Seas—resins, camphor, beeswax, and exotica such as the birds' nests from the caves of the northern Borneo coast that were highly valued as the ingredient of a delicate soup. European markets, however, grew in importance as tin was mined in the states of Negeri Sembilan, Perak, and Selangor and as gutta-percha (a rubber-like resin) was obtained from the forests of the interior. The dependence of Singapore on a steady supply of raw materials from the peninsula and the chronic instability of the Malay states—where succession struggles formed a principal pastime of an idle and jealous nobility—led commercial interests to pressure the British authorities to take a more active role. By the late 1860s only Terengganu and Johore had really stable governments. Both had strong sultans—Baginda Umar in the former and Abu Bakar in the latter—who favored administrative and fiscal reform.

The Chinese were also a destabilizing factor in the states, where they came to work as tin miners under contract to Malay rulers. In 1860 the government of the Straits Settlements had to intervene in the Negeri Sembilan and, two years later, in Perak, owing to conflicts between Chinese miners and Malay rulers. Chinese secret societies, principally the Hai San and the Ghee Hin, enrolled thousands of members who engaged in bloody battles in the tin mining areas, particularly in Perak, and took sides in local succession struggles. Selangor, a state that had been carved up into five bailiwicks by local chiefs backed by Chinese toughs, was another center of violence perpetrated by both Malay and Chinese. By the early 1870s Selangor was a reasonable facsimile of Thomas Hobbes' "state of nature"—life for many of its inhabitants being "nasty, brutish and short." British involvement there grew as an expedition was dispatched in 1871 to deal with Chinese pirates. When tin exports to the Straits Settlements were threatened, Chinese and European merchants petitioned the government to take a more active role in enforcing law and order.

In the last decades of the nineteenth century, another issue making the old laissez-faire policy increasingly impractical was the perceived threat of rival imperialist powers. The German Empire, established in 1871, wanted its "place in the sun"—a colonial empire—and France had already obtained protectorates in Cochin China (the southern part of Vietnam) and Cambodia by 1868. Also, Holland had initiated a policy of expansion into all corners of the Indonesian archipelago, and its attempts to reduce the sultanate of Aceh on the western tip of Sumatra particularly perturbed the British. Anarchic conditions in the peninsula, imperialists argued, made it an inviting prospect for the intervention of other European powers.

The 1874 Treaty of Pangkor

The January 1874 Treaty of Pangkor marks what is commonly regarded as a watershed in the constitutional development of the peninsula. Thereafter, British control, though formally indirect, was more firmly established and resulted in the transformation of the political and economic systems of the Malay states. The treaty was concluded between the British and one of the several pretenders to the throne of Perak, Raja Abdullah. In exchange for British recognition and support, Abdullah, as sultan of Perak, accepted a British resident (appointed by the governor of the Straits Settlements) whose counsel "must be asked and acted upon on all questions other than those touching Malay custom and religion." Residents were also established in Sungai Ujung—one of the nine entities of the Negeri Sembilan—and in Selangor. This simple, though in practice not always unambiguous, formula preserved and co-opted the Malay rulers and the upper ranks of the nobility.

The new residency system got off to an inauspicious start. The first resident of Perak, W.W. Birch, was so zealous in his attempts to push reforms on Malays, particularly in reference to the issue of slavery, that conservatives, on Abdullah's approval, had him assassinated in November 1875. Although Birch's behavior, particularly his penchant for "dressing down" Malay notables in public, aroused hostility, there seems to have been in the first years of the residency system a mutual difference of perception between British and Malays concerning the real nature of the resident's role. For the latter, he was an adviser only, and his insistence on involving himself in government was deeply resented. Upon Birch's death, a British expedition was dispatched to Perak to depose Abdullah and establish a rival as regent. The throne would remain empty until 1887, when the regent, Raja Yusuf, was made sultan. Fighting also took place in Sungai Ujung. There the British supported their client, the Dato' Kelana, against his conservative rivals.

Given Singapore's economic interests, it was not surprising that the residency system was first established in the tin-producing states—Perak, Sungai Ujung, and Selangor. This, along with continued piracy, was the occasion for intervention in Selangor. The central role in establishing the institutional bases for British indirect rule was taken by Hugh Low, resident of Perak between 1877 and 1889. Low, who had experience as an administrator in Sarawak under the "white raja," Sir James Brooke, worked on the assumption that stable government could be established only through winning the support of the ruler and the most important nobles (see Developments on Borneo, this ch.). Rulers' opposition to fiscal reforms and the abolition of slavery had been largely inspired by fear of the loss of revenue; in exchange for reforms, the British granted them generous subsidies. This had the further happy result of putting a stop to that perennial Malay pastime, the succession struggle. The established ruler had revenue and British force to back him up against any prince who might envy his throne. The British, moreover, scrupulously maintained the etiquette and ceremony of Malay courts and gave government employment to the *anak raja* and other members of the nobility.

The most important political institution in what became known as the "protected" Malay states was the State Council, a consultative body that consisted of the ruler; important nobles and chiefs; a representative of the Chinese community; and the resident, who nominated council members other than the foregoing, who had to be approved by the governor of the Straits Settlements. Although religious affairs and those pertaining to Malay custom remained the prerogative of the ruler, Western concepts of modern administration were introduced. On the local level, British district officers supervised administration in conjunction with the *penghulu* (district headman). Before the residency system was established, the *penghulu* had been powerful local rulers, but they were now simply appendages of British rule. Sultans and princes had formerly possessed independent armed forces and sources of revenue from trade, taxes, and piracy and maintained personal ties with their subjects. Now they were figureheads or functionaries and, as such, lost popular esteem and support. Yet the transformation was not a particularly violent one, at least compared with Burmese resistance to the British or Vietnamese resistance to the French around the same time, and there were relatively few outbreaks of significant Malay resistance to the extension of British rule.

One instance, however, was in Pahang, the large Malay east coast state whose ruler had requested a British resident in 1888. After a resident was appointed, a number of Pahang's chiefs, disappointed with declining revenues under British auspices, organized a rebellion that lasted until 1895. Its most determined leaders were forced to flee to the Thai vassal-state of Kelantan, where they were arrested and deported to Bangkok. In 1895 all nine Minangkabau states, including Sungai Ujung, agreed to accept a resident who would be responsible for a single administrative unit, the Negeri Sembilan.

Over the next two decades the administration was centralized in the interests of efficiency and the promotion of development in Pahang and the poorer regions of the Negeri Sembilan. These reduced still further the authority of the Malay rulers. In 1896 Frank Swettenham, at that time resident of Perak, persuaded the rulers to sign the Treaty of Federation, which established a federal government with its own administrative and fiscal apparatus at Kuala Lumpur (a town, destined to be the federal capital of Malaysia, which had begun its existence ingloriously in the mid-nineteenth century as a tin miners' settlement). The governor of the Straits Settlements was also designated high commissioner for the Federated Malay States, and a resident general (the first one being Swettenham) was placed in charge of the residents of each of the Federated Malay States. In 1909 a further step was taken with the establishment of the Federal Council at Kuala Lumpur, which took over the important responsibilities of the state councils. Although the rulers were invited to participate in conferences (*durbar*) in 1897 and in 1903, they were now decorous bystanders. As critical historians of British Malaya have pointed out, the new constitutional arrangements continued to provide the appearance of Malay rule while gently depriving the sultans and chief notables of the reality.

The Unfederated Malay States and Johore

British interest in the northern Malay states of Kedah, Terengganu, Kelantan, and Perlis grew with the apprehension that some other European power capitalizing on the weakness of Siam might intervene there. In 1897 the British concluded a secret agreement with Bangkok that they would continue to recognize Thai supremacy over the states as long as no other power established a presence there. Although King Chulalongkorn desired to maintain Thai supremacy, he was dependent on British goodwill as a counterweight to France (which controlled neighboring Indochina, while Britain ruled Burma to the west). In 1909 the king signed a treaty transferring the states to the British sphere of influence (though Patani to the north remained a part of Siam). Despite British prodding, the four sultans refused to join their states to the federation. They received British advisers, who differed significantly from the residents of the Federated Malay States in that they did not have de facto executive power and were obliged to use persuasion with the sultans on matters of policy. The Unfederated Malay States of Kedah, Kelantan, Perlis, and

Terengganu were the poorest and least developed of any on the Malay Peninsula; their rulers, however, maintained a modicum of independence, and while the rest of the peninsula was transformed by colonial social and economic forces, they remained havens of traditional Malay ways of life and culture.

Johore also remained outside the Federated Malay States, despite its close economic ties with Singapore and the fact that it was hemmed in on sides by "protected" states. Its able ruler, Abu Bakar, had reformed his administration along Western lines and was on close and friendly terms with the British. He insisted, however, that his own state remain independent and politely resisted pressures to accept a resident. In 1885 he went to London to gain assurance that Johore's special status would continue to be recognized, and in 1895 he promulgated a constitution that expressly forbade the surrendering of Johore's sovereignty to any foreign power. Abu Bakar's son Ibrahim came into conflict with the British over control of the railroad line being built through his state from Singapore to the Federated Malay States and over other issues in which he sought to assert Johore's independence of Singapore and London. In 1909, however, he accepted a British "financial adviser" who had wide-ranging powers, and in 1914 the state's general adviser was made responsible not to the sultan but to the Singapore governor. Although its independence by this time was much diminished, Johore never joined the federation.

After the Johore question was settled, the Malay Peninsula was divided into 10 political entities: the Straits Settlements (which after 1844 included the island of Labuan, which had been granted to it by the sultan of Brunei), four Federated Malay States, and five Unfederated Malay States (see fig. 3).

Developments on Borneo

The establishment of the "white rajas" of the Brooke family in Sarawak along the northern Borneo coast is one of the more colorful episodes in Malaysia's colonial history. This region had come under the control of the sultan of Brunei in the sixteenth century; by the early nineteenth century, however, Brunei's power was substantially in decline, and the coast and river estuaries were infested with Ilanun, Orang Laut, and Iban pirates. Malays, tied by old allegiances and the Islamic religion to Brunei, were concentrated along the coast, while the Iban (called Sea Dayak by Europeans because of their skill on water), lived upriver behind the coastal ranges and had a well-deserved reputation as fierce fighters and headhunters. The Iban and a smaller group, the Bidayuh, or Land Dayak, were animist. Although broadly characterized by

Source: Based on information from Kam Hing Lee, "Malaya: New State and Old Elites," in Robin Jeffrey, ed., *Asia: The Winning of Independence*, New York, 1981, 217; Kim Wah Yeo, *The Politics of Decentralization*, Kuala Lumpur, 1982; and Francis Robinson, *Atlas of the Islamic World since 1500*, New York, 1982, 152.

Figure 3. Malaya under British Rule

Europeans as tribes or ethnic groups, the Iban and Bidhayuh before the colonial era identified themselves primarily with their village and longhouse communities, where headmen ruled in accordance with customary law. Unlike the Brunei Malays, they could claim no central political authority.

James Brooke, a former British East India Company officer and man of independent means, sought a life of adventure in the East and in 1839 sailed in his own ship, the *Royalist*, to northern Borneo to explore the area. There he became involved in a civil war between the sultan of Brunei and some of his chiefs, offering his assistance to the former. The rebellion was suppressed with the aid of Brooke's naval guns, and the sultan rewarded him with a stretch of territory in return for a small annual payment. This was nothing new in Malay history, but Brooke was the first European to be so honored; in September 1841 he was installed as "raja" of Sarawak with his capital in the small Malay town of Kuching. With classic understatement, Brooke wrote in his diary, "I have a country but oh, how beset with difficulties." The major one was piracy. During the next few years, with British Royal Navy assistance, he occupied himself with its eradication. In 1849 he defeated a flotilla of 100 Iban war boats at Batang Mura. For this, the sultan granted him more territory along the coast on the condition that Brooke remit half its revenue to him. His services were highly appreciated in Singapore, whose commerce had been greatly affected by a resurgence in piracy; but accusations of atrocities perpetuated against the Iban circulated in London, and it was not until 1854 that a royal commission exonerated him. In fact, Brooke managed to gain the allegiance of most of the Iban chiefs, and when Chinese secret societies initiated a bloody uprising in Kuching in 1857, it was the raja's Iban allies who were most helpful in suppressing it.

Brooke died in 1868 and was succeeded by his nephew, Charles Brooke, whose reign as Sarawak's second raja lasted 50 years. During this time, Sarawak's territory continued to expand as the sultan of Brunei was bribed and cajoled into granting more land. Eventually, the sultan was left with only two small slivers of territory, which compose present-day Brunei. Sarawak's international status was an issue of some ambiguity. Though the Brookes were British subjects, they ruled what was in effect an independent country. The Dutch looked on its expansion with suspicion and hostility, and London itself was reluctant to see the Brookes swallow up the Brunei sultanate. With the threat of French or German intervention, however, the British government concluded a protectorate arrangement with Sarawak, Brunei, and the British

North Borneo Company jurisdiction in 1888. These states would allow London to formulate their foreign policy in exchange for security guarantees.

Sarawak under the Brookes was a laboratory for later political arrangements on the Malay Peninsula. These were essentially conservative in nature. From his days in India and in the China trade, James Brooke developed the conviction that Asians were best isolated from Western influences, and as raja he operated on the premise that each group ought to have a fixed economic and social role. Thus, Malays were encouraged to pursue small-scale agriculture, Chinese were brought in as traders and shopkeepers, and the Iban served as the raja's soldiers under his personal command. By 1867 Brooke had established the State Council and had set up a system of European residents throughout his domains, working in conjunction with indigenous local leaders. After 1874 both the institutions and the underlying conservative intent of these were adopted in large measure on the peninsula.

The region of Borneo north and east of Brunei, known after 1878 as North Borneo and after 1963 as Sabah, was a kind of imperialists' football in the late nineteenth century. Two indigenous rulers, the sultans of Brunei and Sulu, claimed it, with amusing consequences for Western entrepreneurs. In 1865 a United States venture, the American Trading Company of Borneo, leased it from the sultan of Brunei. After this company's attempt at development foundered, the lease was taken over by Alfred Dent, a British merchant based in Hong Kong, and Baron von Overbeck, Austro-Hungarian consul general in that city. The total grant was 17.3 million hectares, ceded on the condition that the Brunei sultan and his minister of war receive an annual payment totaling 15,000 Straits dollars. Dent and von Overbeck soon discovered, however, that this immense chunk of territory was not the sultan of Brunei's to give; its local chiefs only recognized the authority of the sultan of Sulu, and a second agreement, also involving an annual payment, had to be concluded with him.

The situation was complicated by the determination of the Spanish in the Philippines to conquer Sulu and annex all the territory under its control. In 1878 a Spanish gunboat was dispatched to Sandakan, where a representative of Dent and von Overbeck had established a residency to enforce the claim. Spain's effort failed, as did subsequent Dutch attempts. In 1881 the British government granted a royal charter to Dent's enterprise, the British North Borneo Company. (Von Overbeck, having failed to convince his superiors in Vienna that Malays, Kadazans, and Chinese would make as good Habsburg subjects as Hungarians, Czechs, and Bosnians, sold his share to Dent.) The company, similar to those chartered by the British in Africa, had the responsibility of administering and developing the territory on the proviso that it would not be alienated to a foreign power and that its foreign relations would be under British control. A treaty concluded by Britain, Spain, and Germany in 1885 recognized Spanish control of the Sulu Archipelago in exchange for renunciation of its claims to any territory in Borneo. In 1891 a border agreement was signed by Britain and Holland, although the border was not fully mapped and surveyed until 1912. As the historian D. G. E. Hall comments, "these dates form an intriguing commentary upon the urgency of the matter."

Like Sarawak, North Borneo had a population of Malays on the coast and animist peoples, chiefly the Kadazan, in the forested interior. Its most important products were timber and, in the twentieth century, tobacco. Overall, the company's administration was a patchwork affair, employing a medley of British residents and indigenous chiefs who lacked the dynamism that a strong leader like the first two Brooke rajas were able to provide in Sarawak. The region remained a conglomeration of different tribal groups in which unity and direction remained elusive. The ambitions of entrepreneurs to unlock a vast hoard of wealth in the Borneo interior remained largely unrealized. In Sarawak this was due to the Brookes' unwillingness to disturb indigenous ways of life by promoting economic development; in North Borneo it was more a result of the company's general ineffectiveness.

Colonial Economy and Society

During the nineteenth and twentieth centuries, economic development occurred largely along the west coast of the Malay Peninsula; the east coast, particularly the Unfederated Malay States, and the Borneo territories were less affected by modern transformations. From at least as early as the time of the Malacca sultanate, small communities of Chinese traders and shopkeepers had lived in the Malay- and European-controlled entrepôts. During the eighteenth century Malay and Buginese rulers began inviting Chinese—many of them refugees from the Dutch persecution of their community in Java following the 1740 Chinese revolt there—to set up plantations for the cultivation of cash crops, such as pepper, gambier (a resinous substance used in tanning), and tapioca (a derivative of cassava root used to make puddings). These were small holdings, although their total area during the nineteenth century may have been as much as 200,000 hectares.

They were located principally in Johore, the Minangkabau states of the Negeri Sembilan, and Selangor, as well as in the Straits Settlements.

It was tin, however, that spurred a revolution in both the economy and the demographics of the west coast of the peninsula. This metal had been one of its earliest exports. Malays had panned it from riverbeds for centuries, but in the nineteenth century the ownership and operation of more modern tin mines were predominantly Chinese. The discovery of rich deposits of tin ore in the Larut district of Perak in 1848 and in the Kinta district of the same state in 1880, coupled with growth in demand for tin in the industrialized nations in the late nineteenth century, led Malay and British rulers alike to encourage the large-scale immigration of Chinese laborers to work the mines. By 1890 some 80,000 had come from southern China by way of the Straits Settlements to Perak, and another 60,000 had come to other tin-producing areas. Chinese mine owners adopted new technology from abroad, principally Australia, and adapted their own extensive experience in irrigation to make the mines more productive. By the end of the nineteenth century, the Federated Malay States were the world's largest exporter of tin.

In the twentieth century large European and British mining firms expanded into the tin sector at the expense of the Chinese. New technology, particularly the bucket-dredge, which made it possible to dig deeper and exploit poorer deposits of ore over a large area, required investments on a scale that the old Chinese firms could not manage. In 1913 only one-quarter of all mines were European owned, but 25 years later the proportion had risen to two-thirds. Another development was flagging demand for the metal on world markets, particularly during the world depression of the 1930s. In 1931 the International Tin Control Scheme among producer nations was ratified, although a number of revisions were to follow.

Upon the establishment of British rule in the Federated Malay States, the government involved itself actively in the promotion of the mining sector. Land surveys were conducted, roads built, and by 1895 railroads had been built connecting the tin mines to the west coast. By 1918 a railroad running from the Siamese border to Johore Baharu, the capital of Johore State, connected the tin districts with the Straits Settlements. The Mines Department was responsible for control of waterworks in tin-bearing riverbeds and streambeds and the enforcement of safety regulations.

Compared with tin, the establishment of rubber plantations on a large scale was a recent phenomenon, although rubber surpassed tin as the peninsula's most profitable export by 1961. H.N. Ridley, appointed director of the Singapore Botanical Gardens in 1888, was principally responsible for promoting its cultivation. He developed methods for extracting latex from the trees of the *Hevea brasiliensis* variety, which had originally grown wild in Brazil, and, with a single-minded devotion that earned him the nickname "rubber Ridley," encouraged skeptical planters to grow them. His cause was helped by poor markets for Malayan coffee; European planters began to abandon coffee in favor of rubber, particularly after the invention of the automobile opened up a vast market potential. If the Industrial Revolution had run on steel and steam, the "motor age" ran on oil and rubber. In 1900 only about 2,000 hectares were planted in rubber. Following the first of a number of "rubber booms," however, the number increased to 109,000 hectares by 1908. In 1913 it was 322,000 hectares. By 1920 the peninsula was supplying 53 percent of the world's rubber.

The rubber sector was dominated by large-scale plantations backed by European and, to a lesser extent, Chinese investors. The ease with which *Hevea brasiliensis* could be grown, however, soon attracted smallholders, including Malays, who planted the trees around their regular crops. Given the more developed infrastructure of the west coast, the rubber-growing sector was concentrated there, although trees were planted in every Malay state, and rubber was an important export for Sarawak and North Borneo.

Like the price of tin, the price of rubber fluctuated with unstable world demand, the depression again causing the greatest distress. In 1934 Malaya joined other would producers to establish the International Rubber Regulation Committee in a largely futile effort to control production. On the eve of World War II, the peninsula had some 1.3 million hectares planted in rubber, of which about three-fifths were in large estates.

Weak markets for rubber after World War I stimulated the planting of still another crop, oil palms. Palm oil is used in the manufacture of soap, margarine, lubricants, and even fuel. By 1939 the peninsula supplied about 11 percent of world production.

Although British investments on the peninsula were about 70 percent of total Western investment (£116.5 million in 1930), there were important United States-backed enterprises, particularly rubber plantations, and Australian interests in the tin sector. Chinese investments at that time totaled more than £41 million. Iron mines in Johore and Terengganu states were Japanese owned.

The Immigrant Communities

The present-day traveler in the old Straits Settlements city of George Town on Penang will find impressive evidence of the multiethnic nature of Malaysian society. Nowhere else, it seems, has the very human trait of dividing up a common humanity been carried out with such single-mindedness. This is particularly evident in places of worship. There are not only mosques, but mosques serving congregations from the different Muslim regions of the Malay Archipelago and the Indian subcontinent. Hindu and Buddhist temples reflect a similar ethnic and regional differentiation, while Chinese temples and clan halls attest to the bewildering diversity of clan and regional affiliations within a community that is often viewed, by outsiders, as homogeneous. Food stalls and restaurants, moreover, provide a kind of religious and cultural cafeteria where different dietary restrictions and preferences are carefully observed.

During the nineteenth century the Chinese community on the Malay Peninsula was popularly seen as divided into two groups. One consisted of the Babas (or Straits Chinese), born in the country and found for the most part in the Straits Settlements, where their fathers or grandfathers had come to enjoy British law and order. (Some had settled in Malacca, however, as early as the Dutch period.) The other was the Singkeh (a corruption of the Chinese term for "new guest"), recent immigrants whose numbers swelled with the development of the tin sector. The Babas were settled merchants, craftsmen, and shopkeepers. Many had become exceedingly rich and were described as being proud of their status as British subjects. They had come to regard Malaya, rather than China, as their native land and were in some cases Western-educated, fluent speakers of English and even converts to Christianity. Yet most had not forsaken Chinese customs and ways of life. Loyalty to family and clan, counseled by Confucian ethics and also extremely practical for the extension of business contacts throughout the peninsula and other parts of Southeast Asia, was a value that gave the Chinese community strength and flexibility.

The Singkeh came, not unnaturally, into the country on the bottom of the heap. Although the Manchu Ch'ing Dynasty had prohibited the emigration of its subjects, apparently to prevent centers of resistance from being established overseas, this was easily evaded in the southern maritime provinces of Kwangtung and Fukien, where the great majority of the newcomers (like the ancestors of the Babas before them) originated. Turbulence in their homeland—the Taiping Rebellion, by the time it was suppressed in 1864, had cost 20 million lives and devastated China's southern and central provinces—stimulated emigration, as did dreams of making a fortune in Southeast Asia. Like emigrants elsewhere, not a few Singkeh were fleeing the law, creditors, or personal enemies. A few were able to pay their own passage to the Straits Settlements and the peninsula, but a majority were brought over on what was known as the credit ticket program; recruited by Straits Chinese employers, the Singkeh were obliged to pay them for their passage and thus were bound to them by a relationship of indentured servitude.

In 1877 the British government established the Chinese Protectorate, a special agency to deal with abuses within the Chinese community, and a cadre of Chinese-speaking British officials grew up separate from the local district officers in the Federated Malays. Both British and Singkeh shared the assumption that the latter were only sojourners in Malaya. The immigrant's dream was to make money, return to his native village in south China, and be buried in the earth of his ancestors. Many did return to China, but by the twentieth century a large, permanent Chinese population was established. There was increased female immigration from China, especially during the 1930s, and the growth in the proportion of the Malaya-born rose from 22 percent in 1911 to 63 percent in 1947. When the first census for Malaya (excluding Singapore) was held in 1911, Chinese formed about 30 percent of the total peninsula population of 2,329,000; by 1947 this proportion had increased to over 38 percent.

The Indian, Arab, and Eurasian Communities

The Indian population of the Malay Peninsula, which included immigrants not only from present-day India but from what are now Pakistan and Sri Lanka, reflected the diversity of the subcontinent and the tendency, well established in British Malaya and further bolstered by Indian caste discriminations, of linking groups with occupations. Indians had been in contact with the peninsula and the northern Borneo coast since before written historical records. The present population, however, is largely the result of British advances. Until 1867 the Straits Settlements were a part of British India, and a small number of Indians had come to serve in the colonial government or set up retail establishments. Sikhs, from the Punjab region (later partitioned between India and Pakistan), had a reputation as fighters and served in the first British police and armed forces on the peninsula. The

Malay States Guides, the only local defense force in the Federated Malay States from their establishment in 1896 to the end of World War I, was composed of Sikhs. They also served in "martial" occupations such as truck, bus, and taxi driving (lines of work requiring, in Malaysian traffic, a good measure of courage,) night watchmen, and bank guards (still to be seen toting shotguns in front of financial establishments). The Chettiars, from the southern Indian state of Madras, were moneylenders and bankers on a small scale who came to play an important role in the local economies of Malaya. They had a reputation for honesty and conscientiousness but, unlike Chinese moneylenders who were occasionally moved by the Confucian virtue of "human heartedness," have been described as hard bargainers who never let sentiment get in the way of the collection of principal and interest. Bengalis, from the region around Calcutta (the capital of British India until 1912), were prominent in the lower levels of the civil service as functionaries and technical personnel, although they shared clerical posts with a small, educated class of Jaffna Tamils from the northern region of Ceylon.

South Indians, and particularly Tamils from the state of Madras, were far more numerous than north Indians. In 1921 over 82 percent of the total Indian population of the peninsula was Tamil. A great majority of these were laborers who were under contract to work on the plantations. In 1872 Indian migration to the Straits Settlements was legalized, as it was 12 years later to the Federated Malay States (then the "protected" states). Rubber, however, was to the Tamils as tin was to the Chinese. Large-scale Indian migration did not occur until the "rubber booms" of the early twentieth century. There were only about 30,000 Indians on the peninsula in the 1870s, but by 1911 the population, swelled by Tamil labor immigration, was 239,000, or 10 percent of the total (excluding Singapore); 20 years later it was 571,000, or more than 15 percent of the total.

Most Indians were Hindu, but there was a Muslim minority whose religion gave them a basis of community with the indigenous Malays. The small community of Malay-speaking Jawi Peranakan (Indo-Malays), children of Indian fathers and Malay mothers, served as teachers, government clerks, and shopkeepers in cities such as Singapore and Penang. As an elite class and a bridge between Malays and the outside world, they played a formative role in the development of Malay national feeling in the twentieth century.

Another important community, whose influence was far in excess of its numbers, was the Arabs, most of whom came from the

Hadramaut, in what is now the People's Democratic Republic of Yemen (Yemen [Aden]). Many assumed the status of Sayyid, a group or class who, along with the imams, claimed descent from the Prophet and had great influence among the Malays. Like the Jawi Peranakan, they were a link to a broader world outside the Malay states. The oldest group of Eurasians living on the peninsula were the descendants of the Portuguese. A few hundred still live today in their own community near Malacca; they are Christians who speak a sixteenth-century dialect of Portuguese known as "Cristao." Eurasians served as government clerks or professionals. They lived on the fringes of both European and Asian societies, however, victims of the race-consciousness of colonial rulers and ruled alike.

The Malay Response

In 1911, when the first census for the Malay Peninsula was taken, there were 1,370,000 Malays, or 59 percent of the total of 2,329,000 (excluding Singapore). As in the case of the Chinese and the Indians, a closer look at this group reveals a great diversity. All were Muslim, although, of course, not all Muslims were Malay. Within the Malay community there had long been a distinction between the *anak negeri* (the "children of the country"—the local people owing allegiance to the ruler) and the *anak dagang* (the "children of commerce"—outsiders who were Muslim but who came from different parts of the Malay Archipelago). The former included not only the Malays with ties to the Malacca sultanate and its successors but also the Buginese and the Minangkabau, who had begun settling in the peninsula in the late seventeenth and eighteenth centuries; the *anak dagang* immigrants from the Dutch East Indies included Javanese, recruited by the British in large numbers as manual laborers; Acehnese and Bataks from Sumatra; Boyanese, or Baweans, from the island of Bawean, north of the Indonesian island of Madura; and Sumbawa islanders from east of Java.

An overwhelming majority of Malays were rural villagers; the census of 1921 reveals that only 5.8 percent lived in settlements of over 1,000 people. Those few who did live in the cities tended to be separated into largely self-sufficient kampongs (villages or compounds) according to their geographical subgroup. In Singapore these kampongs were often organized around the residences of rulers or dignitaries, such as the sultan and the *temenggong* (war minister) of Johore. Although the British were quick to characterize the "real" Malay as indolent and without initiative, the kampongs were centers of a lively, if small-scale, economy.

Buginese traded goods from the eastern Malay archipelago; immigrants from Bengkulu on the southern coast of Sumatra grew vegetables to sell in city markets; Javanese ran food stalls and coffee shops; and the Boyanese carved a niche for themselves as coachmen and, in the motor age, as chauffeurs.

The Islamic religion and the Malay language, still the medium of commerce in the region, provided a basis of unity among these diverse groups. Yet the obstacles to the development of a single Malay community were considerable. The fragmentation of the Malay world before the imposition of British rule resulted in the localization of loyalties. In the widely scattered rural and coastal villages, the people did not regard themselves as members of a single Malay "nation" but as the subjects of a certain ruler. Unity was further undermined by the institutional, economic, and social differences between the Federated and Unfederated Malay States. Moreover, in the period before World War II the most influential Malays, those close to the sultans and the small group of Malay civil servants in the colonial administration, perceived their interests as tied to the continuation of British rule.

Although the elite remained secure in what one writer has called "a Tory Eden in which each man is contented with his station, and does not wish for change" and the rural majority was apathetic, a small group of intellectuals began to call for reforms within the Malay community. In the prewar period this movement was not political and did not challenge British colonial rule. It sought cultural, social, and economic changes in response to the threat posed by the economically dominant foreigners but was moralistic rather than political in its emphasis.

Developments in the Middle East, the heartland of the Islamic world, stimulated urban Malay intellectuals in the opening years of the twentieth century. A number had studied Islamic law in Mecca or at schools and universities in Egypt. There scholars of a "Modernist" persuasion sought a reconciliation of their religion with modern trends. Singapore, a major stopover for Malays and Indonesians on the pilgrimage to Mecca, was a meeting place for Islamic scholars and teachers (including Arabs and Jawi Peranakan, who were the dominant groups among educated Muslims) and was also a center for Malay-language publishing, journalism, and literature. The Modernist periodical *Al-Imam* (The Leader), established in 1906 and modeled on publications in Egypt, was an early forum for Malay reformist opinion. It called for ethnic unity based on religion and transcending British and Dutch colonial borders (it had a readership in the Dutch East Indies as well as Malaya) and complained that Malays grew poor while foreigners prospered in their homeland. It also criticized the ulama, the established Islamic authorities in the Malay states, as corrupt and narrow-mindedly conservative. An important theme of *Al-Imam,* and a basic tenet of Modernism, was that Malays could foster modern education and economic development without coming into conflict with the principles of Islam as set forth in the Quran and hadith. An attack on established Islam formed the basis of the controversy between the Kaum Muda (Young Group) and the Kaum Tua (Old Group), which preoccupied this generation of intellectuals. Although the issues were primarily religious, there were political implications because the ulama were appointed and subsidized by the Malay rulers in accordance with the residency formula giving them control over Malay custom and religion.

Kaum Muda were diffused throughout the peninsula in the many *madrasah* (Modernist Islamic schools) established in the early part of the twentieth century. Classes were taught in Arabic, but the curricula included such subjects as science, mathematics, and English. Many of the best Islamic schools were in the Unfederated Malay States, and the teachers of Kelantan—particularly To' Kenali, who is described by one scholar as employing a "Socratic" method of teaching—enjoyed an especially high reputation.

Associations of a nonreligious nature had a slow and uncertain development. One of the first was the Singapore Malay Union, founded in 1926. Its president, the journalist Eunos Abdullah, repeatedly affirmed its loyalty to the British government and carefully avoided political issues. Yet the union campaigned to have land reserved in Singapore for the exclusive use of Malays and criticized Arabs and Jawi Peranakan for exploiting their poorer Islamic brothers. One of the most significant prewar Malay movements was the Friends of the Pen (Sabahat Pena), which began in April 1934 as a newspaper correspondence club for young people. The club grew rapidly, holding a national meeting in November 1934 at Taiping in Perak and within the year having a membership not only throughout the peninsula but also in Sarawak. By mid-1937 it had some 20,000 members, having transformed itself into an association known as the Brotherhood of the Friends of the Pen. Its significance lies in its "pan-Malay" nature. Like the Singapore Malay Union, it studiously avoided politics, concentrating on culture, education, and self-development. It was particularly interested in questions relating to the Malay language and in 1938 established the Language Council (Lembaga Bahasa) to promote Malay literature and language reform.

Developments in Indonesia during the 1920s and 1930s, when

nationalists were vigorously criticizing Dutch rule, injected a radical note into Malay intellectual life. In the words of the historian William Roff, "the barrier between British- and Dutch-controlled territories was a porous membrane. . . . Ideologically there was steady seepage from the stronger and more active solution to the weaker." Malay and Indonesian students at the Islamic Al-Azhar University in Cairo had jointly edited and published a journal, *Seruan Azhar*, and journals published in Indonesia enjoyed a wide readership on the peninsula. Some Malays had connections with the Islamic Union (Sarekat Islam) movement, which appeared in Indonesia in 1912. During the 1920s and 1930s the ties deepened, and concepts of a "Greater Indonesia" (Indonesia Raya) and "Greater Malay World" (Melayu Raya) developed. These sentiments were strengthened by the decision of Indonesian nationalists in the 1920s to make Malay the national language of a future Indonesian nation comprising both the peninsula and the archipelago. For Malays, the attractions of Greater Indonesia were demographic—the huge Malay-Indonesian population of the archipelago would offset the concentrations of Indians and Chinese in the peninsula who by 1931 were slightly less than one-half the population, excluding Singapore.

In 1938 Ibrahim bin Haji Ya'acob established the Union of Young Malays (Kesatuan Melayu Muda), an avowedly radical organization, along the lines of Sukarno's Indonesian Nationalist Party, which espoused a Greater Indonesia, "racial" unity, and opposition to foreign exploitation. It was particularly explicit in its criticism of the co-opted Malay traditional elites. The Malay man in the street, however, continued to view political activity and treason as synonymous; as the Indonesian communist Tan Malaka discovered in the 1920s, the peninsular Malays were hopelessly conservative and apathetic, and he argued that revolution could come only from the Chinese and Indian communities. Malays of both humble and elite stations remained largely immune from the appeal of revolutionary Marxist ideologies; the small group of radicals that did emerge at this time were largely journalists and schoolteachers, particularly graduates of the Sultan Idris Training College in Tanjong Malim, Perak, where Indonesian nationalist ideas had great influence.

The Malay Associations (Persatuan Melayu) that were founded in 1938 in various parts of the peninsula were conservative counterparts of the Union of Young Malays. Composed to a large extent of Malay civil servants, including graduates of elite Malay College, they were vocal in their loyalty to Britain, particularly following the outbreak of war in Europe in September 1939.

Among association members, politeness was a virtue lest they be confused with communists or the Kaum Muda. Yet they advocated changes in land policy pertaining to Malays, greater participation of Malays in the defense of the colony, including the establishing of a Malayan air force, and the ban on further alien immigration (exempting Indonesians). National congresses of the Malay associations were held in 1939–40 and included representatives from Brunei and Sarawak.

War, Emergency, and Independence

A few days after the attack on Pearl Harbor, which crippled United States sea power in the Pacific, Japanese forces advanced southward to land at Kota Baharu in Kelantan and Singora in southern Thailand. British defense plans relied on numerical superiority (some three or four British, Australian, and Indian troops for each Japanese) and the supposed impregnability of the Singapore naval installations. The sinking of the British cruiser, H.M.S. *Repulse* and the new battleship, the H.M.S. *Prince of Wales*, on December 10, 1941, was a major blow, and British aircraft were unable to operate effectively against larger numbers of more advanced Japanese fighters. The commander of the invasion force, General Yamashita Tomoyuki, earned himself the nickname "the tiger of Malaya" through the bold and effective use of tank and infantry units (many of the latter using bicycles, which proved a remarkably efficient means of troop transport). The Japanese advance proceeded down the peninsula without significant reverses. Singapore fell on February 15, 1942. Its guns, pointing out to sea, could not be used against invaders coming overland from the north. British forces, including the Malay Regiment and a unit of Chinese volunteers, fought bravely but were poorly led. The loss of Malaya, which might have been prevented by better planning and more decisive leadership, shattered the myth of British invincibility; the hasty evacuation of Europeans, including government officials, seemed to many Asians like an act of desertion and did permanent damage to British prestige.

Japanese objectives in Malaya and Borneo were both economic and strategic. Rubber, tin, and other peninsula commodities were vital to their war effort, and there were oil fields in Sarawak and Brunei. Control of the Strait of Malacca gave Japanese naval forces access to the Indian Ocean. Singapore, renamed Shōnan ("Brightness of the South") was made the center of an administrative unit, including both the peninsula and Sumatra. In 1943 the northern Malay states of Perlis, Kedah, Kelantan, and Terengganu were given to Thailand (official name was Siam 1855–1939 and 1946–49), which had become an ally of Japan the previous year.

All ethnic communities suffered during the Japanese occupation, which lasted until the end of the war in August 1945, but the Japanese policy of treating the groups differently created an antagonism, particularly between Malays and Chinese, that persisted long after the war. In retaliation for Malayan Chinese support of China's war of resistance, the Japanese military authorities executed thousands soon after occupying Singapore, and throughout the occupation, they treated the Chinese community with unremitting harshness. In the new order of things, Malays occupied a privileged position. They were given offices in the administration left vacant by the British and were encouraged to anticipate Malaya's inclusion in an independent Greater Indonesia. Before the war the Japanese had made contact with Ibrahim bin Haji Ya'acob, leader of the Union of Young Malays, and during the occupation he became head of a paramilitary group, Our Country's Avengers (Pembela Tanah Ayer—PETA). In 1945 Ibrahim formed a second group, the Kesatuan Ra'ayat Indonesia Semananjong (KRIS), to promote Malayan-Indonesian unity, after meeting with wartime Indonesian leaders Sukarno and Mohammad Hatta. There was an attempt to garner conservative Malay support as well; the Japanese conferred on the Malay rulers a status similar to that which they enjoyed under the British in 1943. The Indians, as foreigners, could not enjoy the privileges of the Malays but fared better than the Chinese. Their support was needed for the Japanese-sponsored Indian National Army, led by Subhas Chandra Bose, who had set up an anti-British Indian government in Singapore in 1943 and planned to accompany the Japanese advance into India. Thousands of Indian laborers, however, were forcibly recruited to build a railroad between Thailand and Burma and never returned.

The main resistance group in the peninsula was the Malayan People's Anti-Japanese Army (MPAJA), which was predominantly Chinese. The core of the MPAJA was the Communist Party of Malaya (CPM), which had been active in organizing Anti-Japanese National Salvation Associations among the Chinese after the Sino-Japanese war had begun in 1937. In principle open to all ethnic groups, the CPM before its reorganization in 1930 had been the Nanyang (South Seas) branch of the Chinese Communist Party. As in other Southeast Asian countries, communists, by means of their extensive underground organizations and skill in evading colonial police forces, were in the best position to fight the occupiers. The MPAJA numbered about 5,000 and maintained contacts with the British, who provided them with arms. Two strategies that it adopted in conducting a guerrilla war made it a particularly tenacious force—its success in setting up and maintaining support groups within the civilian population, known as Anti-Japanese Unions, and its system of bases in densely forested and thinly inhabited regions of the peninsula. By 1945 the anti-Japanese war took on a markedly ethnic character as the Japanese ordered Malay police and auxiliary units against the MPAJA. Mutual hatreds grew as Islamic religious leaders organized "Holy War Armies" that attacked MPAJA units and Chinese civilians alike in retaliation for MPAJA executions of Malays as pro-Japanese collaborators.

After Japan's surrrender on August 15, 1945, the occupation was followed by what was, in the eyes of many, a British "reoccupation." The war had shattered the "Tory Eden" of the years before 1941, and the new British military administration faced a situation of growing volatility and uncertainty.

The Malayan Union and the Growth of Political Movements

In the closing months of 1945 the Malay rulers were pressured by the British into signing treaties renouncing their old powers and privileges. In January 1946 the Labour Party government published its Malayan Union scheme, a constitutional redefinition of political institutions on the peninsula that would make the Federated and Unfederated Malay States, along with Penang and Malacca, a single crown colony under a British governor rather than separate protectorates. Singapore, with its strategic naval base, would be a separate crown colony and Britain's major military installation east of Suez. This was seen as the first step toward a self-governing Malaya. Under the union arrangement, which was implemented on April 1, 1946, the Malay rulers were no longer regarded (even formally) as sovereigns of separate political entities. A second provision was a common citizenship for the inhabitants of the peninsula, regardless of ethnicity; this was granted to all persons who had been born there or who fulfilled certain residence requirements. Naturalization was possible for those residents who spoke English or Malay.

The union proposal reflected changed British attitudes toward Malays owing to the Malay leaders' wartime collaboration with the Japanese. It completely undermined their prewar special status, making them a minority among citizens in the new state. This prompted an immediate Malay reaction. In March 1946 a meeting of Malay Associations in Kuala Lumpur established the United Malays National Organization (UMNO), with Dato' Onn bin Ja'afar, chief minister of the state of Johore, as its president. UMNO, the first and most important Malay political party in the full sense of the term, demanded that the Malayan Union proposal be scrapped and warned its followers that "the Malay people would be like *lalang*—long grass which cannot stand up to the elements but is flattened by every wind that blows."

A united front of left-wing groups and non-Malay community leaders, known as the All-Malayan Council of Joint Action (AMCJA), supported the spirit, if not the letter, of the union. The British, however, feared growing communist influence (the CPM was part of the council) and were impressed by the forcefulness of UMNO demands and those of former colonial officials who argued for reaffirmation of the special status of Malays. In May 1947 a plan for the Federation of Malaya was published. In the new proposal the rulers retained their former powers; the nine states, along with Penang and Malacca, were joined together in a federation in which each would have a measure of autonomy, particularly in the sphere of Malay custom and religion—the old Pangkor formula. Singapore was to be separated from the federation (the AMCJA had demanded their merger), ensuring a majority of Malays in the new political unit. Citizenship was to be based on place of birth, according to the principle of jus soli, but made more stringent than the liberal union proposal (except for Malays, who became citizens automatically). The AMCJA and a left-wing Malay front, the Center of People's Power (Pusat Tenaga Ra'ayat), organized strikes to oppose the federation proposal, but it was implemented by the British on February 1, 1948.

The Emergency

Between 1945 and 1948, during its "legal" phase, the CPM had been active both in the constitutional controversy and in trade union activities, controlling the largest labor group, the Pan-Malayan Federation of Labor. In 1947 the federation initiated some 300 strikes. A number of factors, still not perfectly understood, contributed to its decision to go underground in 1948. Loi Tak, the CPM's general secretary, who advocated peaceful struggle, absconded in March 1947 with a large amount of party funds, and it was later revealed that this enterprising gentleman had been an agent of both the Japanese and the British. His successor, Ch'in Peng, seems to have been more receptive to Cominform (the Communist International in Moscow) directives to initiate revolutionary armed struggle in concert with communist movements in other parts of Southeast Asia. Party frustration with the outcome of the constitutional issue, moreover, may have strengthened his hand. Federation had raised more ethnic questions than it had resolved, and large numbers of Chinese and Indians were distinctly uneasy about the prospect of living in a Malay (rather than Malayan) Malaya.

The British government proclaimed a state of emergency on June 18, 1948, following CPM attacks on European rubber plantations. The objective of its armed force, the Malayan Races Liberation Army (MRLA), was to cripple the economy by attacking plantations and tin mines in isolated parts of the country and cutting off roads and railroads. To borrow Maoist terminology, the "water" in which the MRLA "fish" swam were the Chinese communities, paricularly the squatter settlements where Chinese had migrated since before the war. There local support groups, the Min Yuen, were organized. In 1948 there were as many as 500,000 Chinese squatters living for the most part in fringe areas between the population centers of the peninsula and the interior, where the CPM had its bases. This gave the communists optimum flexibility, forcing the government to undertake a costly and prolonged campaign to isolate and eliminate the guerrilla forces and uproot their local bases of support.

The communist armed offensive was most decisive in the 1949-51 period, which culminated in the assassination of the British high commissioner, Sir Henry Gurney, on October 6, 1951. The CPM was poorly organized, however, and outside of the Chinese squatter areas enjoyed limited support. Malays remained aloof to the CPM's appeals, and the Malayan Chinese Association (MCA), which had been founded in 1949, provided a noncommunist alternative for conservative Chinese.

An important factor in the failure of the communist movement was the "Briggs Plan," drawn up by General Harold Briggs, the commander of the counterinsurgency forces. The plan called for moving the Chinese out of the squatter areas into New Villages, which were securely under government control. By 1952 some 400,000 had been moved into 400 New Villages. Although these provided better health, sanitation, and educational facilities than the squatter areas, relocation imposed severe hardships. The government was also successful in infiltrating the communist apparatus and through a succession of sweeps in the late 1950s covered the map of Malaya with "white" (guerrilla-free) areas. By 1960, when the Emergency was declared at an end, the MRLA had been forced into the border area of southern Thailand, where the terrain provided ample hiding places for a beaten and dispirited, but still viable, guerrilla movement.

The Alliance and Independence

The British had promised in the Federation of Malaya Agreement of 1948 that Malaya would eventually be granted self-rule. Two obstacles to this were the security situation and the continued suspicions and animosities of the different ethnic communities. By the mid-1950s the guerrilla problem was largely under control. The problem of fostering a genuine sense of national unity was a more complex and difficult one. What the British feared most was an outbreak of communal strife such as that which had accompanied their withdrawal in 1947 from India.

British policy was to encourage dialogue among noncommunist ethnic leaders. In 1949 the Communities Liaison Committee was established, and it became an important medium through which postfederation compromises on citizenship and other constitutional matters were hammered out. Gradually a consensus developed that the Malays would share political power with the other groups only if the non-Malays assisted them in improving Malays' economic position in the postindependence society. The working out of details, however, proved a complex and time-consuming task.

The most important political associations remained communally based—UMNO, the MCA, and the Malayan Indian Congress (MIC), which had been founded in 1946. Dato' Onn bin Ja'afar had attempted unsuccessfully to convert UNMO into a multiethnic political party and in 1951 resigned from UMNO to set up his own Independence of Malaya Party (IMP). He was succeeded as UMNO leader by Tengku Abdul Rahman, a graduate of Cambridge University and member of the royal family of Kedah. The failure of Onn's IMP to gain popular support in the elections that were held over the next few years suggests that ethnic identity would remain a major factor in politics for some time to come.

Municipal elections for Kuala Lumpur were held in 1952. Tengku Abdul Rahman and MCA leader Tan Cheng-Lock, with British encouragement, formed a working coalition of the MCA and UMNO, running Malay candidates in Malay wards and Chinese candidates in Chinese wards. The partnership won the election and, calling itself the Alliance (later known as the Alliance Party), captured 94 of the 124 seats contested in various local elections held thoughout Malaya between 1952 and 1954. In 1955 the MIC joined the Alliance, and in the election for a Malay-wide federal legislature held the same year, the Alliance won 51 of the 52 seats contested. Its success gained it the role of agent for

Malayan interests and opened the way for independence.

An Alliance delegation led by Tengku Abdul Rahman went to London in January 1956 to arrange for the transfer of power. The date of August 31, 1957, was set for the independence of Malaya (Singapore would remain a separate crown colony with its own system of internal self-government), and a Constitutional Commission was convened between June and October 1956.

The resulting document was a masterpiece of compromise. Citizenship was defined according to jus soli, being granted automatically to all persons born on the peninsula; naturalization was possible for others. To satisfy UMNO, Malay (Bahasa Malaysia) was recognized as the national language, English serving as an official language for a period of at least 10 years. The problem of the status of the rulers was resolved by establishing a constitutional monarchy. In a unique arrangement designed to reconcile Malay tradition with representative government, the Constitution provided for a monarch or paramount ruler, the *yang di-pertuan agong,* to be elected for a five-year term from among the nine Malay rulers on the basis of seniority. Although the paramount ruler and the other rulers in their states would retain certain privileges, they were made subordinate in most matters to the prime minister, who was to be chosen by a popularly elected House of Representatives (Dewan Rakyat). The Constitution provided for a nonelective Senate (Dewan Negara) having limited powers similar to those of the British House of Lords.

Islam was made the state religion, although the freedom of other religious communities was guaranteed. The Constitution provided for the retention of special privileges for Malays in the civil service, scholarships, business enterprises, licenses, and the reservation of some land for their exclusive use, while ensuring that the rights of non-Malays could not be hindered by prejudicial legislation or government intervention. The issue of Malay privileges was a sensitive one, and it was not until June 1957 that a final compromise was worked out between the Alliance, the Malay rulers, and the British. On August 15, 1957, document was ratified by the Federal Legislature, and on August 31—right on schedule—the independence of Malaya was announced.

In Indonesia, Vietnam, Burma, and many other former European colonies, the transition to independence was a violent struggle, led by armed revolutionaries with a large peasant following. Their counterparts in Malaya, the CPM, were by independence more of a nuisance than a threat to the status quo, although the Emergency would not be officially proclaimed as over until three years later. The Alliance was conservative in its orientation.

Tengku Abdul Rahman, Tan Cheng-Lock, and other Malayan spokesmen were members of the administrative and financial elites. Their education at prestigious Western-style institutions, such as Raffles College in Singapore and Malay College in Kuala Kangsar, and universities in Britain provided them with the basis for mutual understanding. Although UMNO was broadly popular among Malays, neither the MCA nor the MIC had significant membership among the poorer classes of Chinese or Indians. Mutual accommodations had been made, however, and in the postindependence period the Alliance strove mightily to build a broader and more permanent basis for national unity.

Sarawak and Sabah

The third Brooke raja, Vyner Brooke, lacked the assertiveness of his predecessors and spent much of his time in Europe rather than attending personally to affairs in Sarawak. In 1941 he promulgated a constitution, but during the war the territory was occupied by the Japanese. In 1946 Raja Vyner ceded Sarawak to Britain as a crown colony. There was, however, strong sentiment against cession, particularly among Malay chiefs who feared that their status under British rule would be diminished. In 1949 the British governor, Duncan Stewart, was assassinated by anticessionists. A constitution, however, was proclaimed by the British for Sarawak in 1957, and in 1959 the first political party was established—the Sarawak United People's Party (SUPP), a multiethnic, left-wing group with largely Chinese leadership.

The situation in North Borneo was more placid, although after the war and Japanese occupation, the British North Borneo Company was dissolved and the territory became, like Sarawak, a British crown colony. The disunity of the various indigenous ethnic groups and the company's slowness in initiating reforms, particularly in education (there were no secondary schools), made political development after the war a slow and uncertain process. According to former British civil servant Stanley Bedlington, who worked in the area, the political vacuum was so complete that the British governors were obliged to seek out for themselves men with potential as political leaders. By the mid-1950s the two most important political leaders were Donald Stephens, a Christian Kadazan, and Datu (later Tun) Mustapha, a Muslim Sulu chief.

The Creation of Malaysia

A formal initiative to consolidate the Federation of Malaya and

Singapore was made by Singapore in 1957 and again in 1959, but Malay leaders continued to be reluctant, given their uneasiness about Singapore as a hotbed of left-wing politics and the fact that merger would result in a Chinese majority in the new state. To reduce these fears, the Singapore government tried to develop a "Malayan" consciousness among its Chinese citizens. Lee Kwan-Yew, Singapore's chief minister and head of the left-wing People's Action Party (PAP), advocated the merger of the territory with Malaya.

In 1960 Lee Kwan-Yew and Malayan prime minister Tengku Abdul Rahman held a series of talks with the British secretary of state for commonwealth relations. The scope of the proposed association was enlarged to include Sarawak, North Borneo, and the state of Brunei. This proposal neutralized Malay opposition by providing an ethnic composition for the projected federation in which the indigenous people (counting both Malays and Borneo communities such as the Iban and Kadazan) would maintain their majority. In arriving at this balance, the somewhat optimistic assumption was made that the interests of Malays and the indigenous peoples of northern Borneo were very similar. The road to the creation of the Federation of Malaysia, however, was fraught with many obstacles. After Tengku Abdul Rahman announced the plan publicly on May 27, 1961, opposition was expressed not only by leaders of indigenous non-Muslim communities in Sarawak and North Borneo but also by antimerger groups in Singapore. The proposal also became a focus of international controversies involving Indonesia and the Philippines.

Britain supported federation because it believed that neither Singapore, a crowded island with no natural resources of its own, nor the economically underdeveloped and politically inexperienced Borneo territories (including the tiny protected state of Brunei) could stand on their own after British withdrawal. By offering continuous cooperation and protection, the British also hoped to maintain most of their vital military bases and economic interests.

The comment of one North Borneo leader, "Why should we be forced to exchange one form of colonialism for another?" was typical of initial reaction on Borneo to the Malaysia plan. British colonial officials in North Borneo and Sarawak were ordered, in Bedlington's terms, to "sell" Malaysia to the people, and the British government-appointed Cobbold Commission reported in July 1962 that the majority favored merger. According to Bedlington, only the Muslim one-third of the population really supported the idea; others were either opposed or indifferent.

In fact, formidable opposition to federation came from the Chinese-dominated SUPP, which was strongly supported by labor and Chinese farmers. SUPP opposition to merger stimulated a closer cooperation of the pro-Malaysia forces. Profederation Chinese and Malays joined with Iban and other indigenous peoples in forming the Sarawak Alliance, which together with pro-Malaysia independent candidates won 73 percent of the votes in the June 1963 district elections. No such struggle ensued in Borneo, where the pro-Malaysian North Borneo Alliance Party won 90 percent of the vote in that territory's first election in December 1962.

Substantial compromises had to be made in order to gain local support. Both states were given control over immigration, including that from the Malay Peninsula. Indigenous peoples, claiming the status of Bumiputra (see Glossary), would enjoy the same privileges as peninsular Malays, and special funds would be reserved for the Borneo states' economic development. Although Malay would be the national language, the states could use English (an official language) as a medium of instruction and official correspondence until they decided otherwise. The 1957 constitution was amended to allow for these accommodations and became the Constitution of Malaysia.

In a referendum held in September 1962, Lee Kwan-Yew's promerger platform had won 71 percent of the vote, although the socialist opposition put up a strenuous fight. The state of Brunei, however, decided to stay out of the federation. Its sultan was unhappy with the prospect of being only one among 10 Malay rulers in the federation (wishing to have senior status) and was loath to share his substantial oil revenues with anyone. On September 16, 1963, the Federation of Malaysia, consisting of Malaya, Singapore, Sarawak, and North Borneo (now the state of Sabah), was proclaimed. Its prospects, however, both internally and externally, were highly uncertain.

External Threats: "Confrontation" and the Philippine Claim to Sabah

The greatest threat to Malaysia in the first years was the Confrontation campaign of Indonesia. That country's president, Sukarno, vilified the new federation as "neocolonialist." The old dream of a Greater Indonesia, combined with Sukarno's need to consolidate domestic political support behind a popular issue, brought forth a movement with much smoke and a little fire. Sukarno, in his unique grandstanding style, vowed to prevent federation and, when this failed, to "crush Malaysia." A strategy of infiltration was implemented as Indonesian troops landed in

Sabah, Sarawak, the peninsula, and even Singapore.

Sukarno had become involved in northern Borneo politics by supporting the unsuccessful revolt of A.M. Azahari against the British protectorate in Brunei in December 1962; but his promise to provide 100,000 Indonesian "volunteers" to help establish the state of Kalimantan Utara (which Azahari envisioned as comprising the state of Brunei, Sarawak, Sabah, and even parts of the southern Philippines) never materialized. The Confrontation policy was officially announced in January 1963. Yet adverse foreign reaction and the hope that Indonesia and the Philippines might act to delay the creation of Malaysia prompted Sukarno to strike a conciliatory note and to give theoretical consent to the federation in May 1963. Negotiators of the three countries met in Manila in June and agreed to propose to their governments the creation of a consultative arrangement for collective defense within the framework of MAPHILINDO (Malaysia, the Philippines, and Indoesia) and the submission of the Borneo problem to the United Nations (UN), which would send a commission to carry out an assessment of public opinion in Sarawak and Sabah.

Although Tengku Abdul Rahman accepted both the United Nations commission proposal and MAPHILINDO, he pressed ahead with federation, signing a final agreement with Britain on July 9, 1963, setting August 31 as the date for the formation of the Federation of Malaysia. This infuriated Sukarno and brought the two countries close to war. A summit meeting was held in Manila in late July, and Philippine president Diosdado Macapagal served as intermediary. Tengku Abdul Rahman, meeting with Sukarno, agreed to postpone federation for two weeks to allow the United Nations (UN) sufficient time for assessment. In mid-August nine UN delegates hastily began their tast of gauging public opinion in Sarawak and Sabah. They reported that two-thirds of the population favored Malaysia, basing their conclusion on a review of election results and on interviews with 4,000 people. Its findings were repudiated, however, by both Indonesia and the Philippines.

Violence broke out within hours of the proclamation of the Federation of Malaysia on September 16. Indonesian demonstrators, encouraged by the Sukarno regime, attacked the Malaysian and British embassies in Jakarta. There were increasing numbers of incidents along the borders of the two countries in Borneo, and infiltrators carried out acts of sabotage and terrorism on the peninsula and in Singapore. Sukarno hoped that infiltrators would spark a popular revolt against the government, but in fact the Confrontation strengthened popular support for Malaysia in both the eastern and the western halves of the country. The Indonesian alternative to "neocolonialist" Malaysia won few supporters; the indigenous peoples of Borneo, although still unhappy over some of the conditions of federation, had only to look over the border to see the economic and administrative shambles of Sukarnoist Indonesia.

International attempts to bring Indonesia and Malaysia together failed in 1964; Britain, New Zealand, and Australia sent troops and other military aid in accordance with their defense arrangements to help the Malaysian armed forces. A diplomatic boost came in December 1964 when Malaysia was elected to one year's rotating membership on the UN Security Council. Countering Confrontation was expensive and diverted funds from economic development plans that had been envisioned as necessary to bring the rural Malays and other indigenous peoples closer to economic equality with the Chinese. Yet Malaysia's economy was booming. Tin had an exceptionally good year on international markets in 1965, rates of growth in Sabah were impressive, investment in manufacturing was increasing, and inflation was kept under control. Sukarno attempted to place a trade embargo on Malaysia, but smuggling, particularly to Singapore, flourished.

Sukarno was forced to step down from power following an abortive left-wing coup on September 30, 1965. Gradually, it became apparent that Indonesia's new military leaders were instigating a fundamental change of direction. On August 11, 1966, a peace treaty between Malaysia and Indonesia ended the hostilities.

The Philippines also opposed the federation of Malaysia on the grounds that it had a prior claim to the territory of Sabah, based on the fact that Sabah had previously been part of the sultanate of Sulu. Manila argued that it had been leased, rather than granted, to the British North Borneo Company in 1878 and that the sultan's right of ownership passed to the independent Republic of the Philippines following the Spanish and American occupations. The claim hinged on a linguistic point—the translation of the Malay-Arabic term *pajak,* which unhelpfully can be rendered as either "lease" or "cede." (The English translation of the 1878 agreement gave North Borneo to the company "forever and to the end of time.") Macapagal had raised the issue in 1962 and joined Indonesia in recalling its diplomatic representatives from Kuala Lumpur after the September 16, 1963, proclamation. Although the Philippines resumed diplomatic relations in June 1966, Manila continued to press the Sabah claim. In September 1968 the government enacted a bill redefining the national boundaries. A new Philippines map was published, including much of the territory of Sabah. Kuala Lumpur suspended relations, and they were not restored until the December 1969 ministerial conference of the Association of Southeast Asian Nations, to which both countries belonged. Relations were further strained by the support given by Sabah's erratic chief minister, Tun Mustapha, to Muslim insurgency movements in the southern Philippines until he was voted out of office in April 1976.

The Secession of Singapore

In addition to the problems created by Confrontation and Philippine claims to Sabah, the new federation also had to cope with developing conflicts between Singapore and the other states of Malaysia. As part of the arrangements for federation, Singapore agreed to accept substantial underrepresentation in the House of Representatives in exchange for keeping most of its revenue and autonomy in education and labor affairs. The agreement also provided that citizens of Singapore, although legally Malaysian citizens, could not participate as full citizens in Peninsular Malaysia without fulfilling stringent naturalization requirements.

Lee Kwan-Yew, however, did not appear to regard this agreement as confining him politically to Singapore. Following the 1959 election victory of his PAP, he had neutralized his former left-wing allies in the Socialist Front, reassured skeptical foreign investors, and established a capable, relatively corruption-free and popular government on the island. He was critical of the conservative Chinese leadership of the MCA, who seemed willing to permit the retention of the special status of Malays. He also saw the MCA as blocking his party's path to further political expansion in the country.

In the 1964 Malaysian federal elections, the PAP ran nine candidates in the Malay states, of whom only one was successful against the Alliance. Its total of 15 seats made the PAP the major opposition group, though the Alliance, winning 89 out of a total of 104 seats in Peninsular Malaysia, had a comfortable majority. Lee Kwan-Yew sought a coalition of opposition parties under the slogan "a Malaysian Malaysia" in which "the nation and the state is not identified with the supremacy, well-being and interests of any one community or race." This was a direct attack on Malay rights. Antagonism mounted further in 1965 when, at a convention in Singapore, Malay members of the PAP appealed for the support of rural Malays against the Alliance's alleged partnership of Malay aristocrats and Chinese capitalists. Bitter debates in parliament followed, in which Lee Kwan-Yew pushed for greater speed in removing special privileges for Malays. In rebuttal, Alliance members argued that racial harmony and a greater role for Malays in the economy were needed first and should precede any attempt to create a noncommunal national society.

Lee Kwan-Yew's "Malaysian Malaysia" appeal was seen by the Alliance as a threat to the delicate balancing of community interests that it had promoted since before independence. Early in August 1965 Tengku Abdul Rahman returned from 12 months abroad and, in secret meetings with Lee Kwan-Yew and members of both the federal and the Singaporean cabinets, arranged for the peaceful withdrawal of Singapore from Malaysia. On August 9, 1965, Singapore became an independent and sovereign state, although the two countries signed an agreement that included the promise to work out arrangements for joint defense and mutual assistance.

The Kuala Lumpur Riots of May 1969 and Their Aftermath

The Federation of Malaya and its successor, Malaysia, had survived communist insurgency, the Confrontation with Indonesia, and the separation of Singapore from the federation; however, the lack of a firm consensus on the basic nature of the state, the substance of national society, and the role of the different ethnic groups (which had made the Singapore issue so volatile) posed a growing threat to the country's still fragile unity. The Chinese had become increasingly discontent over what was perceived as the unwillingness or inability of the MCA to protect the community's interests. Similar sentiments were aired by Indians about the MIC. UMNO was itself exposed to criticism from conservatives both inside and outside the association who demanded stronger pro-Malay policies and often campaigned under the banner of Islamic orthodoxy.

In the federal elections scheduled for May 1969, the Alliance was opposed by the Democratic Action Party (an offshoot of Lee Kwan-Yew's PAP), which had a predominantly Chinese following and advocated the abolition of the special status of Malays and the recognition of English, Chinese, and Tamil as official languages equal with Malay. Two smaller left-wing groups, the People's Movement of Malaysia (Gerakan Rakyat Malaysia—better known as Gerakan) and the People's Progressive Party, also ran on multiethnic platforms and had largely non-Malay support. On the right, the Alliance was opposed by an Islamic party whose power base was centered in the east coast states of Kelantan and Terengganu.

Elections in Peninsular Malaysia were held on May 10, 1969, after an acrimonious campaign in which each side accused the other of ethnic chauvinism and dependence on foreign support. (Elections for Sarawak and Sabah were scheduled to be held through May and June, owing to poor communications in those territories.) The results were a blow to the Alliance; its share of the total vote declined from 58.5 percent in 1964 to 49.1 percent, and the coalition returned only 66 representatives to the lower house of parliament compared with 89 in 1964. The three left-wing parties won a total of 25 seats, making their most notable gains in the urban areas where non-Malays were concentrated. The MCA suffered the greatest losses (13 seats in 1969 compared with 27 in 1964), and UMNO lost three seats to the Islamic party. There was mutual recrimination within the Alliance over the MCA's particularly poor showing, followed by its collapse when the MCA withdrew from the government on May 13.

That same day, jubilant opposition party supporters, mostly Chinese, held rallies and parades in Kuala Lumpur celebrating their gains. They allegedly taunted Malay bystanders with racial epithets, and violence broke out. Although confined for the most part to Kuala Lumpur, communal riots continued over the next two weeks with hundreds of casualties, mostly Chinese and Indian. The violence was the worst since independence, and the government moved quickly to declare a state of emergency. Elections in Sabah and Sarawak were postponed until June and July 1970, parliament was suspended, and a special ruling body, the National Operations Council (NOC) was established with Deputy Prime Minister Tun Abdul Razak serving as its director.

Ruling by decree, the NOC amended the Sedition Act of 1948 to prohibit public questioning of the special status of Malays, the powers of the Malay rulers, the status of Malay as the national language, and the citizenship laws, particularly in reference to non-Malays. Other amendments stipulated that persons violating these provisions could be barred from public office for a period of five years and that associations challenging Malay rights could be dissolved. The Rukun Negara (National Ideology) was formulated, emphasizing five principles: belief in God, loyalty to the king and country, morality, the rule of law, and observance of the Constitution. Its appeal was limited, however, if only because the principle of loyalty to the *yang di-pertuan agong* begged the old question of the status of the rulers among non-Malays who wanted a multiethnic state. When parliamentary government was established on February 20, 1971, the Constitution was amended to incorporate the prohibitions against public discussion of sensitive issues.

The retirement of Tengku Abdul Rahman as prime minister in

September 1970 marked a generational change in UMNO, its new leaders being more assertive of Malay rights. Overall, the government's interpretation of the causes of the May 1969 violence centered on the grievances and frustrations of Malays. The compromise and interethnic balancing of the 1948 Federation of Malaya Agreement and the 1957 Constitution were less clearly apparent after 1969. Yet the new prime minister, Tun Abdul Razak, sought a coalition broader than that of the old Alliance. In August 1972 the Alliance (which the MCA had rejoined) and the Pan-Malaysia Islamic Party (better known by its Malaysian acronym, PAS—see Glossary) initiated talks on possible cooperation, culminating in an announcement in December 1972 of coalition at the state and federal levels. The Alliance partnership with PAS meant the burying of intra-Malay political differences, at least temporarily. This development set the stage for the formation of a more broadly representative National Front (Barisan Nasional) government several months before the federal and state elections of August 1974.

The National Front, composed of 10 political parties, won overwhelmingly in 1974, taking 130 of the 154 federal parliamentary seats and 344 of the 392 state assembly seats in an election that many observers regarded as a de facto national referendum on the front's policies of pragmatic interracial coalition. The UMNO, MCA, and MIC—the mainstays of the old Alliance—substantially improved their position, gaining a combined total of 85 seats in parliament compared with 66 in 1969. Datuk Hussein bin Onn, the prime minister after Tun Abdul Razak's death in 1976, was successful in asserting the authority of the federal government in disputes with independent-minded state chief ministers, who were perceived as presenting a threat to national unity and ethnic accord. Sabah's Tun Mustapha had been forced out of office in April 1976, and the chief ministers of Perak, Kelantan, and Malacca were obliged to leave office the following year. In the 1978 federal elections, the National Front was able to hold its own, winning 130 seats out of a total of 154, despite the withdrawal of the PAS from the coalition the previous year. Yet the Dakwah movement, an Islamic revival having both cultural and political implications which appeared during the 1970s, presented the National Front with a formidable challenge during the early 1980s. Dakwah leaders associated with the PAS have advocated the establishment of a more orthodox Islamic state and a stronger commitment to redistribution in favor of Malays. In 1981, Dato' Seri Dr. Mahathir Mohamad, a forceful advocate of Malay rights, succeeded Hussein Onn as prime minister.

Economic Development and the New Economic Policy

Malaysia, because of its relatively low population densities (particularly when compared with other countries in the region) and abundance of natural resources, has generally enjoyed a prosperous economy; during the 1970s real growth averaged around 8 percent a year. Nevertheless, commodity exports have always been vulnerable to unstable conditions in international markets, and a major portion of the country's enterprises, particularly in mining and manufacturing, has been owned by foreign investors. The most difficult problem, however, remains economic inequality among the ethnic communities; Malays continue to be largely excluded from the modern sectors. In the consensus-building process beginning in the early 1950s, the leaders of the Alliance recognized the need to resolve this problem, but development plans after independence had emphasized growth over other considerations. The ethnic violence of 1969, however, shocked the government into the realization that the issue had to be tackled more aggressively. The result was the New Economic Policy (NEP), embodied in the Second Malaysia Plan, 1971-75.

Rubber and tin had been the pillars of the colonial export economy and remained the two most important exports until the late 1970s; but the prospects for these products had always been troubled, owing to the postwar competition of synthetic rubber and inelasticity in the world demand of tin. Diversification became imperative. By 1966 Malaysia was the world's principal producer of palm oil, and other important crops included pepper and pineapples. By 1974 palm oil accounted for 11 percent of exports by value, while timber accounted for 13 percent. In 1980 petroleum from new fields that opened off the coast of Terengganu, as well as from older fields off Sarawak, became the most important export. Earnings from oil were M$7.2 billion (for value of the ringgit—see Glossary) compared with M$4.8 billion for rubber. Another promising export was natural gas, obtained from fields off Sarawak.

The NEP, coming in the wake of the 1969 crisis, sought to redress imbalances that had their roots in the early nineteenth century and had become institutionalized under British colonial rule. Statistics revealed (and continue to reveal) that the household income of Malays, particularly in the rural areas, lagged behind that of the Chinese (although Indians were in some cases as poorly off as Malays). Chinese, moreover, predominated in ownership of domestic-owned enterprises in the modern agricultural and industrial sectors. To improve the economic position of the Malays, a number of public enterprises were established in order to expand their role in commerce and industry. This would be accomplished in large measure through buying up shares in enterprises to be reserved for the Bumiputra (both Malays and the indigenous peoples of Sabah and Sarawak). These enterprises included the Trust Council for Indigenous Peoples (Majlis Amanah Rakyat—MARA), the National Corporation (Perbadnan Nasional), the Malaysian Industrial Development Authority (MIDA), and the State Economic Development Corporation. The NEP set a goal of 30 percent Malay ownership in the commercial and industrial sectors by 1990; non-Malays would control 40 percent. Both were increases over 1970 figures, to be achieved by drastically cutting foreign participation to 30 percent of the total by 1990.

The NEP had social and cultural as well as redistributive implications. Scientific, technical, and vocational education was stressed for Malays through a system of schools and institutes, such as MARA's Institute of Technology, the National Productivity Center, and vocational colleges. A large number of Malays were sent abroad to study technical and business subjects. It was hoped that a new generation of Malays would overcome traditional preferences for white-collar government employment and play a more active role in the productive sectors. Mahathir's "Look East" policies of the early 1980s, which stressed emulation of industrially successful countries such as Japan and the Republic of Korea (South Korea), had social, cultural, and educational, as well as technical and economic, implications for the Malays.

* * *

Informative general histories of Malaysia include Barbara Watson Andaya and Leonard Y. Andaya's *A History of Malaysia;* Stanley Bedlington's *Malaysia and Singapore: The Building of New States;* John Gullick's *Malaysia: Economic Expansion and National Unity;* and Harry Miller's *A Short History of Malaysia*. The sections devoted to the Malay Peninsula and Borneo in D.G.E. Hall's *A History of South-East Asia* are helpful. O.W. Wolters' *The Fall of Srivijaya in Malay History* is a discussion of the founding of the kingdom of Malacca and its Srivijayan antecedent, and A.C. Milner's *Kerajaan: Malay Political Culture on the Eve of Colonial Rule* considers the political, ideological, and economic systems of precolonial Malay states. *The Golden Chersonese and the Way Thither*, written by the indomitable traveler Isabella Bird, provides a vivid and entertaining account of conditions in the Malay Peninsula in the late nineteenth century.

On economic development during the colonial period, G.C. Allen and Audrey G. Donnithorne's *Western Enterprise in Indonesia and Malaya: A Study in Economic Development* and Donald R. Snodgrass' *Inequality and Economic Development in Malaysia* are useful. One of the best accounts of pre-World War II political and cultural developments in the Malay community is William R. Roff's *The Origins of Malay Nationalism*. Anthony Short's *The Communist Insurrection in Malaya, 1948-1960* is a detailed history of the Emergency. On the Brooke dynasty of Sarawak, Steven Runciman's *The White Rajas: A History of Sarawak from 1841 to 1946* is helpful. Nicholas Tarling's *Sulu and Sabah* is a historical study of British involvement in what is now the state of Sabah. (For further information and complete citations, see Bibliography.)

Chapter 2. The Society and Its Environment

Wooden carving from a palace in Terengganu. A flowery motif girds a verse from the Quran.

MALAYSIAN SOCIETY IS a complex mosaic of regions, social classes, rural-urban divisions, and ethnic communities. The most central alignment is ethnicity, which serves to define the plural society of Malaysia—plural in the sense that ethnic boundaries coincide with most social spheres and institutions. Within Malaysia ethnicity is closely related to religion, politics, culture, residence, and socioeconomic position. In the two and one-half decades since independence in 1957, there has been progress toward the creation of a common national (Malaysian) identity and some lessening of interethnic disparities. Nonetheless, the pervasive influence of ethnicity continues to affect all spheres of social life, from food taboos to priorities for government expenditures. Contemporary ethnic differences did not simply arise from primordial passions but were reinforced in part through official policies of the colonial era. With independence and the rise of social aspirations, competition in the economy and polity has often centered on questions of ethnic representation and equity. Yet, even with the high degree of ethnic consciousness and occasional episodes of ethnic violence, there is also a large measure of tolerance, and close personal ties span ethnic boundaries. Ethnocentrism and stereotypes abound, but virulent racism is largely absent.

According to 1980 census figures, Peninsular Malaysia's ethnic balance is roughly 56 percent Malay, 33 percent Chinese, 10 percent Indian, and a remaining category of 1 percent that includes Eurasians, Thais, and other small nationality groups. In Sabah and Sarawak—which together with the states of Peninsular Malaysia comprise Malaysia—there is an even greater level of ethnic diversity. The 1980 population of Sabah was divided primarily into Pribumis (83 percent) and Chinese (16 percent); Indians and others made up the remainder. The Pribumi category is a broad classification of indigenous peoples that includes Kadazan, Murut, Bajau, Malays, and Indonesians. In Sarawak the major ethnic divisions are Iban (30 percent), Chinese (29 percent), Malays (20 percent), Bidayuh (8 percent), Melanau (6 percent), various indigenous peoples (5 percent), and others (1 percent).

Persons are counted in the census as Malay on the basis of self-identification. Individuals simply report the ethnic community to which they belong. To be identified as Malay according to the

Constitution, however, one must profess Islam, habitually speak Malay (Bahasa Malaysia), follow Malay customs, and fulfill certain conditions of birth. Qualifications for Malaysian citizenship status are also specified in the Constitution.

Social life is also influenced by a broad array of other features and institutions, including family structure, economic roles, traditional and modern schooling, religious belief and organization, language use, the mass media, and the availability of medical services. In all spheres of social life, some aspects reflect continuity with the past; however, there is also a strong presence of modernization and change. The most powerful influence on Malaysian social life has been the rapid pace of economic development over the past 25 years. The effects of this development are not only evident in higher levels of consumption but are also visible in the physical transformation of Kuala Lumpur and other large cities and in the pervasive influences of modern curative medicine, telecommunications, and education throughout the country. These changes are most evident in Peninsular Malaysia, but there have also been significant changes in the states of Sabah and Sarawak. Malaysia is also in the midst of a demographic transition from high birth and death rates to lower levels of both vital indicators. Population growth remains high during this transitional period, for mortality has declined more rapidly than fertility. If fertility continues to decline in the coming years as it has in the past, population growth should begin to level off in the coming decades. Past and present changes in demographic processes and structures affect ethnic composition, urban-rural balance, and family structure, as well as demands for education, employment, housing, and other dimensions of economic and social life.

Social change in Malaysia is often glacial in character but often not clearly visible to contemporary observers. However, in recent years economic development has led to truly revolutionary change. Although modernization is transforming many attributes of Malaysian society, the evolving patterns may not necessarily follow Western models. The examples of Japan and other Asian societies, the influence of Islam and other religious traditions, and the unique characteristics of Malaysia's past and present may well lead in new directions.

Environment

The total land area of the country is approximately 330,000 square kilometers—about the same size as Vietnam or the Philippines. On the mainland of Southeast Asia is Peninsular Malaysia, which represents 40 percent of the total land area of the country. The balance of the land area is found in Sabah and Sarawak, the two states on the northwestern side of the island of Borneo. Peninsular Malaysia is separated from the states of Sabah and Sarawak by a 650-kilometer span of the South China Sea. Located just north of the equator, Malaysia enjoys a hot and humid tropical climate marked by seasonal variations in rainfall. The topography varies from coastal swamps to mountainous interiors, and numerous rivers and narrow plains lie in between. The soils of the country are not particularly fertile but are well adapted to tree crops, including rubber and oil palm. The interior is covered with thick foliage and jungle. Malaysia is well endowed with natural resources, including tin, oil, and natural gas. Sparsely settled, the country's population, as counted in the 1980 census, was about 13.1 million, of whom 10.9 million—or 83 percent—lived in Peninsular Malaysia.

Topography

Peninsular Malaysia extends 804 kilometers from its northern border with Thailand to its southern connection—a causeway across the shallow Johore Strait—to the island-state of Singapore (see fig. 4). The peninsula is separated from the Indonesian island of Sumatra by the Strait of Malacca. Although the Kra Isthmus in southern Thailand just above Peninsular Malaysia's northern border is only 64 kilometers wide, the width of Peninsular Malaysia approaches 330 kilometers at its broadest point. Peninsular Malaysia covers a land area of 131,590 square kilometers. There are many small islands off both the east and the west coasts of the peninsula, most of which are largely rural and contain a number of small fishing villages. The one exception is the island of Penang off the northwest coast of the peninsula, which is the location of a major port city.

The central core of the peninsula is dominated by a series of mountain ranges and associated highlands. Over half of the land area is 150 meters or more above sea level. The Main Range is the largest, widest, and most prominent of the major mountain ranges down the spine of the peninsula. It is primarily composed of granite and spans over 480 kilometers from the Thai border to Negeri Sembilan. It has an average width of 48 to 64 kilometers. The highest peak in the Main Range, at 2,188 meters, is Korbu Mountain, but the elevation for the entire length of the range rarely drops below 914 meters. The highest peak on the entire peninsula is Tahan Mountain in Pahang, which rises to 2,207 meters.

Figure 4. Topography

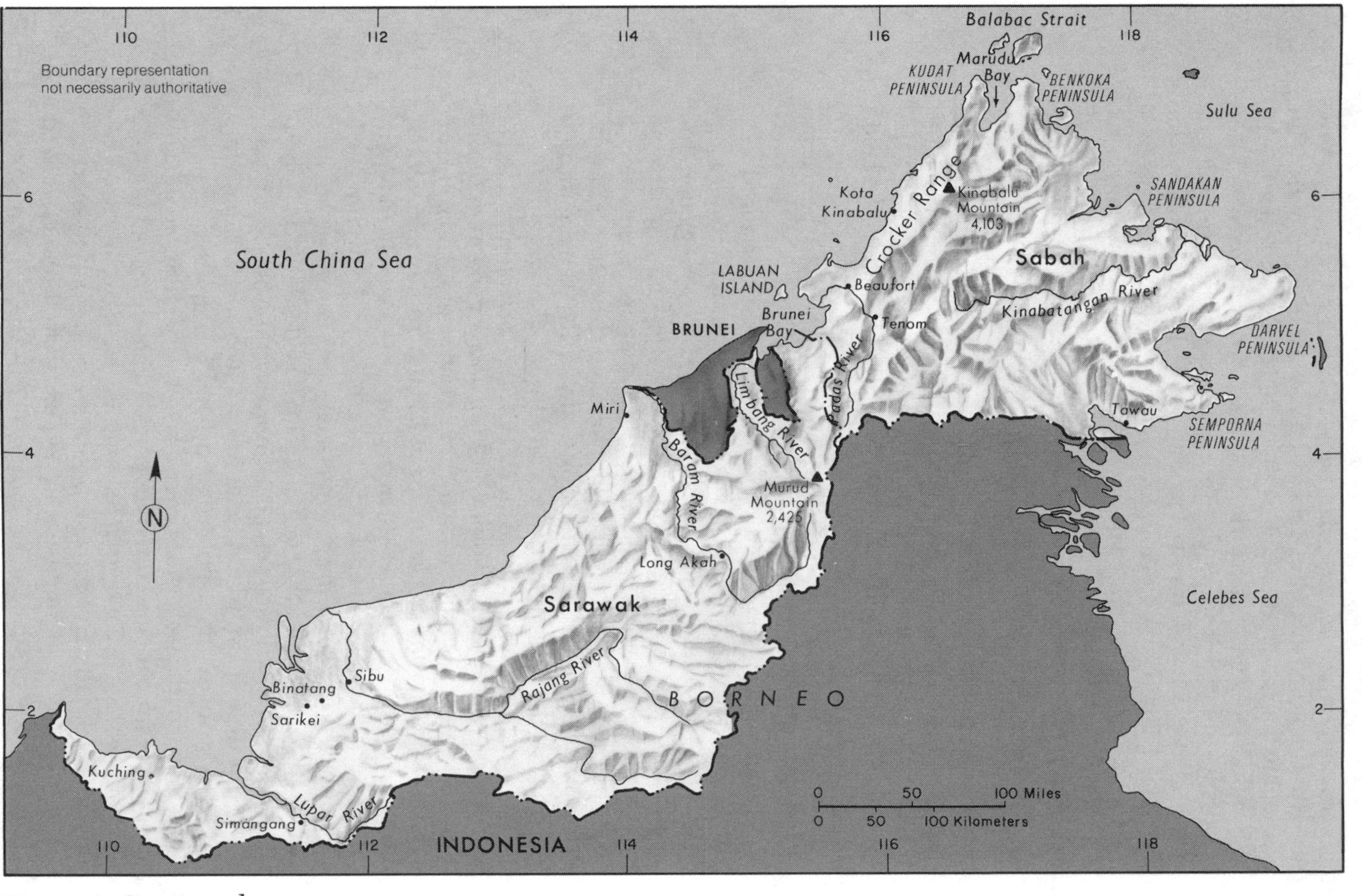

Figure 4. Continued.

These mountain ranges effectively divide the northern two-thirds of the peninsula into east coast and west coast regions. The coastal lowlands on either side of the mountainous interior are 15 to 80 kilometers wide. Historically, these two regions have been relatively isolated from each other because of the difficulty of communications and transportation. Only in 1982, when the East-West Highway was completed, was an overland route between the two northern coasts opened. Large extensive plains that make for intensive *padi* (irrigated rice) cultivation are found in Kelantan and in Kedah but are not the typical landscape of most of Peninsular Malaysia. Much of the lowlands landscape is covered by gentle hills broken by rivers and small streams. Mangrove swamps from the coastline of most of the west coast from Perlis to Johore, while the east coast typically has sandy beaches. The east coast is fully exposed to the South China Sea, unlike the west coast, which is sheltered from the Indian Ocean by the landmass of Sumatra.

Generally running east and west from the interior to the sea are a series of major rivers which were, until modern times, the principal means of transportation. The longest is the Pahang River, which runs for 434 kilometers; other important rivers are the Perak, the Kelantan (which flows north), the Terengganu, the Endau, the Muar, and the Muda. Because of the high, year-round precipitation, these rivers never run dry and are nearly always navigable, although extensive silting in many rivers limits navigation to canoes and rafts. Historically, rural villages were located along the banks of the major rivers and their tributaries.

The two contiguous states of Sarawak and Sabah on the island of Borneo are about 1,120 kilometers long and a maximum of 270 kilometers wide. Sabah has a total land area of 73,711 square kilometers. Sarawak has a landmass of 124,449 square kilometers, almost equal to Peninsular Malaysia. Brunei, a newly independent state, occupies two enclaves along the coast between Sabah and Sarawak. The coastline of some 2,254 kilometers is generally regular in Sarawak but is broken and deeply indented in Sabah. The land border with Kalimantan (Indonesian Borneo), which occupies the rest of the island, is approximately 1,450 kilometers long. Because of the wild, rugged, and unexplored country through which it passes, the border has never been surveyed; and because the area is constantly under cloud cover, aerial photography has not succeeded in determining a definite line. Indigenous peoples of the area move freely from one region to another.

The topography of Sarawak shows a flat coastal plain followed by a narrow belt of hills, then a sharp rise of the mountainous mass that borders Kalimantan. Murud Mountain, near the junction of Sarawak, Sabah, and Kalimantan, is Sarawak's highest mountain at 2,425 meters. The hills that extend the full length of Sarawak are usually less than 300 meters above sea level but are broken by a few mountain groups of about 760 meters; some of the mountains extend to the coast and terminate as sea-formed cliffs. The coastal region is a flat alluvial plain several meters above sea level. The plain is often swampland, and its width varies from less than two kilometers at Miri in the north to over 160 kilometers at some points farther south but is generally 32 to 64 kilometers wide. The alluvial deposits are mud or a deep and extensive mantle of peat. Some moderately productive *padi* land can be found on the banks of river deltas.

The Sarawak coastal waters are very shallow and , coupled with the regular coastline, afford no significant harbors. Moreover, the silt-laden rivers deposit large amounts of allivium, which forms great bars that effectively obstruct the passage of large vessels upstream. The higher elevations, where the hills extend to the sea, can support some farming and permanent settlements, but the muddy beaches fringed by thick mangroves and nipa palm swamps discourage economic activity elsewhere along the coast.

The rivers of Sarawak are numerous and of considerable volume because of the abundance of rainfall in the area. All rivers rise in the interior and descend through gorges until they reach the flat coastal plain, where they change character completely and meander to the sea. Major rivers of Sarawak include the Rajang and the Lupar, both in the south. The Rajang, which is 560 kilometers long, is the country's largest and probably most important river. It is navigable by small ocean vessels for 96 kilokmeters and by shallow-draft riverboats for 240 kilometers from its mouth. The Lupar extends inland for 230 kilometers. Farther north, the Baram River, 400 kilometers long, drains the north-central area and empties into the sea just north of Miri; the Limbang River flows for 196 kilometers between and beyond the two enclaves of Brunei. These and other rivers are the only effective avenues for inland travel. Jungle paths connect their headquarters, and a few trails pass over the watershed into Kalimantan.

The terrain in Sabah is superficially similar to that in Sarawak, but several important differences can be noted. The coastline, for example, becomes progressively more irregular from west to east until, in the east facing the Sulu Sea, it is boldly and deeply indented. The Sunda Shelf, which accounts for the shallowness off Sarawak, reaches its northern limit near Brunei Bay, and eastern Sabah offers many excellent deep-water ports and anchorages.

On the South China Sea, Labuan Island, 56 kilometers from the mainland entrance at Brunei Bay, has a sheltered harbor that is the major terminus for seaborne traffic destined for Sarawak and Brunei, as well as Sabah.

The mountains of Sabah differ from those of Sarawak. The interior mass, particularly where it borders Kalimantan, is the same complex arrangement of highly dissected ranges and occasional peaks of over 2,135 meters, but the ranges lie much closer to the sea and tend to be less complex. The coastal plain in the west along the South China Sea reaches inland only 16 to 32 kilometers, giving way abruptly to the only continuous range in Malaysian Borneo. This backbone, known as the Crocker Range, is really the southeastern extension of the chain that created the islands of the Philippines. It averages somewhat higher elevations than those in Sarawak, particularly in its northern reaches, where spectacular Kinabalu Mountain, 4,103 meters high, towers over everything else in the country; no other peak in Sabah reaches 2,440 meters.

East of the Crocker Range, a series of parallel but lower ranges extend from the elevated interior core to the Sulu Sea. Wide valleys separate the ranges, and the sea has formed long, deep bays along the east coast. The ridges form a series of peninsulas, including Kudat and Benkoka, which enclose Marudu Bay in the extreme north, and Sandakan, Darvel, and Semporna, which define the bays of Labuk, Sandakan, Darvel, and Cowie in the east.

Sabah is drained by many rivers. Those in western Sabah, with one exception, empty into the South China Sea and are relatively short because the mountains are so near the coast. The one exception is the Padas River, which has cut a deep gorge through the Crocker Range and drains a large section of interior lowland. All western rivers carry silt that is deposited on the narrow coastal plain, where it forms good agricultural land. The other rivers of Sabah drain into the Sulu or Celebes seas. The 564-kilometer-long Kinabatangan River is the largest and most significant internal waterway of Sabah. Rising in the southern part of the Crocker Range, it flows generally east-west through the middle of Sabah and empties into Sandakan Bay.

Climate and Vegetation

Peninsular Malaysia, Sabah, and Sarawak lie in the same latitude range, are subject to the same movement of air masses, and have very similar climates. Local variations in temperature and rainfall occur because of elevation or proximity to the sea, but the basic features are heavy rainfall, high humidity, and year-round uniformity of temperature, ranging from 21°C to 32°C. There are two monsoon periods when rainfall is much heavier than average (there is no distinct dry season without rainfall). Both monsoons are wet and hot, and the major difference between them is the direction from which the rains arrive. The more robust period is that of the northeast monsoon, which prevails from the beginning of October until the end of February. Its strong, regular winds sweep southward at a rapid pace until they reach about 5° north latitude, where they become stalled or even retreat slightly, so that the rains that accompany them often persist for days. Exceptionally heavy rainfall during this period occasionally leads to serious flooding, particularly on the east coast of Peninsular Malaysia. The most destructive flood within living memory occurred in December 1970. The southwest monsoon blows from mid-April to about mid-October and is slightly milder but less predictable. It is a period marked by sudden squalls and thunderstorms of such great intensity that rivers in Sabah may rise by as much as 15 meters above normal level in a few hours.

The annual mean rainfall in Peninsular Malaysia is about 2,540 millimeters, with most of the precipitation occurring during the southwest monsoon. In recent years meteorological measurements in Kuala Lumpur have recorded 1,807 to 2,316 millimeters of annual rainfall, including 178 to 196 days of rain. Comparable measurements yield 2,015 to 3,273 millimeters and 171 to 188 days of rain in Kota Kinabalu in Sabah, and 3,868 to 5,293 millimeters and 239 to 264 days of rain in Kuching, Sarawak. The heaviest rain in Sabah and Sarawak fall during the northeast monsoon. On the peninsula, local averages range from 1,630 millimeters in a year at Jelebu in Negeri Sembilan to over 5,000 millimeters in the Larut Hills near Taiping in Perak. Whereas the west coast is wettest during the southwest monsoon, the higher elevations of the interior receive most of their rainfall during the short, eight-week transition period between monsoons. In Sarawak, climatological stations at Kuching and Sibu have reported a difference of over 1,350 millimeters of rain in areas that are only 161 kilometers apart. Farther east at Long Akah in the mountains of the upper Baram River, an annual mean rainfall of 6,000 millimeters makes Long Akah the wettest place in Malaysia.

In lowland Malaysia, the average daily temperature for most of the year is between 26°C and 28°C. Maximum and minimum temperatures are slightly more varied. Highland areas have somewhat cooler temperatures. Cameron Highlands has a temperature range generally between 17°C and 18°C and a recorded absolute minimum temperature of 2°C.

Under the favorable influence of its hot, humid climate, Malaysia is a land of lush and verdant plant life. Woody varieties constitute most of the growth, but lianas, ferns, low shrubs, flowering bushes, and countless epiphytic plants, deriving their nutrients from the air and rain and usually growing on another plant, abound in all areas. Cleared land exists only in major settlement areas along the coast or on the banks of rivers for varying distances inland. Much of the land that has been cleared has been replaced by palm and rubber tree plantations so that if these regions are added to those naturally covered, the forest area reaches about 90 percent of total land area. The type of vegetation in the forests is as varied as it is extensive.

All uncleared areas are commonly referred to as "jungle," but this is not entirely accurate. The mangrove and nipa palm areas are really swamp forests that are treacherous underfoot and almost impenetrable. The major portion of the rain forest is characterized by towering, bare-trunked trees, mostly hardwoods. Most of the trees are about 30 meters high, and occasional giants rise as high as 60 meters. Trees are so close and the canopy is so dense that the floor of the forest is in perpetual shade, allowing only a thinly scattered undergrowth of flowers and low shrubs to exist. In other areas of the rain forest where the soil was derived from underlying strata of limestone, the trees are not as tall, the canopy is more open, and the undergrowth is so luxuriant that a true jungle exists.

Malaysia's forests have always been a major resource of the domestic economy. In recent years, the forest resources of Malaysia have increasingly entered the international market. During the 1970s Malaysia became the world's largest exporter of tropical hardwoods. Because of slow efforts at reforestation and environmental damage associated with timber extraction, there is growing concern about the long-term management of Malaysia's forest reserves.

Natural Resources

Mineral resources have been a key element of Malaysian history and modern development. Gold, tin, and iron ore have been mined in Peninsular Malaysia for centuries and were important items of trade within the regional economy. The development of the tin industry in the late nineteenth century established the colonial economy's main source of wealth. Petroleum and natural gas resources have been a major source of economic growth (see Mining, ch. 3).

The deposits in the tin belt of southeast Asia—centered on Peninsular Malaysia—are the richest and most extensive in the world. In the early years of the tin boom in the late nineteenth century, Peninsular Malaysia provided half of the world's supply; at present, Malaysia remains the world's largest producer, accounting for 30 and 35 percent of the world's production in the 1970s. Although tin deposits are located in the east coast states of Kelantan, Terengganu, and Pahang, the major tin fields have been in the west coast states of Perak and Selangor. The Kinta tin field near Ipoh in the state of Perak has yielded nearly one-half of Malaysia's recorded production and is the world's single most productive tin field. Other minerals, including coal, iron ore, bauxite, gold, and manganese have been commercially mined.

The Miri oil field in Sarawak was developed early in the twentieth century and was the source of considerable production, peaking at 5.5 million barrels per year in 1929. In the late 1960s and early 1970s there were major finds of petroleum and natural gas reserves in Sarawak and Sabah, mostly offshore. Further exploration has led to the discovery of reserves off the east coast of Peninsular Malaysia. By 1983 crude oil production had risen to 365,000 barrels per day and had become an important component of the economy and of government finance.

Transportation

Historically, waterways were the primary means of transportation, both along the coast and by rivers from the coast to the inland settlements. On the peninsula, major rivers and their tributary streams were the traditional avenues of trade, taxation, and political influence. Since the development of roads and railroads, inland waterways have become of only marginal significance on the peninsula. However, rivers remain major transportation arteries in Sabah and Sarawak.

In addition to the established major ports for sea transportation at Kelang and Penang in Peninsular Malaysia, new ports have recently been developed at Johore Baharu and Kuantan. Facilities have also been significantly upgraded at Kelang and Penang. The major ports of Sabah—Kota Kinabalu and Sandakan—were expanded in 1976 to 1977 (see Transportation, Communications, and Other Services, ch. 3). Kuching and Sibu, the major ports of Sarawak, were upgraded, and a new port was constructed in 1979 in Bintulu to handle general cargo as well as natural gas products.

The transportation network of roads and railroads built during the colonial era was centered on the sites of the export economy (rubber plantations and tin mines) and the major cities of the west coast of the peninsula. Although the network was considered to be a relatively advanced transportation system for its time, it provided little service for the majority of the population, including the populous but poorer rural hinterlands. Since independence, the Malaysian government has made road- and bridge-building in the rural areas a major priority. Of the country's 31,450 kilometers of roads in 1981, 22,622 kilometers were hard surface, 7,541 kilometers were gravel, and 1,287 kilometers were earth roads. By 1981 Sabah had 4,747 kilometers of roads (1,883 kilometers hard surface); Sarawak had only 3,070 kilometers (793 kilometers hard surface).

The roads of Malaysia are generally in good condition, although flooding will sometimes make certain roads impassable. An extensive program of road construction and rehabilitaton was undertaken in the 1970s. Major projects incluuded the East-West Highway (which links Kota Baharu in Kelantan to Gerik in Perak) and extensive development of major transport arteries in the Kuala Lumpur-Petaling Jaya-Kelang metropolian complex. Also, there have been thousands of kilometers of development and feeder roads to serve rural areas, especially Federal Land Development Authority (FELDA) schemes.

The main railroad line in the country runs north from Singapore and then divides into two lines running along the west and east coasts. Both lines connect with the State Railway of Thailand. The total length of both lines, plus the feeder lines serving ports and urban areas, is 1,666 kilometers; most are single track. The rail network of Peninsular Malyasia was completed in 1931, and no major additions have been made since then. Beginning in 1971, however, the government-owned Malayan Railway Administration began a long-term program of replacement, rehabilitaiton, and modernization of its lines and equipment. The Sabah State Railway runs 155 kilometers from Kota Kinabalu to points south (see fig. 7). There is no rail service in Sarawak.

Air transport in the country is provided by the Malaysian Airline System (MAS), owned by the government since its initial incorporation in 1947 as Malayan Airways. It has been known under its precent name since 1972 when service under Malaysia-Singapore Airlines ceased. The major cities of Peninsular Malaysia and many towns and administrative centers in Sarawak and Sabah are well linked by domestic and international connections. Air service is particularly important to the transport systems of Sarawak and Sabah.

Regional Divisions

In addition to the two states of Sabah and Sarawak on the island of Borneo, Malaysia contains 11 states plus the Federal Territory on the peninsula. The Peninsular Malaysian states are Johore, Kedah, Kelantan, Malacca, Negeri Sembilan, Pahang, Penang, Perak, Perlis, Selangor, and Terengganu. The Federal Territory, which is coterminous with the city of Kuala Lumpur, was created in February 1974 from part of the state of Selangor (see fig. 9) Under the federal system of Malaysia, each of the states has its own elected legislature as well as shared responsibility for administration with the federal government (see The Federal Government, ch. 4).

At the time of British political intervention in the 1870s, the west coast states had relatively small populations, whereas the northern states of Kedah, Kelantan, and Terengganu (subsequently considered to be relatively underdeveloped in the twentieth century) were the most populous. But the economic developments of the late nineteenth century, particularly in tin mining and plantation agriculture, shifted the economic balance to the west coast of the peninsula. The west coast states, particularly Perak and Selangor, developed the features of a modern economy through the growth of cities and major investments in the physical infrastructure, including roads. These were also the areas of the largest Chinese and Indian population settlement. For many reasons, the socioeconomic and cultural gaps between the east and west coasts continued to widen throughout the twentieth century. Even after independence, regional differences were accentuated by control of the Kelantan and Terengganu state governments by an opposition political party.

The plans for regional development during the 1970s appeared to be intended to break some of the geographical disparities created by earlier trends. Major improvements in communications and transportation, including all-weather roads and bridges, serve to lessen the isolation of many rural areas in both the east and the west coast regions. Moreover, the policies of extensive agricultural development in the interior, and of regional growth centers, should more closely knit the economic and social ties across the map of Peninsular Malaysia (see Government Planning and Policy, ch. 3).

In Sabah and Sarawak, the historical impact of development has been less pronounced. Settlement has been concentrated near coastal areas, and other localities near water transport. In Sabah the majority of the population, the urban areas and development have been centered in the west coast zone. This zone is primarily agricultural, but there are also a number of towns, including the state capital of Kota Kinabalu. The very large eastern zone of Sabah is sparsely settled except for the coastal cities of

Sandakan and Tawau. The majority of Sarawak's population continues to live in the western region, which includes the First and Second divisions and the western part of the Third Division. This area includes the capital city and major port of Kuching, as well as the areas of extensive agricultural development around Sibu, Binatang, and Sarikei.

Population Growth and Distribution

In historical times, the Malaysian peninsula and the island of Borneo were sparsely settled because their environment was not particularly favorable to extensive *padi* cultivation. Despite several decades of rapid population growth caused by immigration, the 1911 censuses counted only 2.3 million people in Peninsular Malaysia (British Malaya, excluding Singapore). Immigration from China, India, and Indonesia (then the Dutch East Indies) continued at a high pace for the next 30 years until the Japanese occupation during World War II. After World War II, immigration ceased to be a major element of population growth. Nonetheless, a high level of population growth has continued through natural increase—an excess of births over deaths.

In the most recent census of Malaysia, in 1980, a population of 13,137,000 (unrevised figure) was counted. When census undernumeration—as estimated by official sources—is taken into account, the 1980 population of Malaysia is reported to be 13.7 million. Because of the lack of detailed data adjusted for the census undercount, actual census figures are used both for 1980 and for preceding censuses. Although these population figures are probably 4 to 5 percent too low, the basic population patterns and trends will not be affected.

Of Malaysia's population of 13.1 million in 1980, 10.9 million were in Peninsular Malaysia, 1 million in Sabah, and 1.2 million in Sarawak. At the time of independence in 1957, the population of Peninsular Malaysia (then the Federation of Malaya) was 6.3 million. Growing at a rapid pace that averaged 2.6 percent per year, Peninular Malaysia's population reached 8.8 million in 1970. From 1970 to 1980, the average rate of population growth slowed somewhat to 2.2 percent per year, although this is still a fairly rapid rate by international standards. Within Peninsular Malaysia, the Malay fraction of the total population increased from 50 percent to 56 percent. The Chinese and Indian populations have also been growing rapidly, but the average rate for each decreased from 2.3 percent per year from 1957 to 1970, to 1.5 percent per year from 1970 to 1980 (see table B).

In spite of the varied pace of population growth across ethnic communities, the demographic underpinning of the Malaysian ethnic balance remains essentially unchanged. The Chinese minorities of 33 percent in Peninsular Malaysia, 16 percent in Sabah, and 29 percent in Sarawak are considerably larger (in a relative sense) than in any other southeast Asian country, with the exception of Singapore. Their economic and political roles cannot be ignored. Moreover, the political balance does not shift on the basis of a few percentage points change in relative ethnic compostion. The complex and delicate nature of ethnic relations in Malaysia will not be fuundamentally altered by modest changes in ethnic composition.

Mortality, Fertility, and Family Planning

The most important cause of rapid population growth since World War II has been the dramatic decline in mortality levels. In Peninsular Malaysia the crude death rate (the number of annual deaths per 1,000 population) dropped from 20 in 1947 to six in 1975. Over the same period, the infant mortiality rate declined from 102 to 33 (deaths of infants less than one year of age per 1,000 births). Improvements in nutritional levels, preventive health programs, and greater accessibility to curative medicine have probably contributed to this decline in mortality. With the exception of Singapore, Peninsular Malaysia has the lowest mortality level of any country in Southeast Asia. Because of weakness of the vital registration system in Sabah and Sarawak, it is not possible to give an accurate reading of current mortality levels in these states.

Beginning in the late 1950s and early 1960s, fertility levels in Peninsular Malaysia began to decline. At first the decline was rather slow, but it accelerated in the 1960s and has continued into the 1970s. The magnitude of these declines is most clearly illustrated by trends in the total fertility rate (TFR). The TFR is a summary measure of annual fertility that is interpreted as the total number of children that a woman would have if she were subject to the current age-specific fertility rates throughout her childbearing years. At the beginning of the fertility transition around 1960, the TFR was well over seven children per woman among the Indian population, over six children per woman among Chinese, and somewhat fewer than six children per woman among Malays.

Fertility declines were most rapid among the Indian and Chinese populations; thus by 1970 fertility was highest for Malay

Table B. Population Size and Growth by Ethnic Group, 1957–80

Ethnic Group	Population (in thousands) 1957[1]	1970	1980	Average Annual Growth Rate (in percentage) 1957–70[2]	1970–80
Peninsular Malaysia					
Malays	3,126	4,672	6,132	3.1	2.7
Chinese	2,334	3,131	3,651	2.3	1.5
Indian	696	936	1,093	2.3	1.5
Other	123	70	69	-4.3	-0.2
Total Peninsular Malaysia[3]	6,279	8,810	10,945	2.6	2.2
Sabah					
Pribumis	344	500	792	3.7	4.6
Chinese	104	139	155	2.9	1.1
Indian	3	7	5	8.0	-2.9
Other	2	7	3	10.7	-8.6
Total Sabah[3]	454	654	956	3.6	3.8
Sarawak					
Malays	129	181	249	3.4	3.2
Melanau	45	53	70	1.8	2.7
Iban	238	304	368	2.4	1.9
Bidayuh	58	84	105	3.7	2.3
Other indigenous	38	51	67	2.9	2.8
Chinese	229	294	361	2.5	2.0
Other	8	10	16	1.8	4.9
Total Sarawak[3]	744	976	1,236	2.7	2.4
TOTAL	7,477	10,440	13,137[4]	n.a	n.a

n.a.--not available.

[1]Sabah and Sarawak figures from 1960.

[2]Sabah and Sarawak figures from 1960–70.

[3]Figures may not add to total because of rounding.

[4]The government's revised 1980 population total was approximtely 13,745,200, broken down as follows: Peninsular Malaysia 11,426,600; Sabah 1,011,000; and Sarawak 1,307,600.

Source: Based on information from Malaysia, Department of Statistics, *1980 Population and Housing Census of Malaysia: General Report of the Population Census*, Kuala Lumpur, 1983, 17.

women, who registered a TFR of 5.2 children. The rate was 4.8 and 4.9 for Chinese and Indians, respectively. Fertility declined even more dramatically in the 1970s; by 1980 the TFR were 4.6, 3.3, and 3.6 respectively, for the Malay, Chinese, and Indian populations (see table 2, Appendix). Although the Chinese and Indian declines in fertility have been amazing (about 30 percent declines in the 1970s), the fertility transition is also significant among the Malay population. The higher concentration of the Malay population in rural areas explains, in part, their slower pace of demographic change. Current levels of Chinese fertility are comparable to those experienced in the United States during the 1950s.

Further detailed analysis of age-specific fertility rates reveals the sources of changing demographic patterns in Peninsular Malaysia. Almost all of the declines in Malay fertility have been among women younger than age 25. This suggests that a trend toward a later age at marriage has been the key factor in lowering Malay fertility. For Chinese and Indians, there have been major reductions in fertility levels across all ages of childbearing. This pattern is consistent with an interpretation that rising age at marriage and an increasing practice of family planning within marriage are both important causes of declining fertility.

In spite of wide variation, there is a consistent trend toward marital postponement for men and women in both urban and rural areas as well as across all ethnic communities. Among Malaysians age 30 to 34 in 1980, most of whom had already married, the median age at first marriage was 25 for men and 20 for women. These figures represent an increase of about two years in the average age at marriage within a generation. Urban men and women marry even later at age 26 and 22, respectively. Across ethnic communities, the Malay population married youngest—the median age at first marriage was 24 for men and 19 for women. These figures, however, represent a postponement of about two years within a generation.

Use of modern forms of contraception has also played an important role in fertility reductions in Peninsular Malaysia. The National Family Planning Board was set up by the government in 1967 to distribute family planning information and contraceptive materials. In addition, there is an active private sector family planning association, and contraceptives are widely available through commercial outlets. Results from a 1974 survey indicated that one-half of Chinese and Indian married women aged 25 to 44 were currently using contraception and about one-quarter of married Malay women were. Oral contraceptives are the most widely used birth control method in Peninsular Malaysia.

Sabah and Sarawak have somewhat higher levels of fertility than does Peninsular Malaysia. However, comparison of 1970 and 1980 census data reveals a trend toward lower fertiltity and delayed marriage in both Sabah and Sarawak. These demographic changes during the 1970s are fairly modest, especially in Sabah. If the experience of Peninsular Malaysia can be taken as a guide, the patterns of a demographic transition should more clearly emerge in Sabah and Sarawak during the 1980s.

Population Distribution by State

The population of states in Peninsular Malaysia ranges from 1.7 million in Perak and 1.6 million in Johore to only 145,000 in Perlis. If the population of the Federal Territory (920,000) were to be counted with Selangor (1.4 million), which completely surrounds it, Selangor would form the largest state. Indeed, more than one-half of Peninsular Malaysia resides in Johore, Selangor, Perak, and the Federal Territory (see table 3, table 4, Appendix). Chinese and Indians are more highly concentrated in the urbanized states of the west coast. The less developed states of Peninsular Malaysia include Perlis and Kedah in the northwest and Kelantan, Terengganu, and Pahang on the east coast. Over 44 percent of the Malay population lives in these five, mostly rural states, while only 13 percent of the Chinese and Indian populations does.

Another way to consider regional distribution is to examine the ethnic composition of the different states. Malays form over 90 percent of the population in both Kelantan and Terengganu, almost three-quarters of Kedah's, and two-thirds of Pahang's population. In most of the other states, the proportion of Malays is about one-half of the total population, sometimes a bit above 50 percent (Johore and Malacca), and sometimes a bit below (Negeri Sembilan, Perak, and Selangor). In Penang and the Federal Territory, the Malay proportion is only one-third of the total population, and the Chinese population comprises the majority. These variations in ethnic composition among states have a major influence on political divisions and other aspects of social life.

Urbanization, Urban Growth, and Internal Migration

Peninsular Malaysia has a relatively balanced pattern of urban development and a good number of medium-sized and smaller towns. Although Kuala Lumpur, Ipoh, and George Town are considered the major metropolitan centers, they are not primate cities in the same way that Bangkok dominates the urban hierar-

Kuala Lumpur (above) and George Town (below)
Courtesy Malaysia Tourist Development Corporation,
Ministry of Trade and Industry

chy of Thailand. At the time of independence in 1957, 80 towns had populations of more than 5,000; by 1970, the number of such towns had grown to 113. The relatively well-developed transportation system of Peninsular Malaysia, as well as the extensive involvement of the rural population in market production, e.g., small-holding rubber, appears to have been especially favorable for the establishment of small- and medium-sized market towns.

Although there is no official figure that designates the minimum population of urban areas in Malaysia, the definition of 10,000 or more has been the standard in the 1970 and 1980 population censuses. According to this criterion, the percentage of the population of Malaysia living in urban areas rose from 27 percent in 1970 to 34 percent in 1980 (see table 4, Appendix). Although international comparisons of urbanization are plagued by problems of definition, Malaysia appears to be one of the more urbanized societies in Asia.

Further comprehensive research and data provide a fuller analysis of urbanization and urban growth in Peninsular Malaysia than for Malaysia as a whole. According to the definition of an urban area as having a minimum population of 10,000, the percentage of the population of Peninsular Malaysia in urban areas increased from 19 percent in 1947 to 27 percent in 1957, to 29 percent in 1970, and to 37 percent in 1980. Much of the urbanization during the 1947–57 period was precipitated by the resettlement program during the Emergency of 1948-60. Approximately 400,000 to 500,000 rural villagers, mostly Chinese without formal title to their agricultural lands, were forced to resettle in so-called New Villages, most of which were adjacent to existing small towns. Over the years, many of these New Villages were absorbed into the larger urban environment. From 1957 to 1970 the level of urbanization had shifted moderately (from 27 to 29 percent), although most urban areas were growing at a fairly rapid rate of 2 to 3 percent per year. Rural areas, however, were growing just as fast, so the rural-urban balance did not shift appreciably. From 1970 to 1980 the level of urbanization in Peninsular Malaysia jumped from 29 to 37 percent. The proportion of all Malays in urban areas rose from 15 to 25 percent, of Chinese from 48 to 56 percent, and of Indians from 35 to 41 percent.

Another way to examine the process of urbanization is to compare the average annual growth rate of urban and rural areas from 1970 to 1980; the growth rate of urban areas increased on average by 4.7 percent as compared with a 1.2-percent growth rate for rural areas during this period. The urban Malay population increased at a rate of 8 percent per year, compared with a growth rate of only 1.4 percent per year of the rural Malay population.

Among Chinese and Indians, the urban populations were growing at 3.2 percent per year, whereas their rural populations were essentially stable. The proportionately greater contributions of Malays to urban growth as compared with that of Chinese and Indians was of special interest (table 5, Appendix).

From the available data, it is not possible to provide a complete explanation of the urbanization process during the 1970s. Clearly, rural to urban migration must have been a major factor for all groups as new economic opportunities were created in the cities and as rural occupations became less remunerative. Another potentially important factor was the outward shift of urban boundaries (and additions to the number of urban places). Many towns and cities annex adjacent areas, including small towns, during the process of urban expansion. More refined analysis in the coming years will allow for a more comprehensive interpretation of urban change.

The pace of urbanization has been moving in the same direction in Sabah and Sarawak, although starting from a smaller base. By 1980 about one-fifth of the population in Sabah and Sarawak lived in urban areas. The rate of urban population growth was greater in Sabah (6 percent per year) than in Sarawak (4 percent per year), but in both states urban population growth was double that of rural growth.

Data from the 1980 census suggest that there was much migration during the 1970s; more than 2.5 million people reported they had moved from one locality to another during that decade. Almost half of these moves were from one rural area to another. Fewer than one out of five moves were from a rural location to an urban destination. There are very clear patterns of interstate migration, and it is the Federal Territory, Selangor, and Pahang that have gained through internal migration. Company state of birth with state of current residence, and subtracting out-migrants from in-migrants, the Federal Territory gained almost 200,000 net-migrants, Selangor 180,000, and Pahang over 160,000 according to the 1980 census. Sabah and Sarawak have gained modest numbers through migration but all the other states of Malaysia have experienced net out-migration.

Because the suburban areas around Kuala Lumpur, including Petaling Jaya, are part of Selangor, it seems reasonable to consider the major influx of migrations to Selangor and the Federal Territory as a response to the boom of Kuala Lumpur during the 1970's. The migration to Pahang is undoubtedly tied to the major land development projects undertaken by the government. Such developments not only attract settlers but also create additional opportunities which, in turn, encourage migration.

Ethnicity and the Plural Society

Patterns of Immigration

Early settlements established 500 to 1,500 years ago were small and were concentrated in a few towns along the seacoast. The countryside was thinly populated by Malay peoples who were primarily engaged in wet-rice cultivation and fishing along the major river valleys of the peninsula. Farther inland in the uplands and mountains were small aboriginal populations who were pushed to the interior when the Malay population settled the lowlands about 1,000 to 2,000 years ago. The Malay population, which is thought to have originated in South-Central Asia, migrated southward in prehistory and populated the Malay Peninsula, the Malay Archipelago, and much of the rest of Southeast Asia. The rise and fall of several maritime empires, as well as the ease of migration throughout the region, probably generated ebbs and flows of population movement between the peninsula and neighboring islands.

Colonial penetration and the development of the export economy in the nineteenth century set the stage for the emergence of the plural society of the twentieth century. As tin mining and plantation agriculture began to expand in the mid-nineteenth century—often as the result of alliances between Malay rulers on the peninsula and Chinese merchants from the Straits Settlements (see Glossary)—the shortage of labor was a major constraint on economic development. The western Malay states were very thinly populated; moreover, relatively few Malay peasants were willing to assume the role of cheap labor. The terrible working conditions, low remuneration, and authoritarian environment in the early mines and plantations did not present attractive economic opportunities to the Malay peasantry. The result was an extraordinary wave of immigration from China and India and from Sumatra, Java, and other islands of the Malay archipelago.

At the peak of immigration to British Malaya, approximately from 1880 to 1930, there were several hundred thousand arrivals annually. Although the annual outflow of emigrants was often as high as the number of immigrants, a sizable number of the Chinese and Indians (and probably most of the Indonesians) developed local roots and settled permanently in British Malaya. By 1911, when censuses of all states in British Malaya were conducted, the population was composed of almost 35 percent Chinese and 10 percent Indians—figures very close to the contemporary ethnic balance. Non-Malays formed the majority in most of the west coast states.

Immigration was slowed by the worldwide depression of the 1930s and virtually ceased after World War II. Although the immigration streams from China and India were composed mostly of young men, more women began to arrive in the early decades of the twentieth century, and a second generation of locally born Chinese and Indian residents emerged. By 1947 about two-thirds of Chinese and one-half of Indians in the country had been born in Malaya or Singapore. By 1980 more than nine out of 10 Malaysian Chinese and Indians were native-born.

The Malay world of historical Southeast Asia included the peninsula, the east coast of Sumatra, and parts of Borneo; thus the large numbers of culturally related immigrants from Sumatra, Java, and other Indonesian islands have been largely absorbed into the Malay community. However, the pace of assimilation has been of quite a different character for the descendants of Indian and Chinese immigrants. The structure of colonial society may well have served to widen rather than narrow ethnic divisions.

Colonialism and Its Impact on Ethnic Relations

The Portuguese conquest of Malacca in the early sixteenth century marked the first case of European intervention in the area of contemporary Malaysia. The century of Portuguese colonial rule and the following 150 years of Dutch colonialism in Malacca appear to have had only a minor effect on subsequent developments. The first century of British imperialism in the area, beginning with the occupation of Penang in 1786, appeared to represent only a slight variation in the typical European role in the region—the maintenace of port facilities for long-distance shipping and participation in the very profitable aspects of regional trade. However, increased European economic involvement in the mainland of the peninsula during the nineteenth century, along with growing Chinese entrepreneurial activities, led to full-scale political intervention. From 1874 onward, in conformity with an agreement between the British and one of several pretenders to the throne of Perak, direct colonial rule expanded throughout the peninsula until all the Malay states were incorporated by 1909 (see Federated and Unfederated Malay States, 1826–1909, ch. 1)

Although British authority in Malaya spanned a relatively brief historical period of 75 years—interrupted by the Japanese occupation of 1942–1945—it created the plural society of modern Peninsular Malaysia. Not only did the early decades of the colonial era see the ethnic balance shift with the heavy immigration from China and India, but colonial policies also reinforced ethnic cultural differences, created structural divisions along ethnic lines, and nutured ethnic stereotypes that continue to haunt contemporary society.

Before the major wave of Chinese immigration in the late nineteenth century, the Chinese community had assimilated Malay culture by adopting such elements as dress, language, and cuisine. The descendants of these early Chinese immigrants, known as Baba, or Straits Chinese, remain a distinctive community within the Malaysian-Chinese population. Other settlements of Chinese in predominantly Malay areas also evince considerable social and cultural assimilation. But the massive wave of Chinese immigration in the late nineteenth century led to the creation of large Chinese settlements that had little or no contact with the indigenous Malay community. In such an environment it is not surprising that Chinese settlers, even after a generation of Malayan residence, considered their primary identity to be Chinese. It is also possible that the major wave of Chinese immigration led to a greater sense of Chinese identity on the part of the Malayan Chinese community.

In addition to these informal processes, colonial policies reinforced communal solidarity by failing to acknowledge the Chinese in the Malay states (outside the Straits Settlements) to be sojourners, filling a temporary labor need. This policy allowed the colonial administration to defend its political role in alliance with the traditional sultanates (whose subjects were the Malay community) and to avoid governmental expenses for Chinese education, community needs, and the like. Under such conditions, the Chinese community experienced considerable social and political autonomy, financed its own schools and community services, and developed a strong ethnic and cultural identity.

British colonial administrators co-opted the Malay aristocracy into a dependent role through recognition of their symbolic positions and through generous pensions. Before British intervention, the west coast states had experienced considerable political instability as rivals for the sultanships fought for political dominance and the economic gains of office. All of this ceased with colonial rule. In order to maintain the fabric of feudal Malay society, traditional economic and social roles. As a booming export economy based on tin and rubber was being created, and as government revenues expanded enormously, the colonial government provided only modest educational opportunities to the rural Malay population. Rural schooling was purposely limited to the primary level and to the Malay language (not English) in order to discourage social mobility as well as migration to urban areas. Peasants were discouraged from growing rubber (a much more profitable crop than rice) on their farms or from entering the capitalist economy. As colonial Malaya developed in the twentieth century, relatively few Malays were prepared to enter the urban economy. Chinese and Indians in urban areas had a definite advantage in gaining access to English schools and to the emerging economic opportunities.

In addition to the economic and social policies that caused Malays, Chinese, and Indians to inhabit separate social, economic, and geographical spheres, the colonial era also legitimized ethnic stereotypes. Colonial administrators, in both their official and unofficial writings, created images of Malay, Chinese, and Indians that compared unfavorably with European society. These perceptions were then used to explain and to justify the social discrimination by Europeans in colonial Malaya. This Eurocentric interpretation of Malayan society became the dominant ideology of elites of all ethnic communities and even reached deeply into all social strata. In 1984—decades after independence—Malaysians in all ethnic communities still believed that Malays are inherently less ambitious, that all Chinese have extraordinary economic motivations, and that ethnic strife is just beneath the surface. More than bridges and roads, schools and hospitals, the real legacy of colonialism is the "racial" ideology of the country.

Ethnic Antagonism and Conflict

The economic and geographical structure of Malaysian society has served to separate ethnic groups into different residential communities. Historically, most Malays have lived in rural villages and the majority of Chinese and Indians were concentrated in tin-mining settlements, rubber plantations, or in the towns and cities throughout the country. Even within urban areas, ethnic communities tended to be residentially segregated. Because schooling was largely organized along vernacular lines (with the exception of the English-medium stream), children were largely exposed to ethnically homogeneous environments. Most interethnic contacts were in the market, where Chinese and Indian merchants predominated. Most rural Malay villages participated in the market economy, not only to purchase consumer goods but also to sell their agricultural products—especially rubber. Given such a situation, it is somewhat surprising that ethnic antagonism has been largely kept in check for most of the twentieth century.

During the two decades before British political intervention in the west coast states, periodic warfare broke out between Malay villagers and Chinese settlers. Most of the episodes, however, did not occur along ethnic lines. The potential wealth of tin mining, as well as the unsettled political conditions, led to frequent violent clashes. But often a Chinese group in alliance with a Malay chief was opposing another Chinese-Malay alignment.

It is clear that Malay social and political leaders in the early twentieth century were disturbed with the growing non-Malay—particularly Chinese—role in the country. The most common reaction was to urge Malays to be more competitive in the growing urban economy and to appeal to the British to expand opportunities for Malays. Chinese leaders, especially the English-educated, were often outspoken in their belief that colonial policies tended to discriminate against their political aspirations. One of the justifications for the maintenance of colonial rule was that democratic processes would unleash ethnic animosities by opening up competition in the political arena. However, there seem to be almost no reports of interethnic violence during most of the colonial era.

The first clear episodes of Malay-Chinese violence occurred during the Japanese occupation of Malaya during World War II. The resistance army against the Japanese, the Malayan Peoples Anti-Japanese Army (MPAJA), was predominantly Chinese. During the occupation, some MPAJA soldiers killed Malays (and Chinese) who were thought to be Japanese collaborators. One such incident in February 1945, near Batu Pahat in Johore, resulted in a backlash, and Malays attacked nearby Chinese settlements. Initially, the Japanese encouraged such violence but finally intervened to stop it. After the Japanese surrendered in August 1945, the MPAJA emerged as the dominant political authority in many towns and cities until the British military administration was set up in September 1945. During this interregnum, there were numerous MPAJA executions of Malays and Chinese who were thought to have been Japanese collaborators. These incidents and the memories of them led to considerable fear of interethnic hostility in the postwar era.

There have been a few other episodes of ethnic violence in the postwar era, such as in Singapore in 1964. Most significant, however, were the riots of May 1969 in Kuala Lumpur (see The Kuala Lumpur Riots of May 1969 and Their Aftermath, ch. 1). In retrospect, it seems that this episode of ethnic conflict marked a critical turning point in the postwar era.

The election of 1969 had aroused considerable ethnic expectation and fear. The opposition non-Malay parties had not run on anti-Malay sentiments; indeed, there seemed to be a fair degree of Malay support for the People's Movement of Malaysia (Gerakan Rakyat Malaysia—better known as Gerakan.) Nonetheless, the modest success of the opposition parties (which came largely at the expense of the Malayan Chinese Association [MCA]), encouraged a number of non-Malays to make public comments that denigrated Malays. A series of hostile events then led to full-scale riots, which took several days for the authorities to contain. The May 13 incident was limited to Kuala Lumpur and largely confined to some aparts of the city. Nonetheless, the stories of atrocities and the shifting of the government's public policies made deep imprints on public thinking.

Ethnic Composition and Subdivisions

Although the census classification of ethnicity appears to suggest clear-cut divisions among ethnic communities, a more detailed examination reveals considerable ambiguity. One factor to be considered is the heterogeneity within each ethnic community. Although outsiders tend to perceive each ethnic group as a unified bloc, the reality is one of considerable internal differentiation by place of origin, language, and cultural characteristics. And, though the census classification includes few Orang Asli (aboriginal peoples in the interior of Peninsular Malaysia) under the Malay category, few Malays or Orang Asli see themselves as part of a larger ethnic community. The cultural characterists of an ethnic community are even more difficult to enumerate. Each ethnic grouping is crosscut by many other dimensions, including rural-urban residence, religion, language of formal education, number of generations of Malaysian residence, and socioeconomic position. Cultural characteristics identified by an ethnologist in one area at one time can only be loosely generalized to other social aggregates.

Malay Society

Together with the Orang Asli and the indigenous peoples of Sabah and Sarawak, the Malay population is identified as Bumiputra—literally, sons of the soil (see Glossary). The connotation is that, as the indigenous peoples of the modern states, they possess an entitlement to represent the social and cultural core of the national identity.

The claim that Malays are the indigenous peoples is certainly true in a relative sense, given the nature of the Malay world of historical Southeast Asia. United by a common language and shared cultural features, there was continual interchange and mobility of peoples among the traditional states of the Malay world. However, except for occasional periods, there was no united polity that could claim sovereignty on the basis of Malay identity.

As a modern state was formed under colonial direction, the map did not follow cultural boundaries. Although the northern states of Kedah, Perlis, Kelantan, and Terengganu were wrested from Thai control, the Malay state of Patani remained part of Thailand, as present-day Pattani. Sumatra was joined with Indonesia. The inclusion of Sabah and Sarawak added a broader variety of ethnic communities in addition to the Malay Muslim populations in each state. This formal division of international boundaries by the colonial powers meant that regional migration became defined as international migration. Thus the claim that many Malays are descendants of Indonesian immigrants can be best understood as an element of the present debate over the definition and entitlement of the Bumiputra community.

There are few records of the volume of migration from Sumatra, Java, and other Southeast Asian islands to the Malay Peninsula during the late nineteenth and early twentieth centuries, although it appears to have been substantial. Not only did such migrants come independently (outside of the normal immigration channels) but many have also gradually been assimilated within the broad Malay community, although anthropological studies reveal continued differentiation in some areas. About 5 percent of the Malay population of Peninsular Malaysia reported their ethnic community as Indonesian (Javanese, Buginese, and the like) in the 1970 census.

In addition to those who claim Indonesian ethnic identity, state of origin is probably the key subdivision within the Malay community. There are some structural and cultural features that differentiate the Malay population among states, but there are also informal ties related to common schooling or kinship that link individuals together, even after migration to new environments. Malays from the east coast states, particulary Kelantan, claim to have a distinct identity. This may be influenced, in part, by the fact that the Malay population forms the overwhelming (90 percent or more) majority of the population in the east coast states.

Malays of Negeri Sembilan are also considered to be unique because of their customary law *(adat)* that recongnizes matrilineal descent and inheritance. Negeri Sembilan was also quite different from the other Malay states, in that elections were part of the process of selecting individuals for political office.

Standard accounts of Malay cultural values suggest that respect for authority (those with higher status), strong familiar ties, and the performance of proper social behavior are of paramount importance. There are many words in the Malay language (Bahasa Malaysia) as well as parables that emphaize these and other traditional cultural themes. Yet, it is difficult to confirm the degree of continuity of these values because external forces such as education have influenced successive generations in new ways. Moreover, ethnographic accounts typically report "ideal" forms of behavior rather than the considerable variations in behavior that are actually acceptable.

Perhaps the one universal element of Malay culture is the Muslim faith. Although all Malays are not equally devout in their behavior, there are practically no Malays who deny Islam.

There are some Javanese who are unorthodox Muslims and a few who are Christians. Historically, becoming a Muslim has often meant acceptance within the Malay community. The line between Indian Muslims and Malays is often a narrow one, and there has been considerable intermarriage as well as shifts in ethnic identity.

Divisions within the Malay community are based on aristocratic-commoner status, wealth (including landownership), language ability, and urban-rural residence. Although Malay identity spans these and other alignments, there are significant internal variations. In all of the states of Peninsular Malaysia except Penang and Malacca, there is a sultan, usually with a large extended family. Members of the royal family are usually treated with great deference, which includes elaborate ritual and special terms of address. Rarely are the social divisions between royalty and commoners bridged, except on ceremonial occasions, for the two groups inhabit separate social worlds. In the traditional Malay village, the *penghulu* (a part-time local government administrator) and the headman are usually given great respect and social deference, as are religious officials and village elders.

Traditional authority is often aligned with other bases of social stratification. In Malay villages the primary determinant of economic position and social status is landholding. Although comprehensive data on land tenure in Malaysia are unavailable, many case studies have revealed considerable inequality in landownership and a sizable number of landless peasants in many villages. Many villagers own a small amount of land, and some rent more from larger landowners. Land tenancy is more of a problem in *padi* than in rubber areas (see Land Use and Tenure, ch. 3). In many cases, the landlord-tenant relationship is crossed by ties of kinship with mutual obligations.

In the last generation new bases of leadership and status have arisen within the Malay community. Most important are the political leaders. Officials of Malay-based political parties and elected reperesentatives to the national parliament and the state assembly play very important social and economic roles in many areas throughout the country. These "new leaders" can influence government administrative decisions and often sponsor their followers.

Other significant factors that are shaping Malay social organizations are the spread of primary and secondary schooling throughout the country as well as the rising share of Malay urbanization. The traditional characterization of the Malay population as rural peasants with little or no schooling no longer fits. By 1980 one-fourth of Malays lived in urban areas, and the majority of Malay youth would undoubtedly complete secondary schooling. The impact of such modernizing factors on Malay culture and social organization is not at all clear.

Chinese Society

The role of China in Southeast Asia extends back into prehistory. Trade with China and the recognition of China were central to the early empires of the region, including Malacca. But the major wave of Chinese settlers came later, coinciding with the development of the export economy and colonial intervention. Francis Light, the founder of the first British settlements at Penang, reported 3,000 Chinese settlers in Penang in 1794. Chinese also came by the thousands to Singapore after 1819 when it began to develop as the British-ruled entrepôt of regional and long-distance trade. In successive decades, Chinese arrived by the tens of thousands to work as laborers in pepper and gambier (see Glossary) plantations and then in the tin-mining settlements of the west coast.

Chinese immigration to Southeast Asia came largely from the two southern Chinese provinces of Kwangtung and Fukien. Suffering from poverty in the relatively overpopulated villages in China, the Chinese were lured away by stories of great economic opportunities in "Nanyang" (the South Seas.) Although a few struck it rich, most could barely eke out a living as laborers before being forced to return to China almost as poor as when they had left.

Although originating mainly from several southern provinces of China, the immigrants were quite diverse linguistically, and as they settled in Malaysia, the various dialect groups concentrated in certain occupational lines or geographical areas. Accordingly, in the mid-twentieth century the largest Chinese dialect groups in Peninsular Malaysia were the Hokkien, the Cantonese, the

Village in coastal Sarawak (above) and traditional market in Sabah (right)
Courtesy Embassy of Malaysia, Washington

Hakka (Khek), and the Teochius. Small groups included the Hainanese, the Kwangsi, and the Hokchiu. In Sabah the major Chinese dialect groups were the Hakka (more than half), the Cantonese, and the Hokkien. In Sarawak the Foochow and the Hakka were the largest groups, followed by smaller numbers of Hokkien, Teochius, and Cantonese.

Historically, dialect groups within the Malaysian Chinese community were considered the major subethnic division (subdivided by clan and surname groups), and formal and informal organizations often followed linguistic subgroupings. However, the passage of time, the use of the Chinese national language—Kuo Yu or Madarin—in Chinese schools, and the societal perception of Chinese as one population have eroded the boundaries among dialect subgroups. Although Hokkien continues in 1984 to be the lingua franca among Chinese in Penang, and Cantonese serves the same role in Kuala Lumpur, many Chinese no longer see their mother-tongue community as a major reference group. Intermarriage across dialect groups appears to be very common.

A wide variety of formal organizations, ranging from benevolent societies (providing community assistance) to occupational guilds and chambers of commerce, link many Chinese. In earlier times, so-called secret societies were a key element of Chinese social organization and were often engaged in struggle with other Chinese groups.

Perhaps the most significant division within the Malaysian Chinese community has been between the Chinese- and English-educated. Generally, the English-educated are middle class and have a close contact with Malays and Indians of similar status. The Chinese-educated are the much larger community and often live and work in ethnically homogeneous areas. Although most of the Chinese in this latter group consider themselves Malaysians, they maintain a high degree of identity—both politically and socially—with China and Chinese concerns.

Whereas the Malay kinship system is bilateral, most Chinese in Malaysia maintain the traditional Chinese patrilineal system. There is great emphasis on the maintenance of the male line. If family circumstances permit, married sons are encouraged to spend at least some period of residence in their paternal household.

Indian Society

The Malaysian Indian community is the most heterogeneous of the three primary ethnic groups of Peninsular Malaysia. The overwhelming majority of Indians (over 80 percent) are descendants of Tamils from the Indian state of Madras (now Tamil Nadu) and of the Hindu faith. However, there are also smaller Indian populations from many of the other Indian states, speaking other languages, including Telegu and Punjabi. The distinctive Sikh community, in which many men wear turbans, are Punjabi speakers. Also included within the Indian community are descendants of immigrants from Sri Lanka (formerly Ceylon). The Malaysian Sri Lankan community includes both Tamils (primarily Hindu) and Sinhalese, who are Buddhist. Religion is the major element of differentiation within the Indian community. There are a significant number of Indian Muslims, some of whom consider their ethnic identity to be Pakistani. Other Muslims, particularly from southern India, consider themselves to be of Indian origin. There is also a small group of Indian Christians.

Most Indian immigrants, particularly the Tamils, came in response to the need for labor in the rubber plantation sector during the colonial era. The major wave of Indian immigration began in the last years of the nineteenth century and continued for the first three decades of the twentieth century. Until 1910 a system of indentured servitude was the predominant means of Indian immigration within the colonial system. After 1920 a quasi-indentured servitude mechanism, or *kangany* system, was used. The *kangany* received a commission for each recruited laborer. Although abuse was probably lessened, the main features of the old system continued—the use of false pretenses to attract labor and the obligation to work for several years to repay passage and other recruiting expenses.

In addition to the migration of laborers to the estate sector, there were also other streams of Indian migration. Indians were recruited by the colonial government to work in the construction of roads and railroads and in telecommunications. Indians were also employed as clerical employees in many government departments, particularly in the railroads. To the present day, Indians are overrepresented in the public works, transportation, and communications sectors of the government.

Urban Indians have been active in commerce, participating in small-scale retailing as well as dealing with large firms that trade with India. A good proportion of Malaysia's middle-class professionals, in both the private and the public sectors, are from the urban Indian community.

Other Ethnic Communities in Peninsular Malaysia

The Orang Asli are classified in Malaysian censuses under the inclusive Malay category. In everyday terms, however, the

Orang Asli are considered to be a separate ethnic community or, more properly, a number of separate ethnic communities. The 1970 census counted over 52,000 Orang Asli, the largest groups being the Semai and the Temiar. Smaller groups include the Jakun, the Semelai, and the Negrito. Historically, the Orang Asli have lived as nomadic groups engaged in hunting and in shifting cultivation (see Glossary) in the interior jungle of the peninsula. Periodically, the government has encouraged the settlement of the Orang Asli in permanent farming villages but has had only modest success.

The largest of the ethnic groups in the "Other" category is the Thai community, which numbered 27,000 in 1970. Most of the Thai live in rural villages in Kedah and Kelantan. The next largest "Other" community, the Eurasians, numbered 14,000 in 1970. Many live in Malacca and are descendants of the Portuguese colonialists of the sixteenth century. There are also small numbers of Erasians in many of the urban areas throughout Peninsular Malaysia.

Pribumis of Sabah

The listing of the Pribumi category in the 1980 census represented an effort to encompass the diverse indigenous ethnic communities of Sabah. The detailed ethnic classification included 28 separate categories under the Pribumi category. The single largest group is the Kadazan (formerly known as the Dusun) who inhabit the lowlands from the coastal plains to the mountainous interior. They live in stable villages and are predominantly engaged in *padi* and rubber cultivation. Farther inland are the Murut, who occupy the hilly southwestern uplands as well as part of Indonesian Borneo. Along the coastal plains are the Malay Muslim peoples whose ancestors probably came form the histortic sultanates of Sulu in the southern Philippines, Brunei, or elsewhere in the archipelago. The number of Muslims has increased sharply in recent years as a result of continued immigration and of conversion of indigenous peoples.

Indigenous Peoples of Sarawak

Sarawak is also a multiethnic state with a mosaic of indigenous languages, cultures, and religions. The Muslim peoples are located mainly along the coastal areas—the Sarawak Malays in the First and Second divisions, and the Melanau in the Third and Fourth divisions. Malays are not migrants from the peninsula but are descendants of indigenous peoples who converted to Islam. The largest single ethnic group is the Iban (formerly known as Sea

Dayak), who live in longhouses up the rivers of the Second and Third divisions. Most Iban engage in shifting rice cultivation and are known for their independent and self-confident culture. The Iban have taken advantage of educational opportunities and have played an important role in state politics. The other large ethnic community is the Bidayuh (formerly known as the Land Dayak), who are concentrate in the First Division and across the border in Indonesian Borneo.

Ethnic Socioeconomic Inequality

Socioeconomic inequality among the ethnic communities of Peninsular Malaysia has been at the root of much of the political debate and ethnic antagonism since independence. The question is not only the degree of inequality but also the interpretation of its causes and its potential resolution. In spite of considerable social science research on the topic, the issues are far from resolved. But larger than academic debates are the political controversies over the appropriate public policies in Malaysia.

Most socioeconomic indicators show that Malays are the most disadvantaged population in the country. Generally, Chinese tend to have higher levels of schooling, a more diverse occupational structure, and above-average incomes. Indians tend to hold an intermediate status between Chinese and Malays. Although detailed data from the 1980 census have yet to be analyzed, earlier research suggests that Malays have made relative gains. The gap in educational attainment between Malays, Chinese, and Indians had been narrowed sharply among the younger age-group who received their schooling after independence. In terms of occupational patterns, the gains of Malays had been fairly modest up to 1970 (see Income Distribution and Living Standards, ch. 3).

In the analysis of these differences, there is a debate between the cultural and structural interpretations. The cultural interpretation suggests that ethnic values toward achievement are the primary reason for the differential socioeconomic attainment. The standard presentation of the cultural interpretation contrasts Chinese emphasis on economic success and thrift with the more relaxed and noncommercial orientations of the Malay community. According to the logic of this explanation, cultural values are transferred across generations through socialization and are fairly resistant to change. The structural interpretation stresses the unequal opportunities, or differential social structures, encountered by each ethnic community. The structural interpretation does not deny the presence of cultural values but argues that they are as much the product as the cause of socioeconomic roles. In other words, Malays and Chinese are exposed to both differential values and differential opportunities. Historically, most Malays found it very difficult to acquire the skills and experience necessary to become successful in the urban commercial world. The structural interpretation suggests that cultural continuity is the result of unequal opportunities.

Although a comprehensive review of the literature provides some evidence for both sides of the cultural-structural debate, the structural interpretation appears to have more substantial social scientific support. Historically, Malays have been responsive to economic opportunities, most notably in the planting of smallholder rubber during the colonial era. Moreover, multivariate statistical analysis shows that a significant share of the socioeconomic differences between Malays and Chinese (in education, occupation, and income) is a result of the higher level of rural-agrarian origins of Malays.

Constitutional Issues

Although the colonial government claimed to represent the interests of the Malay community, the historical record is mixed. The prestige of the Malay aristocracy was maintained, and some Malays were allowed to enter the junior ranks of the colonial civil service. In large part, however, the colonial objective was to isolate the rural Malay peasantry from the development and growth of the export economy and urban areas. As independence approached in the 1950s, a more activist government role for promoting Malay interests was planned.

A number of elements that marked a shift in the role of government were incorporated into the 1957 Constitution. The document was written as an agreement among the elite of each ethnic community representing the interests of their respective communities. A "bargain" was struck with generous allowances for citizenship of the non-Malay communities in return for official recognition of the government's role in Malay sponsorship. It is often suggested that subsequent ethnic antagonism has been the result of forgetting the delicate balance of ethnic interests and rights formulated in the Constitution of the Federation of Malaya.

The distinction between persons ethnically defined as Malay and the larger body of Malaysian citizens has important political implications. Under Article 153 of the Constitution the *yang di-pertuan agong* is given the responsibility for safeguarding the "special position" of the Malays and, since the creation of Malaysia in September 1963, of the natives of Sabah and Sarawak as well. Article 153 entrusts the paramount ruler to protect the "legitimate interests of other communities." Malaysian citizenship can be acquired in four ways; qualifications are spelled out in Articles 14 through 22 of the Constitution (see The Politics of Communalism, ch. 4). A Malay is defined under Article 160 as being a person who professes the Muslim religion, habitually speaks Malay, and conforms to Malay customs. There are additional requirements, such as birth before Merdeka Day (Independence Day, August 31, 1957) in the Federation of Malaya or in Singapore, birth to a parent who was born in the Federation of Malaya was domiciled on Merdeka Day in the Federation or in Singapore, or the issue of such a person. Note that the definition allows for a Malaysian Chinese or Indian to enjoy Malay status (via changes in religion, language, and custom) and also excludes Indonesians who share religion, language, and custom unless they (or their parents) have a history of residing in Malaya.

The Constitution officially sanctions preference for Malays and natives of Sabah and Sarawak in a number of public spheres, while balancing these actions with guarantees of non-Malay rights. For instance, the articles establishing Islam as the official religion and Malay as the sole national language are joined with constitutional rights of religious freedom and prohibitions against any restrictions on the teaching or learning of any language. When parliament reconvened in 1971, the first act to be passed was a constitutional amendment that banned any public discussion—even in the legislature—of all "sensitive issues" relating to ethnic constitutional rights. The list of sensitive issues includes citizenship, the national language, the rights to use other languages, the special position of Malays and the natives of Borneo, the legitimate interests of other ethnic communities, and the sovereignty and prerogatives of the rulers. Other legislation makes it a crime under the Sedition Act of 1948 to question publicly any of these matters.

Under Article 153 of the Constitution, the government has the responsibility to promote Malay interest (and those of the indigenous peoples of Sabah and Sarawak) by reserving positions in the federal public service and in places of higher education and by favorably distributing licenses or permits (necessary for certain economic activities). There is wide latitude in the implementation of these official preferences. For most of the periods up to 1970, Malay preference had only a modest impact on non-Malay opportunities. For instance, the widely quoted preference of four Malays for one non-Malay in the federal public service had been limited to Division One officiers (the highest rank) in the Malaysia Home and Foreign Services (formerly the Malaysian Civil Service) and the police force. A three-to-one ratio is supposed to hold for Division One officers in the Judicial and Legal Service Commission and the Customs Service. Looking at the entire public sector or even at Division One officers in the entire federal service, non-Malays formed the majority of employees as of the late 1970s.

Economic Policy, 1957–70

After independence in 1957 the government changed its role as a passive manager to that of a direct promoter of development. Public expenditures, especially for health and education, were sharply increased. In promoting the interests of the Malay community, the government largely pursued indirect strategies. In addition to the expansion of Malay-medium schooling, rural development was seen as the primary means of improving the economic opportunities of the Malay community. This included programs of rural public works, such as road-building and village-level building projects, increased investments in small-holding agriculture, and the opening up of new agricultural lands through resettlement schemes for landless peasants.

Although these programs certainly brought benefits to many rural Malays, there seemed to have been very little change in the relative economic positions of Malays and non-Malays. In fact, many of the benefits of an expanded urban economy and increasing university enrollments went primarily to non-Malays. Chinese and Indians were in a better position to take advantage of the emerging opportunities based on their higher educational qualifications. Most of the nonagricultural sectors of the economy, including manufacturing and commerce, were left entirely to private initiative. Because most private businesses were owned and managed by non-Malays, the natural process of employing kin and personal acquaintances probably gave non-Malays an informal advantage in the modernizing sectors of the economy.

Some observers have suggested that ethnic grievances on both sides—from non-Malays who resented the governmental sponsorship of Malay interests, and from Malays who were frustrated by their lack of socioeconomic progress during the 1960s—contributed to the tensions that led up to the riots of May 13, 1969.

New Economic Policy

The New Economic Policy (NEP), formulated in the wake of the 1969 riots as part of the Second Malaysia Plan, 1971–75, put forth a 20-year plan to eradicate poverty and to eliminate the identification of ethnicity and economic roles. Toward these goals, the government engaged in a much more activist role in the economy and showed direct preferences for Malay socioeconomic advancement. Specific programs included a series of state economic enterprises in a number of key sectors of the economy. Eventually, these enterprises were expected to become privately owned, but in the meantime they provided an opportunity to promote Malay entrepreneurs and mangers and to accumulate capital for the Malay community (see The Corporate Sector, ch. 3).

The NEP seeks to redistribute income so that ethnic inequality is eliminated. There is no concern with modifying the capitalist structure of the economy or in redistributing income within ethnic communities. No group or community is intended to experience an absolute loss of income or any sense of deprivation in consequence of it. The most specific goal of the NEP is to ensure that Malays and other indigenous people will manage and own at least 30 percent of the total commercial and industrial activities in the country by 1990. This goal of creating a Malay business elite has been a source of domestic controversy. Some charge that a capitalist class cannot be created by government initiative. Other critics see this priority as overshadowing another major goal—that of eliminating poverty among Malays and non-Malays alike.

For most of the 1970s the vigorous public spending program (made possible by relatively good commodity prices and the development of oil and natural gas resources) brought significant economic growth and probably some relative gains for the Malay population. Although detailed data have not yet been made available to analyze progress toward the NEP targets, it does seem that some progress has been made, even if not at the pace hoped for by planners in Malaysia (see Patterns of Development, ch. 3).

Language

As in plural societies throughout the world, language use and language policy in Malaysia have been issues of contention. Malay became the national language when independence was gained, but many other languages are widely spoken throughout the country. English remains an important language and is still used among the middle class in urban areas. The various Chinese and Indian dialects continue to be widely used in households and in informal communication, as well as in schools, the mass media, and in ethnic associations.

Malay (Bahasa Malaysia)

Malay is the mother tongue of the Malay population of the peninsula, the eastern coast of Sumatra, and for many of the coastal regions of Borneo. Historically, it was the lingua franca of maritime Southeast Asia and could be understood by many individuals throughout the Malay Archipelago and the southern Philippines.

There are a number of dialects of Malay, although most are mutually intelligible. In each state the use of words and the intonation vary. The east coast dialect spoken in Kelantan and Terengganu, which is fairly similar to that spoken in Pattani (the Malay-speaking region of southern Thailand), is the most distinctive Standard Bahasa Malaysia, as used in the schools and mass media, is based on the Johore-Riau-Malacca dialect. Nonnative speakers often pick up the rudiments of Malay in the market and from informal conversation. This form is called Bazaar Malay and often contains a mixture of Chinese and English words.

Jawi, an Arabic script, continues to be taught in the schools but has become secondary in importance. Many books and a national newspaper, *Utusan Melayau,* are published in Jawi. A romanized script of Malay, called Rumi, has become the official form. Beyond the standard Malay, there are also literary forms, both traditional and modern, that contain style and forms of expression rarely used in conversation.

Chinese Languages

Of the various mutually unintelligible mother tongues spoken by the Chinese of Malaysia, the most important are Hokkien, Cantonese, Hakka, Foochow, Teochius, and Hainanese. Depending on the homogeneity of the Chinese in a local area, individuals may speak several dialects. For instance, nearly all Chinese in Kuala Lumpur speak the locally dominant dialect, Cantonese, even if they have a different mother tongue. The Baba (or Straits) Chinese community largely lost its original language. Most speak Malay or English as their mother tongue.

The adoption of Kuo Yu as the official language of China in 1918 spread to the Chinese in Peninsular Malaysia. As of the early 1980s, Kuo Yu was the language of instruction in all Chinese schools. For the Chinese-educated it had become the medium of communication across dialect groups. There was only one form of written Chinese used by speakers of all dialects. Chinese-language books, magazines, and newspapers catered to a large audience.

Tamil and Other Languages

Tamil is the mother tongue of the majority of Malaysian Indians. This is also the language used in the Indian vernacular primary schools. Other Indians speak a variety of dialects, including

Malayalam, Telegu, Punjabi, Urdu, and Gujarati.

There are many other languages spoken in contemporary Malaysia as well. Each ethnic community of the Orang Asli has its own mother tongue (sometimes with several dialects), as does each of the indigenous ethnic communities of Sabah and Sarawak. In many cases some form of Malay serves as the interethnic medium of communication. The younger generations, exposed to formal schooling, are acquiring literacy in Malay.

Language Policy

During the colonial era English was the language of the elite in all ethnic communities. English-language schools, both primary and secondary, were widespread throughout the peninsula. Because English was the language of government and all other official circles, there was great motivation to acquire English fluency. For non-Malays, acquisition of Malay fluency (other than Malay as spoken in the bazaar) was of little utilitarian value.

The formation of national language policy turned into one of the central political debates of the postindependence period. The dispute was basically over the exclusive use of Malay in official settings. Some non-Malays hoped that English would remain indefinitely on a par with Malay and there would be liberal provisions for the use of other languages. But as part of the communal bargain of the 1957 Constitution, Malay was declared the national language, with the provision that English could be used for official purposes for a period of 10 years. The National Language Act of 1967 declares that Bahasa Malaysia must be used for all official purposes; however, there are still exceptions when English can be used. At the formation of Malaysia in 1963, the states of Sabah and Sarawak were given considerable autonomy in the implementation of the national language policy.

Through a variety of activities, the federal government has tried to strengthen the national language and to encourage its acceptance. The Language Council, a government-sponsored bureau, promotes the development of the national language and publishes educational and popular materials in Malay. The governments of Malaysia and Indonesia have agreed to standardize their spelling systems to increase interchange between the two countries.

Perhaps the most important influence on developing the national language has been the substitution of Malay for English as the main medium of instruction in all lower and mid-level secondary schools (see Education, this ch.). Chinese- and Tamil-language schooling is only available at the primary level; thus,

Chinese and Indian students have had to learn Malay to continue their education. The effects of this change are clearly evident throughout Malaysia, for the younger generations of all ethnic communities are fluent in Malay. According to the 1980 census, 41 percent of Malaysian Chinese and 61 percent of Malaysian Indians (age 10 and over) are literate in Malay. The 1980 figures are approximately double those of 1970.

Religion

Islam is the official religion of the country, but Article 11 of the Constitution provides that every person has the right to profess and practice his or her own religion. The propagation of any other religion to Muslims is forbidden by state laws. According to the 1980 census, 53 percent of the population is Muslim, 17 percent Buddhist, 12 percent Confucian, 7 percent Hindu, 7 percent Christian, and the balance (about 4 percent) adhere to another or to no religion. These figures differed according to geographical area and ethnic composition. For instance, 56 percent of Peninsular Malaysia's population is Muslim, 51 percent of that of Sabah, and 26 percent of that of Sarawak. Only 2 percent of the population of Peninsular Malaysia is Christian, but the corresponding figures for Sabah and Sarawak are 27 percent and 29 percent, respectively. Religion correlates closely with ethnicity in that in varying degrees of religiosity, all Malays adhere to Islam; Chinese embrace elements of Buddhism, Taoism, and Confucianism; and nearly all Indians adhere to Hinduism. About 4 percent of the Chinese and about 8 percent of the Indian communities profess Christianity.

Because religion largely coincides with ethnicity, it tends to reinforce communal divisions. For instance, intermarriage is very rare between Chinese and Malays; Islam does not sanction religious intermarriage.

Islam

Islam spread throughout the Malay world during the Malacca sultanate of the fifteenth century. Adapting to and being modified by its local environment, indigenous beliefs and the earlier influence of Hinduism shaped its structure and evolution in Malaysia. Before British intervention, local religious leaders had considerable autonomy and secular authority. But the formation of the civil state and the limitation of the sultan's authority over matters of Malay religion and custom served to centralize religious au-

Ubudiah Mosque in Kuala Kangsar (above) and National Mosque in Kuala Lumpur (below)
Courtesy Malaysia Tourist Development Corporation, Ministry of Trade and Industry

thority within each state (see The British Colonial Presence, ch. 1).

Under the Constitution the ruler of each state (with certain exceptions) is the highest ranking Islamic authority in that state. Religious questions pertaining to the entire country are decided by the Conference of Rulers (see The Federal Government, ch.4). In Penang and Malacca, neither of which has a sultan, and in the Federal Territory, these duties are assumed by the supreme head of the federation, or *yang di-pertuan agong*, who is also the religious head of the state from which he is elected. In certain cases he may act for the Conference of Rulers in religious matters affecting the authority.

In each of the Muslim states the supervision of religious affairs is the responsibility of the Religious Affairs Department. These departments are responsible for issuing opinions and rulings on religious questions and supervising such matters as collecting special taxes imposed on Muslims—the annual tithes required by religious law. The Constitution reserves to the Muslim states—as distinct from the federal legislature—almost all power to legislate on Muslim affairs, including regulation of such matters as inheritance, betrothal, marriage, divorce, dower, maintenance, legitimacy, guardianship, and trusts. In addition to special tax liabilities, Muslims are subject to penalties for violating religious injunctions, e.g., failure to attend Friday prayers, consumption of intoxicating liquor, contempt of religious authorities or of Islam, and others.

Islam has no ordained clergy; local religious functionaries—those who lead public prayers, preach sermons, and call the faithful to pray—are generally chosen within the community from those who have achieved religious authority through knowledge, scholarship, piety, or through making a pilgrimage to Mecca. Religious authority is rooted within the locality served by a mosque (in the larger villages or towns) or the smaller prayer house *(surau)*, and religious officials generally form most of the local elite. These factors had implications in the mobilization of support for the country's principal Islamic political party (see Opposition Parties, ch. 4)

The sultans of the various Malay states are the "defenders of the faith" and the highest religious officials. The sultans appoint the state religious legal adviser or judge (mufti), who is assisted by several magistrates presiding over Islamic courts. Part of the responsibilities of these officials is to rule on conflicts between Islamic law (sharia) and customary law, which frequently differ on such basic matters as inheritance.

Although state officials were nominally responsible for supervising religious life, it appeared that such control rarely affected the mosques, which generally served several villages and had religious jurisdiction over an entire subdistrict *(mukim)*. The imam (prayer leader) of more numerous prayer houses—often built by pious villagers or well-to-do peasants—appeared to be almost completely independent of the formal state hierarchy. The prayer house was also a ritual center and the most important focus of village religious life; along with the local coffeehouse it was also the social center.

Elementary instruction in the Quran is provided at the prayer house as well as in the mosque; instruction ordinarily consists only of memorizing parts of the scriptures, but it formally establishes the children in the community of Islam. Advanced training can be obtained at one of the several religious schools *(pondok)* that developed around particularly well known and learned teachers (gurus) and served regional rather than local areas.

Among several religious festivals, the two most important are the Pilgrimage Festival (Hari Raya Haji) and the Fast-Ending Festival (Hari Raja Puasa). The former celebrates the time when pilgrimages to Mecca are customarily made and the latter, the end of the month of fasting (Ramadan). These festivals and the celebration of the Prophet Muhammad's birthday are national holidays.

Malays belong overwhelmingly to the Sunni branch of Islam. Their duties are spelled out in the Five Pillars of Islam (declaration of faith in Allah and the divine messenger, the Prophet Muhammad; ritual prayers and ritual purification; distribution of alms; fasting during Ramadan; and the pilgrimage to Mecca), in addition to which there are a variety of other obligations. Much as in all religions, there is considerable variation in individual behavior. However, for some duties, such as the injunction against eating pork, there is universal adherence.

Islam has had a major influence on the development of Malay political thought. During the 1920s and 1930s, religious scholars returning from Cairo (and other centers of Islamic reform) influenced a generation of Islamic activists in Malaya. These activists criticized both the unorthodoxy of local Islamic practice and secular authority. This debate between Kaum Muda (Young Group) and Kaum Tuda (Old Group) created the seedbed of subsequent nationalist activity in Malaya. The strongest opposition party in contemporary Malaysia, the Pan-Malaysia Islamic Party (better known by its Malaysian acronym PAS—see Glossary), relies on religious appeals to build its political base, usually in Malay-dominant areas (the east coast states and the northwest) (see Opposition Parties, ch. 4).

During the 1970s an Islamic revival movement caught hold, especially among some highly educated youth. Although there is considerable variation in philosophy and organizational settings among persons caught up in the revival, all are labeled as being part of a so-called *dakwah* (missionary activity or, literally, an invitation) movement.

Two elements are common to most *dakwah* followers—a change in dress and a questioning of secular society. Although male *dakwah* members typically do not dress differently, women have begun to cover their entire bodies, usually with a headdress and some with a veil. Some adherents also tend to avoid contact—including informal conversation—with members of the opposite sex. Because Malay women had never followed the custom of seclusion, this represents a marked change. Most *dakwah* followers believe that Malays should purify Islamic practices (eliminate traditional influences) and also maintain strong religious principles in secular life.

There is, however, considerable variation in the goals and strategies of the several *dakwah* groups in Malaysia (see The Creation of Malaysia, ch. 1; Internal Security and Public Order, ch.5). Some seek to escape from the corrupting influences of modern society and to create new communities based on Islamic belief. Others seek to redeem society through political activities and a variety of self-help programs, including schools for Malay youth. Some leaders stress the Islamic principles of social justice and equality that include non-Muslims. Nonetheless, most non-Malays and many Malay elders fear the *dakwah* movement is hostile to authority, intolerant of the nation's multiethnic and multireligious society, and insensitive to its fragility.

Chinese Religions

The three great religious streams among the Chinese—Confucianism, Taoism, and Buddhism—are not sharply differentiated, and the religious life of most Chinese is likely to embrace elements of all three, the emphasis depending in part on the area of China from which the family originally came. Confucianism strengthens and sanctifies family life; Taoism seeks freedom from social constraints and personal power through the use of ritual exercises and potions; and Buddhism preaches a doctrine of reincarnation, promising salvation for all beings. Although they offer enlightenment, spiritual guidance, and—in Buddhism and Taosim—such institutions as temples and monasteries, the three traditions are practical rather than mystical and are oriented to the problems of everyday life rather than to cosmic or metaphys-

Chinese temple in Penang
Courtesy Malaysia Tourist Development Corporation Ministry of Trade and Industry

ical concerns.

The forebears of Malaysian Chinese came to the peninsula as poor laborers or petty tradesmen. They brought with them a strong folk religion, the main element of which was a personal and individualized ancestor cult—as influenced and systematized by Confucianism, Taoism, and Buddhism. The ancestor cult was based on the assumption that the living can communicate with the dead and that the dead are affected by and can influence events in the world of the living. It is incumbent on the living, therefore, to venerate and protect their ancestors and to live their own lives in a way that would benefit their ancestors and ensure their own well-being in the afterlife. The eclectic character of Chinese religion includes belief in spirits and the worship of numerous deities and saints, some of whom are taken from ancient Chinese mythology and others who are drawn from Buddhist and Taoist pantheons.

Certain particulars, if not the broad outlines, of religious practices have been modified as a result of Chinese isolation from their homeland, the influence of their new environment, and their initial circumstances of cultural, spiritual, and family deprivation. An ancestral tablet (or a substitute, such as a photograph) is still kept in a special shrine or on a shelf, which may also house certain deities and is the object of ritual attention in domestic worship.

However, more elaborate beliefs relating to the division of the soul after death, fixing part of the soul in the ancestral tablet, and requirements for periodic rituals of kinship solidarity, have been simplified. Just as it is unthinkable to neglect one's parents or grandparents while they live, so it is unthinkable to neglect and forget them after death. As an expression of filial piety for deceased parents, children pay their respects and provide for their welfare in the afterlife through the medium of ritual.

In Malaysia, as in China, the Goddess of Mercy appears to be the most popular deity. Some gods acquired entirely new personalities and functions in Malaysia. Moreover, the elaborate and rigid bureaucracy of gods and their functionaries, once a part of the Chinese belief system, has become less important than the more adaptable system of deified local heroes and spirits of the dead who can intervene to protect the economic interests of the Chinese community.

The Chinese express their piety by a quiet adherence to the positive virtues sanctioned by the spirit world. More overt manifestations of religious feeling appear in the domestic rites before the household gods and ancestors. Traditionally, ceremonies take place before the tablets on the first and fifteenth days of the lunar calendar month, during which incense is burned or candles lit. Special rites are observed at certain times of the year—New Year, Feast of Tombs, Dragon Boat Festival, Month of Good Brothers, Birthday of the Kitchen God, Winter Festival, and the times of death or marriage. Some of the calendar observations, such as the Dragon Boat Festival, are occasions for large-scale public celebrations, but these are not of primary importance from a religious viewpoint. Chinese ritual is essentially family centered, and the family or household rites have the greatest significance. This is true even in the death ceremonies although the community offers support to the bereaved family in its attempt to carry out the duties of filial piety.

The frequent and important rites practiced in the home are commonly carried out by the women—primarily by the senior woman—who bear the main responsibility for them. Because children are often made to help the women in the simple daily and monthly rounds of lighting incense, it is common to see little boys playing their part. Adult men, however, take little direct interest in domestic religious affairs.

Temple priests are usually associated with the cults of the various deities. A benevolent or regional association may have a section dealing with death and burial benefits and may support a temple in its graveyard. There may also be a section for those interested in the cult of a specific deity with another temple supported for that purpose. Buddhism and Taoism are represented by separate cults and their associated priesthoods, which offer their services—especially for funeral rites—to anyone who will pay the fees. These two religions are not clearly distinguished in temple organization; in most temples both Buddhist and Taoist images are found, although they are often placed in separate rooms or shrines. Although the gods of these temples have jurisdiction over a relatively fixed area, the congregation is not defined as being from a specific area. In the countryside a local temple may maintain a more fixed relationship with the people who live near it, but generally individuals may worship in the temple of their choice.

Hinduism

Hindu Indians worship a plurality of gods and adhere to a comprehensive range of ideals, rituals, and beliefs. The orthodox Hinduism of the present day is divided into six sects, the most important being Sivaism and Vishnuism. The Indians who migrated to Malaysia brought a religion connected with the cultivation of the land, the welfare of the family and kin group, and the deification of the place of family or kin group residence. Migration weakened this pattern, if only because of the impersonal nature of employment on the large rubber estates and the lack of familiar deities associated with the land.

An attempt has been made to continue some of the old forms in the new setting. Each estate has at least one temple dedicated to a god—usually derived from the Hindu pantheon—who serves as a guardian deity for the estate workers. However, if one of the gods seems unpropitious, the workers have no hesitancy in turning to another deity. The temple is regarded not as a place for communal worship but as the abode of a deity. The worshipers take no part in the temple ceremonies and merely enter the temple to attain spiritual uplift and blessing and to give offerings to the gods through its priests.

Christianity

Of the 915,000 persons who reported their religion to be Christianity in the 1980 census, more than 60 percent lived in the states of Sabah and Sarawak. More than 25 percent of the population in these two states professes Christianity, while only 2 percent of Peninsular Malaysia's population is Christian. In spite of the small numbers in Peninsular Malaysia, Christian churches and ministers are visible in almost every city and town throughout the country. Although the incidence of Christianity is higher among Indians than among Chinese (8 percent to 4 percent), a majority of Christians in Peninsular Malaysia are Chinese (owing to their larger share of the total population).

The major Christian churches in Malaysia are Roman Catholic, Methodist, Anglican, Presbyterian, and Seventh-Day Adventist. During the colonial era, Christian missionaries were active in establishing English-language schools and hospitals in many urban areas. The association of Christian missionaries with English schools was thought to have discouraged Malay school attendance. Although as Muslims Malays were skeptical of the influence of other religions, this presented no problem to most Chinese with their syncretic religious background.

Education

Education is a key government priority. In 1980 some 3.2 million students were attending school (almost one-fourth of the total population), up by 40 percent from the 1970 enrollment of 2.3 million students. School attendance in Sarawak increased by over 80 percent from 1970 to 1980. Approximately one-fifth of government revenues—about 6 to 7 percent of the total gross national product (GNP—see Glossary)—is spent on education. The Malaysian government sees education not only as an important investment for socioeconomic development but also as a means to unify is multiethnic society. The low median age of the Malaysian population and its rapid growth over the last few decades have put enormous pressure for expansion on the educational system. The system had grown to provide almost universal education at the primary level and significant increases in capacity in secondary and tertiary educational institutions.

Changes in educational content and emphasis have accompanied expansion. Because instruction in Malaysian schools follows national syllabi, central coordination is not a problem. The major change has been the conversion of the English-language educational stream to Malay-medium, which began in 1970 and was completed in stages in a little over a decade. There has been renewed emphasis on the teaching of English, science, and mathematics, accompanied by a new initiative to inculcate values and norms in line with the principles of the Rukun Negara (National Ideology)—the national philosophy espoused by the government, which emphasizes belief in God, loyalty to king and country, upholding the Constitution, rule of law, and good behavior and morality).

A Historical Perspective

There was little formal eduction in the country before the British colonial period. Islamic education was dominant and included village-level schools and higher schools for educating religious teachers. Students attending a *pondok* religious school could board at the teacher's house (or with neighbors) and work on the teacher's farm in lieu of school fees.

As state revenues began to grow in the early years of colonial intervention, a small percentage of funds was allocated for public schooling. The limited goal of schooling in Malay villages was literacy in the Rumi and Jawi versions of the Malay language. A few English-language schools were begun in the urban areas by the government and by missionary bodies. Although government budgets for education remained modest throughout the colonial era, the numbers of Malay and English schools grew in the late nineteenth and early twentieth centuries. English schools in the urban areas were attended by students from all ethnic backgrounds, although Chinese predominated because of their numbers in urban areas.

The goals of colonial education evolved in the late nineteenth century. On one hand, there was the obvious necessity of training a sufficient number of English-literate Asians (regardless of ethnic background) to fill the manpower needs of the bureaucracy and the export economy. On the other hand, there was the fear that too much schooling would lead to a questioning of existing political, social, and economic institutions. As a result, a paternalistic policy was implemented to provide the minimal amount of Malay-language education to the rural peasantry. This policy was expressed by an early British colonialist as follows: "Vernacular education is in my opinion useful in so far as it makes the Malay regular and clear in his habits, but where it exalts boys, as it often does, above the calling of their fathers, who for the most part will remain small agriculturists or fishermen, it does more harm than good."

An alternate path for select Malay youth primarily of aristocratic origins was residential Malay College at Kuala Kangsar. Instruction at Malay College (often called the "Malay Eton") was in English and was designed to train a small number of elite Malay youth to serve as junior officers in the colonial administrative state. The only secondary educational institution having Malay as the language of instruction was the Sultan Idris Training College (SITC) in Tanjong Malim, Perak. The SITC was the training college for Malay schoolteachers in the 1920s and 1930s and developed into an intellectual center for Malay literary and political activity in the pre-World War II era.

Providing vernacular education for Chinese and Indian youth was not regarded as a high priority for the colonial government. Largely supported by private funds from the Chinese community, a Chinese-language school system was formed. Its educational content was China-centered, and the teachers were recruited from China. Rubber plantations were obligated to provide some primary schooling for the children of their largely Indian labor force. The European management of the plantations provided only the bare essentials of primary-level schooling in the Tamil language, and most children dropped out of school to begin work by age 10.

It was possible to transfer from vernacular primary school to an English-language secondary school by attending "Remove Classes" which provided intensive English-language training to facilitate the transition. Very few students, though, were actually able to move in this direction. For most students, vernacular schools were dead ends, and English schooling was the channel for social mobility.

During the 1950s and 1960s, both before and after independence, a series of committees and national commissions studied Malaysian schooling. Major policy changes were made to coordinate educational planning with national objectives. These changes included common syllabi for instruction in all schools and the establishment of Malay-medium secondary schools. Many Chinese leaders feared that these and other changes would reduce the autonomy of Chinese-language schools, and some Malay politicians saw too many concessions to multilingualism.

The central issue in the Malaysian educational dilemma was the future of English-language schools. Although earlier reforms had led to the creation of Malay-medium secondary schools, few Chinese or Indians chose to attend them. English-language schooling remained the most prestigious and most effective channel for socioeconomic mobiltiy. Malay graduates of Malay-medium schools had trouble finding jobs after leaving school. Multilingual schooling served to maintain diversity and to provide an excellent English-language educational system for the urban middle class, but it did not help to eliminate ethnic inequality or to further integration. The issue was settled in the wake of the Kuala Lumpur riots when the minister of education unilaterally announced that the English-language schools would be converted to Malay-medium, one grade per year, beginning in

A typical example of school buildings being built throughout the nation to meet the expanding demand for education Courtesy Embassy of Malaysia, Washington

1970. Although this policy shift aroused considerable political consternation, the transition appears to have been more or less successful.

Educational Expansion and Inequality

During the colonial era Malay educational attainment was considerably below the levels attained by Chinese and Indians. As noted earlier, the popular explanation for this was that Malays were less interested in educational advancement and did not encourage their children to pursue it. As one scholar put it, "Most Malays were peasants and fishermen. Their environment was not conducive to education and their culture did not induce them to want it." Detailed analysis, however, reveals that the primary obstacle to Malay educational advance was access. In the west coast states where schooling was available, Malays enrolled at the same rates as other ethnic communities. Moreover, they were just as likely to continue schooling once they began. The overall lower attainment of Malays was linked to lower attendance levels in areas where schooling opportunities were scarce and to the difficult transition from primary to secondary schools. Instruction in almost all secondary schools was in English, and the schools themselves were in urban areas. After independence, when the expansion of schooling in rural areas became a major priority, educational differentials in schooling largely disappeared. Along with this change, the traditional difference in educational attainment between boys and girls has largely been eliminated.

A study of school discontinuation (dropouts) undertaken in the early 1970s revealed major socioeconomic inequality in educational opportunity and attainment , but ethnic variation was insignificant.

Educational expansion in the 1960s and the 1970s has been extensive. Enrollment in all primary schools in Peninsular Malaysia (Malaya) in 1938 was slightly over 200,000. By 1947, when the country was still recovering from the Japanese occupation, enrollment had risen to over 450,000 pupils. By 1956, on the eve of independence, the figure had almost doubled, and by 1981 over 3 million students were enrolled.

Secondary school expansion was even more rapid. From 17,000 secondary school students in 1947, to 90,000 in 1956, the numbers then grew seven fold to 706,000 in 1974. The 1980 census shows that among young adults (ages 15–19) in 1980, three-fourths will have attended lower secondary schools and over one-third will have attended upper secondary or postgraduate schools.

Malaysia inherited from the British an elitist educational system that was geared to screen out all but the most able students from higher education. The most prominent feature of the system is a series of national examinations given at regular intervals. Examinations at the end of primary school were abolished in 1964 but as of the early 1980s continued to be mandatory at the end of lower secondary (after nine years of schooling—Standards 1–6 and Forms 1–3), middle secondary (11 years—Forms 4 and 5), and at the completion of upper and lower divisions. Grading of the examination was once done in Britain. The Malaysian Examination Council gradually took over this function, however, and by 1982 the procedure was being done wholly in Malaysia.

Higher Education

In 1949 two prewar institutions of higher education in Singapore, Raffles College and King Edward VII College of Medicine, were joined to form the University of Malaya. In 1959 a branch campus of the University of Malaya was formed on the outskirts of Kuala Lumpur. Several years later the Kuala Lumpur campus became fully autonomous and has retained the name of the University of Malaya (the Singapore campus was renamed the University of Singapore and in 1983 the National University of Singapore). The University of Malay enjoyed a reputation for excellence. From the Malaya perspective, however, the picture was clouded by the relatively low enrollment of Malays (only 21 percent in 1963–64). Furthermore, the virtual absence of Malays in the faculties of science, medicine, and engineering aroused considerable concern.

In the early 1970s four new universities were created: the Science University in Penang, the National University in Bangi, the Agricultural University of Malaysia in Serdang, and the Technology University. The latter two universities were created out of diploma-granting colleges. In addition, the Institute of Technology has university-equivalent programmed degrees. As a result of their establishment, student enrollment in degree-granting institutions increased from 7,677 in 1970 to 20,704 in 1980 and is projected to grow further to 29,540 by 1985. In addition, there were 14,776 students enrolled in diploma-level colleges in 1980, projected to increase to 23,737 in 1985.

Most of the new university enrollment has been disproportionately Malay, even in the University of Malaya. By 1977 three-quarters of all students admitted to universities were Malay. In response to declining opportunities for university education in the nation, reflecting the imposition of quotas by the government, the Chinese community petitioned to start a privately funded Chinese-language university to be named Merdeka University. Controversy over this proposal simmered for a number of years before it was finally rejected by the government in 1978. In June 1979 the government promised to increase the ratio of non-Malays to Malays in the university system.

Overseas university education is another mechanism for middle-class non-Malays to further their education. The government estimates that nearly 40,000 Malaysian students at all levels (many of them government-sponsored scholars) were studying overseas in 1980. Sixty percent of these, however, were estimated to be Chinese as compared with 23 percent Malay. Most of the government scholars were Malay.

Household and Family Structure

In all societies, the family is a pivotal institution that maintains social continuity through reproduction and socialization of successive generations. The web of family relationships and obligations is strongly felt in most Asian contexts. This arises partly from the continuing economic, as well as social, functions that the family performs. In most Asian farm households and small businesses, all family members—including small children—are active economic participants. Moreover, the extended family is typically the primary source of assistance in times of need. It is expected that successful family members will sponsor the mobility of other kin. For instance, remittances to one's family of origin are obligatory (if possible) and are typically used to finance the education of siblings and other relatives. As society modernizes, family structures change, and stresses become more manifest. This does not necessarily imply a disappearance of Asian family patterns, although there are bound to be some revolutionary shifts.

According to the 1980 census, there were 2.5 million households in Malaysia, compared with 1.9 million in 1970. The average household size was 5.2 persons, lower than the 1970 average of 5.5 persons. Households tended to be slightly smaller in urban areas than in rural areas and were also smaller in Peninsular Malaysia than in Sabah and Sarawak. Interestingly, Malay households are smaller than Chinese households in rural as well as urban areas. This difference is not owing to variations in fertility, for Malay fertility levels are higher than either Chinese or Indian levels.

Malay Households and Families

Malay family structure is bilateral, and there are strong kinship ties to both the wife's and the husband's extended families. Extended family residence is not uncommon, but there is a cultural preference for a nuclear household. In most Malay villages, housing units are typically clustered together in close proximity, so separate housing units do not necessarily limit social interaction or prevent villagers from sharing meals together. House construction in rural villages can be relatively simple, using easily available materials and making only a modest labor investment. One study found a higher incidence of extended family residence in urban areas than in rural areas. A possible interpretation of this pattern of households in urban areas is that the higher costs of independent housing in urban areas constrain younger couples to double up with relatives.

Residence in the wife's or the husband's village (or household) seems to be shaped by economic opportunity rather than by custom. If land is available with the family of one spouse, then the couple is likely to reside nearest that family. Women tend to play an active economic role in rural Malay households. In addition to the management of household responsibilities, Malay women are often active in *padi* cultivation, vegetable gardening, and rubber tapping.

Malay family structure is in the midst of major change resulting from trends in marriage and divorce patterns. Thirty years ago the average Malay marriage was between a young woman of 16 or 17 having little or no schooling and a man several years older possessing minimal schooling (but more than his bride). By the 1980s the typical Malay bride was in her early twenties, her husband was in his mid-twenties, and both were likely to have had elementary and perhaps secondary schooling. It was also increasingly likely that the wife had worked before marriage. These factors have not only been responsible for the declining fertility of Malay families but have also probably modified the character of Malay family life and the social relationships between husbands and wives.

Changes have been even more dramatic in the level of divorce among Malays. Malay marriages have tended to be very unstable, and about one-third have ended in divorce. Divorce was most common in the east coast states of Kelantan and Terengganu, where divorce rates were probably the highest of any society in the world. Although divorce is a very simple procedure in Islamic law, the high incidence of divorce seems to be more a feature of the Malay cultural environment than Islamic influence. Most divorces occur within a year or two after marriage, and remarriage is the norm. Some evidence suggests that although men have greater formal authority to divorce than wives, it was often the wife who initiated the divorce process. Divorce rates have dropped sharply in the last few decades. The postponement of age at marriage, greater self-selection of partners, higher education, and reform movements may have influenced this decline in divorce. Polygamy has been fairly rare in Malay society and seems to have declined in recent years.

Chinese Households and Families

During the early years of Chinese settlement in Malaysia, the demographic composition of the largely immigrant community precluded a traditional Chinese household and family structure. As late as 1931 there were still twice as many males as females in Peninsular Malaysia. The large number of young single men probably contributed to the potential for vice and secret society activity during the colonial era. During the 1930s the colonial authorities allowed for greater numbers of Chinese female immigrants. This factor, plus the increasing population of second-generation Malaysian Chinese, created the basis for a more settled population in the post-World War II era.

The traditional Chinese family structure is patrilineal and patriarchal. The bride is supposed to move into her husband's house-hold and to be subservient to elder members of the family. Maintenance of the family surname through male descent is so highly prized that sons are much preferred over daughters. If there are many daughters, they are sometimes given up for adoption to Malay families.

The strong corporate nature of the extended Chinese family has been reinforced by entrepreneurial activities. Children and other relatives are typically hired in the many small Chinese-owned firms throughout Malaysia. Moreover, kinship links are the bases of sponsorship and of access to credit, supplies, and markets. A business environment based on Chinese kinship is one of the primary barriers to Malay economic mobility.

Chinese family structure has also adapted to the conditions of the Malaysian environment. Economic factors, residential mobility, and the lack of available relatives means that conformity with Chinese tradition is not always possible. For instance, only 32 percent of Chinese households in 1980 contained an extended family. Half of all households contained only a nuclear family, and the balance were of other types (one person, related persons, or unrelated persons)

At one time Chinese generally married at a later age than Malays and Indians. Even in 1947, median age at first marriage was 20 for Chinese women and 25 for Chinese men. But by the middle 1970s age at marriage was typically about 23 for Chinese women and 26–27 for Chinese men. The later age at marriage among Chinese can be explained partly by urban residence, higher educational attainment, and early work experience. In the 1950s Chinese fertility was very high in spite of a pattern of older age at marriage, with an average of six to seven children per woman. However, a further rise in age at marriage and increasing use of contraception had lowered fertility to moderate levels by 1980. There is a very low level of divorce among Malaysian Chinese.

Indian Households and Families

There is a deep division between rural and urban Indians. The rural Indian community lives primarily on rubber estates. In this environment traditional Indian family structure evolved in particular ways. Women married young and had very high levels of fertility but were also active members of the labor force, working as wage laborers on the estates. In urban areas Indian women were much less likely to work outside the home.

The demographic transition and the changes in marriage patterns have had a marked effect. The average age of marriage of Indian women has been increasingly deferred, and Indian fertility, which was the highest of any ethnic community in the 1950s, declined dramtically in the 1960s and 1970s. By 1980 Indian fertility levels were only slightly above those of the Chinese.

* * *

The standard reference work on geography is Ooi Jin-bee's *Peninsular Malaysia* (latest edition is 1976). Although rather dated, the best comparable works on Sabah and Sarawak are Lee Yong-Leng's *North Borneo (Sabah): A Study in Settlement Geography* and *Population and Settlement in Sarawak*. An edited volume with current summaries on developmental topics is E.K. Fisk and H. Osman-Rani's *The Political Economy of Malaysia*. The basic demographic patterns of the 1980 census are contained in the official Malaysian publication *1980 Population and Housing Census of Malaysia: General Report of the Population Census*. More scholarly demographic analyses are reported in Manjit S. Sidu and Gavin W. Jones' *Population Dynamics in a Plural Society: Peninsular Malaysia* and Charles Hirschman's "Demographic Trends in Peninsular Malaysia, 1947–75" in *Population and Development Review*.

Donald Snodgrass' *Inequality and Economic Devlopment in Malaysia* is a masterful survey of most of the social science literature on ethnicity. For two quite different views on the Malay community, Dr. Mahthir Mohamad's (as of late 1983, the prime minster) *The Malay Dilemma* and Syed Husin Ali's *The Malays: Their Problems and Future* are helpful. The best work on the Chinese community remains Victor Purcell's 1948 classic, *The Chinese in Malaya*. An excellent survey of the Indian community is S. Arasaratnam's *Indians in Malaysia and Singapore*. Readers wanting a general survey of the country will find a good introduction in John Gullick's *Malaysia: Economic Expansion and National Unity* and Stanley S. Bedlingon's *Malaysia and Singapore: The Building of New States*. The latter includes a thorough discussion of Sabah and Sarawak. (For further information and complete citations, see Bibliography.)

Chapter 3. The Economy

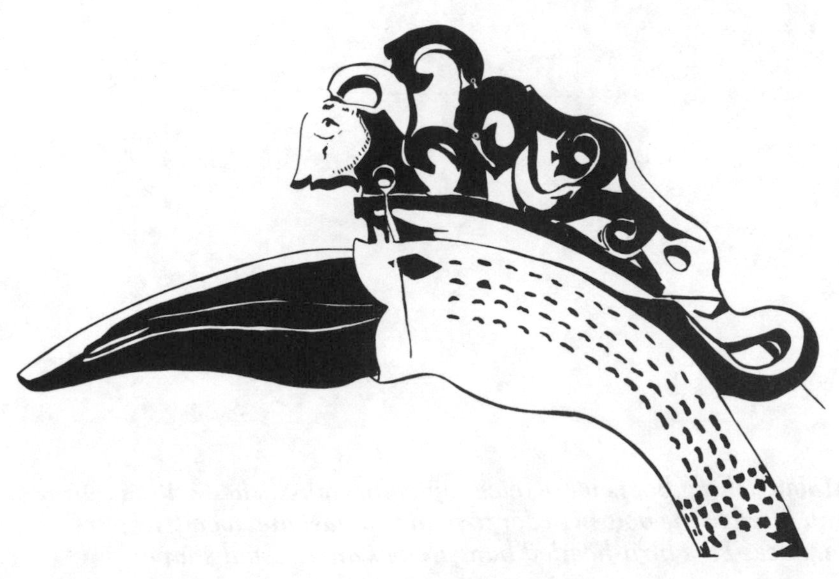

Malay fishing boats were once typically embellished with a bangau fitted to the bow in order to hold the mast and wooden spars in place. This bird-headed bangau was an unusual shape.

LOW POPULATION DENSITIES and abundant natural resources have blessed the Malaysian economy at least since the nineteenth century, when it began to modernize. Even in the 1980s earnings from primary exports such as rubber, tin, timber, and palm oil, have enabled the country to pay for its many import needs. Primary production in agriculture, forestry, fishing, and mining accounted for 28 percent of the gross domestic product and 38 percent of employment in 1982. Malaysia has also established viable domestic industries and service enterprises to cater to the needs of one of the wealthiest populations of consumers in the so-called developing world. Manufacturing, construction, and utilities production accounted for 26 percent of the gross domestic product in 1982; other services accounted for 46 percent. The per capita gross national product was equivalent to US$1,792 in 1982—sufficient to rank Malaysia among the wealthiest one-quarter of developing countries. The growth of this per capita income was above the average for this group of countries.

The distributive aspects of economic growth have been prominent in government policy since 1971, when the New Economic Policy was unveiled in the aftermath of ethnic riots in 1969. The principal goal of development thereafter was twofold: the elimination of poverty, particularly among the farmers and fishers, who together formed more than one-half of the households in the country as late as 1980, and the eradication of the economic bias that had held back the progress of Malays and other indigenous ethnic groups. Malays, who accounted for about one-half of the population according to the 1980 census, were concentrated in rural occupations that produced lower than average income. The Chinese minority, which made up 32 percent of the population, had what was considered an advantageous economic position in modern mining, manufacturing, commerce, and services.

During the 1970s programs that were developed under the New Economic Policy to promote manufacturing (especially for export), construction, and public services, as well as continued support for rural development, created better paying jobs for Malays and reduced the incidence of poverty. In the early 1980s, however, the public expenditure program that had enabled this progress encountered balance of payments difficulties, rising international interest rates, and worldwide recession. The openness of the economy to foreign commerce and its dependence on international markets had finally caused it to be dragged downward with the world economy. The expansion of government-owned corporations, in what was essentially a private sector economy, was also causing some concern.

The outlook in early 1984, however, was hopeful. The prices of the nation's export commodities were beginning to rise, as was demand from the reviving industrial economies of Japan, North America, and Western Europe. The government debt, though growing, was far from the crisis stage, and the debt to foreign creditors was well below that of other countries. Despite the nationalist tone of some government policies, foreign investors were still attracted by the freedom with which the government allowed financial capital, including profits, to move in and out of the economy and by the nation's continuing political stability. Oil and natural gas produced from offshore wells began to be exported in significant quantities. Less encouraging was the initial response to schemes to sell some inefficient government-owned enterprises to private investors. The government continued to invest in new ventures with the private sector to build heavy and intermediate industries.

The long-term problems were many. Cheap labor was becoming scarce, and if the country could not improve the skills of its work force and modernize industry to justify higher wages, the economy would fall behind other producers for the international marketplace. Dato' Seri Dr. Mahathir Mohamad, Malaysia's fourth prime minister, cited nations like the Republic of Korea (South Korea), which had a smaller per capita income than Malaysia but a much more modern industrial base. By contrast, Peninsular Malaysia had large undeveloped and impoverished areas, particularly on its eastern coast, while Sabah and Sarwak—the two states on the island of Borneo—remained rustic frontiers despite a decade of rapid progress. Underlying these areas of concern was perhaps the realization that the overall distribution of income remained extremely skewed in favor of a small minority in all ethnic groups and that efforts to build a large middle class beyond the urban centers must be redoubled.

Patterns Of Development

The formation of Malaysia's modern economic structure began in the late nineteenth century when Britain took an active interest in developing the territory's tin deposits. Soon railroads, roads, and other modern facilities linked the "tin belt" with a new capital in Kuala Lumpur through the Federated Malay States of Perak, Selangor, Pahang, and Negeri Sembilan. Rubber plantations set up in the early twentieth century spread the modern economy beyond the mining centers but still concentrated development in what became Peninsular Malaysia. The continued immigration of Chinese to work the tin mines and Indians to cultivate the rubber plantations tended to isolate the Malay majority from the mainstream of economic development.

Tin and rubber carried the economy through boom and bust until the nation's independence in 1957, by which time the Federation of Malaya was probably better off than any other area in Southeast Asia, with the possible exception of Hong Kong. The states of Sabah and Sarawak, which with Singapore joined the federation in 1963 to form the nation now known as Malaysia, were much less developed, but they had significant timber, petroleum, and copper resources to attract some important investment.

The colonial legacy was not all beneficial. The export sector, dominated by British and local Chinese interests, contrasted sharply with the rural Malay subsistence sector. Capital accumulation took place exclusively in, or for the benefit of, the export sector, which depended on Britain for nearly all of its capital, technology, and management needs. The participation of Malays was negligible. The rural Malay economy was based on rice growing, smallholder rubber cultivation, fishing, and fruit cultivation. Although the rural economy was monetized, its techniques were poor, productivity was low, and investment was minimal. Ethnic Chinese, who lived chiefly in the urban centers, oftern served as intermediaries between the big European trading firms and Malays, collecting smallholder produce and distributing imported goods. The official policy of noninterference in the indigenous social system at least indirectly condoned the relative isolation and poverty of Malay peasants (see Colonial Economy and Society, ch. 1).

After independence the government became committed not only to the promotion of economic growth but also to the equitable distribution of the gains from that growth among its peoples. The laissez-faire approaches inherited from the British, however, soon appeared to be more suited to the former than to the latter objective.

During the 1960s economic growth per se was favorable; the gross national product (GNP—see Glossary) increased by 4.8 percent per year on average (see fig. 5). The economy's resilience in the face of the confrontation with Indonesia, the separation of Singapore in 1965, and fluctuating international prices for its exports

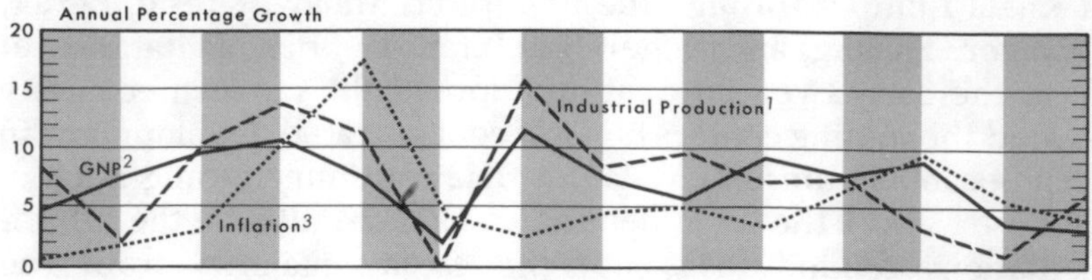

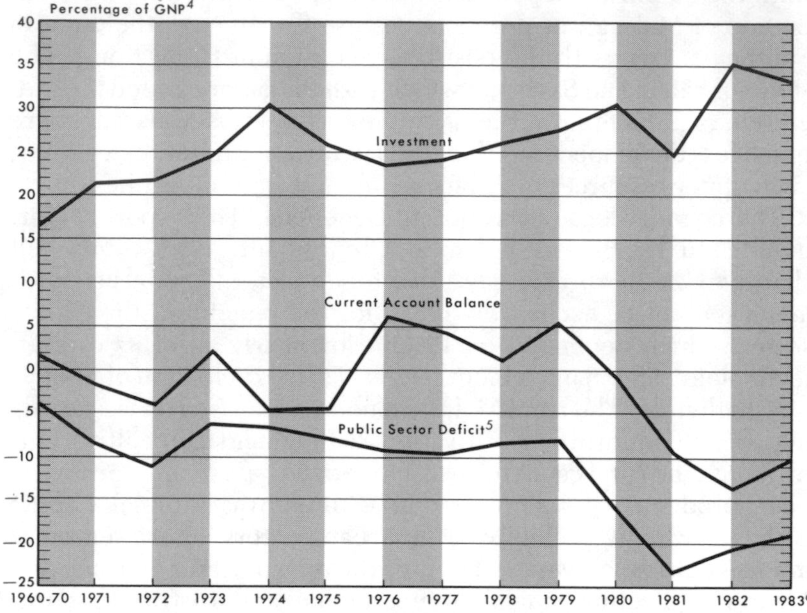

[1]Changes in industrial production index for large enterprises in Peninsular Malaysia, using weights for 1968 as base.

[2]Gross national product (see Glossary) adjusted to real terms to account for inflation in a variety of inconsistent ways depending upon different price series. Data are in accordance with price indexes having 1967 or 1970 as base year.

[3]Changes in consumer price index for Peninsular Malaysia based on prices in 1967 for 1960-81 period and on 1980 prices thereafter.

[4]GNP at market prices, unadjusted for inflation.

[5]Consolidated deficit of national and state governments and selected public authorities and government owned enterprises, including net lending from national government.

[6]Preliminary estimates.

Source: Based on information from *International Financial Statistics Yearbook, 1983*, Washington, 1983, 304–307; and Malaysia, Ministry of Finance, *Economic Report, 1983–84*, 12 Kuala Lumpur, 1983, xii-xiii, xxxii-xxxiii.

Figure 5. Major Economic Indicators, 1960–83

was remarkable. The economy diversified from its traditional reliance on rubber and tin to palm oil, timber, and manufacturing. The latter, which had a later start, expanded from about 9 percent of the gross domestic product (GDP—see Glossary) in 1960 to some 13 percent 10 years later. Most of this growth was spurred by the substitution of imported consumer manufactures with domestic industry—a process commonly called import substitution. The weakest aspect of the economy was the low level of investment, which fluctuated around 16 percent of GNP through 1970 and threatened the long-term prospects for growth. This performance was particularly disappointing because the country had ample financial resources and had barely tapped the international loan market.

Despite some government successes in promoting smallholder agriculture and rural development, large estates—employing mainly Indian labor—still produced about one-half of Peninsular Malaysia's rubber production and over 90 percent of palm oil output in 1970. The low-income traditional sector remained about 80 percent Malay. Accordingly, during this decade of development the gap in living standards between Malay and non-Malay groups and between rural and urban areas was perceived to widen. There was resentment that over 95 percent of all corporate assets in Peninsular Malaysia were in the hands of Europeans and non-Malay Asians. According to government statistics for the same year and area, the average household income for Malays was less than one-half that of Chinese and less than 60 percent of that for Indian households.

The ethnic riots of 1969 in Kuala Lumpur catalyzed the government to take action to redress these economic inequalities. In 1971 it set forth the New Economic Policy (NEP), having the two-pronged objective of "eradicating poverty irrespective of race" and "restructuring society to eliminate the identification of race with economic function." All this was to be accomplished by 1990, when Malays and other indigenous groups, collectively referred to as Bumiputra (see Glossary), were expected to "own and manage at least 30 percent of the total commercial and industrial activities of the country in all categories and scales of operation and become full partners in the economic life of the nation." The restructuring of wealth and employment was not to be accomplished through radical measures, such as the expropriation of property, but through positive programs, loans, and investments.

During the first decade of the NEP, the economic structure changed in several important ways. Manufacturing became the lead sector, growing at an average rate of 12.5 percent per year and accounting for 20.5 percent of GDP in constant prices (see table 6, Appendix). The generating of employment in manufacturing was also impressive, expanding by some 7.6 percent per year to reach 15.8 percent of all employment. The employment of Malays in what the government called secondary industry—mining, manufacturing, construction, and transportation—expanded much more rapidly than for other ethnic groups, and Malay unemployment was reported to drop from 8.1 to 5.1 percent of the Malay work force. The share of the agriculture, forestry, and fishing sector decreased from 30.8 to 22.2 percent of GDP, while the service sector, especially government services, expanded rapidly to counterbalance this decline.

The stimulus for GNP growth, which averaged 7.8 percent per year during the decade, came chiefly from public expenditure, investment, and exports. Fixed public investment rose from 6 to 11 percent of GNP (in current prices), while public consumption increased from 16 to 18 percent of GNP. Overall, government expenditures, including those from public corporations, accounted for nearly one-third of the growth of GNP. Private investment expanded from 13 to 19 percent of GNP, but private consumption decreased its share from 61 to 54 percent. Although exports did not grow as rapidly as imports on average, primarily because of the increased importation of investment goods and materials, they expanded from 45 to 62 percent of GNP. Crude petroleum, copper, palm oil, and manufactures led this expansion. Manufactured exports increased their value especially during the second half of the decade as the government implemented export-oriented industrial policies.

Many of the shifts in the compostition of demand were caused by price changes, particularly after the oil crisis and price increases of 1973–74. The effects of inflation, however, did not alter the underlying trends of the 1970s toward increased investment, public consumption, and exports relative to private consumption. At the same time, however, expenditures by private individuals and enterprises on consumer goods and services, excluding inflation, rose by some 4.6 percent per year and reached M$1,963 per percent (for value of the ringgit—see Glossary) in 1980. The implied higher standards of living, according to government estimates, reduced the incidence of poverty in Peninsular Malaysia from 49 to 29 percent of all households. Also in Peninsular Malaysia, the household income of Malays increased slightly more than that for other groups. The position of the poorest 40 percent of all households, however, improved at a slower rate than the average for all groups.

Despite the resilience of the economy in the wake of the oil shock in 1973, the second round of major oil price increases in 1979 and the world recession of the 1980–82 period strained the economy seriously and may have subverted some of the progress toward the goals of the NEP. In 1981 the value of the nation's exports dropped significantly below that of imports for the first time since 1972, and the combined current account deficits for 1981 and 1982 averaged 11.8 percent of GNP. The government budget swung more deeply into deficit to make up for the anticipated lack of external demand, reaching 23 percent of GNP in 1981 before falling to about 20 percent the next year. Fearing a round of double-digit inflation similar to that experienced after the first oil crisis, the government prepared austere budgets for 1982, 1983 and 1984. The effect of the external economic environment and government policies was to reduce real per capita private consumption by 9 percent from 1980 to 1982, suggesting a lower standard of living. The sluggish performance of agriculture, which grew less rapidly than all other sectors except mining, implied that rural Malays were hardest hit during the recession.

The recession was ill timed for Malaysia's policymakers. Arguing that the basic industrial structure was undeveloped compared with that of other Asian countries having lower incomes than Malaysia, Prime Minister Mahathir launched another phase of import substitution to develop heavy industries based on the country's resources of energy and raw materials. Wishing to emulate the performances of Japan and South Korea, Mahathir urged his compatriots to "Look East" and build a "Malaysian Incorporated" (see Relations with Selected Countries, ch. 4). His strategy was to construct a nucleus of indurstries producing vehicles, basic engineered products, cement, refined petroleum and gas, and petrochemicals around which smaller enterprises could flourish. The industrial policy fit in with the goal of developing the poorer regions of the country and, according to the government, was the best hope for upgrading the status of Bumiputra, most of whom lived in the less-developed areas. The "Look East" approach was also based on Mahathir's long-held desire to change the Malay work ethnic to one as vigorous and competitive as that of other East Asians.

Some economists have criticized the ambitiousness and potentially high investment costs and risks of the prime minister's goals and strategies. Others have rankled at the growing influence of government-run enterprises, which proliferated in the 1970s and crowded out the private sector in the scramble for financial resources. Alternative economic strategies proposed by the government's critics emphasized the mechanization and intensive development of agriculture, the expansion of metal-products industries to fashion the machinery for this and other modernization programs, and the development of small-scale industries. In fact, as financial capital became scarce in the early 1980s, the government itself has explored less costly alternatives to the heavy industrialization program and has deferred its investment plans. It has also announced plans for the so-called privatization of some government-owned enterprises.

To a great extent the preoccupation with industrialization reflected the influence of the emerging Malay middle class and its impatience for an expanded role in business management. The Malay perception has been that government-owned businesses have the most room for Malay managerial talent. Industrial expansion seemed unlikely to reduce the interethnic rivalries for wealth and power, which, if the pattern of earlier development was any indication, far outweighed the importance redistributing economic assets from the richer to the poorer elements of the society.

Employment and Income

Patterns of employment and income distribution have varied considerably by region and occupational category as well as by ethnic group. Although government labor statistics were incomplete and not always consistent, by 1980 at least, they showed that Malaysia had achieved some progress toward equalizing economic opportunities and alleviating the poverty of many disadvantaged households. The evidence did not suggest, however, that government policies had moderated significantly the unequal distribution of income between and within different groups and regions. The government feared, moreover, that slowing rates of economic expansion in the 1980s could undermine some of the gains of the previous decades.

Employment and Labor Relations

The labor force was projected to grow by 3.1 percent per year during the 1981–85 period, meaning that some 167,000 new jobs would have to be created each year to keep the jobless rate at the level reported in 1980—some 5.3 percent. The estimated rate of growth of the work force would be about one-quarter less than that registered in the 1970s and heralded a period of labor scarcity

Textiles (above) and battery assembly: two examples of Malaysia's fast-growing light manufacturing sector
Courtesy Embassy of Malaysia, Washington

and continued immigration. Toward the end of the 1970s there were reports of labor shortages on some farms and in scattered industrial and construction projects. Meanwhile, immigrants—legal and illegal—continued to arrive from nearby countries to work on the plantations. Ironically, many laborers from Johore commuted to Singapore to work. The lack of skilled workers and managers was a major problem, and the government estimated that only two-thirds of the needed technicians could be trained during the 1981–85 period to meet its investment plans. As a result, the Ministry of Labor has attempted to improve its planning and training capabiltities, and the government has looked to private industry to provide on-the-job training.

In spite of some shortages—caused chiefly by poor communications, transportation, and skill levels—the unemployment rate rose to 6.2 percent of the work force of approximately 5.9 million persons in 1982. The rate of underemployment—defined by the government as the percentage of workers employed for fewer than 25 hours a week and seeking additional work—was not available after 1978, when it was recorded at 2.6 percent. Underemployment was primarily a characteristic of rural areas. According to studies from the 1970s and the 1980 census, the rate of unemployment among Malays was twice that of Chinese and one-quarter higher than that for Indians, who constituted another important minority. Women were 75 percent more likely to be unemployed than men.

Employment in agriculture, forestry, and fishing continued to decline in the early 1980s as rural laborers were attracted to urban markets; such employment accounted for some 38 percent of all employment in 1982. The mining sector likewise has shrunk, making up only 1.4 percent of the total. Manufacturing's share was virtually unchanged from 1980, at about 15.5 percent. The fastest growing employment sectors continued to be government services and construction, which accounted, respectively, for 15.7 and 5.9 percent of all jobs in 1982. In some urban areas, public sector employment made up as much as 40 percent of all jobs. A government hiring freeze instituted in 1982 and a downturn in the private housing industry were slowing some of this growth in 1983. The service industries—ranging from small-scale retailing to sophisticated business and finance—supplied a large and moderately growing number of jobs.

During the 1970s the structure of employment within economic sectors also changed. According to the government, most new jobs in the agricultural sector were created on public land development schemes, livestock farms, and forestry projects—generally higher paying than other agricultural enterprises (see Land Development and Technical Support, this ch.). In manufacturing, labor-intensive and export-oriented industries, such as those producing electonic equipment and textiles, expanded most rapidly. Construction and service employment boomed primarily because of public expenditures on housing, education, health, defense, and infrastructure development.

Labor union membership increased slightly faster than the employment growth rate during the 1970s and numbered 595,000 workers organized into 366 unions in 1982—about 10 percent of the work force and 15 percent of all salaried employees. Most of the unions were small; the largest, the National Union of Plantation Workers, had about 100,000 members. Labor federations have been the principal national representatives of labor, and one such federation, the Malaysian Trade Union Congress, has claimed more than three-fourths of all union membership. The Congress of Unions of Employees in Public and Civil Services represented virtually all of the rest and was of obvious interest to the government.

Union activity has been circumscribed by increasing government controls. Although the Trade Union Ordinance of 1959 and the Industrial Relations Act of 1967 permits strikes, the government usually refers industrial disputes to binding arbitration as quickly as possible, at which time they become illegal. In the wake of a particularly debilitating slowdown and strike by the nations's airline employees in 1978 and 1979, the government passed controversial changes to the labor laws in 1980. The amendments enhanced the powers of the Ministry of Labor and affiliated regulatory agencies. The labor federations backed down from a threatened general strike in response to the new legislation partly because the government modified some of the provisions. The yearly economic damage caused by strikes decreased from about 109,000 to 10,000 lost work days from 1976 to 1982. The government has proposed that in-house unions rather than industrywide labor organizations be the norm; the labor federations have vehemently opposed this suggestion, citing it as another attempt to oppress the workers.

Labor legislation also contains important safeguards for Malaysian workers. There is no general minimum wage, but the government has the right to designate minimum wages in select industries. The amended laws require overtime pay on rest days at thrice the hourly wage; an annual bonus calculated as part of the basic wage; minimum maternity leave of 60 days; 10 paid holidays; annual leave of at least eight days; and sick leave of at least 14 days. The average workweek is 48 hours, and overtime is not to exceed 32 hours per month. The ability of the authorities to enforce these regulations was doubtful but apparently better than in most other developing countries. The labor regulations covered about 60 percent of the work force in 1980.

Income Distribution and Living Standards

According to government statistics, based on an unspecified minimum standard of living, the total number of poor households in Peninsular Malaysia decreased from about 792,000 in 1970 to 666,000 in 1980 (see table 7, Appendix). The worst incidence of poverty occurred among agricultural households outside of the estate crop and irrigated rice-farming sectors. Except in mining, however, the poverty rate fell for all groups during the 1970s.

The traditional association of economic occupation with ethnic origin continued to keep Malay incomes low. In 1979 the average household income of the poorest 40 percent of Malay households was one-half that of similar Chinese households and only a slightly larger proportion of that of Indian households. The gap between Malay and Chinese households had, however, narrowed; in 1970 the poorest Malay households had earned only 42 percent of that by Chinese households. Several scholars have shown, moreover, that when household income was adjusted to account for the size of the families, leisure-time activities, and work hours, the position of Malay households relative to others improved substantially. Indeed, rural Malay and Indian households, the latter engaged primarily on plantations, tended to be equally poor.

Income distribution and poverty have had strong regional biases (see table 8, Appendix). According to the only detailed survey of poverty, conducted in 1976, rural households were almost three times more likely than urban households to be poor. Only the Federal Territory had less than 10 percent of its people living in poverty, and only surrounding Selangor had less than one-fourth of its population in poverty. Johore, Penang, Malacca (Melaka), and Pahang had less than one-third in this category, while the rest of the states had higher percentages. The worst case was Kelantan, in northern Peninsular Malaysia, where more than 55 percent of the population lived in poverty.

The government has addressed the issue of regional development in many of its policy pronouncements, but the needs of industrial development have not always permitted it to take sufficient measures. The planned public expenditure program for the

1981–85 plan period, for example, was supposed to take into consideration the level of per capita income, the rate of growth of GDP, and the incidence of poverty for each state during the previous decade. The planned expenditure for the Federal Territory, however, was two and one-half times the economic investment and more than seven times the social expenditure needed to meet these criteria; by contrast, Perlis, Penang, Negeri Sembilan, Malacca, Terengganu, Sabah, and Sarawak were underfunded. resource limitations and political constraints therefore shaped the government's regional development policies as much as ideal considerations of economic equity.

In general, the labor market distributed income rationally according to skill levels. The major exception was the case of women, who were usually economically disadvantaged. According to one government survey conducted in 1979, women earned about 20 percent less than men in the same occupational categories. There were also wage differentials between employees of large companies and those in smaller firms, but most of these were based on skill. Credentials, however, have been very important in Malaysia; sometimes regardless of performance, having the right degree from the right school has meant a better job and better pay.

Although there has been real progress in the elimination of poverty and some improvements in the position of the Malay ethnic group, there appeared to be some deterioration in the distribution of income in general. The latest available household income survey, conducted in 1973, showed that incomes were highly skewed: the bottom 40 percent of the income ladder earned 11.2 percent of the national income, while the richest 20 percent earned 56.1 percent of the income. Other government data, showing that the mean household income had risen faster than the median income during the 1973–79 period, however, suggested that the top one-half of the income distribution was expanding its wealth more rapidly than the bottom. This gap was especially large among Chinese households.

Despite these somewhat disturbing trends, Malaysians remained much better off than the citizenry of most developing countries. Modern durable consumer items were pervasive (see table 9, Appendix). The Employees' Provident Fund and the Social Security Organization provided pension and insurance benefits to 4.2 million employees and 2.2 million low-income workers, respectively, in 1982. Contributions to the former fund were 20 percent of a worker's salary, of which the employer provided 11 percent. Together with improved health care and educational services, these benefits have significantly improved the standard of living.

The nation's consumers have further benefited from the lobbying efforts of an independent consumer advocate group, the Consumers' Association of Penang. Founded in 1970, the organization has since increased its visibility in the media and its effect on government agencies. Partly in response to the association's efforts, the Ministry of Trade and Industry has strengthened its consumer protection division, and the government has upgraded the Department of the Environment to the status of a ministry. In 1983 the group criticized the abuse of pesticides, excessive hospital fees, insurance fraud, harmful additives in beverages, and some questionable practices on the stock and commodity exchanges. The regional office of the United Nations-sponsored International Organization of Consumer Unions was also based in Penang and worked closely with its Malaysian affiliate.

The Corporate Sector

Restructuring the society so that Bumiputra might have greater influence in the economy has been accomplished primarily through government efforts to alter the ownership and management of corporate enterprise. Although incorporated enterprises accounted for only a part of the economy—issues of corporate stock were equivalent to 53 percent of GNP in 1980—it was politically and psychologically important to the government to change the pattern of ownership and control. The goal of the NEP was for Bumiputra to own 30 percent of all corporate stock by 1990, while the shares of other Malaysians (primarily Chinese and Indians) and foreigners would represent 40 percent and 30 percent, respectively. Bumiputra, moreover, were to take on managerial positions in proportion to their number in the total population. One consequence of these policies, however, has been the expansion of government-owned enterprises, which has caused some resentment from the private sector and concern on the part of many public officials, including the prime minister.

Government involvement in corporate enterprise nearly tripled the share of stock owned by Bumiputra after 1971 to 12.4 percent of the total in 1980. Some two-thirds of this share, however, was held in trust by government agencies, such as the Trust Council for Indigenous Peoples (Majlis Amanah Rakyat—MARA), established in 1966, and the National Trust (Permodalan Nasional—PERNAS), founded in 1978. Some PERNAS ventures were considered to be private enterprises in 1983 because they were actively being sold to small investors, but nearly all were public enterprises. In addition, each Malaysian state has established an economic development corporation to channel federal and state funds to Bumiputra entrepreneurs. According to the minister of trade and industry, as of June 1983 Bumiputra entrepreneurs owned 29 percent of the nearly 381,000 companies registered in Malaysia.

The transfer of corporate shares to Bumiputra has been hampered by the tendency of many shareholders to resell their stock to other Malaysians for a quick profit on the stock exchange (see Finance and Monetary Policy, this ch.). In order to arrest this trend, PERNAS created a subsidiary trust fund in 1981 that offered shares costing only M$1 each, whose value in exchange would be frozen until 1990. The guaranteed return on this investment was 15 to 18 percent per year and would be distributed in the form of new shares.

The government also provided assistance to increase the ranks of Bumiputra managers and professionals. MARA's Institute of Technology and the nation's universities trained some 25,000 Bumiputra professionals in 1980—more than three times the number in 1971. Courses in bookkeeping, management, and marketing were provided to another 22,000 Bumiputra—a tenfold increase during the same period. As a result, about 54 percent of the technical and professional jobs created in Peninsular Malaysia in the 1970s went to Bumiputra. Some 43 percent of the new administrative and managerial positions were filled by Malays. By the end of the decade Malays were well represented at the professional and technical levels. Chinese continued to predominate at the middle levels, where they occupied 62 percent of the slots in 1980. Malays and Indians represented 32 percent and 6 percent of all managerial and administrative positions, respectively, in 1980.

Many difficulties faced companies that seriously tried to comply with government directives to employ representative numbers of Bumiputra at all levels of management. Many Malays simply lacked the requisite skills, and those who were well trained were quickly lured to better paying jobs in other companies or in the government. Often Malay employees lacked a deep commitment to their employer because they felt they were hired only to fill a quota. More importantly, the majority of Malays lived outside of the urban areas where most managerial employment was created.

In 1980 Malaysian citizens not qualifying for Bumiputra programs owned slightly more than 40 percent of all corporate equity. They have aggressively defended their assests. After the passage of the Industrial Coordination Act of 1975, which gave the government discretionary powers to regulate the ownership and management of private enterprises, Chinese business leaders joined together to form Multi-purpose Holdings, a company to shelter and merge smaller Chinese enterprises. By 1983 the company had grown to become the second largest firm listed on the stock exchange. Its bid to take over the third largest commercial bank in 1981 brought it directly into conflict with PERNAS. The government eventually intervened to create an equal partnership between PERNAS and Multi-purpose Holdings in the management of the bank. In addition to Multi-purpose Holdings, some 50 smaller holding companies have been formed by the numerous Chinese guilds and dialect associations (see Ethnic Composition and Subdivisions, ch. 2).

The chambers of commerce and industry, which represented the interests of the business community, were organized along ethnic lines—one each for Malays, Indians, Chinese, and foreigners. Other employers' associations and groups representing financial enterprises and specific manufacturing industries, however, were organized according to functional specialties rather than ethnic affiliation. The association of some industries with certain ethnic groups—the Chinese with tin mining, for example—continued, however, into the 1980s and perpetuated ethnic competition in the business community.

By 1983 most Chinese and other Malaysians outside of the Bumiputra community seemed basically satisfied with amendments to the Idustrial Coordination Act and the pragmatic approaches of the government; foreign-owned companies, however, were increasingly on the defensive. Foreign stock ownership declined from 62 percent of corporate equity in 1971 to 47.5 percent in 1980. Although the government had maintained that its target for restructuring would not be applied to individual companies, it made several moves in the early 1980s that unsettled some investors. In April of 1982 the government required foreign insurance companies to submit plans to reduce immediatly the foreign share of their equity to less than one-half of the total and to lower it further to 30 percent by 1990. Indirect pressure prompted the two largest foreign commercial banks to announce plans for local incorporation in the same month. In addition, PERNAS and other trust agencies have quietly accumulated controlling and noncontrolling stakes in some of the largest foreign-owned firms, including the largest plantations. Joint ventures between government and private firms and foreign companies were also becoming common.

If because of lingering anticolonialist sentiments foreign companies still remained the "bogies," as the minister of finance declared in 1980, they have nonetheless been welcome to invest in Malaysia. After a long period of stagnation from 1968 to 1975, when the net inflow of foreign investment averaged from 2 to 3 percent of GDP, the average rose to nearly 4 percent in the 1976–80 period. It jumped dramatically to over 9 percent and 12 percent of GDP, respectively, in 1981 and 1982. Most of this increase came from a surge in portfolio investment, particularly in government bonds. Direct private investment also rose significantly from 3.5 percent of GDP in 1976 to 4.7 percent in 1982. The development of free-trade zones and numerous fiscal incentives helped to attract investors (see Fiscal Policy and Incentives; International Finance and Trade, this ch.). Much of the foreign investment has been in the petroleum industry (see Mining, this ch.).

Until the 1970s Malaysia was overwhelmingly a private sector economy, and the expansion of the public sector has not altered the fundamental nature of the system. From 1970 to 1980 the private sector's share of total fixed investment decreased from about 68 to 67 percent. This moderate trend masks some significant cyclical variations, however. After the Petroleum Development Act of 1974 and the Industrial Coordination Act were passed, investment dropped dramatically before recovering later in the decade. The recessionary conditions of the early 1980s caused the private sector's share of investment to fall temporarily to about 57 percent of the total.

Public enterprise and investment expanded rapidly during the 1970s, primarily as a consequence of the Bumiputra promotion campaigns. By 1983 the government had established 115 enterprises, statutory authorities, research institutes, and other agencies under the control of government ministries. The Ministry of Public Enterprises, founded in 1974, oversaw the activities of 26 enterprises and trust agencies that controlled, in turn, some 500 companies chiefly employing Bumiputra managers. In 1980 the government contributed more than 8.2 percent of the paid-in capital of the corporate sector, compared with 1.7 percent in 1971.

Prime Minister Mahathir has called for genuine cooperation between the public and private sectors. The cooperative effort was supposed to coalesce in the "privatization" campaign, a program to sell many government-owned enterprises to private interests. By late 1983 the government had demonstrated its good faith by allowing the formation of the first private television network, opening bids to private investors for control and management of the planned elevated mass transit system for Kuala Lumpur, and announcing that it would allow bids for the existing Kelang Port Authority. The National Electricity Board and the Telecommunications Corporation have both announced plans to let private enterprises undertake and own future projects.

The major labor federations united in opposition to the plan for Kelang in 1983, however, and some economists have argued that the government's divestment plans were nebulous and naive. Many of the enterprises under consideration for divestiture—including the railroads, airline, and shipping companies—have shown declining profits or losses for a number of years. Poor profitability and the sheer size of some of these corporations would make them prohibitively expensive and risky for private investors. It was also unlikely that enough Bumiputra capital could be found to keep the privatization program from undermining some of the progress of the NEP.

Government backing of Bumiputra enterprises has also come under attack from critics who complained that the beneficiaries of public enterprise were usually well-heeled Malays. According to their view, powerful politicians, senior bureaucrats, and businesspeople having political connections have developed into a class of so-called bureaucrat capitalists. Its members—predominantly Malay—cooperated with Chinese and foreigners who were willing to go along with the Bumiputra promotion campaigns as long as their profits were protected. Such an appraisal would view the scandal involving the government-owned Bank Bumiputra as a natural consequence. In 1983 a subsidiary of this bank stood accused of a serious misallocation of loans to a Chinese real estate magnate in Hong Kong. The situation was becoming a political embarrassement for the prime minister.

Government Planning and Policy

The competence and confidence of the Economic Planning Unit (EPU), attached to the Prime Minister's Department have grown during the preparation and evaluation of four five-year economic development plans since 1966. Each subsequent plan, moreover, has included more detailed regional information in an attempt to plan the spatial development of the country. The Second Malaysia Plan, 1971–75, enumerated the goals and strategies of the NEP, and its mid-term review, published in 1973, included the Outline Perspective Plan, which spanned the entire 1971–90 period. The Third Malaysia Plan, 1976–80, incorporated a major effort to integrate studies conducted by individual urban and regional planning authorities with national macreoeconomic projections. The Fourth Malaysia Plan, 1981–85, offered the most detailed account of regional development priorities by state and filled in many of the earlier statistical gaps.

Although the implementation of these development plans has uncovered inevitable shortcomings in both the planning process and government policies, the plans formed a strikingly comprehensive, consistent, and level-headed approach to economic development. The sectoral strategies have concentrated on increasing the productivity of agriculture, expanding and diversifying the industrial base, modernizing the financial and service sectors, and varying the sources of economic growth. Stimulating investment and exports has been particularly important to the planners, as has been locating efficient import-substituting industries to form linkages to the rest of the economy.

Balanced social and economic development among the states has been another major priority. In particular, the government has planned to limit the growth of the Kuala Lumpur-Kelang areas as much as possible, leave Penang to enjoy its own dynamism, and stimulate investment in Malacca, Johore Baharu, and especially in regional development centers on the eastern coast of Peninsular Malaysia. Eight major regional development areas had been established as of late 1982.

The sine qua non of Malaysian development planning, however, contiuned to be the NEP. Every investment in agriculture, industry, services, or labor development had to be justified in terms of the twin goals of the eradication of poverty and advancement for the disadvantaged ethnic groups.

The EPU was by far the most important planning agency. It served as the secretariat of both the National Development Planning Committee, composed of the heads of the economic ministries, and the National Economic Council, a cabinet commitee. The Prime Minister's Department also included specialized agencies that drafted plans for manpower, social, and public service development; other ministries also had planning departments. Each state had planning units as well as development offices for formulating specific projects. A housing and population census, conducted in 1980, and the installation of an integrated data system were enhancing the statistical bases for planning. But the complexities of the rapidly growing economy and the number of planning agencies at the national and local level presented coordination problems.

Fiscal Policy and Incentives

Although private investment has accounted for at least one-half of the economic development of the country, public sector planning has allocated increasing expenditures to economic purposes. During the first half of the 1970s, public development expenditure was the equivalent of 11 percent of GDP—three percentage points higher than in the 1960s. This share rose to nearly 13 percent in the second half of the decade, and the government planned to sustain at least this level of expenditure throughout the Fourth Malaysia Plan, 1981–85. Federal government agencies spent over 82 percent of the total development funds during the 1970s, state governments about 10 percent, and public authorities the remainder.

The composition of development expenditures has changed according to planning priorities, although it has seldom been exactly as targeted. Before 1970, spending on infrastructure facilities such as transportation, communications, and utilities, accounted for the largest share of expenditure—about 45 percent Agricultural and rural development programs received about one-fifth of all development expenditure, while industry and commerce accounted for only 2 percent. In the 1970s the share devoted to commerce and industry rose to 13.5 percent, and that for infrastructure development decreased to about 21 percent (see table 10, Appendix). Development spending for social service facilities decreased slightly to about 14 percent of the total. The major changes for the Fourth Malaysia Plan were the relative expansion of development expenditure for electricity and water facilities, agriculture and rural development, and defense (see Defense Spending and Industry, ch. 5). As a counter-recessionary measure, the government abruptly expanded its investment in housing construction in 1981 and 1982.

According to government data, about 32 percent of the expenditure allocated during the Second Malaysia Plan went toward the goals of the NEP. During the Third Malaysia Plan, this percentage dropped to less than 29 percent. The projected allocation for the Fourth Malaysia Plan was some 36 percent. The vast majority of these expenditures was devoted to reducing poverty, but during the 1981–85 period the government hoped to raise the amount expended on increasing the economic power of Malays to one-third of the total. It should be noted that these percentages were based on allocations rather than actual expeditures.

During the 1975–81 period operating expeditures also expanded rapidly in order to maintain the new facilities constructed by development expenditures. About one-third of operation expenditures went toward wages. Subsidies for rice and petroleum products, transfers to state governments, pension contributions, and payments on the national debt were also important. In 1982 and 1983, in the face of revenue shortfalls and higher borrowing costs, the government was trying to slow the growth of operating expenditures primarily by restraining some wages and contributions to statutory funds (see table 11, Appendix).

Total revenues of the federal and state governments expanded rapidly during the 1970s, although not as rapidly as expenditures. In 1981 and 1982, however, the rate dropped precipitously as income from export duties on rubber, tin, and palm oil declined. Revenues in 1982 were about 6 percent less than the amount planned in the budget. As a result, the government had to curtail development expenditures in fiscal years 1982, 1983, and 1984. The cutbacks involved postponing some development projects—notably an oil refinery in Malacca, a military air base, expansion of the Kuala Lumpur-Johore highway, and retracking of the railroad.

The public debt of the national government increased by 33 percent per year from 1980 to 1982, when it reached M$41.5 billion—some 69 percent of GDP, compared with 45 percent in 1980. Whereas during the 1975–80 period over 71 percent of the additonal debt was financed by domestic borrowing—in the form of government securities and treasury bills—nearly 45 percent of the newly acquired debt in the early 1980s was financed by foreign borrowing (see International Finance and Trade, this ch.). Nevertheless, government securities continued to dominate the stock market, accounting for 90 percent of the new funds raised in 1982. The bulk of the securities issued had long-term maturities of 15 or more years.

The tax structure served not only to raise revenues but also to direct economic activity in favored directions. The Investment Incentives Act of 1968, as revised in 1978, provided for incentives to be granted to all sectors, including agriculture. There were seven major investment incentives: for industries receiving a "pioneer status"; for industries in designated "locational incentive areas"; for export industries; for businesses employing more than 50 Malaysian employees; for modernizing and expanding existing investment for hotels; and for selected agricultural industries. "Pioneer status" incentives have been the most popular.

The incentive system suffered from a complex administration

that led sometimes to less than desirable investment patterns. The Malaysian Industrial Development Authority (MIDA) was theoretically the sole conduit for incentive approvals. It was assisted not only by the Foreign Investment Committee but also by other economic ministries and agencies, most of which had a representative on MIDA's decisionmaking board. Applications were handled on a case-by-case basis requiring lengthy documentation and approvals from many quarters. The government recongnized the need to streamline these procedures and to develop automatic mechanisms but had unveiled no such measures as of late 1983. It was especially important to correct the large bias in favor of companies locating in free-trade zones, which could double their incentives by qualifying for "pioneer status" as well.

Finance and Monetary Policy

Banking and finance has been one of the fastest growing sectors in the economy and a major conduit for the government's campaigns to promote businesses on its priority list. During the 1971–82 period, commercial banks, of which 22 were incorporated locally and 16 overseas, tripled their staff to more than 31,000 and increased their assets ninefold to about M$49 billion—some 46 percent of the assets of the entire financial system. The Central Bank of Malaysia (Bank Negara Malaysia), various employee and social security funds, some 40 finance companies, 12 merchant banks, a national savings bank, and 64 insurance companies accounted for nearly all of the remaining assets. Numerous regional, specialty, and rural credit institutions made up a small fraction of the total. In addition, a vigorous stock market added depth to the financial system.

Commercial bank lending has been directed disproportionately toward commerce, finance and business services, real estate, construction, and manufacturing, compared with the share of these sectors in the general economy. Government regulations, however, required that Bumiputra individuals and enterprises receive at least 18 percent of the total outstanding credit in 1982, small-scale enterprises 12 percent, home buyers 10 percent, and food producers 5 percent. The banks met these guidelines as a group, although the share devoted to small-scale and agricultural businesses was barely sufficient. Some individual banks, moreover, had to be penalized for failing to meet the targets. The government created the Credit Guaranty Corporation in 1972 to insure commercial loans to small businesses, including petty traders and hawkers having assets less than M$250,000. In 1981 the corporation opened a new facility to offer loans of up to M$50,000 at even more concessional terms than before. During 1982 some 17,000 borrowers availed themselves of this facility.

Rural credit institutions included a special agricultural bank, cooperatives, and government agencies, as well as the larger financial intermediaries of the banking system. Agricultural loans extended in 1982 were about M$695 million, compared with M$1.4 billion in 1981 (see Land Development and Technical Support, this ch.).

The Central Bank actively promoted the development of primary and secondary markets for financial instruments other than deposits during the 1970s, introducing bankers' acceptances and negotiable certificates of deposit. The former were particularly attractive because they could be rediscounted at the Central Bank. The interbank market of call money, loans, and other instruments has grown about twice as rapidly as the overall money supply (see Glossary).

The market for corporate securities has also expanded as the Kuala Lumpur Stock Exchange, separated from the Singapore market in 1973, has matured. Private corporations raised some M$900 million through new issues on the exchange in 1981—equivalent to about 19 percent of the net new credit extended. The government was considering setting up over-the-counter operations in 1983 in order to stimulate issues and trading of the stocks of small companies not listed on the main board.

Monetary policy was the preserve of the Ministry of Finance as advised by the Central Bank, which was also the implementing agency. Although the Central Bank had effective command of its own assets and the liquidity of the banking system, it has had less control over government lending and borrowing and changes in the balance of payments, two other major influences on the money supply and inflation. During the 1960s the government borrowed only lightly from the banking system, and the money supply expanded relatively slowly. In the early 1970s, however, increased development expenditures, financed from the large balance of payments surpluses and the banking system, caused the money supply to grow by more than 20 percent per year. Inflation, often underestimated by the government index, averaged over 9 percent per year and peaked at 17 percent in 1974.

After first lowering and then raising the government-administered interest rates, liquidity ratios, and statutory reserve requirements, in order to achieve the perfect blend of expansionary and deflationary policies during the 1973–78 period, the government has embarked on a major reform of the financial system.

Late in 1978 the government changed the regulations to allow banks to determine their own interest rates and to permit merchant banks to accept deposits. Further changes in 1982 enabled the Central Bank to impose credit limits on individual borrowers, prohibited loans to bank staff and relatives, and required senior bank officials to declare their personal assets periodically. Some of these measures were relaxed in 1983. Through tax incentives, the government has also encouraged the lengthening of the average maturity on deposits and loans. Partly as a result of the financial reforms, the rate of inflation moderated to an average of 6 percent per year during the 1976–82 period.

International Finance and Trade

The government's generally free-market approach to international finance and trade has resulted in few balance of payments crises. During the 1961–80 period the merchandise trade balance was positive in every year, and current account surpluses, achieved in most of these years, more than compensated for the deficits. At the same time, the net inflow of investment capital averaged about the same as the net outflow of profits and wages.

The international recession of the early 1980s, however, brought record deficits to the balance of payments. The most important balance, that on the current account, registered a deficit equivalent to 13.3 percent of GDP in 1982. The burden of servicing the external public debt more than doubled to 6 percent of the value of export earnings. Official borrowings from overseas in 1983 increased another 12 percent over those for 1982. Although the debt-service ratio was low compared with other developing countries and lower even than in Malaysia's own experience, the government was clearly disturbed at the need to scramble for financing.

The recession in the industrialized world was most responsible for the poor performance of Malaysia's exports in 1982. Exports of petroleum, natural gas, and timber—the only buoyant commodities—did not increase rapidly enough to offset decreases in the value of rubber, palm oil, and tin (see table 12, Appendix). The volume of exports declined for rubber and tin, while unit prices dropped for all of the major exports except timber. Manufactured exports continued to grow rapidly in value as they had throughout the 1970s and made up 27 percent of all merchandise exports in 1982, compared with only 11 percent in 1970. The downturn in prices for the nation's primary commodities was probably temporary, and prices for rubber and palm oil were already rising in late 1983.

Malaysia participated in two important commodity arrangements. As the world's largest producer of rubber, the country was a founding member of the Association of Natural Rubber Producing Countries, established in 1970, and the host of the International Natural Rubber Council. The latter was an association of producing and consuming countries set up in 1980 to manage a buffer stock of some 550,000 tons. Likewise, Malaysia has been a long-time member of the International Tin Council, based in London, which has administered the terms of six successive tin trading agreements since 1956. In June 1983 the country became a founding member of the Association of Tin Producing Countries, to be based in Kuala Lumpur, and by October the association had six members, accounting for 93 percent of world production. Malaysia was accused of "illegally" organizing a massive buying campaign on the London tin market in late 1981 and 1982 to support the plummeting price of tin, sparked in part by the decision of the United States General Services Administration to unload its so-called strategic stockpile onto the world market (see Relations with Selected Countries, ch. 4). A new tin agreement, which came into force in 1982, set up export controls for producers and increased the buffer stock to nearly 50,000 tons.

In 1980 the government passed the Commodities Trading Act and set up the Kuala Lumpur Commodities Exchange in an effort to gain some control over the prices of its export commodities. Trading in palm oil futures began that year and by 1983 exceeded the total volume of production. Foreign brokerages were becoming more and more active, and about one-quarter of those operating in 1983 did some international trading. Trading in rubber futures was introduced on the exchange in September of 1983, and the government planned to begin trading in tin by mid-1984. Although considerable skepticism surrounded the development of the exchange, the success of palm oil futures buoyed the optimism of the government.

Manufactured exports have been boosted by the establishment of free-trade zones. The duty-free zones accounted for more than 60 percent of manufacturing employment growth since their introduction in 1972 and employed some 73,000 people in 1982. About three-quarters of these workers were young women who performed the relatively simple manual tasks of sewing garments or assembling electronic equipment. The latter made up 50 percent of the value of manufactured exports in 1982 (see Manufacturing, this ch.)

On the import side of foreign trade, consumer items have steadily decreased their relative share of the total, while investment and intermediate goods have increased. In the late 1970s the relative share of investment goods declined in favor of intermediate goods to supply earlier investments but regained importance in the early 1980s. Parts and raw materials, especially for manufacturing, represented 48 percent of all imports in 1982.

The level of protection offered domestic industries by the application of tariff and other import restrictions has been significant but less restrictive than in other developing countries. Exemptions from tariffs on intermediate and investment goods were common for specific firms and industries. Data from the late 1970s suggested, however, that the case-by-case approach of the government's tariff adminstration tended to discriminate against export-oriented firms. The 1984 budget included substantial increases in protection for domestic garment and food manufacturers and for the proposed automobile factory (see Manufacturing, this ch.).

The direction of trade and financial flows demonstrated both the openness of the economy to commerce with all nations and its particularly close relations with other members of the European Economic Community (EEC), especially Britain. Economic relations with the former colonial power, however, have diminished in importance since the early 1970s, in keeping with the government's goal of enhancing its independence. Singapore remained by far the most important economic partner (see table 13, Appendix). Preferential trading arrangements between members of ASEAN governed less than one-half of 1 percent of Malaysia's exports to the group, but a comprehensive review by member states was under way in 1983 to promote further cooperation.

So-called countertrade arrangements, a form of international barter trade, received the prime minister's blessing in 1983 as a means of skirting increased protectionism from the industrialized countries. As of early 1984 Malaysia had negotiated barter deals with South Korea, Burma, Pakistan, Brazil, and Yugoslavia. The government has directed all economic agencies and affiliated corporations to introduce countertrade provisions in their procurement contracts.

Agriculture, Forestry, and Fishing

Long the mainstay of the traditional and colonial economies, the agriculture, forestry, and fishing sector continued to support

Tin mine: tin is becoming a less important export commodity for Malaysia, one of the world's oldest and largest producers. Courtesy Embassy of Malaysia, Washington

one-half of all Malaysian households in 1983. Favorable land and water resources provided for a diversity of activites, from less productive forms of shifting cultivation (see Glossary) to modern plantation agriculture. The vast majority of agricultural households, however, worked small landholdings of rubber trees, rice, coconuts, and oil palms. The methods and technologies employed on these smallholder farms depended on what they produced and how near they were to modern services and markets. The long-term trend, however, has been toward increased modernization and commercialization.

In early 1984 the government was preparing to announce the National Agricultural Policy, a program that had been debated for more than a decade, to improve the economic efficiency and equity of the farming sector. The government was concerned that the sector had grown by only 4.1 percent per year during the 1976–82 period compared with 6.2 percent during the much longer 1960–72 period. Controversy surrounded the policy, especially between those who argued for heavier investment in tree crops for export and those who favored food crops, more than one-half of which came from imports in 1982. Uneconomic cropping patterns, the small size of most smallholder farms, and the duplication of effort and disorganization of government agricultural authorities were major constraints on development. The new policy, however, was expected to be a set of government priorities for the future rather than a detailed program for investment.

Land Use and Tenure

The government has estimated that a little more than one-half of the 33 million hectares of land territory in Malaysia could eventually be cultivated, although an independent scholar has suggested that only 13.8 million hectares might be suitable. As of 1979, however, only 4.6 million hectares were under permanent cultivation, principally in the coastal and riverine lowlands and on the gentler of the upland slopes (see Environment, ch. 2). In Peninsular Malaysia about 4.1 million of 6.4 million hectares of potentially cultivable land were cropped, while in Sabah and Sarawak merely 453,000 out of an estimated 8.8 million hectares suitable for agriculture were cultivated. The figures for Sabah and Sarawak probably excluded extensive areas affected by shifting cultivation, and much of the undeveloped area consisted of upland terrain suitable primarily for tree crops. During the second half of the 1970s, some 80,000 hectares of new lands were brought into permanent cultivation each year on the peninsula; an average of 136,000 hectares were added each year to shifting and permanent cultivation areas in Sabah and Sarawak. This rate of expansion would probably continue in the 1980s until it seriously impinged on the nation's forests and watersheds (see Forestry, this ch.).

Shifting cultivation has persisted, either as an integral part of the culture of certain Malaysian ethnic groups or as one of several farming methods chosen for economic reasons. The growing of upland rice by this method has been essential to the ritual and belief systems of many Iban communities in Sarawak and to most of the Orang Asli (see Glossary) of the peninsula. Other groups, such as the Negrito of Peninsular Malaysia and the Punan of Sabah, have remained largely dependent on hunting and gathering. Many of the Temuan, Bajau, and Kadazan groups have used shifting cultivation as a supplement to what has become a basically sedentary form of agriculture.

The Food and Agriculture Organization (FAO) roughly estimated in 1980 that shifting cultivation supported 390,000 people on 1.6 million hectares of land in Sabah and 1.3 million people on

3.3 million hectares of territory in Sarawak. There were perhaps 44,000 shifting cultivators on the peninsula. Only one-tenth of the area affected by shifting cultivation was actively farmed in a given year because of the long period of fallow required. In some cases it was possible that the rotation cycle was longer than 10 years.

Upland or "hill" rice has been the principal crop for most shifting cultivators. Cassava and other food crops, however, might be cultivated as hedges against a poor rice harvest or for special purposes; rubber and pepper have tended to become permanent, but there was little information in 1983 suggesting the rate of changeover from shifting to settled agriculture. During the 1970s state agencies in Sabah and Sarawak developed 58,000 and 77,000 hectares of land, respectively, for permanent farming. The government planned to double this rate of development for Sabah and reduce that for Sarawak during the Fourth Malaysia Plan period.

Smallholder farm households numbered more than 636,000 in Peninsular Malaysia in 1980 and occupied more than 2 million hectares of land. About 426,000 households cultivated rubber trees; some 151,000 grew wetland rice; another 34,000 tended coconut trees; some 25,000 raised oil palms; and an unspecified number cultivated minor tree crops, managed small truck gardens, or reared livestock. The size of smallholder farms averaged about 2.2 hectares, but this average was biased upward in government statistics, which included holdings having as many as 40 hectares. The average wetland-rice farm, for example, was only 1.2 hectares in size. The most commercialized smallholder farms were those specializing in tree crops, market gardening, and livestock raising.

Plantation or estate agriculture was developed during the colonial period and concentrated almost exclusively on tree crops. In 1980 plantations covered about 608,000 hectares and averaged about 400 hectares per farm. Estate workers formed about 113,000 households, a 24-percent decrease since 1970. Many of the estates have broken into small holdings or smaller estates since the nation's independence. All but 64,000 hectares of foreign-owned plantations had been bought out by Malaysian interests as of 1982. Although the conditions on the larger estates have improved since the 1960s, there were reports in 1983 that workers on some small estates were abused.

Land tenure patterns were difficult to document in early 1984 because the relevant census and survey data were limited and out of date. The legal concept of private property was poorly developed among shifting cultivators, but communal ownership had also been rare. Generally, each extended family or household within a family established exclusive farming rights to the land it cleared. These rights of usufruct were passed on to the heirs in perpetuity. There was no basis, however, for holding or transferring legal title.

Smallholder tenure systems, by contrast, were based on a well-defined sense of property ownership, and tenancy arrangements have long existed. According to the 1970 census, in Peninsular Malaysia about 65 percent of all smallholder farms were operated by the owners themselves, some 24 percent were run by tenants, and the rest were run by a combination of owners and tenants. The size of the holdings in these categories average 2.3 hectares, 1.6 hectares, and 2.8 hectares, respectively. Exclusive of government land development schemes, Malays owned 58.6 percent of all smallholder farms, Chinese about 37.8 percent, and Indians another 2.8 percent. Malays occupied most of the government land development projects. Malay farm holdings averaged only 1.8 hectares in size, compared with 5.9 hectares for Chinese small holdings, many of which were actually small estates.

Land Development and Technical Support

Numerous federal and state agencies have been involved in the development of newly established and long-standing farms. In fact, coordinating the various programs for clearing new agricultural lands, constructing and maintaining irrigation facilities, supplying farm inputs, disseminating information about farm technologies, and storing and marketing produce has been a major chore for the Ministry of Agriculture and other agencies. Increasingly, the government has emphasized integrated approaches to agricultural development in specified project areas.

Land development and resettlement projects have been the most visible of the agricultural development programs. During the 1970s over 866,000 hectares of new land were developed, or about 97 percent of the targeted area. Three national agencies—the Federal Land Development Authority (FELDA), the Federal Land Consolidation and Rehabilitation Authority (FELCRA), and the Rubber Industry Smallholders' Development Authority (RISDA)—together accounted for 53 percent of the developed area. State agencies and private companies often acting in conjunction with government agencies developed the rest of the area (see table 14, Appendix). Federal and state programs resettled some 72,200 families during the decade; other programs employed some 142,000 workers. Public expenditure on land development averaged M$4,310 per hectare, whereas the annual return

Oil palms (left) are fast outpacing rubber (right) as the backbone of the agricultural economy.

Courtesy Frederica M. Bunge and Malaysia Tourist Development Corporation, Ministry of Trade and Industry

for beneficiary families on federal schemes averaged between M$800 and M$1,600 per hectare.

FELDA, which was established in 1958, has developed areas principally for oil palm and rubber production but has also established sugarcane, coffee, and, increasingly, cocoa farms and plantations. FELCRA was established in 1966 to rehabilitate and consolidate previously alienated lands that had fallen into disrepair or disuse. Legal problems concerning the agency's authority to redesign and consolidate holdings already under title forced the agency to duplicate some of FELDA's functions by developing unalienated lands near existing farms. RISDA has also concentrated more on rehabilitation and replanting than on new land development. The plan for the 1981–85 period was to increase the area developed to more than 108,000 hectares per year and to shift the emphasis from FELDA to FELCRA, state-run, and private operations.

Water supply and control have been the most important determinants of agricultural productivity in Malaysia, and since 1932 the Drainage and Irrigation Department has worked to modernize and expand the area served. During the 1970s the agency constructed 68,000 hectares of irrigation works, bringing the total coverage to 165,000 hectares serving 136,800 farm households in 1980. Almost all of these systems served rice farms. Drainage facilities have been important for tree crops, which are susceptible to root rot from water logging. Improved facilities were provided for 99,500 hectares during the 1970s, bringing the total area to 305,300 hectares. The work program for the 1981–85 period envisaged the addition of 9,000 hectares of irrigated land and the improvement of 16,000 hectares of existing facilities each year.

Other measures for improving the productivity of the farmland have included the introduction of high-yeilding crop varieties, agricultural chemicals, mechanized farm equipment, and new farming techniques. During the 1970s government agencies devoted 6.5 percent of the agricultural development budget to replanting some 302,900 hectares of crops, chiefly with improved varieties. This achievement represented about 77 percent of the area targeted. The consumption of chemical fertilizer expanded by more than 11 percent per year since the late 1950s to about 78 kilograms of nutrients per hectare in the late 1970s; gross consumption was about 1.3 million tons in 1982. Mechanization has become increasingly important, particularly on double-cropped rice fields, where power tillers have become common. New cropping techniques consisted of the miltiple cropping of rice and other crops, intercropping of food crops on tree-crop farms, and the complementary raising of livestock wherever possible.

The impetus for agricultural development came from a number of institutional arrangements and incentives. The government-run Agricultural Bank of Malaysia and various cooperative banks provided M$225 million of loans to finance farming activities in 1982. Outright subsidies on the procurement of farming supplies accounted for 2.2 percent of all agricultural development expenditures during the 1976–80 period and were expected to average 6 percent during the 1981–85 period. A national agricultural extension program completed during the 1970s trained nearly 6,000 agents, and their services reached 400,000 farm families in 1980. RISDA and other specialized agencies maintained their own extension staff. Six institutes and the Agricultural University of Malaysia trained an average of 37 professional and 1,400 technical staff each year during the 1970s. The nation's agricultural research facilities, spearheaded by the Malaysian Agricultural Research and Development Institute (MARDI), had a competent staff of favorable international repute.

In order to coordinate and integrate its support activities, since

1973 the government has been creating multipurpose farmers' cooperatives, which were under the national leadership of the Farmers' Organization Authority (FOA). The policy of the FOA was to delineate special development areas, which encompassed 2,000 to 4,000 hectares and served 1,000 to 2,500 smallholder households. In each area, one centrally located cooperative and development center was to provide facilities for the many agencies involved in agricultural support. The central cooperatives incorporated smaller unit cooperatives, many of which had been established years earlier. By the end of 1979 some 218,000 farmers belonged to 202 farmers' cooperatives, and an additional 123,000 farmers were associated with subsidiary cooperative societies that specialized in the processing of agricultural commodities. In early 1984 the government was developing 13 new integrated agricultural development authorities around the country at a level of organization larger than the cooperative.

Farm Production and Trade

The cultivation of rubber, oil palm, rice, and coconuts continued to dominate Malaysian agriculture in 1983 (see table 15, Appendix) Tree crops in particular generated the bulk of agricultural earnings at home and abroad. Although the prospects for Malaysia's exports of commercial crops seemed good even in the long run, the government nonetheless longed for the country to become self-sufficient in food production—still a distant goal. In 1980, for instance, the value of net food imports—excluding fish—reached about US$734 million, roughly 22 percent of the net value of commercial crop exports. This percentage was sharply lower than in 1975, but the cost of food imports had risen by nearly 11 percent per year during the five-year period.

Food and Livestock

Rice, in both its wetland and its dry-land varieties, has long been the dietary staple. Production in 1982 reached some 1.3 million tons of milled rice, compared with the consumption of 1.8 million tons for the year. The share produced locally was virtually unchanged from that in 1970. The shortfall, however, was primarily the result of drought conditions, and in 1980 as much as 92 percent of the nation's needs had been grown domestically. Production had increased by about 2 percent per year since the 1969–71 period. More than two-thirds of the increase could be attributed to improved yields, which reached about 2.8 tons per hectare in 1981—low by Asian standards. Yields on wetland farms, which made up 88 percent of the planted area, were some four and one-half times larger than those on dry-land farms. About 60 percent of the wetland area was double cropped, the off-season harvest accounting for about 37 percent of production.

In Peninsular Malaysia, which contributed about 86 percent of all rice production in the 1982 crop year (see Glossary), rice farms were clustered on the marshy lowland of Kedah and Perlis on the western side of the peninsula and on the steeper and drier plains of Kelantan on the eastern side (see fig. 6). In the west the 96,000 hectares of rice land managed by the Muda Agricultural Development Authority produced 35 percent of the nation's rice harvest in the 1982 crop year and had previously contributed more than 40 percent. In Kelantan an integrated project under the Kemubu Agricultural Development Authority spanned some 57,000 hectares of farmland and has produced from 7 to 8 percent of the annual crop. Virtually all of the farms in these projects were irrigated and double cropped, and yields were slightly higher than for other wet-rice areas. Although every state has developed some wet-rice cultivation, the area was especially small in Johore and the easternmost parts of Sabah and Sarawak. Almost all of the dry-land cultivation took place in Sabah and Sarawak, chiefly in the latter.

Most farmers sold their rice surpluses to private shopkeepers and agents from processing mills, but the influence of cooperative and government purchasing agents has grown steadily. The National Paddy and Rice Authority, established in 1971, was the sole importer of rice and also maintained a price-support system for domestic producers. Subsidies on the price of rice reached M$165.4 per ton on about 1.1 million tons purchased by the agency in 1982. The subsidy element alone in that year was equivalent to the export price of rice in neighboring Thailand. Even given the support price for rice, however, only those farmers who were able to grow two crops a year could normally earn enough income to stay above the government's poverty line. Rice farmers in the Kemubu project area staged violent protests in January 1980 to press for higher subsidies, and the government remained concerned about such sentiments in 1983.

Cassava, maize, sweet potatoes, sago, yams, and taro were less important starches than rice. Total production of such roots and tubers was about 507,000 tons in 1981 and had been growing slightly more rapidly than rice. Sago and cassava were especially important to the people of Sabah and Sarawak.

Sugarcane was grown for local consumption in most parts of the country, but only in Perak, Perlis, Negeri Sembilan, and, to a lesser extent, Johore was it of commercial significance. After dec-

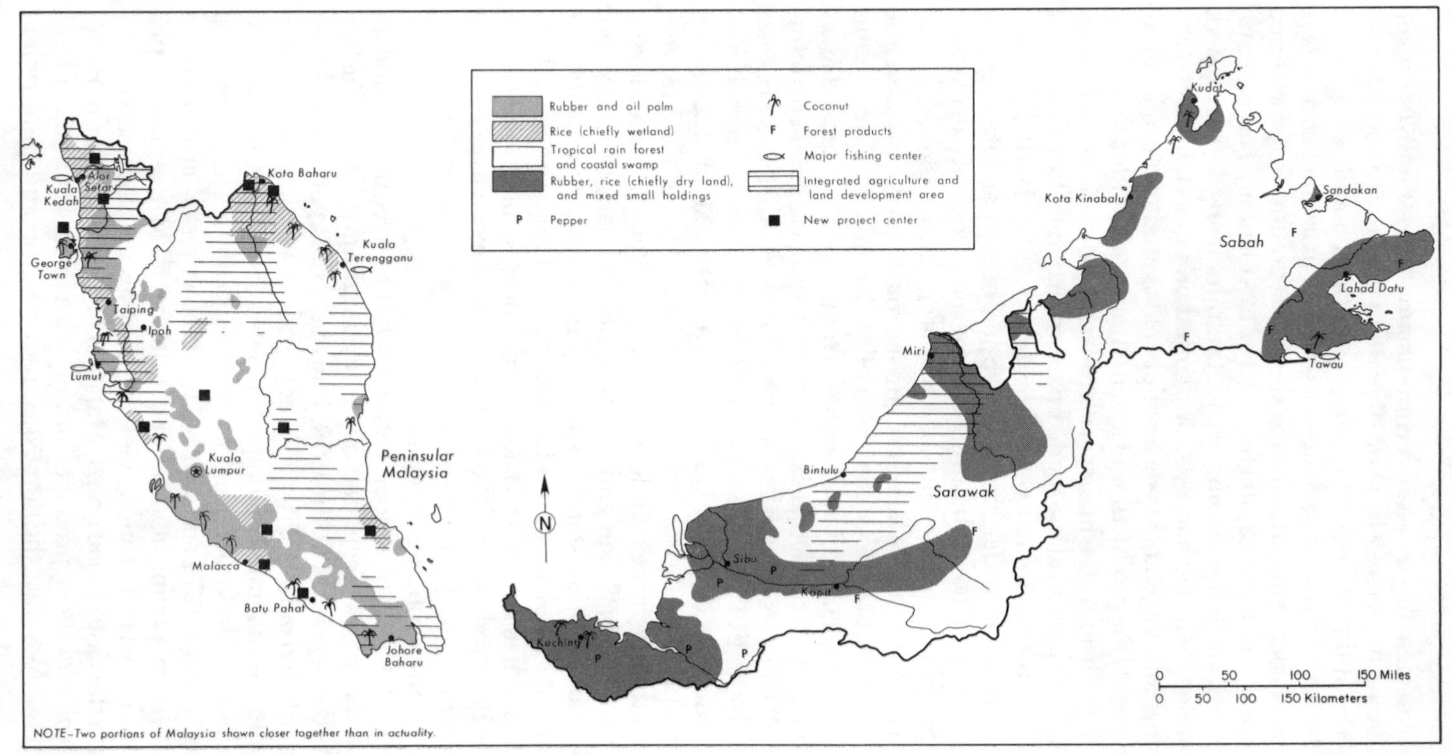

Figure 6. Agricultural Activity, 1983

ades of neglect, renewed government support in the 1970s caused production to increase by over 19 percent per year to 850,000 tons in 1981—still insufficient to meet domestic demand.

Oilseeds and pulses have been eschewed in favor of coconuts to produce cooking oils, but during the 1970s groundnut production expanded rapidly to 23,000 tons in 1981. Kelantan, Terengganu, and Perak were the leading areas, the nuts being intercropped, grown between rice harvests, or planted on upland fields.

Fruits and vegetables were widely cultivated in a profusion of varieties. Most production originated on smallholder farms, except for pineapples, which were grown on plantations for export. Banana production alone made up more than one-third of the 1.4 million tons of fruits and vegetables harvested in 1981.

Coconuts, like coffee, tea, and pepper, occupy an intermediate realm between food and purely commercial crops. An extremely versatile plant, the coconut may be eaten raw or cooked and its milk used to prepare Malaysian curries, or it may be pressed into copra for eventual processing into oil. Coconut trees are ubiquitous in Malaysia, and because small stands are often tucked away in settled areas, the actual extent of cultivation is difficult to determine. Estimates of the larger stands suggest that the area has grown little, if at all, to about 250,000 hectares in the early 1980s. Production has declined slightly on average to about 1.2 million tons of nuts in 1981, from which about 208,000 tons of copra were extracted. In contrast to developments in Peninsular Malaysia, new planting in Sabah and Sarawak has dramatically increased production in these states, especially from state-run plantations in Sarawak. Elsewhere, production was primarily from smallholders, who managed mixed stands of pepper, coconut, coffee, and cocoa. The production of the latter increased by nearly 22 percent per year during the 1970s to 35,000 tons in 1981, primarily because of intercropping programs.

The marketing of all food crops, with the exception of pineapples and rice, was regulated by the Federal Agricultural Marketing Authority (FAMA). In 1979, however, the agency purchased and marketed only M$2.9 million of produce—paltry by comparison with the amount sold on private markets. FAMA had also established seven processing centers for coffee, coconuts, and groundnuts by 1979 and was busy establishing other centers for cocoa, banana chips, and other products. FAMA regulated private trade by issuing and reviewing licenses for wholesalers.

As in the case of food crops, Malaysia has been a net importer of livestock and dairy products and of substantial amounts of livestock feed. Whereas the domestic production of pork, poultry, and eggs expanded rapidly in the 1970s to meet most of the nation's needs and to produce some 80 percent of the value of all livestock production, Malaysia imported 60 percent of its beef, about 75 percent of its mutton, and nearly all of its dairy requirements in 1981. Most of the increase in poultry and pork production has come from large, specialized farms having more than 40,000 chickens or 3,000 pigs per farm. Virtually all of the pork produced and consumed was accounted for by the Chinese ethnic community.

The Department of Veterinary Services under the Ministry of Agriculture and the National Livestock Development Authority were engaged in a large-scale program to import and crossbreed beef and dairy cattle and disseminate new breeds and management techniques around the country. The latter agency set up government-owned ventures to raise and market livestock and dairy products; the former concentrated on extension services, research, and development programs and has also set up milk collection centers.

Rubber and Palm Oil

Malaysia continued to be the world's largest producer and exporter of natural rubber in 1983 and has supplied routinely between 40 and 50 percent of the world's trade. In 1982 some 525,000 hectares of rubber trees were planted on private estates, about 389,000 hectares on public land development schemes, and some 1.1 million hectares on smallholder farms unaffiliated with government schemes. The area under private estate cultivation declined from over 64,000 hectares in 1970 as owners switched to oil palm and other crops or parceled off their holdings to small producers. Production declined after 1977 in the face of weak international demand until it stabilized at around 1.5 million tons during the 1981–83 period. Almost all of production was exported or stockpiled for future export.

About 84 percent of the planted area and 98 percent of production came from farms in Peninsular Malaysia, where yields were higher than in Sabah or Sarawak. The major areas were Johore, Selangor, and Negeri Sembilan, in decreasing order of importance. Replanting was taking place at the rate of about 7,000 hectares per year on estates and 23,000 hectares per year on small holdings. Yields averaged about 801 kilograms per hectare on small holdings and 1.3 tons per hectare on estates and have increased as improved varieties of trees came to represent 87 percent of the area planted in 1982. RISDA provided a replanting subsidy of M$5,436 per hectare for holdings under four hectares in size and a grant of M$3,707 per hectare for larger farms. Those replanting with oil palm or other crops could receive a smaller subsidy. The government reduced the export duty on cheaper grades of rubber in 1982 to reduce further the burden on poor smallholders.

The recovery of the automobile industry in the major industrial economies in 1983 was boosting the price for natural rubber internationally, and the government felt free to raise the export duty slightly. The recession of the early 1980s, however, caused many smaller producers to go bankrupt. Factory managers complained that fewer smallholders were coming forward to deliver supplies of needed raw material, and plantation owners found it difficult to employ sufficient numbers of tappers. Many hectares of rubber trees were abandoned by smallholders migrating to construction sites and urban areas. Others have been replaced with oil palm, a plant that takes about half the time to mature and for which prices have remained strong.

During the recession of the early 1980s many Malaysians came to call oil palm their "golden crop" because of its strong international demand. Almost all of the 3.5 million tons of palm oil produced in 1982 was exported and represented about 80 percent of the world market. For the first time, in 1982 palm oil earned a larger share of the nation's export revenues than rubber. From 1970 through 1981 production expanded by nearly 19 percent per year and jumped 24 percent in 1982. Most of the increase resulted from the expansion of the area under cultivation, but farmers have achieved substantial increases in yield by introducing weevils to pollinate the trees. The yields averaged 3.8 tons of oil per cultivated hectare in 1982.

The total area planted covered some 1.1 million hectares in 1982, of which some 908,000 were mature plants. Some 115,000 hectares were located in Sabah and 23,000 hectares in Sarawak, where yields were increasing most rapidly from a small base. Production estimates from 1978 showed that Johore and Penang each accounted for more than one-fourth of the area cultivated. Nearly 59 percent of the planted area that year was on private estates, and the remainder was on land development schemes. The latter were operated similarly to private estates, although smallholders could receive title to some of the land. The government was developing oil palm processing facilities so rapidly that it developed serious overcapacities in 1983.

The outlook for oil palm brightened in late 1983. Because of shortfalls in the production of soybeans in North America and coconuts in the Philippines, palm oil prices were rising. The possible uses for palm oil—normally to produce margarines, fats, lubricants, soaps, and plastics—were multiplying as scientists furthered their research. Drought conditions and some complications from the introduction of weevils, however, caused production to decline slightly in 1983.

Forestry

Timber, including sawn timber, continued to be Malaysia's second most important export in 1982, generating US$1.9 billion of revenue and representing 40 percent of all world trade in 1981. Sabah and Sarawak accounted, respectively, for 33 and 28 percent of production and for 54 and 40 percent of export volume. The depletion of easily accessible forest areas has caused production in Peninsular Malaysia to decline since 1980. The most common species extracted were dipterocarps—tropical hardwoods indigenous to Southeast Asia.

Ownership of the nation's forests rested chiefly in the hands of the state governments, but in practice the federal government has managed forestry production and conservation in Peninsular Malaysia while Sabah and Sarawak have maintained some autonomy. In 1978, however, the national government promulgated the National Forestry Policy to coordinate conservation activites in all the states, establish permanent forest reserves, slow the so-called logging rate, and rehabilitate logged-over areas. The policy proposed to reduce progressively the annual logging rate from about 366,000 hectares in 1978 to 149,000 hectares by 1985. Foresty rehabilitation was to equal the rate of deforestation.

As of 1983 some 4.6 million of the 6.3 million hectares of forests in Peninsular Malaysia had been classified as permanent forest reserves; about 1.9 million hectares were completely protected from forestry producers, while 2.7 million hectares were classified as productive and open to concessionaires. In Sabah there were 3.7 million hectares of permanent reserves and in Sarawak about 3.3 million hectares; the total forested area was unknown. The Forestry Department, which maintains offices in each state in Peninsular Malaysia, managed intensively an estimated 500,000 hectares of forested land in 1980. State authorities in Sarawak likewise managed production on 2 million hectares of forest reserves; Sabah had yet to set up carefully controlled reserves.

According to one government report, the logging rate for Malaysia as a whole decreased to about 176,000 hectares in 1982. The FAO estimated the rate of deforestation, that is, the transformation of forestland into agricultural and other uses, at about

90,000 hectares per year in Peninsular Malaysia, some 42,000 hectares per year in Sabah, and 86,000 hectares per year in Sarawak during the 1980–85 period. The annual rate of forest degradation (the destruction of forest through shifting cultivation and the overextraction of timber and charcoal resources) was estimated to be virtually nil in Peninsular Malaysia, with the exception of some valuable hardwood *meranti* species. Another FAO study has indicated considerable damage—from 14 to 40 percent of the forest cover—in logging areas in Sabah; extensive but indeterminate damage was also occurring in Sarawak.

Reforestation activities, by contrast, have been mediocre. During the 1971–80 period, only 4,770 hectares on average were reforested each year, and merely 1,270 hectares a year were newly planted. Most of the activity was confined to the peninsula, where additionally, some 7,000 hectares of industrial plantations had been established by 1980; the government hoped to develop 12,000 hectares of new plantations each year in the 1981–85 period. In Sabah there were some 18,000 hectares of plantations in 1980, and the government hoped to add 70,000 hectares of new plantations through 1985. Sarawak had developed no such plantations but was researching this matter. Most of the plantations were of tropical softwoods.

The major focus of conservation efforts in the 1980s was to control the felling of trees. As of 1982, however, production in Peninsular Malaysia was still 22 percent above the planned average of 8 million cubic meters per year for the decade as a whole. In the mid-1990s the annual output was supposed to stabilize at around 5.3 million cubic meters per year. Similar utilization plans had yet to be formulated for Sabah and Sarawak.

Fishing

Before the 1960s fishing remained basically a traditional economic activity confined to inner coastal waters and to small, unmotorized craft. Since Malaysia's independence, and especially in the 1970s, public and private investment has developed commercial trawling both within and beyond the Exclusive Economic Zone (see Glossary), which covered 138,700 square nautical miles to depths of 100 meters. The exploitation of these excellent marine resources, together with the development of a small fresh- and brackish-water aquiculture industry, caused the total fish catch to double from 1970 to 1982, reaching an estimated 683,000 tons. The catch, however, had been as high as 755,000 tons the year before. Fishery exports, chiefly of quality products such as prawns, generated about M$160 million in 1982.

Sawn timber is a major export commodity, especially from Sabah and Sarawak.

Courtesy Embassy of Malaysia, Washington

The government's development programs, spearheaded by the Fishery Department and the government-owned Fisheries Development Authority of Malaysia, have tended to benefit the operators of larger, modern vessels. There were some 30,000 fishing vessels under license in 1982, of which over 80 percent were motorized, but only 4,400 were trawlers. During the 1970s about 21,000 fishers—some 22 percent of the total number—received government subsidies averaging M$2,360 per person for the purchase of modern vessels and gear. The government also disbursed M$16.3 million to fishing cooperatives, which were reorganized in 1979 into 30 regional cooperatives serving 3,900 vessels. Fish-handling complexes were constructed at four sites and begun at five others in order to reduce the post-harvest spoilage rate, which in 1983 remained at between 10 and 20 percent of the total catch.

The management and conservation of fishing grounds were becoming increasingly important in the 1980s as resources along the coasts were depleted. The west coast fishery in the Strait of Malacca, where most of the fishing vessels operated, was particularly damaged. The government has restricted trawling to areas more than five nautical miles from the shore and announced that the area would be extended to 15 nautical miles by 1985. The government has also required that the mesh of trawling nets be more than 3.8 centimeters wide. The nation lacked sufficient marine police, however, to enforce these regulations to the letter. The growth prospects for the east coast fisheries of the peninsula and those off Sabah and Sarawak seemed good, but the fleet operating in those areas was the most antiquated.

Malaysia had nearly 1 million hectares of inland water bodies suitable for aquiculture, but as of 1978 it had failed to develop more than 10,000 hectares. The small aquicultural harvest of only 1,690 tons in 1982 suggested that little had been done to develop this potentially important fishery.

Industry and Services

Tin mining and rubber processing formed the basis of industrial development even in the early postcolonial period, but the manufacturing industry has spurred economic growth in the 1970s and 1980s. Much of manufacturing, however, depended on supplies of raw materials from domestic farms, mines, and oil and gas wells. Basic industry to produce the equipment and materials for light industry, moreover, relied to a great extent on imported components and was the main target for investment in the 1980s. Construction, transporation, communications, and other service industries grew primarily in response to developments in industry but were often critical themselves to the success of industrial ventures. The development of all of these nonagricultural sectors in areas outside of Kuala Lumpur, Penang, and other urban centers where they had been concentrated in the past was a major thrust of economic policy.

Manufacturing

Continued import substitution in industries producing processed foods, household appliances, furniture, and clothing, together with export promotion in those producing wood products, rubber products, textiles, and electric machinery, propelled the manufacturing sector to grow by some 12.5 percent per year during the 1970–80 period—about twice as fast as GDP (see table 16, Appendix). Emphasis on light industry helped generate new employment at more than one-half this rate of growth and reduce the nation's dependence on imported consumer products. Manufactures increased their share in the country's merchandise exports from 12 to 20 percent of the total value. The basic industrial structure, however, remained somewhat underdeveloped compared with some neighboring countries having lower per capita incomes than Malaysia. The industries developed in the 1970s remained dependent on imported components, contributed only modestly to the development of better technologies and skills, and did not attract sufficient numbers of domestic investors.

In the early 1980s the government launched a program of heavy industrialization designed to develop the internal economic linkages necessary for future growth. Making maximum use of the country's natural gas and hydroelectric resources and fostering the development of so-called ancillary industries, the program aimed to establish strategic heavy industrial projects in the less-developed areas of the country.

The main instrument for implementing the industrialization program was the Heavy Industries Corporation of Malaysia (HICOM), established in 1980. By 1983 HICOM had studied eight projects and had signed letters of intent with foreign contractors valued at M$3.3 billion. Four projects were under construction: a M$800-million sponge-iron and steel-billet plant located between Kuala Terengganu and Paka, a M$430-million cement plant on Langkawi Island in Kedah, another sponge-iron plant on Labuan Island in Sabah valued at M$450 million, and an automobile plant in the Federal Territory to cost M$560 million. Government and private investors were spending an additional M$3.6 million in 1983 to develop the infrastructure for these projects. Plans for an oil refinery and cold steel rolling plant were shelved indefinitely in 1983 as a result of the continuing economic recession and budgetary austerity measures.

The automobile plant, a joint venture with Japan's Mitsubishi Corporation, was expected to begin production in 1985 with a capacity of 80,000 vehicles per year; by 1988 production was projected to rise to 120,000 units. The venture would compete directly with the seven existing assembly plants that built some 80,000 cars per year in the early 1980s. The existing industry was extremely fragmented and, despite persistent government efforts to increase the local content, used imported components for some 85 percent of its final products. Critics of the government's ambitious plans have cited the need for heavy tariff protection, implemented in 1983, and the small size of the domestic market as evidence that the project would ultimately prove uneconomical.

The steel mill, to be fired by natural gas pumped from off the coast of Terengganu, was to produce 560,000 tons of billets from 600,000 tons of sponge iron, beginning in 1985. One other combined government and foreign joint venture and numerous smaller producers had 950,000 tons of capacity in 1983, mostly in the production of steel bars. The planned sponge-iron plant in Sabah was to produce solely for export. Both projects have come under criticism because of the potentially high cost of fuel and transportation and the less-than-optimal scale of production.

The cement industry, at least in Peninsular Malaysia, was in danger of building up too much capacity. Total capacity from the three big producers on the peninsula was about 2.8 million tons in 1983, just above domestic demand, but expansion projects and two new ventures would add at least 3.3 million tons by 1985. Domestic consumption, despite the strong demand from the construction industry, was expected to reach about 4.6 million tons that year. The HICOM undertaking included the construction of a port to enable substantial exports, and the success of this enterprise would depend on an increasingly glutted international market.

Other projects were developing in conjunction with the petroleum and gas industry. Chief among them was the natural gas liquefaction plant at Bintulu in Sarawak, where production was expected to reach 1.7 million tons in 1983 and to increase to 6 million tons by 1986. Although most of the liquid natural gas was to be shipped to Japan as part of a contract with a major investor, some would be diverted to a large-scale urea plant also to be located at the complex. The urea plant was a joint venture between Malaysia and other ASEAN members and would produce about 1,500 tons of urea per day beginning in 1985. Construction began in mid-1983, but until the plant was finished, the country would continue to be a net importer of chemical fertilizer. The National Petroleum Company (Petroliam Nasional Berhad—PETRONAS) began refining petroleum at its own small facility in Terengganu in 1983; the capacity was about 30,000 barrels per day (bpd). Two other refineries were foreign owned.

Private foreign investment caused the local electronics industry to boom in the 1970s, basically in the packaging of semiconductor chips produced and finished overseas. In the 1980s, however, new sophisticated products and processes were being developed in Malaysian factories, which remained, nevertheless, labor intensive. One large Hong Kong company was building a plant to produce computer peripherals on Penang Island that would employ 3,000 people starting in 1984. In order to make up for the lacking support industries, the investor was building plants to perform metal casting, stamping, and plating and automatic plastic molding. The scarcity of electrical engineers and the poor communications infrastructure in many of the industrial parks were hindering the development of these and other manufacturing industries.

Special incentives and relatively cheap and literate labor attracted much of this investment. Although a very rough indicator and an example of the poor state of industrial statistics, the record of investment approvals made by MIDA showed that M$15.3 billion had been earmarked for manufacturing during the 1970s. Most of these funds went to the food-processing industry but also in significant quantities to textile, electronics, and nonmetallic mineral manufacturing. Only 55 percent of the 4,226 ventures approved, however, were implemented. In 1981 and 1982 MIDA approved 1,094 projects totaling M$10.8 million; nonmetallic minerals, wood products, chemicals, food products, fabricated metals, textiles, and electronics were the major areas. About 42.5 percent of the investments in 1982 were to be located in the less-developed areas: Kedah, Perlis, Pahang, Kelantan, Terengganu, Sabah, Sarawak, and southeastern Johore.

Some of the incentives were associated with special free-trade zones and industrial parks (see International Finance and Trade, this ch.). By late 1982 Malaysia had developed nine free-trade zones, covering 434 hectares (see fig. 7). Four of the zones were completely filled, and the zone in Malacca was being expanded. The government has opened 45 industrial parks around the country, of which 26 were full to capacity in 1980. Despite these attempts to disperse industry, however, as of late 1983 only eight of the country's 107 largest manufacturers were located in the less-developed areas.

Small-scale firms, by far the most numerous form of manufacturing enterprise, have benefited little from government support relative to larger enterprises. The more than 10,000 manufacturers employing fewer than 50 workers received less than M$204 million in special government loans during the 1970s. Medium- and large-scale manufacturers received more than twice the amount of commercial loans per worker than did small enterprises. In an effort to streamline its programs for small manufacturers, in 1983 the government decided in principle to integrate the activities of 10 separate agencies into one small-scale enterprise corporation.

Mining

During the 1970s the mining sector experienced a fundamental structural shift as output from the fledgling petroleum industry increased to 63 percent of the total value. Petroleum exports rose to 21 percent of all foreign exchange earnings in 1980, surpassing rubber and tin, the previous leaders. The value of tin production, by contrast, decreased from 53 percent of all output in 1970 to 33 percent in 1980; tin exports represented just over 12 percent of export earnings in 1980. Part of this shift was financial, representing simply the rapid inflation of the price of crude petroleum after 1973; most of the increase, however, came from expanded physical output. The production of minerals of lesser importance, such as copper, iron ore, and bauxite, has declined on average.

Although the early inhabitants of Sarawak had used bituminous seepage to caulk their dugout vessels and to fuel primitive lanterns, not until the twentieth century did commercial production of petroleum begin in Malaysia. Exclusively under the control of foreign companies, production from one field in Sarawak peaked at 15,000 bpd in 1929 but declined through World War II and never fully recovered thereafter. Only in the 1960s, when exploration moved offshore, did the efforts of foreign oil companies pay off once again. By 1972 reserves totaling some 1.5 million barrels of crude oil had been located off Sabah, Sarawak, and Terengganu.

After the oil crisis of 1973, the Malaysian government moved to capture a greater share of the inflated profits of the oil industry. PETRONAS, created in 1974, required all foreign firms to sign production-sharing contracts that, including taxes, effectively channeled 92 percent of oil profits into government coffers. Because of the harsh terms, only two of the companies remained in Malaysia until the 1980s; these were the only two producers in 1983. Five foreign companies, however, were actively exploring blocks covering 31,450 square kilometers of the South China Sea in 1983. In addition, a PETRONAS subsidiary was exploring 19,800 square kilometers of territory. PETRONAS raised its estimate of recoverable crude oil reserves in 1982 to 2.5 billion barrels.

PETRONAS initially counseled the government to take a conservative approach to the depletion of the nation's oil reserves, suggesting that the optimal depletion rate would be about 250,000 bpd. The fall in international prices for the nation's exports, however, prompted the government to abandon this policy. Production was allowed to rise from 280,000 bpd in 1980 to 365,000 bpd in 1983 and was expected to reach 400,000 barrels per day by late 1984. In 1982 the local subsidiary of Shell Petroleum produced 58 percent of all crude output from more than 90 wells off Sarawak and four wells off Sabah. The subsidiary of Exxon Corporation expected to surpass Shell's level of production in 1983 by doubling the number of production platforms to 12 in its fields off Terengganu, where 110 individual wells were already in operation.

Natural gas was even more important to Malaysia's economic future than petroleum. Estimates in 1983 put the total commer-

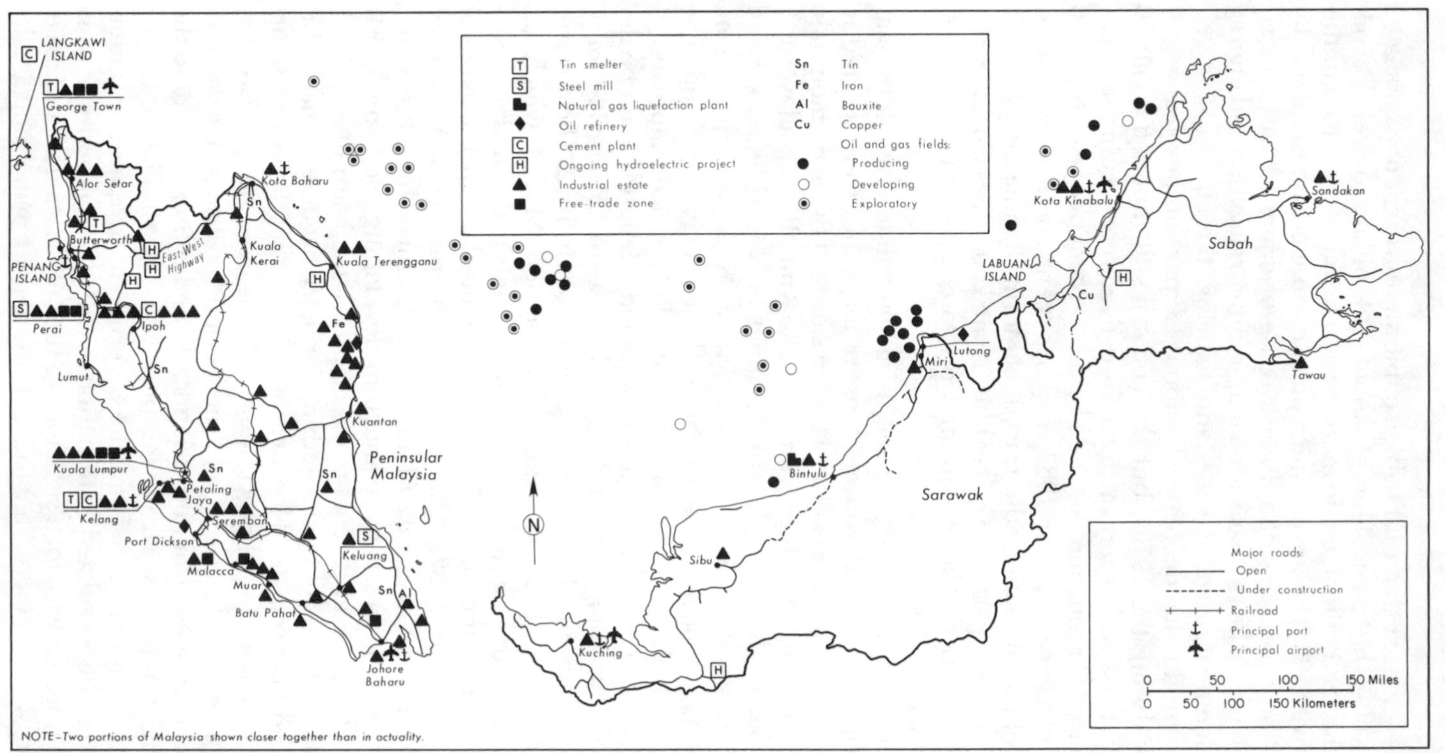

Figure 7. Industial Activity and Transportation, 1983

cial reserves at about 1.1 trillion cubic meters of gas not associated with oil—the equivalent of about 7.4 billion barrels of oil. Another 283 million cubic meters were estimated to be commingled with oil. The government planned to increase dramatically both the export and the domestic use of liquefied natural gas, which was to be the basis for a major industrialization and energy development program (see Manufacturing, this ch.).

Tin production decreased by about 1.8 percent per year on average during the 1970s, but the country still supplied about 30 percent of world exports. After a short-lived recovery in the 1977–80 period, production declined by 5.5 percent per year to 52,300 tons of concentrate in 1982; exports were about 48,600 tons. Gravel-pump mining, the traditional form dominated by ethnic Chinese, was particularly hard hit; some 250 mines closed in the 1980–82 period. The tin-mining work force fell from over 39,000 in 1980 to 28,500 in 1982.

The majority of the tin came from alluvial deposits both near the surface and underwater. Most of the mines were located in Perak and Selangor near the western slopes of the main mountain range; the chief producing area was the Kinta River Valley south of Ipoh. In the 1970s, however, mines in Negeri Sembilan and Pahang also became important. Mining was concentrated on lands having poorer grades of tin or those previously mined. The total available reserves were unknown, but if prices improved, it was possible that large undergrouond lode deposits could be developed economically. Altogether there were 521 gravel pump, 43 dredging, and 62 other mining operations in 1982. The government-owned Malaysian Mining Corporation (MMC), which has taken over the expired leases of foreign mining companies, was the largest in the world. The MMC produced over 16,000 tons of concentrate in 1982.. The largest mining project under way in 1983 was located at Kuala Langat in Selangor, where the MMC and private interests were joined in developing a lode mine that might produce 15 percent of the country's total output in 1985.

The problems of the tin-mining industry have been many. Investment has remained low because of fears that the international price might again fall precipitously. Costs have also increased as the price of oil has risen, and the federal tax structure tended to discourage states from releasing lands under their control to the mining companies. Heavy taxation was also stimulating the activities of smugglers, costing the government revenue and undermining the regulated international prices. Competition from China, which was not a signatory to the International Tin Agreement, was also increasing (see International Finance and Trade, this ch.). International buyers, moreover, were constantly developing new ways to economize on the use of tin.

In response to these problems, the government has introduced numerous measures to protect the declining industry. Taxes have been reduced and special production quotas granted to marginal producers. The government has subsidized the cost of diesel fuel and granted exemptions on the import of certain mining equipment. Despite the industry's problems, these measures and the nation's overwhelming resources were likely to maintain Malaysia's position as the world's largest producer for many years to come.

Copper, bauxite, and iron ore were the most significant of the many other lesser minerals produced in Malaysia. The nation has produced enough copper to export a small surplus since 1968, but only after the opening of a major mine in Sabah did production boom to nearly 129,000 tons of ore in 1982. In 1980 the estimated reserves were about 83 million tons of sufficient grade to produce 500,000 tons of copper concentrate. Bauxite production from two mines in Johore peaked at 1 million tons in 1970 but declined steadily to about 600,000 tons in 1982 after a drop in international demand. Diminishing iron ore reserves caused a steady decrease in production from about 950,000 tons of ore in 1971 to 342,000 tons in 1982. Sizable deposits of high-grade coal have been located in Sarawak but had yet to be tapped.

Construction and Utlitiies

Boosted by private and public investment, the housing industry expanded rapidly in the 1970s. Private developers tripled their production of medium- and high-priced houses to 40,000 units per year in the 1976–80 period and to 68,000 units in 1980; production fell to 20,000 units per year in the next two years. Public agencies constructed housing at a rate of 21,000 units per year over the decade; the government planned to increase production to 35,000 units per year in the 1981–85 period but was fulfilling only three-fourths of this goal in 1981 and 1982.

According to the 1980 census, about 17 percent of all urban households lived in apartments or rooms, and 44 percent were renters. About 24 percent of the dwellers in the Federal Territory—or 45,000 households—were illegal squatters. According to a private survey conducted in Peninsular Malaysia in 1979, only 9 percent of the whole population lived in detached or semidetached houses; about 21 lived above shops or in the increasingly popular complexes of row houses; only 4 percent resided in apartments or rooms; and the vast majority lived in traditional thatch- and tin-roofed houses. The number of households per dwelling unit was low by international standards: about 1.08 households in Peninsular Malaysia, 1.09 in Sarawak, and 1.10 in Sabah.

Investment in commercial facilities and public works projects also stimulated the construction industry, which grew more rapidly than GDP even during the recession of the early 1980s. The commercial area in the nation's four largest urban centers expanded by more than 50 percent in 1982. The public construction program continued to be spearheaded by the work on a bridge from the peninsula to Penang Island and by highway projects. The construction industry, however, was suffering from shortages of skilled labor.

Energy production, chiefly in the form of electricity, dominated the utilities industries. The demand for electricity grew by roughly 13 percent per year in the 1970s and exceeded 10,000 million kilowatt-hours in 1983. In July of that year, however, the minister of energy, telecommunications, and posts claimed that the country's total generating capacity of 2,400 megawatts exceeded the required level by 1,100 megawatts. About 89 percent of this generating capacity was located in Peninsular Malaysia, virtually all at facilities operated by the National Electricity Board; some 130 megawatts were installed at an independent utility in Perak and in small industrial plants. Sabah and Sarawak had their own separate utilities comprising about 160 megawatts each. Some 71 percent of the electrical capacity came from petroleum-fired plants, about 25 percent from hydroelectric facilities, and the remainder from gas-fired turbines.

Electricity investment in the 1980s was geared toward rural electrification programs. As of the end of 1980, only 55 percent of all rural households in Peninsular Malaysia had access to electricity, compared with 85 percent of urban households. The least developed states in Peninsular Malaysia were Pahang, Kelantan, Kedah, Johore, and Terengganu, where from 40 to 55 percent of all households were connected. Electricity reached only 29 percent of rural households in Sabah and a mere 2 percent in Sarawak. The government was undertaking a project financed by the World Bank (see Glossary) to provide 130,000 households in Kedah, Kelantan, Terengganu, and Pahang with electricity as part of a larger program to reach 300,000 additional households by 1985.

In order to ensure an adequate supply of electricity for industry and to reduce the dependence on oil-generated facilities, the government was developing a 900-megawatt gas-powered plant at Paka in Terengganu. In addition, there were major hydroelectric projects under construction in Perak, Terengganu,and Sabah, as well as numerous mini-hydroelectric schemes.

The water supply system also expanded rapidly in the 1970s, increasing to 59 percent the share of the population having access to safe water in 1980. Over 90 percent of all urban dwellers had such access, while rural coverage extended to 47 percent of the population in Peninsular Malaysia, some 25 percent in Sarawak, and 18 percent in Sabah. Modern sewerage systems, however, reached only 14 percent of the urban population on the peninsula—chiefly in Kuala Lumpur and George Town (also known as Penang). Investment in the 1980s was to continue the emphasis on water supply in the rural areas and smaller towns.

Transportation, Communications and Other Services

The number of motor vehicles in operation increased nearly fourfold from 1970 to 1982 to some 2.8 million, of which 1.7 million consisted of motorcycles, about 868,000 cars, and the remainder commercial vehicles. Such a rapid expansion of traffic, particularly in Peninsular Malaysia, required steady progress on the road network, which spanned some 32,000 kilometers in 1982. About 72 percent of the network was paved, chiefly in Peninsular Malaysia; less than half of the network in Sabah and Sarawak was paved. The major accomplishment of the roadbuilding program was the completion in 1982 of some 115 kilometers of the East-West Highway through rugged and hostile territory in Perak and Kelantan (see The Security Setting and the National Defense Concept, ch. 5). The new road would reduce the road distance from Butterworth to Kota Baharu by about two-thirds. The major projects for the 1981–85 period were the completion of the road from Kuala Kerai to Kuala Lumpur and the upgrading of the trunk networks in Sabah and Sarawak.

Railroad transportation expanded only half as rapidly as road transportation in the 1970s but remained important for bulk-cargo and long-distance passenger traffic. The Malayan Railway Administration, a government-owned company, began a long-term modernization program in 1971 and by 1982 had replaced some 90 steam engines with 138 diesel locomotives. In the late 1970s, however, there were an average of more than 100 derailments each year, and the west coast line, particularly between Kuala Lumpur and Seremban, was in dire need of double tracking. The precarious financial position of the railroad corporation, worsened by increased competition from the roadways made such an investment difficult. A small state-run railroad in Sabah was in even worse condition, handling a declining number of passengers and a stagnating volume of freight traffic. New equipment purchases in the mid-1970s, however, were maintaining it as a supplemental form of transportation in the 1980s.

Sea transportation has been essential to the economy, and the total volume of freight doubled during the 1970s to 21.9 million tons. Sabah and Sarawak handled 2.8 and 2.9 million tons of this volume, respectively. The government-owned Malaysia International Shipping Corporation expanded its fleet more than twelvefold during the 1970s and 1982 had vessels totaling more than 1.1 million deadweight tons, including five liquid natural gas tankers for the Bintulu export project (see Manufacturing this ch.). Despite this expansion, in 1980 the national carrier hauled only 18 percent of the total volume between Malaysia and Europe and had even smaller shares on other lines. Ongoing expansion projects at the ports of Kelang, Penang, Kota Kinabalu, Bintulu, and Sandakan were expected to increase their handling capacity from 17.4 million tons in 1980 to 20.7 million tons by 1985.

Air transportation, beginning from a smaller base of development than the other transportation networks, increased its traffic about fourfold during the 1970s to 6.5 million passengers and 52,000 tons of freight in 1980. The government-owned Malaysian Airline System (MAS), the only domestic carrier, had a fleet of 19 jets and 15 smaller aircraft in 1982, including five wide-bodied jets. The airports at Kuala Lumpur, Penang Island, Kota Kinabalu, and Kuching were equipped to handle wide-bodied craft, and Kota Baharu was expected to develop this capabiltiy in late 1983. Kuala Lumpur airport was being expanded to two passenger terminals that year.

Telecommunications facilities have improved markedly, the number of telephones increasing from one to almost four telephones per 100 people from 1970 to 1982. About one-quarter of applicants for telephone hookups, however, had to be put on a waiting list in 1980. Separate microwave networks linking all the main towns had been installed in Peninsular Malaysia and in Sabah and Sarawak. The two systems were themselves linked by satellite, radio, and undersea cable connections. The latter has also enabled the expansion of the television network to reach 53 percent of all households on the peninsula, about 35 percent of those in Sabah, and 27 percent of those in Sarawak.

The commercial marketing system that linked producers and consumers was in the hands of private traders, with the exception of some large-scale wholesaling operations in agriculture and mining. Retail outlets were generally small. Some 98 percent of all general-provision stores in Peninsular Malaysia in 1980 had no more than 30 square meters of space; two-thirds has less than 13 square meters. Larger stores, including some 50 supermarkets and about 60 department stores, were confined to the major urban centers of the Federal Territory, Penang, Ipoh, Johore Baharu, and the like. In these areas there was one such large facility for every 6,400 people in 1980.

Other modern sevices, such as finance and real estate, were also largely confined to the major urban centers. Tourism continued to generate about 1.1 percent of the GNP in 1980, and new tourist arrivals grew by more than 14 percent per year in the 1970s. Government services accounted for 14 percent of employment and more than 13 percent of GDP in 1980.

* * *

The most recent and comprehensive survey of the Malaysian economy is E.K Fisk and H. Osman-Rani's *The Political Economy of Malaysia*, in which articles of particular interest are Fisk's overview, "Development Planning." The outline and charting of economic policy and performance are found in numerous government documents, especially in the *Fourth Malaysia Plan, 1981–85* and the annual report from the Ministry of Finance, *Economic Report, 1983/84*. The annual report of the Central Bank of Malaysia (Bank Negara Malaysia), is also an excellent source of statistics and analysis. Numerous articles in the weekly *Far Eastern Economic Review* and the daily *Asian Wall Street Journal* follow the economy regularly. In particular, a special section entitled "Focus: Malaysia '81" in the August 28, 1981, edition of the former journal provides a state-by-state look at the economy. A thought-provoking but somewhat ideological critique of the country's economic development is offered in Jomo Kwanme Sundaram's "The Ascendance of Bureaucrat Capitalists in Malaysia." (For further information and complete citations, see Bibliography.)

Chapter 4. Government and Politics

Enameled porcelains such as this polychrome flower vase were made in China in the nineteenth century for use by ethnic Chinese inhabitants of the Malay Peninsula.

THE POLITICS AND GOVERNMENT of Malaysia bear an imprint of the British constitutional monarchy and parliamentary politics. The highest public official of the Federation of Malaysia is the paramount ruler, or king, but his constitutional role is more symbolic than substantive. The actual, day-to-day process of policymaking, supervision, and implementation with regard to the affairs of the nation is in the hands of the prime minister, who is concurrently the country's dominant political leader. Since independence in 1957 partisan political conflicts and competition have been resolved peacefully through general elections, and the transfer of power from one set of national leadership to another has been accomplished with no crisis of transition. There have been no coup d'etat or countercoups and, unlike the situation in some other countries of the world, the military has not been a significant factor in the political process.

In 1984 the dominant political party remained the United Malays National Organization (UMNO), founded in 1946 by Malay nationalists to safeguard their traditional political prerogatives from encroachment by non-Malays. UMNO was led by Dato' Seri Dr. Mahathir Mohamad, who had succeeded Datuk Hussein bin Onn as prime minister in 1981. As UMNO leader and prime minister, Hussein Onn had been preceded by Tun Abdul Razak (1970–76) and Tengku Abdul Rahman (1957–70).

UMNO's policy objectives were twofold—to consolidate national unity in a multiracial and multicultural society and to accelerate the pace of economic development so that all segments of the population could equitably share the benefits of nation-building. These objectives were dictated by the interracial tensions and the adverse consequences such tensions would have on the stability of civil and political orders. Accordingly, UMNO had found it imperative to soften its initial pro-Malay orientation and to form an interracial coalition with other political parties serving as the vehicles for various ethnic communities.

In 1984 this coalition arrangement worked through the National Front (Barison Nasional), a broadened version of an earlier coalition called the Alliance, first formed in 1952. The philosophical underpinning of the National Front continued to be that the search for national harmony should be carried out through mutual collaboration and with minimal infighting among the various racially inspired political organizations. Equally important was the National Front's commitment to the notion that poverty, perceived to be a major source of tension and disaffection, should be removed from all sectors of society irrespective of race.

Among the factors, actual and potential, affecting the stability of the nation was insurgency by factions of the communist movement. Also to be taken into account were potential backlashes caused either by Malay dissatisfaction with unfulfilled economic promises of the National Front government or by Chinese reaction against any economic or political measures that they might perceive to be blatantly anti-Chinese. From all indications the ultimate success of the coalition government in its efforts to bring about prosperity and interracial harmony appeared to hinge on its economic performance.

Malaysia's gradualist approach to nationbuilding is reflected also in its foreign policy orientation. Peace, moderation, and avoidance of conflicts with other countries remain conspicuous features of its foreign relations. In recent years an increasing emphasis has been placed on the promotion of regional cooperation within the framework of the Association of Southeast Asian Nations.

The Federal Constitution of Malaysia

In 1957 the newly independent Malaya proclaimed a constitution as the basic framework for a strong federation of 11 component states. The document was carefully crafted to nurture a British-patterned parliamentary democracy, to balance the conflicting interests of a racially divided society, and to ensure political harmony among the princely states traditionally ruled by hereditary sultans. The Constitution remained unaltered until 1963, when it was slightly revised and was named the Federal Constitution of Malaysia in order to account for the accession to Malaya of Singapore, Sarawak, and Sabah. When Singapore opted for separation from the federation in 1965, the basic law of the land was revised accordingly. The Constitution has since been amended from time to time to accommodate new political circumstances; the most recent of these amendments occurred in 1983 (see The Politics of Compromise, this ch.). The integrity of the Constitution as the fundamental set of guidelines and prescriptions continued to be respected in 1984 by nearly every segment of the population, regardless of racial or political differences.

The Constitution guarantees fundamental freedoms for peaceable assembly, speech and press, association, political participation, worship, and privacy of home, subject to restrictions by law only on grounds of national security, public order, or public morality. Since independence internal security has been the main reason for limitation of these freedoms. No person is to be deprived of life or liberty without due process of law. A citizen is not to be subjected to arbitary detention, double jeopardy, or retroactive application of criminal laws. In case of detention the arrested person must be expeditiously notified of cause, allowed counsel of choice, and arraigned before a magistrate within 24 hours of arrest; but in a state of emergency, constitutional safeguards may be withdrawn indefinitely unless the law granting emergency powers to the government is revoked by both houses of parliament.

Under the Constitution, Islam is the official religion of the nation, and Malaysian Muslims are legally bound by Islamic law, but other faiths are practiced freely without government discrimination. No one may be taxed to support a religion alien to his or her beliefs, and each religious group is entitled to regulate its own internal matters as it sees fit, to own property, and to establish and maintain its organizations and charities. All faiths are, however, subject to laws relating to public order, public health, and morality. Every citizen has the right to propagate his or her faith, and the freedom of conversion to Islam is not expressly forbidden; but attempts to proselytize among Muslims is banned.

The Constitution empowers the parliament to enact necessary laws to cope with both actual and potenial organized violence, with conditions likely to disturb public order and endanger national security, or with actual or potential situations abetting disaffection against the paramount ruler or any legally constituted authority in the nation. In the event of a grave emergency threatening the security or economic life of the federation or any part thereof, the government may exercise special emergency powers; these powers can be invoked, however, only after a state of emergency is declared by the paramount ruler on the advice and request of the cabinet or of the prime minister. The proclamation of an emergency and any related ordinance promulgated by the paramount ruler must be laid before the parliament for its consent. The proclamation is valid for six months unless revoked sooner by the federal legislature. While the proclamation is in force, the federal government may pass laws on matters that are reserved under the Constitution for a state government. These laws may not apply, however, to "any matter of Muslim law or the custom" in Sarawak or Sabah, nor should it extend to matters pertaining to religion, citzenship, or language.

The question of citizenship is given detailed and lengthy attention because of its broad ramifications. Citizenship comes under the legislative purview of the federal government. Four basic categories are established for acquistion of citizenship. First, citizenship can be obtained "by operation of law," that is, by persons who were citizens before August 31, 1957; by children of Malay parents; by persons born in the federation on or after August 31, 1957, but before October 1962; and by persons born on or after August 31, 1957, if one of the parents was a citizen or a permanent resident of the federation at the time of the person's birth. The second category is "by registration" of wives and children of citizens and of persons over the age of 18 who were born before August 31, 1957, provided they had resided in the federation for at least five of the preceding seven years, as well as those who had resided there for at least seven of the preceding 10 years. "Elementary" knowledge of the Malay language, good character, and a declared intention of permanent residency are also required.

The third category is through naturalization of persons 21 years old and over. Applicants must have good character and an "adequate" knowledge of Malay and have resided in the federation for at least 10 of the last 12 years, including the 12 months immediately preceding the date of application. They must also show intent to reside in the country permanently. Under the fourth category Malaysian citizenship may be extended by law to everyone born or naturalized in any state or new territory acceding to the federation of Malaysia. Citizenship may be terminated when a citizen has acquired the nationality of a foreign country or voted in the elections of other members in the Commonwealth of Nations.

Malaysia is a federation of 13 states. The principle of federalism as envisaged by the framers of the Constitution has a strong bias toward a centralized national government. This is manifest in the primacy of the federal parliament over state legislative assemblies.

The Constitution prescribes three kinds of legislative jurisdictions: federal, state, and concurrent. The federal category covers, inter alia, foreign affairs; national defense; internal security; civil and criminal law; justice; naturalization and citizenship; finance; trade, commerce, and industry; public works; census; science and technology; education; labor; public health; newspapers and publications; and censorship. The state list concerns Islamic law relating to personal and family matter; succession; marriage; maintenence; guardianship; religious courts; endowment and charities; control of missionary work among Muslims; Malay custom; land; agriculture and forestry; local government outside the area of the national capital; and state public works and roads. Sabah and Sarawak may also legislate on matters of native law and custom; operation of native courts; ports and harbors other than those under federal control, and, in the case of Sabah, the Sabah railroad.

The federal and state legislatures may exercise concurrent jurisdiciton over social welfare; child care; protection of women and juveniles; scholarships; protection of wildlife and national parks; animal husbandry; town and country planning; sanitation; and irrigation and soil conservation. For Sabah and Sarawak the concurrent list also covers personal and family law; adulteration of foodstuffs; shipping under 15 registered tons; hydroelectric power; agricultural and forestry research; charities in the states; theaters and films; and midterm local elections.

The concept of federal supremacy pervades the legislative process. The state jurisdiction notwithstanding, the federal government may enact a bill on any state subject—after previous consultation with the state or states concerned—when warranted by the conduct of foreign relations or by the need to promote uniformity of the laws of two or more states (in Peninsular Malaysia only) or when requested to do so by the legislature of any state government. Moreover, the Constitution stipulates that federal law shall take precedence over state law in case of inconsistency or conflict. In an effort to minimize friction, the state governments are directed to comply with any federal law applicable to the states and to refrain from undermining the authority of the federal government. In addition, the subject of national economic development remains under federal direction; the federal government may initiate a development plan in any area or areas in one or more of the states in consultation with the National Finance Council, the National Land Council, and the states concerned.

The Constitution is amended only by an act of the federal parliament. Procedures are complex, but generally a proposed amendment requires approval by a two-thirds majority in each house. Some bills affecting the rulers and governors of the states and the special privileges of Malays can be effected only with the consent of the Conference of Rulers. Some articles of special concern to the states of Sabah and Sarawak must have the concurrence of the governors of these states. Other articles, dealing with relatively unimportant matters, can be amended by a simple majority.

The Federal Government

Malaysia is headed by a constitutional monarch, the titular sovereign of the federation, whose function is analogous to that of Britain's monarch. The head of the government is the prime minister, who by convention enjoys the support of a majority political bloc in the federal parliament. Under the Constitution the power of government divides into the executive, legislative, and judicial categories.

The highest official of the federation is the *yang di-pertuan agong*, variously identified as the paramount ruler or the supreme head of the federation (see fig. 8). The paramount ruler is elected for a five-year term by the nine hereditary sultans of the federation from among themselves. Under the Constitution only these sultans may stand for and vote in the election. As a rule, the most senior sultan (based on dates of accession) is chosen, unless he is a minor, has declined to be elected, or has been determined by his peers to be unfit and incompetent. At least five affirmative votes are needed to become the constitutional monarch. Reelection is not allowed until the sultan of each state has been elected paramount ruler at least once.

The paramount ruler's powers are largely ceremonial. The executive authority of the federation is vested nominally in him, and all laws are supposed to be proclaimed and executed in his name, but he must act on the advice of the prime minister or of the cabinet. He may convene, prorogue, or dissolve parliament when so requested by the prime minister. Another formality is to appoint the prime minister in accordance with the British-influenced parliamentary convention, under which the head of the government is the leader of the majority party or of the coalition commanding a majority in the lower house of parliament.

Among the paramount ruler's other duties are those of giving royal assent to all bills passed by parliament, including constitutional amendments submitted to him for his signature; of exercising the power of pardon and reprieve for offenses triable by court-martial; and of appointing the lord president (chief justice), judges of the Supreme Court (called the Federal Court until mid-December 1983), and judges of the two second-echelon courts—the High Court in Malaya (for Peninsular Malaysia) and the High Court in Borneo (for Sarawak and Sabah).

Once in office the paramount ruler may not exercise any power as ruler of the state from which he originates. The power to amend the constitution of his state government remains unchanged, however. During his absence from the state, the ruler's power is delegated to a regent appointed by him.

The Constitution provides for the office of deputy paramount ruler of the federation, who is elected in the same way as the paramount ruler. The deputy remains the ceremonial ruler of his home state and carries out the functions of the paramount ruler in the event of the latter's disability or absence from the federation lasting over 15 days. In case the paramount ruler dies or resigns, the deputy becomes the first in line of succession by election through the Conference of Rulers.

The Conference of Rulers

The Conference of Rulers is composed of the nine hereditary sultans or rulers and the four state governors appointed nominally by the paramount ruler. Its functions are to elect the paramount ruler and his deputy; to give consent to or withhold it from any parliamentary bill affecting the privileges and honors of the nine sultans; to render advice on appointment involving high-ranking public officers; to agree or object to the extension of any religious acts, observances, or ceremonies to the federation; and to deliberate on national policy—in which case the paramount ruler of the federation and the sultans and governors of the states must be accompanied by the prime minister and the chief ministers of the state governments, respectively. In the election for the paramount ruler and his deputy, the governors are not allowed to vote.

Meeting three or four times a year in sessions lasting three days each, the Conference of Rulers exercises its right to advise and consent on matters affecting the alteration of state boundaries; the privileges, position, honors, and dignities of the rulers; religious questions; and any constitutional amendment bill concerning certain provisions of the Constitution. Consultation is mandatory in matters affecting the special position of the Malays and the natives of Sabah and Sarawak.

The Prime Minister and the Cabinet

The chief executive officer of the government is the prime minister, the leader of the dominant party or bloc in parliament. He must be a citizen of the federation by birth and a member of the House of Representatives, the lower chamber of parliament. The prime minister presides over the cabinet, the highest policymaking body, whose members he chooses from among the members of either house of parliament. The selection process takes into account not only individual talents but also considerations, governing political rewards and racial harmony.

The cabinet is collectively responsible to parliament, and if the prime minister loses the confidence of the lower house, he must either resign along with his cabinet or request the paramount ruler to dissolve the lower house; in either case, a general election must be held within 60 days in Peninsular Malaysia and within 90 days in Sabah and Sarawak. The prime minister is responsible for keeping the paramount ruler informed of the general administration of the federation and for advising him on the appointment of judges, the auditor general, and members of the Public Services Commission and of the Election Commission. He has a broad range of discretionary power in filling senior posts in the civil service.

The cabinet meets once a week in private, its decisions on public issues reached by consensus. Its decisions are implemented under the coordination of the secretary to the cabinet, who is concurrently the head of the Prime Minister's Department, the central office of the prime minister. The secretary is the only civil servant authorized by law to attend cabinet deliberations. Other senior officals of the government may participate by special invitation, depending on issues deliberated. In the absence of the prime minister, his duties are discharged by the deputy prime minister, who can be a member of either house of parliament. By convention the deputy prime minister is also the deputy president of the dominant UMNO and hence the second most powerful official of the government and the first in line of succession to the prime minister.

A cabinet minister is usually aided by three principal officers: deputy minister, parliamentary secretary, and political secretary. Whereas the first two can be members of parliament, the third need not be and may be appointed and dismissed at will by the prime minister. At the start of 1984 there were, apart from the prime minister and deputy prime minister, 22 ministers with portfolios and three without. The ministerial portfolios included agriculture; culture, youth, and sports; defense; education; energy, telecommunications, and posts; Federal Territory; finance; foreign affairs; health; home affairs; housing and local government; information; labor; land and regional development; national and rural development; primary industries; public enterprises; science, technology, and environment; trade and industry; transport; welfare services; and works and utilities.

The policies and actions of various ministries come under the general supervision of the Prime Minister's Department, the most pivotal focus within the bureaucracy. This department attends to the administrative needs of the cabinet and deals with apappointments involving such high-ranking officials as governors,

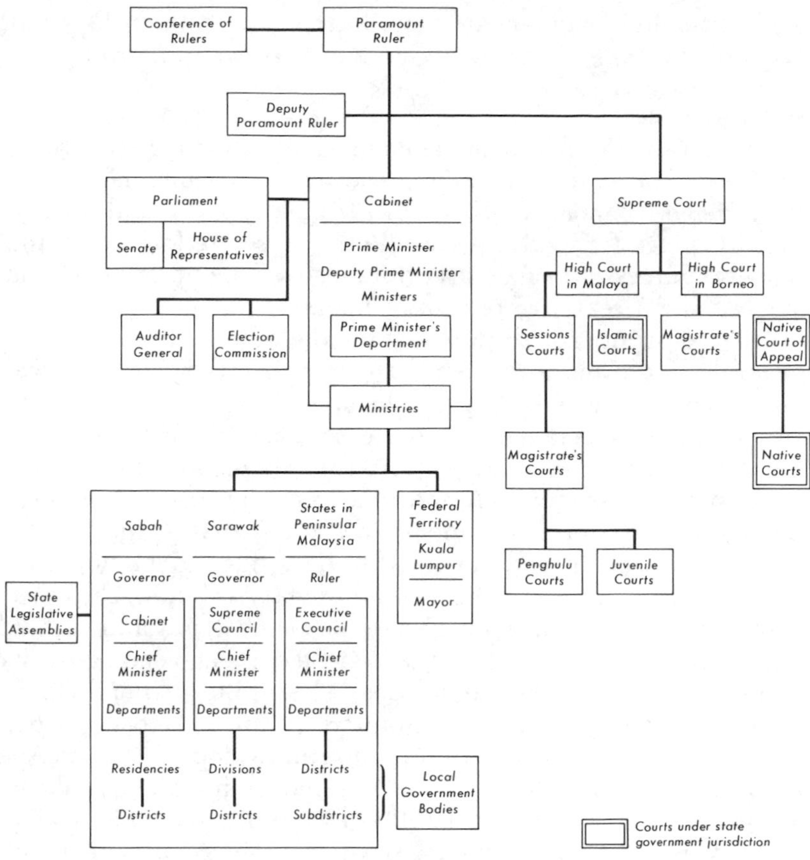

Figure 8. Governmental Organization, 1984

the president of the Senate, the Speaker of the House of Representatives, ministers and deputy ministers of the federal government, members of the Senate, parliamentary and political secretaries, and judges and the members of the constitutionally mandated commissions. This office also handles protocol; general services; administrative reforms and manpower planning; socioeconomic research relevant to economic development planning and living conditions; statistics; public complaints; petroleum development; and national security affairs. Another key function of the office is to monitor and evaluate the implemenation of the New Economic Policy (NEP) projects through its Economic Planning Unit, which serves as the central staff agency for national socioeconomic development planning (see Government Planning and Policy, ch. 3).

Statutory Bodies

There are three regulatory and consultative organs concerning matters of interest to both federal and state governments: the National Land Council, the National Finance Council, and the National Council for Local Government. These are formed by the representatives of the federal and state governments and convene at least once a year or as often as is necessary.

The Constitution also provides for the offices of the attorney general and the auditor general. The former is the principal legal officer and public prosecutor of the federation, rendering advisory opinion on legal matters to the paramount ruler, the prime minister, and the cabinet; the attorney general also drafts government bills for deliberation and enactment by parliament. Appointed by the paramount ruler on the advice of the prime minister, he must be a person qualified to be a judge of the Supreme Court; he may or may not be a member of the cabinet. The office of the auditor general, an independent agency with a sizable staff, scrutinizes the fiscal operations of both federal and state governments and of all public enterprises. The auditor general is formally appointed by the paramount ruler on the advice of the prime minister, and his appointment requires the concurrence of the Conference of Rulers. He can be removed from office only on grounds of misbehavior or disability. His audit reports for the federal government are submitted to the lower house of parliament and those on the state governments to the state legislative assemblies.

The Parliament

The federal parliament consists of two houses: The Senate (Dewan Negara) and the House of Representatives (Dewan Rakyat). The upper chamber has 68 members, of whom 26 are elected by the legislatures of the 13 state governments, two from each, and the balance are appointed by the paramount ruler on nomination by the prime minister. The nominees are those who "have rendered distinguished public service or have achieved distinction in the professions, commerce, industry, agriculture, cultural activities, or social service or are representatives of racial minorities or are capable of representing the interests of aborigines." The Senate is a continuous body, unaffected by the dissolution of the lower house. All of its members sit for six-year terms. The Constitution provides that parliament may increase

Parliament building, Kuala Lumpur
Courtesy Malaysia Tourist Development Corporation, Ministry of Trade and Industry

the number of elective senators from each state to three, change the current method of indirect election to a direct one, or decrease the number of appointive senators or abolish such members altogether. As of 1984 there were no basic changes in the composition of the Senate.

The House of Representatives has 154 members, who are directly elected from single-member constituencies for five-year terms—114 from Peninsular Malaysia and 16 and 24 from Sabah and Sarawak, respectively. The number of the lower house constituencies was raised to 176 under the constitutional amendment of 1983 to reflect a roughly 50-percent increase in eligible voters since 1973.

Each house selects its own officers—president and deputy president of the Senate, and Speaker and deputy Speaker of the lower chamber—and appoints committees for legislative processing. The Speaker may or may not be an elected member of the lower house; if not elected, the Speaker may not vote on any motion; otherwise, he may cast a tie-breaking vote. This procedure is designed to ensure the Speaker's impartiality in the legislative deliberation. Both houses make their own rules and pass bills usually by a simple majority of the members present. Parliamentary immunity is constitutionally ensured, subject to restriction only on the grounds of internal security, public order, or communal harmony. Parliament meets at least once every six months.

Bills may originate in either chamber, but money bills, which are drafted by the cabinet, are processed only by the House of Representatives. All bills are processed in three readings. Parliamentary bills require the consent of both houses before being submitted to the paramount ruler for his signature and publication in the official gazette. The paramount ruler does not have revisionary or veto power, but the Constitution sets no time limit for him to give royal assent. This means that he can block a bill from becoming law by withholding assent as long as he wishes, as was done for nearly five months in 1983 (see The Politics of Compromise, this ch.).

The Judiciary

The administration of justice is patterned after the common law tradition of Britain, as in most other member countries of the Commonwealth of Nations. Both in theory and in practice, the judiciary is independent of executive and legislative control. Except for the traditional Islamic courts, the judiciary is entirely under federal jurisdiction.

Judicial independence and integrity are secured in part by the constitutional provision governing the appointment, removal, tenure, and remuneration of judges. Morever, to prevent the judiciary from becoming embroiled in partisan politics, the Constitution bans parliament from discussing the conduct of a judge of the Supreme court or of the state-level high court, except on a substantive motion of which notice has been served by not less than one-fourth of the total members of parliament. State legislative assemblies may not question a judge's conduct under any circumstances. Barring misbehavior or disability, the judges of the Supreme Court and of the high courts hold office until age 65. They are appointed by the paramount ruler on the recommendation of the prime minister and in consultation with the Conference of Rulers.

The Supreme Court is the highest court of the federation. Its bench consists of the lord president (the chief justice), the two senior judges (called chief justices) of the two high courts, and four other judges. Situated in Kuala Lumpur, it has jurisdiction over appeals from decisions of the two high courts, over the constitutionality of laws enacted by the federal or state legislatures, over disputes between states or between the federal government and any of the state governments, and over constitutional questions referred to it by a lower court. In addition, the Supreme Court renders advisory opinion to the paramount ruler on request on any constitutional issue. The advisory opinion must be made public in open court. The bulk of the work load of the Supreme Court is concerned with appeals from the lower high courts.

Between 1957 and 1975 appeals from the Supreme Court were referred to the Judicial Committee of Her Majesty's Privy Council (Privy Council) in London on criminal, constitutional, and civil cases. Under 1976 legislation, such appeals were terminated for the first two of the cases, effective in January 1978. In 1983 the last of the judicial links with the Privy Council was abolished under a constitutional amendment. Prime Minister Mahathir stated that Malaysian judges had shown themselves to be fully competent to make "fair and wise judgements."

Below the Sureme Court are two courts of equal competence at the state level: the High court in Malaya, sitting in Kuala Lumpur, and the High Court in Boreno, sitting alternately in Kuching and in Kota Kinabalu. The former has 18 judges and the latter, five. These courts have unlimited orginal jurisdiction over criminal and civil cases and also exercise appellate, revisionary, and supervisory functions over all lower courts other than the Islamic and native courts. Decisions of the high courts may be brought before the Supreme Court.

In Peninsular Malaysia, other lower courts include the sessions courts, magistrate's courts, *penghulu* (village headman) courts, and juvenile courts. Located in major cities, the sessions courts try serious criminal and civil cases. The magistrate's courts are divided into first- and second-class categories and have criminal and civil jurisdiction. At the lowest level of the judiciary are the *penghulu* which handle minor village-level misdemeanors and civil disputes, usually through informal out-of-court procedures. At this level, disputes may also be taken to a magistrate's cour Through mutual agreement. The juvenile courts are for offenders under the age of 18. The Islamic courts come under state jurisdiction. Appeals from these courts are submitted to the sultan of the state concerned, the ultimate appellate authority in Islamic affairs.

In Sarawak and Sabah there is a separate system of native courts under the jurisdiction of the state governments. A breach of native law and custom (including Islamic law and custom) involving only natives is settled by the native courts. These courts may assume also a limited jurisdiction over religious and matrimonial cases if one of the parties is a native. Decisions of these courts may be taken to the native courts of appeal, which are presided over by high court judges. In Sabah the district officer may also serve as the final appellate authority. In these two states the federally mandated courts are the magistrate's courts, which divide into three classes, each with competence over criminal and civil cases appropriate to its classification.

The Public Services

Terms of service, salary, career development, pensions, and other benefits of government employees in the public services sector are the responsibility of the Public Services Department, described as the central personnel management agency of the federal government. Recruitment, appointment, promotion, transfer, and discipline, however, are handled directly by one of several commissions. These include the Public Service Commission, the Armed Forces Council, the Judicial and Legal Service Commission, the Police Force Commission, the Railway Service Commission, and the Education Service Commission. Personnel training is done by the National Institute of Public Administration, an arm of the Public Services Department. Employees of the state governments are subject to the operation of their own public services commissions, but some of these states transferred their responsibility for personnel administration to their federal counterpart with respect to certain categories of employees.

In the public services, Malays are given preferential treatment as stipulated in the Constitution, which calls on the paramount ruler to "ensure the reservation for Malays and natives of any of the states of Sabah and Sarawak of such proportion as he may deem reasonable of positions in the public services (other than the public services of a state) and of scholarships, exhibitions, and other similar educational or training privileges or special facilities given or accorded by the Federal Government." Under a constitutional amendment effected in 1971, any public discussion of the issues regarding "the special position of Malays and the legitimate interests of other communities" in the political process of the federation is expressly forbidden in an effort to minimize the possibility of communal disturbances.

State Government

The principle of government organization at the state level follows that of the federal level. The chief executives of the state governments are responsible to their respective assemblies—and by extension to the electorate—and not to the sultans and governors. For administrative purposes the federation is divided into 13 states and the Federal Territory—the national capital region.

Rulers and Governors

The rulers (or sultans) and governors are titular heads at the state level. Under the concept of constitutional monarchy applicable to both the federal and the state levels, the rulers and governors must act on the advice of their state-level cabinets, called executive councils, which are chaired by the chief ministers *(menteri besar)*. The heads of the nine states of Peninsular Malaysia—Johore, Kedah, Kelantan, Negeri Sembilan, Pahang, Perak, Perlis, Selangor, and Terengganu—are chosen through the customary practices of each dynasty. Eight of the nine inherit their titles from their father-predecessors, and the ruler of Negeri Sembilan is elected from among and by nine local Malay chiefs. Seven of the nine are called sultans, and the rulers of Perlis and Negeri Sembilan are known as raja and *yang di-pertuan besar*, respectively. The nine rulers hold office for life under normal circumstances.

Malacca, Penang, Sabah, and Sarawak are headed by governors, all of whom are appointed by the paramount ruler after consulting the states' chief ministers. The governors need not be Muslims but must be Malaysian citizens by birth. Appointed for four years at a time, they may be reappointed and may resign at any time, and they can be removed from office only by the paramount ruler after a resolution to that effect has been passed by the legislative assembly of the state concerned. These four officers are represented on the Conference of Rulers but do not participate in discussions relating to the status of hereditary state rulers or the election of the paramount ruler. The governors are not the titular heads of Islam in their states and hence do not concern themselves with the administration of Islamic law.

Executive Councils

The chief minister presides over the executive council (called the supreme council and the cabinet, respectively, in Sarawak and in Sabah). Invariably he is the leader of the dominant party or coalition whose mandate derives from victory in elections to the state legislative assemblies. His appointment as the executive head of the state administration by the ruler or governor is a foregone conclusion under the British-influenced traditon of parliamentary politics. The ruler's power of appointment here is ceremonial, and the chief minister cannot be removed from his office except through a vote of no confidence against him by the state legislative assembly, of which he is a member. A non-Malay can become a chief minister in a Malay state if he and his party win a state election and if he is a Malaysian citizen by birth.

The members of the executive bodies are named by the chief ministers and are collectively answerable to the legislative assemblies. They must resign in a bloc and be replaced when they lose the confidence of a majority of the legislatures or when the legislatures from which they are drawn are dissolved.

Legislative Assemblies

Each state legislative assembly bears the same relationship to the executive council as parliament bears to the cabinet of the federal level. All legislatures in the states are unicameral, their members elected popularly for five-year terms. They meet four or five times a year. State legislators are granted parliamentary immunity, and their official conduct may not be questioned in any court of law. A bill becomes law when assented to by the ruler or governor, such assent being strictly a matter of routine formality. At times, however, some rulers have withheld their assent to embarrass the state administrations whose chief ministers they did not like (see The Politics of Compromise, this ch.).

Local Government

In Peninsular Malyasia the states are divided into districts, each of which consists of five to 10 subdistricts called *mukim* (*daerah* in Kelantan) (see fig. 9). Each *mukim* is responsible for a varying number of kampongs (villages or compounds). In Sarawak divisions and districts are the main subdivisions, and their counterparts in Sabah are residencies and districts.

In both wings of the federation, the district serves as an important administrative arm of the federal and state governments. As in the British colonial era, it is headed by a district officer, who is popularly viewed as the personification of government authority. In Peninsular Malaysia he is a member of the civil service, reporting to the Ministry of Housing and Local Government through the state government. In Sarawak and Sabah he is a state government official whose activities are supervised and coordinated by an administrator (head of the division in Sarawak) and a resident (head of the residency in Sabah). Each district contains at least one officer on loan from each of the various federal ministries and the departments of state governments.

The district officer remains the most important link between the governing and governed. He is responsible for general administration and tax collection and occasionally exercises the judicial and police powers of a magistrate, though the trend has been to assign the law-and-order function to regular magistrates and police officers. His importance has grown in recent years because of new responsibilities for local development requiring close coordination and cooperation among the federal, state, and local authorities.

The *mukim* in Peninsular Malaysia may be a large, sparsely populated tract of land or may include several villages. It is headed by a *penghulu* (*penggawa* in Kelantan), a part-time official locally elected for five years or appointed by the state government to serve as the principal liaison between the district and the village. Assisted by several appointed functionaries, he reports to the district officer and receives a salary in addition to a remission of at least part of land rent. The village elects a chief (*ketua*).

The pattern of local self-rule varies widely both in name and in practice. For the most part, local bodies are appointed, the election of local councils having been suspended since 1963. They are variously known as municipal councils, city councils, town councils, town boards, district councils, rural district councils, and local councils. Several states of Peninsular Malaysia did away with local bodies for reasons of inefficiency and lack of resources to deal with schools, sanitation, health, roads, and town planning. These functions have been transferred to the district administration. Where the local bodies continue to function, they have limited revenue-fixing powers and are staffed by locally paid officials.

Kuala Lumpur, the national capital, has special status as the political, administrative, commercial, cultural, and educational center of the federation. Its mayor, appointed by the paramount ruler on the advice of the prime minister, is under the Ministry of Federal Territory and is assisted by an advisory board for the general administration of city affairs.

The Electoral System

Elections in Malaysia have been generally fair and free of violence, fraud, and government meddling. They continue to serve as the principal vehicle for peaceful resolution of partisan conflicts. The centrality of elections as the backbone of the federation's parliamentary system of government and politics has not been brought into question in any partisan debates about public issues.

The Constitution provides for an independent Election Commission, whose chairman and three other members may serve until the age of 65. These members are appointed formally by the paramount ruler based on the prime minister's recommendation

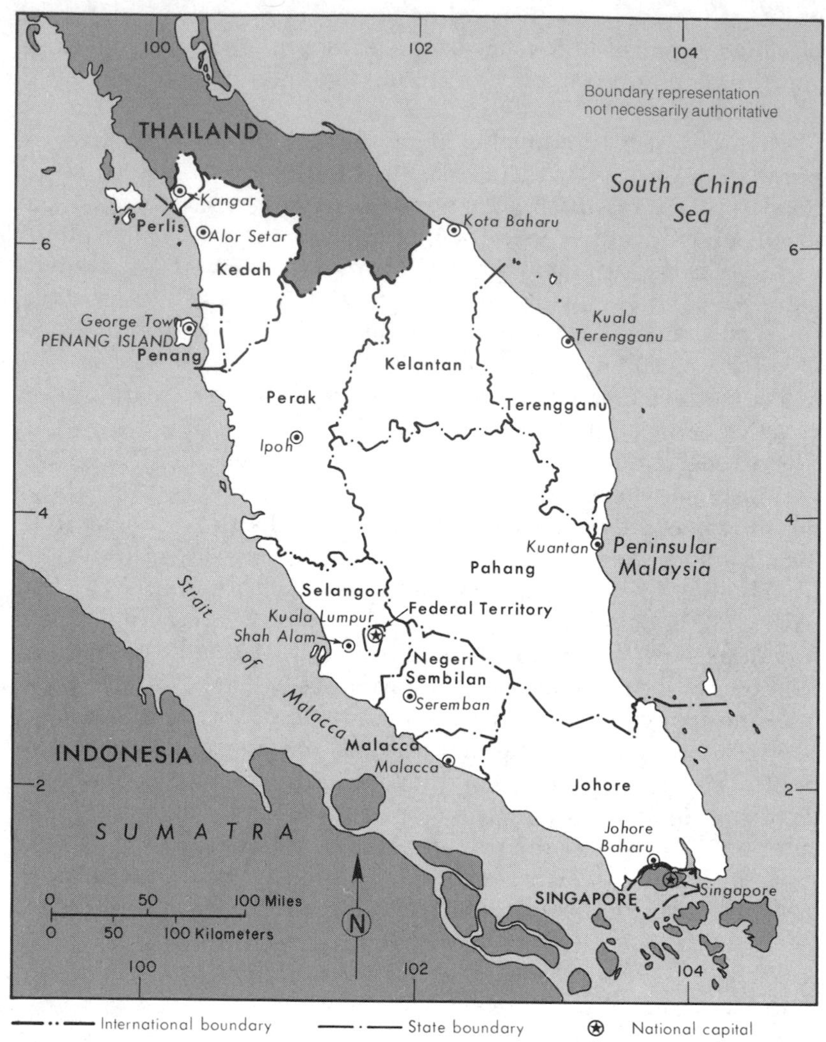

Figure 9. Administrative Divisions, 1984

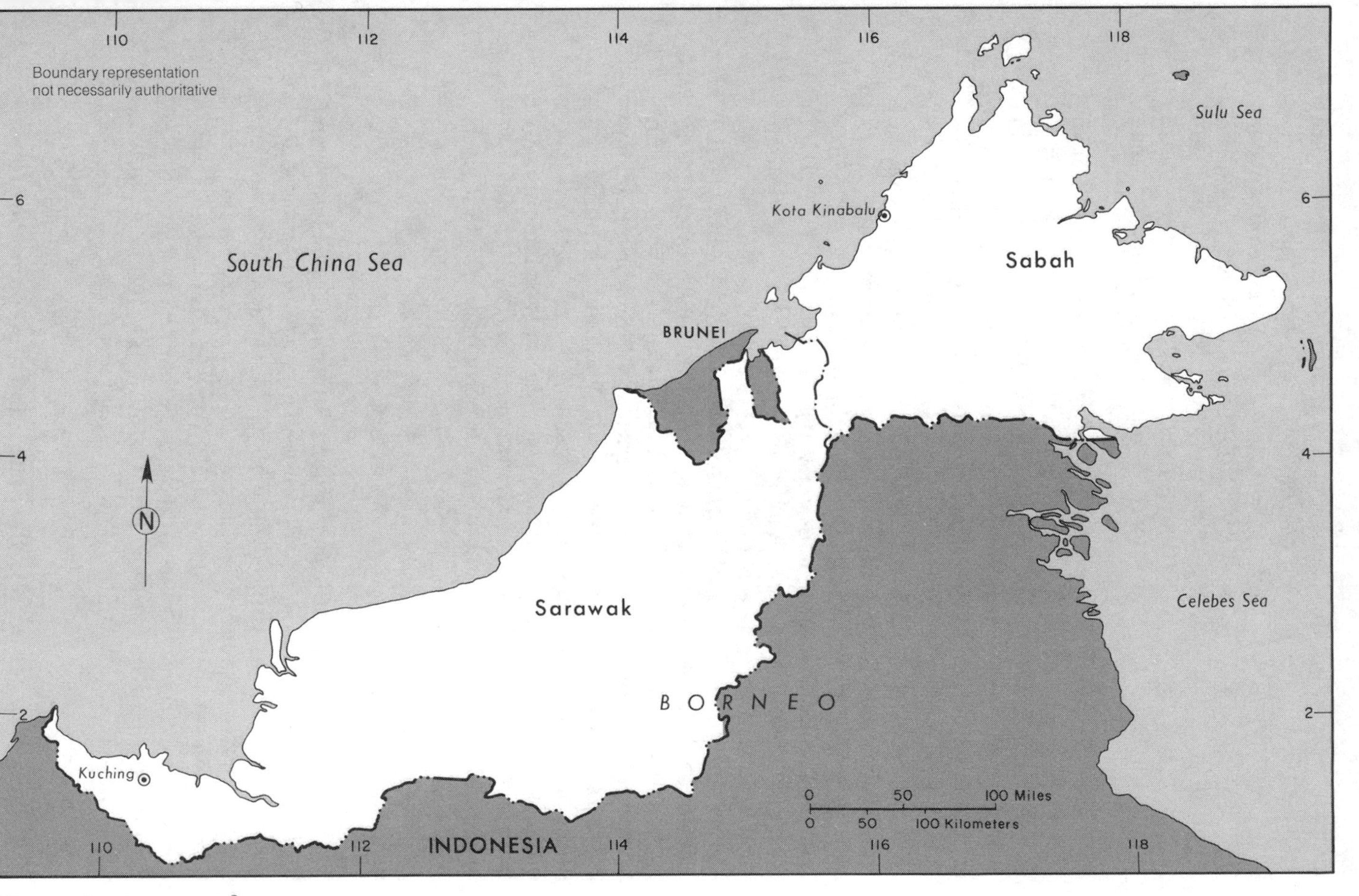

Figure 9 Continued.

and after consulting the Conference of Rulers. Because they are responsible for supervision of elections, nonpartisanship and integrity are essential to their appointment. They may resign at any time and can be removed only on grounds of misbehavior or other constitutionally stipulated reasons. The Election Commission prepares and revises electoral rolls and reapportions electoral constituencies at intervals of not more than 10 and not less than eight years.

In the redrawing of constituency boundaries, the number of voters as a rule must be approximately equal in each single-member constituency. The Constitution states, however, that "in some cases a rural constituency may contain as little as one-half of the electors [voters] of any urban constituency." Ostensibly, this so-called weightage system is necessary in view of what the Constitution calls "the greater difficulty of reaching electors in the rural districts and other disadvantages facing rural constituencies." Actually, this is designed to give the predominantly Malay-inhabited rural constituencies an advantage at the polls over Chinese voters insofar as well over one-half of Chinese in Peninsular Malaysia are urban dwellers.

Elections to the House of Representatives and the state legislative assemblies are held every five years, barring the dissolution of these bodies sooner than the scheduled dates. They are elected by secret ballot on the basis of universal adult franchise. Citizens 21 years of age and over are qualified to vote and to run for the lower house of parliament, state legislatures, and local self-governing bodies. Candidates for the upper house of parliament must be at least 30 years old. Senators are appointive as well as elective; in the latter case, they are chosen indirectly by the state legislatures.

Politics

Malaysian politics is still significantly influenced, as it had been throughout the 1970s, by the multiracial underpinnings of the society. National unity through interracial harmony and economic development continues to be the overriding objective of the multiracial ruling coalition, the National Front. Partisan conflicts are usually resolved peacefully through parliamentary process. Political opposition to the National Front continues to be vocal but has not been able to capture the popular imagination.

The Politics of Communalism

As independence neared, the British and the communal groups

sought in earnest a formula for ensuring interracial peace that they believed was critical in light of the massive communal carnage precipitated by the partition and independence of India in 1947. In the mid-1950s the leaders of the Malay, Chinese, and Indian communities reached an understanding that was to become the underpinning of the Constitution of 1957.

The intercommunal bargain,or compromise, was premised on the notion that the status quo—the political preeminence of Malays and the economic dominance of the Chinese—would not be altered but that in due course Malays would be encouraged to venture into the modern economic sphere, as would the Chinese and other non-Malays into the political domain. Under that bargain, the Constitution decreed that only a Malay could become the paramount ruler of the federation and that Malay sultans' privileges would be inviolable. Moreover, Islam—the faith of Malays—was established as the official religion, and Malay (Bahasa Malaysia) was designated as the national language. Malays, slightly outnumbering non-Malays, were given a two-to-one edge in voting power, assuring them of the dominant voice in the politics of representation. They were also to benefit from the constitutional stipulation for a preferential allocation of positions in the government services, of scholarships and other educational benefits, and of business opportunities. For non-Malays, citizenship qualifications were somewhat liberalized so that they could eventually play a more active role in the political process.

The interracial compromise scheme did little to narrow the communal distance, however. The constitutional provisions for the "special position of the Malays" came under Chinese attack as being discriminatory. Non-Malays argued that they too should be given protection in matters of language, education, and employment. They also contended that the poorest segments of the Chinese and Indian communities would be denied equal protection under the existing constitutional system.

Ranged against non-Malays were ethnocentric Malay militants, clamoring for the elimination of all non-Malay influence from Malay society. A growing number of economically deprived Malays blamed the Chinese for their hardships. In these circumstances the policy of national unity backed by the three-party interracial coalition known as the Alliance came under increasing pressure form both Malay and Chinese chauvinists.

Intercommunal tension continued to figure as a major political issue facing the federation. It led to the separation of Singapore from Malaysia in 1965, the racial rioting on the island of Penang in 1967, and the tragic violence of May 1969 in Kuala Lumpur, which was doubtless a major turning point in contemporary Malaysian politics (see The Creation of Malaysia, ch. 1). The massive rioting of May 1969 was directly responsible for the suspension of parliamentary rule. To prevent future rioting, the Alliance government initiated the New Economic Policy (NEP) as a remedy for the root cause of the riot—poverty among Malays.. The new policy was billed as an economic uplift program for all Malaysians, but it was perceived by non-Malays to be laden heavily with pro-Malay bias.

Parliamentary politics were reinstated in February 1971 under a new set of rules, however, that banned all communally inspired partisan politicking; public discussion of racially charged issues became liable to criminal prosecution under new emergency regualtions (see Security Offenses, ch. 5). The new rules meant in effect the hardening of existing interracial cleavages, giving rise to a flurry of debates among opposition parties on the wisdom of conditional cooperation with the ruling Alliance. Factional infighting within the opposition camp in 1971 and 1972 caused defections and splits, but the Alliance too had factional problems within, evidently because of its unexpected setbacks in the 1969 elections that had preceded the racial riots by three days.

The new National Front into which the Alliance coalition had regrouped in early 1974 consisted of 10 affiliated parties, including the three parties of the old Alliance. In the general election of August 1974 the National Front parties won handily at both federal and state levels; they appealed for popular support, promising the enhancement of interracial harmony. General voting patterns showed that Malays continued to vote for UMNO's Malay candidates, and nearly 50 percent of the urban Chinese cast ballots for candidates opposing the National Front.

Recent Political Developments

The concept of multiracial coalition rule as a gradualist vehicle for national integration remained unchanged under Datuk Hussein bin Onn, who was sworn in as prime minister in January 1976 following the death of Tun Abdul Razak (see The Federation of Malaysia, ch. 1). The Hussein Onn leadership was determined to defuse any racially or religiously motivated tensions, to suppress the communist subversions, to minimize excesses in partisan politicking, and to implement the NEP. In the elections of July 8, 1978, held concurrently at the federal and state levels, the ruling National Front parties won a clear-cut mandate for another five years.

The Hussein era was politically calm, though there were some minor problems. At the end of 1978 the massive influx of "boat people" from Vietnam threatened to become a considerable drain on Malaysia's resources; another complication was that because these refugees were mostly of Chinese origin, the already sensitive racial equation of the federation might become an issue if the boat people were allowed to settle in Malaysia. There was also a potential problem of subversive infiltration through the refugees. The Vietnamese invasion of Kampuchea at the end of 1978 and subsequent incursions by the Soviet Union into Afgahanistan became a concern on the part of Malaysian officials in charge of foreign affairs and national security. In October 1979 the government announced measures for strengthening national security capability. At the same time, Malaysia stepped up its diplomatic efforts regionally and elsewhere to seek a negotiated settlement of the Kampuchean question.

Assertiveness along racial and religious lines remained endemic. In 1978 Chinese guilds and clan associations pressed for the establishment of Merdeka University, a private institution where Chinese would be the medium of instruction. A parliamentary bill to that effect was introduced by the opposition Democratic Action Party (DAP), but it was defeated by an overwhelming margin (see Opposition Parties, this ch.). Another problem that surfaced in 1978 was an indication of Islamic revivalism in the east coast states of Peninsular Malaysia. The government warned of the dangers of Islamic "fanaticism" as a major divisive force.

In March 1979 the paramount ruler of the federation died, and in April the seventh constitutional monarch—His Majesty Tuanku Haji Ahmad Shah Al-Musta' in Billah ibni Al-Marhum Sultan Abu Bakar Ri'ayatuddin Al-Mu'adzam Shah [the sultan of Pahang]—was elected by the Conference of Rulers for a term of five years, expiring in April 1984. The new monarch—Ahmad Shah ibni Sultan Abu Bakar (as abbreviated)—reputedly the first popular constitutional monarch since independence—was formally installed in July 1980.

The Hussein Onn administration continued what might be called a preventive strategy in seeking to ensure fragile communal balance—and by extension political continuity and stability. In 1980 it ordered the Muslim Youth Movement of Malaysia (Angkatan Belia Islam Malaysia—ABIM) to sever its ties with foreign Islamic groups, which the government suspected as a possible source of incipient Islamic "fanaticism" in Malaysia. Another action taken in the year was the enactment of a law empowered the government to intervene in labor disputes, ban partisan politics within the labor movement, suspend unions on security grounds, and prosecute illegal strikers.

In April 1981 the government amended the 1966 Societies Act as part of its effort to depoliticize clubs, societies, and associations numbering in the thousands (see Communal and Social Issues, ch. 5). Under the amendment a group lobbying for changes in the policies or actions of the government would be classified "political," and, once so labeled, that group could not receive money from foreign sources or have noncitizens as members, nor could it have any foreign connections without government permmission. The amended version could also be stretched liberally to outlaw any group, organization, or society without recourse to judicial review. The amended Societies Act was subsequently modified somewhat in response to widespread criticism that as it stood it would have had the effect of banning anyone but politicians and political groups from commenting on political issues. The preventive strategy of the government was also evident in 1981 when the Constitution was amended so that the paramount ruler of the federation could declare a state of emergency in case of an "imminent" rather than actual threat to national security or to public order and peace. Emergency decrees issued while parliament was not in session were not to be challenged in the courts of law. The amended clause did not provide any express stipulation that the proclamation of emergency should be based on the advice of the prime minister and thus left open the possibility that the paramount ruler could act unilaterally. It was this possibility that figured in the government decision to amend the pertinent clause of the Constitution in 1983 (see The Politics of Compromise, this ch.).

An event of major significance in 1981 was the ascension to the prime ministership of Mahathir. This was the fourth time since independence that political power was transferred peacefully without any transitional crisis. The stage was set for this development in Malay 1981 when Hussein Onn announced—citing his ill health—his intention to step down and not to stand for reelection as president of UMNO. In June Mahathir, then deputy president of UMNO and deputy prime minister and Hussein's choice as successor, was elected unopposed by UMNO's general assembly as its new president. By convention the presidency of UMNO, meant automatically the premiership of the government. In a bitterly contested election for the deputy presidency of UMNO, Dato Musa Hitam, minister of education, defeated Tengku Tan Sri Razaleigh Hamzah, minister of finance. Customarily, the deputy president of UMNO fills the position of deputy prime minister on the government side; Musa Hitam assumed this post as

Prime Minister Dato' Seri Dr. Mahathir Mohamad (left) and Deputy Prime Minister Dato Musa Hitam (right) Courtesy Malaysian Information Services

well. The procedure for succession at the highest level of the government is clearly established and proved to be workable over the years.

In July 1981 Mahathir announced a new federal cabinet whose members were selected, as had been true in the past, to ensure the balance of communal interests as represented by the component parties of the ruling National Front. His administration reaffirmed its commitment to continue the basic policies of its predecessor concerning racial harmony and economic development. It was greeted, however, on a note of uncertainty and apprehension. This was because there were lingering suspicions among the Chinese that Mahathir and Musa Hitam were once widely regarded as Malay chauvinists.

The air of uncertaintly was tempered, however, by a vague and yet expectant mood for some reformist changes under the new prime minister. This could be ascribed to the fact that Mahathir had been reared in a political milieu different from that of his predecessors. Unlike the three prime ministers before him, Mahathir was a commoner who had no notable connection with any of the Malay royal houses, and he had not been schooled as a lawyer in Britain. A medical doctor by profession, his political career has been shaped through UMNO for the most part in post-independence years. Businesslike and decisive almost to the point of being blunt, he was regarded by many to be an idealist, reformer, and activist. Although his government did not break any new ground in the framing of policies, it proved more purposeful than its predecessors in its efforts to improve efficiency in government, to stamp out corruption from the public sectors, to scrutinize mismanaged and unprofitable government-owned Bumiputra (see Glossary) enterprises, and to curb political infighting at the federal and state levels.

In March 1982 Mahathir, "a man in a hurry," called a general election for April, more than a year earlier than scheduled by law. Evidently, he was eager to have his own mandate as soon as practicable; he allowed only 15 days for election campaigning. Given the dominance of the National Front, victory for his ruling coalition was a foregone conclusion; however, it was not certain whether the National Front under his leadership could come anywhere near the front's impressive electoral performance in 1974 and 1978. At stake in the election of April 22, 1982, were 154 seats in the House of Representatives and 312 seats in the 11 state legislative assemblies of Peninsular Malaysia. State elections in Sabah and Sarawak were not scheduled until 1984 and 1986, respectively. The National Front parties campaigned for popular support, promising "clean, efficient, and trustworthy" government.

The National Front parties confounded observers by scoring an overwhelming victory, returning 132 of the 154 federal seats and 281 of the 312 state seats. The victory was seen as the most solid mandate given to any administration since independence. The combined share of the vote received by the coalition parties increased from 55 percent in 1978 to 61 percent in 1982. The Mahathir administration claimed that the election results showed "a new awareness and understanding among the electorate of what the National Front government stands for." The 15-day campaign period for the April elections was the shortest since independence. Opposition parties were critical of the way the election was handled by the government, which permitted no outdoor public rallies, for security reasons. Moreover, the National Front candidates had decisive advantages partly because of their ready access to the largely progovernment media and partly because of government generosity in allowing them free use of public facilities for campaigning. The elections were peaceful and were not marred by untoward incidents.

There were some potentially significant developments surrounding the elections. Generally, candidates were younger and better educated than they had been previously. Of the nominees for UMNO, nearly half were new to electioneering, suggesting that the Mahathir leadership would not tolerate incompetence and indolence among the rank and file of UMNO organizations. Also noticeable was a portent of change in the composition of urban voters in larger cities. A growing number of Malays voted in urban constituencies of Kuala Lumpur; for example, Malay voters for the first time outnumbered Chinese voters in the 1982 elections.

Still another notable development was Mahathir's surprising announcement in late March 1982 that Anwar Ibrahim, president of the 40,000-member ABIM, was leaving his organization to join UMNO; shortly afterward, Anwar was nominated as a UMNO candidate for the House of Representatives. One of Malaysia's best known human rights and political activists—and a thorn in the side of the government for years—the 34-year-old Anwar was considered by many to be a moderate within the spectrum of Islamic revivalist movements in Malaysia. Many had also viewed him as a potential future leader of the Pan-Malaysia Islamic Party (better known by its Malaysian acronym, PAS—see Glossary), the main rival to UMNO in competition for Muslim votes. Anwar explained that his decision to affiliate with UMNO was based on his satisfaction with UMNO's commitment to Islamic values and his confidence in Mahathir's leadership in addressing the problems of corruption, inefficiency, and poverty.

As befitting the reputation of "a man in a hurry," the prime minister unveiled his new cabinet within a week after the election. There was some reshuffling in ministerial assignments, but changes were minimal, reflecting Mahathir's apparent desire to maintain political continuity and to embark on reforms in a gradual manner. Prudence was more by necessity than choice, for in Malaysia the cabinet is not just the top executive body of the federation; it is perhaps the most important political focus because it must be formed in a way that accomodates the needs of not only the National Front parties but also the 13 states of the federation. Harmony between the federal and state levels is always important because the roots of power for the UMNO-dominated National Front are embedded in the states (see Power Structure, this ch.).

The second echelon of government leadership showed a number of new faces. One of these was Anwar, a deputy minister who was assigned to the Prime Minister's Department. In September 1982 he surprised many within and outside UMNO by being elected president of UMNO's youth organization and vice president of the parent UMNO at their respective annual assemblies. His meteoric rise to the top of the UMNO machine was unprecedented—cause for dismay for dozens of loyal second-echelon UMNO aspirants to power; these loyalists were mostly in the youth wing of UMNO. In any case, Anwar became the minister of culture, youth, and sports in 1983—an object of speculation as a future prime minister of Malaysia.

The Politics of Compromise

In 1983 Malaysia faced the most serious constitutional crisis in the decades since independence. At stake was not only Mahathir's personal prestige but also the future of constitutional monarchy in a parliamentary democracy—not to mention the traditional Malay practice of resolving sociopolitical conflicts through consultation and consensus-building.

The crisis was occasioned by the passing in August of a constitutional amendment bill that contained changes in 22 clauses of the Constitution. The bill still required the paramount ruler's signature to become law. It had been rammed through parliament in uncharacteristic haste and without publicity, and the Mahathir administration offered no credible rational for some of the proposed amendments. Obviously, the bill was highly sensitive; otherwise, before it was sent to parliament the government would not have taken the precaution of warning the press about possible political backlashes. Prudently, the press avoided reporting on the most controversial aspects of the bill which were aimed, inter alia, at curtailing the formal role of the paramount ruler and other hereditary sultans in the legislative process. Specifically, the proposed bill would oblige the rulers at both federal and state levels to give their assent to legislation passed by parliament within 15 days. The contentious point was that such legislation would become law automatically, even in instances where assent was withheld. Unamended, the Constitution provides for no time limits for royal signature.

The rulers' displeasure was not surprising inasmuch as the constitutional amendment bill would have eliminated what seemed—at least to them, if not to the Mahathir administration—to be their last remaining political prerogative of major substance. Although the sultans are limited in theory to symbolic functions, some of the more strong-willed and independent rulers have been politically meddlesome at times, particularly when they have become disenchanted with the chief ministers of the state administrations over which, under the Constitution, they lacked political control. Unable to dismiss the chief ministers, some of the rulers at times have sought to stymie the state governments, usually by withholding assent to bills passed by state legislative assemblies. In the shadow of hostile palaces, the chief ministers would find it difficult to govern for long or effectively, and they found it necessary to resign. In 1977, for example, the sultan of Perak forced his chief minister to quit. In 1981, shortly after Mahathir became prime minister, two other chief ministers were forced to step down in the face of hostility from the ruler of Johore and Pahang.

It came as no surprise then that in Kuala Lumpur in late 1981 rumors were spreading that the Constitution might be amended soon to eliminate the possibility of royal interference in politics. Evidently, Mahathir and his advisers grew apprehensive about the prospect of a constitutional crisis at the federal level sometimes in or after 1984, The occasion of their concern was that the incumbent paramount ruler would be succeeded at the expiration of his term in April 1984 by the sultan of either Perak or Johore, both of whom were well known for their fierce independence and for their penchant for political involvement. In October 1981 the *Far Eastern Economic Review* was prophetic in its observation: "The new prime minster, seeking his own mandate as early as next year, has the unenviable task of preventing a constitutional crisis without promising that he would indeed like to prevent such crisis by changing the basic law of the land."

The collective displeasure of the state sultans with the constitutional amendment bill was reflected in the paramount ruler's refusal to sign it or, for that matter, any one of eight other parliamentary bills—one of which concerned budget appropriations for the fiscal year (FY—see Glossary) 1984. From sketchy reports, it appears that before the bill had been submitted to parliament in July 1983, Mahathir had been informally assured by the paramount ruler that he would consent to it. Under Article 34 of the Constitution, however, even with the unqualified backing of the prime minister, he alone cannot decided on any issue affecting "the privileges, position, honors or dignities of the rulers. The consent of the Conference of Rulers is required."

Mahathir came under criticism from some of the UMNO's rank-and-file members for handling the amendment issue without proper courtesy to the state rulers. It is not clear whether he wanted to present the amendment bill as an accomplished fact to the rulers or whether he underestimated the depth of likely resistance. It seemed quite probable that, unless resolved soon, the constitutional crisis would have some far-reaching and uncertain ramifications.

Opposition to the amendment bill was focused on another issue of major importance as well. Under the proposed change, the power to declare a state of emergency would be transferred from the paramount ruler to the prime minister in such a way that the latter could exercise that power without having to consult parliament, the cabinet, or the paramount ruler—and without reference to any judicial review. Other proposed changes were for the termination of civil appeal from the Supreme Court in Malaysia to the Privy Council in London, for the reapportionment of electoral constituencies at the federal and state levels, for the increase of parliamentary seats from 154 to 176, and for the renaming of the Federal Court as the Supreme Court.

Intense maneuvering continued on both sides through early December. The opponents argued that the government's amendment tactic was a breach of the Constitution, that "the fault of one or two rulers" should not be used to punish the others, and that the possibility of the constitutional monarchy's being replaced by a republic might no longer be idle speculation if the prime minister's unchallenged emergency power under the proposed amendment was allowed to stand. For its part the Mahathir regime sought to pressure the sultans through extensive publicity and public rallies; these were aimed at demonstrating that the people were behind the government and that the amendment was necessary to preserve the nation's constitutional monarchy. The government's effort in effect amounted to a massive public education campaign on what constitutionalism and parliamentary democracy were all about in Malaysia.

The gathering crisis was tempered by sobering thought on both sides. If unresolved by the end of December at the latest, the stalemate was certain to bring the government to an embarrassing halt, since the appropriations bill for 1984 was one of the bills left in limbo. There were also signs of growing restiveness within the UMNO hierarchy. No less at stake was the image of the royal houses—unflatteringly viewed by some Malaysians as an anachronism and, worse still, as being mainly concerned with preserving their own personal privileges at the expense of the public interest.

In the end, cool heads prevailed, both sides realizing that there would be no victors, only losers, in the constitutional impasse. On

December 15 the paramount ruler signed the disputed amendment bill and other parliamentary bills. There was one modification, however—extending the 15-day limit to 30 days, during which the monarch may send a bill back to parliament for reconsideration. The redeliberated bill, in whatever form, must then be signed within the next 30 days so that the bill may become law—with or without royal assent.

More specifically, as part of the quid pro quo the government promised to drop the clause that would have eliminated the sultans' power of assent at the state level. The paramount ruler reportedly gave a verbal "undertaking" that the sultans should not engage in any obstructionist tactic in state legislation. Another concession promised by the Mahathir regime was to restore the old provision that gave the power to declare an emergency to the paramount ruler; this was done on the paramount ruler's pledge that he would use that power only on the advice of the prime minister—not unilaterally. In January 1984 new legislation modifying the 1983 amendment was passed by an overwhelming majority, as promised by the Mahathir leadership. The crisis of constitutionalism had been defused through the politics of consultation and compromise. The *Far Eastern Economic Review* reported that Sri Delima, a noted Malaysian columnist, commented in the December 17 issue of the *New Straits Times:* "Victory belongs to both sides, to the *rakyat* (people) and to the system—the imperfect, bungling, cumbersome system of democracy we have opted for, grumble about, yet would not want to throw out."

Power Structure

In 1984 political power remained ethnically with Malays and institutionally with UMNO, the dominant Malay organization within the ruling National Front coalition. Although the term *coalition* suggests a partnership of equals, the preeminence of UMNO was beyond challenge, as had been true since independence. The legitimacy of power was confirmed through the constitutionally prescribed instrumentality of parliamentary elections.

The political power elite included a select body of federal- and state-level elected officials, the leaders and officers of the parties affiliated with UMNO, senior career government officials, and heads of the tribal communities in Sarawak and Sabah. Except for Malay royalty, which held a special place in the power hierarchy, access to the elite level was generally competitive, open to all aspirants with proven political skill or professional competence. More often than not, Malay citizenship by birth was essential in the competitive process. Wealth and royal background further enhanced the likelihood of ascendancy to the top layer of the power structure.

In Malaysia there are two axes of power—the politically dominant Malays and the economically dominant Chinese. They are complementary rather then exclusive. Generally, the Malay leaders continue to value, at least in the short run, the economic acumen and resources of the Chinese, who in turn benefit from the constitutional guarantee of free enterprise. As the government-sponsored enterprises for Malays produce beneficial results under the NEP, however, this interdependency will probably undergo a qualitiative change. More Malay ventures and success in banking, commerce, construction, finance, and transportation would likely mean broader bases of power for the Malays.

How soon this might happen remained unclear. The polarization of power into the political and economic categories with ethnic correlation continued in 1984. To be sure, there were a growing number of Malay entrepreneurs making inroads into economic functions previously in Chinese hands; from all indications, however, the pace of change was gradual, ruling out any radical alteration in the existing balance of political and economic powers.

The members of Malay royalty, grouped into the nine separate dynasties of Peninsular Malaysia continued in early 1984 to enjoy socially and politically the most prestigious status in the country. Prestige did not translate into political or economic power automatically, however. Although the sultans were financially well-to-do, their political role was limited to symbolic functions. (This constraint did not apply to other members of the royal houses who, as individual citizens, were entitled to all constitutionally guaranteed rights and freedoms.)

As a consequence of the constitutional crisis of 1983, it was possible that some of the sultans might become less assertive politically. Whatever the case, the sultans and their confidants were likely to remain an integral part of the Malay political elite; they continued to be the standard-bearers of Malay political supremacy, looked upon as the defenders of Malay customs and cultural tradition. Their privileges and honors were among the several matters of principle that were placed above any public questioning under a constitutional amendment adopted in 1971.

Influential members of the power structure consisted of the heads of federal government ministries grouped into the cabinet.

They were drawn primarily from UMNO's Supreme Council—the most powerful organ within that organization—and secondarily from other parties affiliated with the National Front. The composition of the cabinet, as well as the Supreme Council, had to reflect the pragmatic need for interracial balance, not to mention the relative political weight shown by various participant parties in the National Front. Also important was the need to accommodate the political and other interests associated with the 13 local centers of power, each the seat of a state government led by the chief minister. In 1984 all 13 chief ministers of the states were represented on the UMNO Supreme Council.

Below the state level were elected state assembly members, district officers, and village heads. These officials, together with the heads of UMNO branches at the appropriate levels, provided links through which local interests could be channeled to the top of state administrations—and eventually to the cabinet and the Supreme Council in Kuala Lumpur. This was the standard procedure in areas with a large Malay population; in predominantly non-Malay areas, representatives of other ethnic groups, in consultation with the local UMNO branches, articulated their particular interests.

Senior government officials, many of whom were Malays, could be regarded as members of the broadly defined political elite. Their expertise and experience were valuable to administrative and political continuity. Cabinet ministers relied on them for assistance in the formulation of policies and in the drafting of legislation. In order to ensure the professional integrity of the bureaucracy, career officials were forbidden to run for elective office or to take orders from politicians other than those serving as federal or state cabinet ministers. The principle of nonpartisanship applied also to members of the military and police forces. The military has not had a tradition of political activism and remains under civilian control.

Tribal chieftains in Sabah and Sarawak, unlike the Malay royalty of Peninsular Malaysia, have been allowed to retain considerable temporal power over administrative and judicial matters. In most cases they have been appointed by state governments from among those best fit to lead their tribal groups. In an effort to prevent the politicization of these groups, tribal chiefs have been required to step down before engaging in partisan political activities.

Political Parties

Political conflict or cooperation continues to take place largely within a multiparty system, which is characterized by the preponderance of one party, UMNO, over a multitude of minor parties. Most of the parties are affiliated with the ruling coalition, the National Front, and they are for the most part communally organized. Their relative strength, measured in terms of parliamentary representation, tends to correlate with the density of communal populations in different states. UMNO, which is the backbone of, and undisputed senior partner in, the National Front coalition, has by far the largest number of party branches. Other parties are geographically delimited.

The National Front Parties

In 1984 the National Front comprised 11 political parties, of which six were based in Peninsular Malaysia, three in Sarawak, and two in Sabah. Intra-front communications and coordination were handled by the front's top policymaking body, the Supreme Executive Committee. Each of the affiliated parties had at least three delegates on the committee, which was chaired by the president of UMNO—that is, the prime minister of federal government.

UMNO was founded in 1946 by a group of conservative Malays to promote Malay political interests. In 1952, however, it entered into a limited partnership with the Malayan Chinese Association (MCA) and in 1955 also with the Malayan Indian Congress (MIC). This three-party partnership came to be known as the Alliance. The show of intercommunal solidarity was believed to be essential because Malaya was scheduled for independence two years later. In 1974 the Alliance was absorbed into a broader, new coalition called the National Front.

As of early 1984 UMNO continued to return the single largest bloc of members in elections to the House of Representatives (see table 17, Appendix). Its top policymaking Supreme Council consisted of 27 members, including the president, deputy president, and five vice presidents, who were elected every three years by delegates to the general assembly of the party. The general assembly, in theory the highest party organ, meets annually to deliberate on a wide range of issues. By convention senior members of the Supreme Council were also members of the federal cabinet. They continued to have an important say in the distribution of cabinet posts among the various component parties of the National Front; this was also the case in the selection process for UMNO candidates in general elections.

UMNO stood for intercommunal harmony and cooperation but at the same time sought to advance the "case for the Malays." Its leaders were particularly committed to the protection of the Malays' special position with regard to government employment, education, language, commercial licenses, and preferential land policies. Another major concern of UMNO was to propagate the culture and religion of the Malays among non-Malay communites. UMNO's annually reaffirmed platform calls for faith in God, loyalty to the paramount ruler and the federation, justice and discipline, neutrality and self-reliance in foreign affairs, and the establishment of "Malaysian democracy."

As of mid-1982 UMNO had 1 million party members according to its monthly organ, *Merdeka*. This showed a startling increase of 65 percent in less than one year. The monthly claimed that the sharp increase was attributable to growing popular confidence in Mahathir's leadership as well as to the belief of Malays that only UMNO could fulfill their needs and aspirations. Many of the new members were said to be youths and intellectuals. Party members were under the guidance and direction of the Supreme Council, the State Liaison Committee, divisional committees, and branch committees. They were assigned to various party units concerned with such functions as finance, economy, social affairs, education, religion, labor, youth, and women. The UMNO youth group doubled as the principal training ground for future party leadership.

The MCA was formed in 1949 by a group of businessmen as the main political instrument of the Chinese community. In 1984 it remained the major Chinese party. The MCA appeared to have support from a majority of its ethnic constituents, who believed that their interests could best be advanced within the UMNO-dominated government. This view could be changed, depending not only on the MCA's effectiveness as the major communal agent but also on UMNO's ability to assuage both manifest and latent Chinese apprehensions about the government's economic and educational policies.

Undeniably, however, the premise of equating economic security with interracial collaboration has been questioned by a considerable number of Chinese. In the 1950s and 1960s the MCA's partnership with the Alliance was criticized as a sellout by its younger members. From the mid-1960s a growing number of Chinese intellectuals and ethnocentric activists argued that the "capitalist" MCA was unable to address the needs of the poorest sections of the Chinese community. Popular dissatisfaction, coupled with MCA's inability to attract the younger members of the community, was responsible for the organization's electoral setback in 1959 and for the substantial gains of other Chinese-dominated parties campaigning against the Alliance in general and the MCA in particular. In 1974 the MCA made a strong recovery and became the second most important component of the new National Front coalition government.

Within the Chinese community the MCA was opposed after the mid-1960s by the Democratic Action Party (DAP), which proved to be more popular among the younger and the urban Chinese voters. DAP's share of the vote in constituencies with a predominantly Chinese population was roughly equal to that of the MCA. In 1978 it returned seven out of 10 parliamentary seats it contested against the MCA; in 1982, however, the MCA won nine out of 12 seats in head-to-head contests against its arch rival. In both elections the votes received by both parties showed no appreciable change. Generally, the MCA has done better than DAP because it has not fielded as many candidates as DAP. Moreover, the MCA has benefited from being an UMNO partner; its candidates in the rural and semiurban constituencies can get elected with a relatively small number of votes under Malaysia's electoral weightage system, an advantage denied to the largely urban-based DAP (see The Electoral System, this ch.). In the 1982 election the MCA evidently received far more votes from the urban Chinese than in any previous elections. It is suggested that many Chinese became convinced that their suspicion of Mahathir as a Malay chauvinist was unfounded and that therefore a policy of cooperation rather than comfrontation would likely yield more benefits.

A third Chinese group competing with the MCA and DAP for the popular vote was the People's Movement of Malaysia (Gerakan Rakyat Malaysia—more frequently known as Gerakan). Gerakan, led since 1980 by Lim Keng-Yaik, was formed in 1968 by a group of Chinese and Malay politicians and intellectuals as a noncommunal, moderately socialist alternative to the Alliance. Although predominantly Chinese in membership, it appealed to Chinese as well as Malays with a program calling for special aid to the economically depressed Malays and other indigenous peoples. Much of the support for Gerakan came from intellecturals and urban workers; geographically, however, this group was based in the state of Penang and has been unable to attract support from outside of the state. In any case it scored an impressive electoral success in 1969 and won the mandate to rule in Penang, which became the first state in Peninsular Malaysia to be placed under a Chinese chief minister. It was widely believed at the time that the race riots of 1969 were precipitated in part by Gerakan's victory marches and by the inflammatory effects these had had on Malays. In 1972 Gerakan became the first opposition party to enter the Alliance coalition. Two years later it joined the new National Front coalition.

In the early 1980s political competition among Gerakan, the MCA, and DAP was as intense as ever. Personality clashes and difference over issues were frequently sources of factional infighting both within and among the three groups. In 1981, for example, the MCA's former deputy president, Michael Chen, crossed over to Gerakan with a large following. A sizable number of Gerakan and DAP members shifted their allegiance to the MCA in 1981.

Indians, the third major ethnic group, have been represented since 1946 by the MIC. Their primary concern has been to secure representation in the federal cabinet and to raise their living standards within the framework of the NEP. In early 1984 the MIC was led by Datuk Samy Vellu.

The Malaysian Front Islamic Council (better known by its Malaysian acronym, Berjasa) is a Kelantan-based Islamic party. It was founded by Dato Haji Mohamad Nasir in late 1977 after he and his moderate faction broke away from the Pan-Malaysia Islamic Party (PAS). At the time of his expulsion, Nasir was the chief minister of the Kelantan state government. In the elections for Kelantan's state assembly in March 1978, Berjasa entered into electoral alliance with the National Front and returned 11 delegates to the 36-member state legislative assembly. In mid-1980 it became a National Front partner at the federal level but in the parliamentary election of 1982 failed to win any seats.

In the early 1980s politics in Sarawak continued to be dominated by the same parties that had been active in the mid-1970s. These were the United Conservative Bumiputra Party (Parti Pesaka Bumiputra Bersatu—PPBB), the Sarawak National Party (SNAP), and the Sarawak United People's Party (SUPP). All three were affiliated with the National Front at the federal level and together were in control of the Sarawak state government through the ruling coalition called the Sarawak National Front.

The PPBB was formed in 1973 as a merger of parties that had previously represented Malays and indigenous groups in Sarawak. Its political objective is to secure the same special privileges and safeguards for the indigenous peoples of Sarawak as are available for Malays in Peninsular Malaysia. SNAP was organized in 1961 by conservative and ethnocentric Bidayuh and Iban leaders to promote their sociopolitical and economic interests. The SUPP began in 1959 as a multiracial organization seeking support from nearly all races. Initially, it has some support from Iban and Malays, but its leaders and most of its members were Chinese. It remains essentially a Chinese movement, drawing its support mostly from the more ethnocentric elements among the economically weak and undereducated Chinese.

In Sabah the Sabah People's Union (Bersatu Rakyat Jelata Sabah—Berjaya) became the dominant party by winning 10 of the 16 parliamentary seats assigned to that state in the 1982 election. Berjaya (meaning victory or success in Malay) was formed in 1975 with firm encouragement from the federal government to counter the autocratic rule of Datu (later Tun) Mustapha. It joined the National Front coalition in 1976. At the state level it was opposed by the United Sabah National Organization (USNO), which was also a member of the National Front at the federal level. In the 1982 election USNO lost all five seats it contested.

Opposition Parties

In the early 1980s opposition parties continued to have difficulty in mounting an effective show of strength. The National Front parties have had the advantage of being in power at the federal and state levels for over a decade. The difficulty of the opposition has been compounded by the legal restrictions placed on debating communally sensitive issues; public utterance of words interpreted by the authorities as likely to generate feelings of ill will or hostility between ethnic groups has been cause for police arrest and prosecution under the laws dealing with internal security and sedition. Moreover, personality conflicts and policy differences have made it difficult for opposition groups to organize a united front or to enter into an electoral alliance. Electoral pacts were possible in some instances but produced few results.

In 1984 the leading opposition group was DAP. Chinese in leadership, DAP was formed in 1965 as a noncommunal, moderately socialist movement drawing the bulk of its support from intellectuals and non-Malay voters—largely young, liberal Chinese in urban areas and some of the economically weaker rural Chinese as well. It made a strong showing in the 1969 elections at the expense of the conservative MCA. The election results of 1974 indicated that DAP had the support of the majority of urban Chinese voters, suggesting that it became the chief beneficiary of growing Chinese apprehensions about the NEP. The party's electoral support was strongest in Perak, Penang, Malacca, and Negeri Sembilan. In 1978 DAP captured 16 federal seats, but in the 1982 elections it won only nine. One notable aspect of the 1982 elections was that DAP won two federal seats in Sarawak and one in Sabah, thereby becoming the first Peninsular Malaysia-based political party to establish a political beachhead in those states.

PAS is another major opposition group. In 1982 it won only five federal seats (four in Kelantan and one in Kedah) out of the 82 seats it contested. Nonetheless, PAS' potential as a leading challenger to UMNO could not be overlooked, if only because of its identification with Islam, even though such identification also happens to be an important rationale for UMNO.

PAS can be traced back to the late 1940s when it was launched by Islamic leaders, theologians, and ultranationalists as the Malayan Muslim Party. Initially, it worked through UMNO but split from it in disagreement over UMNO's proposal to grant citizenship automatically to all persons born in Malaya, a proposal that would have opened the door to an expanded political role for the Chinese. PAS' electoral strength was noticeable in the predominantly Malay states of Kelantan and Terengganu, and after its strong electoral showing in 1959, PAS not only captured political power in these two states but also laid the groundwork for its challenge to UMNO's claims to be the sole agent of Malay hopes and interests. The conservative Islamic party also showed pockets of strength in Pahang, Perak, Selangor, and Kedah.

PAS' success in 1959 was attributed to a combination of circumstances. Its candidates identified themselves with the hopes and frustrations of poor rural Malays, among whom Islam held a powerful appeal as a vehicle for political mobilization. PAS portrayed UMNO politicians as self-seeking, factionally preoccupied agents of a distant elitist bureaucracy settled snugly in Kuala Lumpur, inattentive and unresponsive to grass-roots problems. They used the mosque as a readily available channel for discussion and articulation of village issues. In 1969 PAS managed to retain power in Kelantan and to improve its strength in Kedah, Terengganu, and Perlis, despite UMNO's efforts to dislodge it from these strongholds. After 1971, however, UMNO's visible shift to a more pro-Malay posture—undoubtedly in reaction to the object lessons of the 1969 elections and riots—might well have put PAS on the defensive. PAS had to reassess its political options in light of the constitutional amendment in 1971, the NEP, and possibly even discreet suggestions by influential UMNO members for UMNO-PAS cooperation. In December 1972 PAS delegates voted for collaboration with UMNO at the federal and state levels and in the following month joined the UMNO-dominanted Alliance. Proponents defended the move as a practical though temporary means of ensuring access to aditional development funds and of bolstering PAS' strength, whereas opponents argued that collaboration was a betrayal of party principles. In 1974 PAS continued its partnership with

UMNO through the new National Front and scored impressive gains in the general elections held in August of that year-winning all but one of the seats it contested—13 parliamentary seats and 49 assembly seats.

The alliance with UMNO did not mean the end of frictions with the senior partner, however. In late 1977 a factional split within PAS involving the National Front led to the formation of a breakaway, pro-UMNO party (Berjasa); furthermore, PAS was expelled from the National Front. In 1978 PAS suffered a major electoral setback at both federal and state levels. The bitter aspect of the setback was that of the 36 assembly seats in Kelantan, PAS managed to return only two as compared with Berjasa's 11; UMNO won 22, and MCA one. PAS losts its strongest power base since independence. In 1982 it was unable to recover its former electoral strength; its share of the popular vote decreased from 17 percent in 1978 to 14.5 percent in 1982. Before the 1982 election PAS had refused the invitation to rejoin the National Front. Its definance was cause for UMNO's charges that PAS' fundamentalist posture was politically divisive.

Foreign Affairs

Malaysian foreign relations have been influenced by diverse factors, such as anticommunism, anticolonialism, opposition to racial discrimination, nonalignment, regional cooperation, and critical dependence on free trade. These factors have dictated the cultivation of friendly relations with all countries irrespective of ideological and political differences. Pragmatism and flexibility remain essential to the formulation and execution of foreign policy.

The Evolution of Foreign Policy

Malaysia's costly struggle against communist terrorism before and after independence was bound to place an indelible mark on the conduct of foreign relations. Because the communists were predominantly Chinese who were suspected of having been inspired and directed by China, Malaysia's foreign policy was cautious toward the communist regime in Beijing. Even though Malaysia had commercial ties with China, it had until 1974 refused to acknowledge the communist Chinese government as the sole and lawful representative of the Chinese people. Nor did it for that matter recognize noncommunist Nationalist China on Taiwan. Anticommunism at home tended to reinforce the country's pro-Western orientation, at least through the mid-1960s.

Despite the legacy of British rule, the country became independent while remaining relatively unencumbered by bitterness toward its former colonial power. Before 1957 the British had generally treated Malay rulers with respect. The internment of Malay nationalists before World War II was resented, but the peaceful British relinquishment of power in the postwar period evoked pro-British sentiments. Many Malaysians saw little inconsistency in retaining links with the British while supporting the cause of anticolonialism elsewhere. Malaysia's image of itself as an emerging and new nation has been reflected in its efforts to identify with the aspirations and needs of other Afro-Asian peoples and countries.

Noninvolvement in Great Power conflicts—or nonalignment, as Malaysia calls it—remains a significant aspect of foreign policy. Wishing neither to alienate nonaligned neighbors such as Burma, India, and Indonesia nor to displease China, Malaysia did not join the anticommunist, pro-Western military alliance, the Southeast Asia Treaty Organization. This did not prevent the country from signing a bilateral mutual defense pact with Britain, however. The official rational was that because it was not concluded in the context of any East-West conflict, this bilateral arrangement did not contradict the nonalignment policy. Malaysia's claim to nonaligned status, however, was given recognition rather belateldly in 1969 when the country was invited to attend a preparatory meeting of nonaligned countries held in Tanzania.

Active interest in regionalism stems partly from its close historic ties with Indonesia, the Philippines, and Thailand and partly from the fluidity of Great Power relationships in Asia. The Association of Southeast Asian Nations (ASEAN), formed in 1967 by Malaysia, Indonesia, the Philippines, Singapore, and Thailand, continues to be the most important of the regional cooperative forums. (Brunei joined in January 1984.) As of 1984 its achievements in a wide range of nonmilitary fields fell far short of goals envisaged by its member countries, but there was no question about the fact that Malaysia, like its other partners in ASEAN, continued to pin high hopes on ASEAN's potentials.

Tin and rubber, the leading foreign exchange earners, have been significant as determinants of Malaysian foreign relations. The critical importance of these commodity exports had underlined the pragamatic need to foster goodwill abroad. This element had been especially compelling in the mid-1960s when the price of rubber continued to drop and Malaysia experienced a concurrent stagnation in exports. Against this background and as Britain and the United States declined in importance as traditional customers, Malaysia in 1967 opened diplomatic relations with the Soviet Union, which by then had become the biggest buyer of Malaysian rubber.

Also since the mid-1960s Malaysian leaders had become concerned about the implications of the Vietnam Conflict and British economic and military retrenchment east of Suez for Southeast Asia in general and Malaysia in particular. Such concern led to Malaysia's two-track policy of supporting the United States military effort in Vietnam—as part of its consistent opposition to any form of communist expansion—and of seeking a peaceful settlement of the war through negotiations. Equally significant, the shifting priorities in British foreign policy spurred Malaysia's efforts to meet its own national needs through self-reliance and regional cooperation. The United States decision, made public in mid-1969, to scale down its military involvement in Asia further accelerated Kuala Lumpur's search for self-reliance and for a new means of ensuring peace and security in the region.

In espousing a nonalignment policy, Malaysian leaders were mindful of the possibility that dependence on, or alliance with, a major power could court the risk of foreign interference and, above all, the danger of Malaysia's being swept into a vortex of Great Power rivalry and conflict. At the same time, however, they were aware of the potential security problems that could arise from a growing Soviet naval presence in the Indian Ocean, the anticipated British departure from Southeast Asia, the United States policy of lowering its military profile in the region, and China's continuing interest in Southeast Asia through its covert aid to the communist rebels in the region.

The Malaysian response to the perceived volatile foreign policy environment was to have a zone of peace created for Southeast Asia—to forestall Great Power intervention in the region and to prevent a power vacuum there at the same time. According to its official perception, Southeast Asia was bound to be a natural target for exploitation and an arena for a power struggle in view of its strategic importance, economic potential and, on the negative note, political fragmentation. This potentially dangerous situation was said to require "clear ground rules" so that the region would never be turned into a pawn of Great Power conflict.

The concept of neutralization for Southeast Asia derives from such considerations. Malaysia let it be known that this concept had been quietly discussed as early as 1966 and 1967 but that it was not until September 1970 that the idea was first publicized internationally. This was done at the Conference of Nonaligned Nations in Lusaka, Zambia, where Malaysia called on the nonaligned

Countries to take a greater interest ina neutrality scheme that hopefully would be subscribed to by the Great Powers themselves—the United States, the Soviet Union, and China. In October 1971 Malaysia elaborated on this concept before the United Nations General Assembly and evidently succeeded in persuading the ASEAN partners to accept neutralization as a desirable, if not immediately practical, goal for the region.

In November 1971 the five ASEAN member nations signed a declaration pledging their "necessary efforts toward the recognition of and respect for Southeast Asia as a Zone of Peace, Freedom, and Neutrality, free from any form or manner of interference by outside powers" (see Foreign Military Relations, ch. 5). They acknowledged at the time that they had no illusions about the "long and difficult road ahead of us" in their efforts to attain the objective expressed in their common manifesto.

Relations with Selected Countries

In bilateral relations, Malaysia maintained, as of 1984, friendly and cooperative ties with many nations, especially its immediate neighbors. There were some issues of potential friction, but these were relatively minor and were unlikely to affect adversely its neighborly ties with Indonesia there were close cooperative economic ties, and the two counties occasionally held joint military exercises. One potential source of tension was the conflicting claim by Malaysia and Indionesia to the islands of Sipadan and Ligatan, off the eastern shore of Borneo, on the area of the border between the two countries. In August 1982 the Malaysian government stated that it was making a new map of Malaysia to give neighboring countries chance to negotiate on frontier issues. It stressed at the time that the negotiations must take place in a spirit of cordiality and goodwill.

Relations with Singapore were affected for many years by the lingering trauma of separtion in 1965. Since 1981, coinciding with the assumption of the prime ministership by Mahathir, the two countries, linked by a causeway across the Johore Strait, have taken steps to mend their differences. These steps relate to the strengthening of ties in economic cooperation, trade, tourism, transportation, and even in the security area.

Malaysia collaborates closely with Thailand in the policing of their common border as part of their joint efforts to suppress communist rebels. The countries are also engaging in barter trade—Malaysian oil for Thai rice. They also agreed in 1982 to explore the possibility of initiating socioeconomic projects for the benefit of the people in the border areas in a mutual effort to ensure that the communist terrorists would find it difficult to penetrate local populations.

Relations with the Philippines were cordial, but in the early 1980s they were still marred somewhat by what Malaysia regarded as the Philippines' groundless claim to Sabah. In 1977 the Philippine government declared its intention to relinquish the long-standing claim to Sabah, but the Malaysian government insisted amend that such a statement was not sufficient and that the Philippines should amend its constitution to make the statement of relinquishment more official. The issue was still unresolved in 1984.

Relations with other countries were general by friendly. Malaysia and the United States maintained close and friendly ties in 1984. The only notable source of friction concerned the matter of American disposal of surplus stockpiles of tin and rubber in the world market. This matter troubled Malaysia for many years because the United States action in disposing of its stockpiles more often than not had an adverse effect on Malaysian exports of tin and rubber. The two countries continued, in the early 1980s, to have mutual consultations so that the problem would not become aggravated.

Ties with China and the Soviet Union were cordial. For many years Malaysia was troubled by its perception of Chinese assistance to the communist rebels inside Malaysia and elsewhere in Southeast Asia. Since 1979, however, the Chinese leadership has publicly expressed its intention to terminate such assistance. The Malaysian government remains somewhat skeptical, however, because China continued to express its intention to lend "moral and political" support to the rebels. With the Soviet Union, relations were perhaps on the cool side. This was because of the Soviet invasion of Afghanistan in 1979 and the perceived apprehension in Kuala Lumpur that the Soviet Union was expanding its influence in Southeast Asia and in the Indian Ocean region in the years after the conquest of the Republic of Vietnam (South Vietnam) in 1975 by the Democratic Republic of Vietnam (North Vietnam). Also troubling to the Malaysian leadership was the endemic fear of Soviet espionage activities in Southeast Asia.

Doubtless the "new orientation" in Malaysian foreign policy in recent years was what the Mahathir administration called the "Look East" policy enunciated in late 1981. Specifically, this policy called for a reduced level of economic linkage with Britain in favor of a more active cooperation with Japan and the Republic of Korea (South Korea). Evidently, the Mahathir leadership believed that Japanese and South Korean successes with economic development merited close scrutiny and emulation. The new orientation was a source of displeasure with Britain, but Malaysia concluded that it had more to benefit from close economic and technological cooperation with Japan—Malaysia's biggest trading partner as well as its largest foreign investor—and South Korea than from continued ties with Britain. The Mahathir leadership apparently was not happy with the way Britain was perceived to be taking Malaysia for granted.

* * *

There are several works on the Malaysian political system that may be of interest to those who seek further information and insight on the subject matter. These include *The Constitution of Malaysia: Its Development, 1957–1977*, edited by Tun Mohamed Suffian, H.P. Lee, and F.A. Trindade; *Malaysia and Singapore: The Building of New States* by Stanley S. Bedlington; *Government and Politics of Southeast Asia*, edited by George Kahin; *Malaysian Politics* by Gordon P. Means; *Malaysia—New States in a New Nation* by R.S. Milne and K.J. Ratnam; and *Democracy Without Consensus* by K. Von Vorys. *The Politics of Islamic Reassertion*, edited by Mohammed Ayoob, may also be instructive for those who are concerned with the place of Islam in the political scheme of Malaysia. The chapter on Malaysia in *Strategies of Survival: The Foreign Policy Dilemmas of Smaller Asian States* by Charles E. Morrison and Astri Suhrke is a concise introduction to the foreign policy of Malaysia.

For more recent information on Malaysia politics and government, perhaps the best sources are the annual summary articles on Malaysia appearing in the *Asian Survey*. Equally informative are the annual summaries in *Asia Yearbook* published by the Far Eastern Economic Review. The weeklies issued by the Far Eastern Economic Review often contain valuable insights and trends relating to the country's politics and foreign policy. A very thoughtful overview of the current trend in the Malaysian politics was presented by K. Das in the February 3, 1983, issue of the *Far Eastern Economic Review* under the title of "Perils of Polarisation." (For further information and complete citations, see Bibliography.)

Chapter 5. National Security

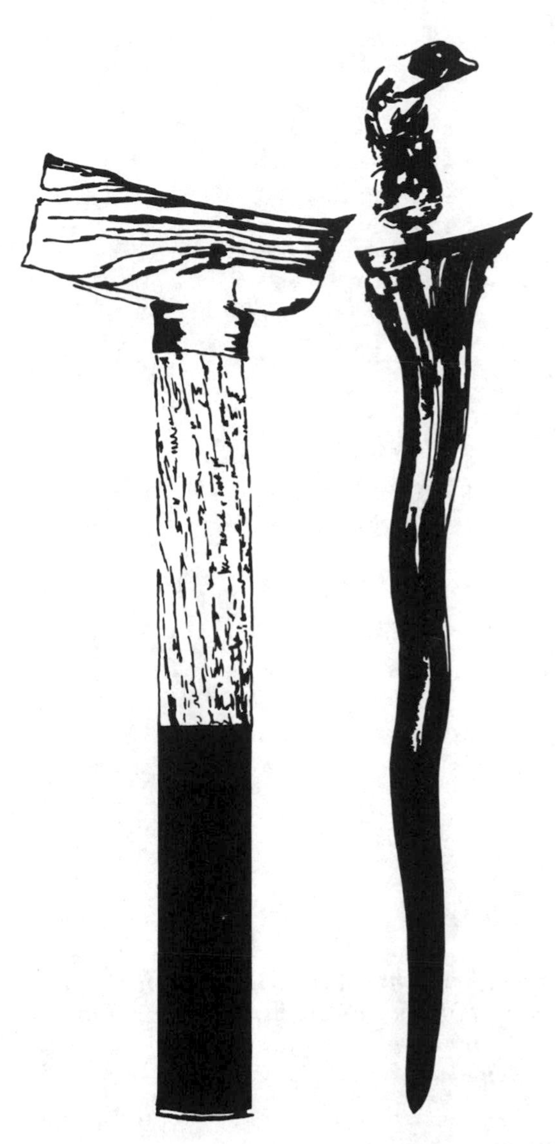

The wavy-bladed kris, shown together with its sheath, is one of the most respected Malaysian cultural objects. Fabulous tales abound about its magical powers, especially the powers of those owned by brave heroes.

CONDITIONS OF INTERNAL ORDER in Malaysia were generally stable and peaceful during the early 1980s. Despite the essentially favorable internal security setting, however, the government had continued to be very sensitive to potential threats to public order. It has strongly defended the need for having a wide latitude of official action in matters that affect national security as defined in very broad terms. Domestic and foreign critics have charged that some enforcement measures were unnecessarily extreme, but government officials have consistently stated that the nation has special security problems and that national development could best be accomplished in an orderly society.

The government has identified several sources of threats to internal security, primary of which was communal tension associated with the attempt to forge a united nation out of separate and often mutually hostile communities of ethnic Malays, Chinese, Indians, and others. As of early 1984 there had been no major outbreaks of ethnic violence since riots erupted in Kuala Lumpur in May 1969, and the government—in which Malays, as the largest of the nation's ethnic groups, dominated—has acted quickly to preclude any issue from escalating into an ethnic confrontation. The riots continued to be regarded as proof, however, that the potential for ethnic antagonism was omnipresent in Malaysian society and that the first priority of public policy must be to remedy conditions—primarily economic—that exacerbate tension between ethnic groups.

The task of maintaining ethnic harmony has been increasingly complicated since the late 1970s by the activities of what the government labeled "religious extremists" who, inspired by the revival of Islam in other parts of the world, sought to modify radically the practice of Islam in Malaysia, to use Islam for political purposes, or to make all Malaysians subjects to Islamic law. Malays were by definition Muslims, but the Chinese, most of the Indians, and several other ethnic groups were not. The government has expressed its sympathy for efforts to pursue a more orthodox approach to the practice of Islam but has drawn sharp distinctions between the pursuit of legitimate religious expression and anything that caused disharmony within the Muslim community, aroused interethnic group tension, or challenged the existing system of government.

Communist subversion has been identified as posing a major threat to internal stability and public order ever since the Communist Party of Malaya first launched armed struggle in 1948 and caused the Emergency of 1948-60. The government continued to insist that although communist insurgency was almost completely contained by the armed forces in the early 1980s, past experience had proved that any letup in anticommunist vigilance would inevitably be followed by a dangerous expansion of communist influence. In early 1984 insurgents appeared to be divided into three separate parties, two of which were confined to areas on both sides of the border between Peninsular Malaysia and Thailand and the third active only in remote sections of Sarawak—which, along with Sabah, was located across the South China Sea on Borneo. All three parties looked to China for ideological inspiration, but none was believed to receive material aid from that nation. The government has also warned that communists affiliated with the Soviet Union have made attempts to infiltrate some organizations in the nation.

As of early 1984 the national leadership anticipated no external military threat developing in the short term but since 1979 had administered a major armed forces development and modernization program designed to build up the capability to meet possible future threats. Most often mentioned in this regard were potential regional instability associated with Vietnamese incursions into Laos and Kampuchea, the growing role in Southeast Asia of the Soviet Union, and, over the long term, the place a modernized China might occupy in regional affairs. Setbacks in the national economy in 1982 led to budgetary retrenchment that affected the defense buildup and all other of government programs; defense planners have attempted to minimize the effect on the development of a modern, balanced defense capability, however, by devoting a major proportion of available resource to the acquisition of modern weapons and platforms, especially for the air force and the navy. The buildup had also focused on supplying the army—the dominant branch of the three military services—with an armored capability. The army has traditionally supported paramilitary units of the police in counterinsurgency jungle operations; starting in the early 1980s, however, all elements of the military initiated training in conventional warfare as well.

Internal Security and Public Order

Malaysia has struck its own balance in reconciling the conflicting human desires for order and freedom by adhering to constitutional provisions that the exercise of certain liberties cannot be absolute even during the best of times. Those liberties most subject to limitation in the interests of societal order and the maintenance of the state include the guarantees of free speech, association, movement, and assembly. The right to equal treatment under the law must also give way to the need to maintain harmony among ethnic groups. In cases involving subversion or during times officially proclaimed as emergencies, the Constitution grants the legislature and the executive branch special powers allowing the use of extraordinary measures that impinge on a citizen's recourse to due process of law and further limit personal freedom. A state of emergency has been in effect since the 1969 riots, even though the orderly functioning of all branches of the government resumed in 1971. The question of emergency powers was a major issue during the 1983–84 constitutional crisis (see The Politics of Compromise, ch. 4). As of early 1984 the government has used emergency powers invoked in 1969 as well as other security legislation, principally the Internal Security Act of 1960 (ISA), to prohibit any activity that, in the judgement of the government, threatened national security and public order.

Foremost of the government's concerns was the threat of subversion. The Constitution broadly defines subversion as action either taken or threatened that would excite disaffection against the head of the federation, cause a substantial number of citizens to fear organized violence, promote ill feeling between ethnic groups, make use of unlawful means to alter anything established by law, or prove prejudicial to the security of the nation. Primary among potential sources of subversion identified by the government in the early 1980s were interethnic group tension, religious extremism, communism from both domestic insurgent groups and foreign movements, and Vietnamese refugees.

The government has also expressed its concern that discussion of controversial social issues or criticism of official policies except through the medium of political parties would promote national disunity, confuse the people, and perhaps even provide issues for subversives to exploit. Accordingly, organizations of all types, certain students studying abroad, labor unions, and occasionally journalists and news media have been closely watched and from time to time subjected to restrictive legislation or repressive measures. Moreover, since the 1969 riots, permission for large groups to assemble for political or other purposes has seldom been granted.

Communal and Social Issues

As was true of nearly every aspect of the national life, interethnic group relations have had a direct bearing on the level of public order in Malaysia. The three major ethnic communities—Malay, Chinese, and Indian—have essentially retained their own separate identities; and cultural, social, and economic integration has been very limited. Politics was conducted almost entirely through the medium of communally based parties that mirrored the ethnic cleavages dividing Malaysian society. At the top, parties governed jointly in the ruling National Front (Barisan Nasional) coalition, which held an overwhelming majority of seats in the parliament. Within the National Front, the United Malays National Organization (UMNO) was dominant. Under this system, representatives of the different ethnic groups have been able to forge a consensus and govern effectively (see Political Parties, ch. 4).

Below the elite decisionmaking level, however, interethnic group relations have often been tense, and ethnic divisions have complicated problems Malaysia has experienced in common with other developing countries, including urbanization, industrialization, rising expectations, and unemployment. Problems were most severe in Peninsular Malaysia, where relations between the Malay and the Chinese communities have been especially troublesome. In Sabah and Sarawak relations between the indigenous (chiefly non-Malay) and nonindigenous (chiefly Chinese) populations have been far less problematic.

The causes of interethnic tension on the peninsula have complex historical roots (see Ethnicity and the Plural Society, ch. 2). In modern times difficulties have most often been expressed in economic terms, namely in Malay resentment over their own comparative economic disadvantage vis-à-vis the Chinese and, to a lesser extent, the Indians. The situation has been complicated by the insistent expression of ethnic pride and identity by all groups, which has on occasion contributed to the development of ethnic chauvinism. One other major factor affecting interethnic group relations was the fact that communist insurgency has been largely a Chinese-based phenomenon.

Since the 1969 riots the government has emphasized policies directed toward easing interethnic group tension and forestalling the outbreak of further violence. The New Economic Policy (NEP) was drawn up in 1970 to combat what the government perceived as the underlying causes of communal tension: poverty and imbalances between the economic status of different ethnic groups. Under the NEP the government has pursued a two-pronged approach to developing the economy by eradicating poverty in all ethnic groups and at the same time correcting economic imbalances between ehtnic communities. In practice, implementation of the NEP has centered on the establishment of quotas, incentives, loan programs, and state enterprises to benefit indigenous ethnic groups—primarily the Malays. In general, nonindigenous groups have supported these policies, although some resistance has occurred, especially when issues relating to education were involved.

In a second major move to defuse potential interethnic tensions in the wake of the 1969 riots, the Constitution was amended to forbid discussion of certain sensitive issues. That amendment makes it illegal even in parliament to debate publicly matters relating to the national language, the special status accorded to indigenous ethnic groups, or the rights and privileges conferred by citizenship.

The concern for maintaining harmony within and between ethnic groups has led the government to evaluate issues not conventionally viewed as public order or internal security matters in precisely those terms. The conduct of religious affairs, particularly the role of Islam, was one such issue. According to the 1980 census, approximately 53 percent of the population was Muslim, about 90 percent of those being Malays, who were by definition Muslims. In recognition of the fact that Islam has had a political association and a special place in the nation since early Malay rulers converted to that religion, the Constitution declares that "Islam is the religion of the nation." At the same time, the Constitution also guarantees all persons the right to profess and practice any religion and not to be subject to the pratices or beliefs of other faiths (see Religion, ch. 2; The Federal Constitution of Malaysia, ch. 4). The framers of the Constitution and all Malaysian administrations have insisted that this would give legal recognition to the importance of Islam in the national life imposing Islam on non-Muslims. The system appears to have worked quite effectively until 1969, when it became clear that Islam had become a political issue and that the politicization of Islam has contributed to the outbreak of ethnic violence.

The situation was quickly brought under control, but by the late 1970s Islam again had become a political issue. This, combined with a general trend toward a more fundamentalist expression of the faith in Malaysia—associated with a revival of Islamic orthodoxy in countries of the Middle East—again made the government wary that the issue of the conduct and role of Islam could pose a destabilizing threat. In part this was because of frustrated aspirations of a minority of Muslims who believed that Malaysia should be made an Islamic state wherein all persons were subject to Islamic law. The government was also sensitive to the potential for public disorder among non-Muslims, who became alarmed by these aspirations and feared that despite constitutional guarantees and official assurances to the contrary, they might be made subject to Islamic law. The government has also expressed concern over the effect on public order of growing divisions within the Muslim community; in the early 1980s there were instances in Peninsular Malaysia where rival Muslim leaders incited their congregations to violence against each other. The divisions within the Muslim community have most often coincided with personal allegiance either to UMNO or to the fundamentalist, Malay-based opposition party, the Pan-Malaysia Islamic Party (better known by its Malaysian acronym, PAS—see Glossary). These divisions and the measures used to control differences between the groups were generally regarded as having political as well as internal security ramifications (see Opposition Parties, ch.4).

National leaders have also expressed alarm over the effect on internal security of Islamic beliefs that hitherto had not been experienced by Malaysian Muslims, the great majority of whom belong to the Sunni branch of Islam. These included what the government has characterized as foreign, extremist, and subversive notions that held that monarchy, the sultanates, and nationalism were incompatible with Islam. The government has also repeatedly expressed its concern that antimaterialism being upheld by some Muslim leaders could undermine the nation's development effort, because believers were being urged to concentrate on preparing for the next life and to forget about working to improve material conditions of their present lives. Finally, government officials have also warned that communist subversives were seeking to infiltrate Islamic organization and manipulate them for their own purposes.

There were only a few outbreaks of violence having religious overtones during the late 1970s and early 1980s, and those that did occur were mostly isolated and on a small scale. Two incidents, however, both shocked and alarmed the nation. In August 1978, five Muslims were caught destroying images in a Hindu temple—sacred to much of the Indian community; four were killed by the temple guards. In October 1980 a police station in Johore was attacked by 15 Muslims who had worked themselves into a trance; eight of the attackers were killed after wounding 23 police officers and civilians. In both instances, the perpetrators were members of groups far outside the mainstream of even the most fundamentalist strain of Islam in Malaysia, but their violent actions worried responsible leaders concerned that cleavages over principles of faith within Islam might adversely affect interethnic relations as well as relations within the Muslim community itself.

In general, the government has dealt with members of these and other groups in one of two ways. Some were treated as common lawbreakers, freedom of religion being guaranteed only within the bounds of the general law relating to public order, public health, or morality. Courts of Islamic law, which had jurisdiction only over Muslims and only over matters pertaining to religion and domestic life, have also commonly been used to discipline individuals or groups that distributed religious tranquillity within the Muslim community (see Criminal Procedure, this ch.). In March 1982, however, in an unusual move, the government used the ISA to place in preventive detention members of a religious group calling itself Crypto. Law enforcement officials apparently acted because they believed the group might lead its followers into violence similar to the 1978 and 1980 incidents. According to the police, the group subscribed to a somewhat bizarre collection of tenets, including the belief that membership in Crypto meant immortality and that the Malaysian government should be a theocracy in which Jews would be supreme. Members were told they could attain unusual power by standing with their arms raised for 10 minutes at 3:00 A.M., or, if that proved unsuccessful, they should try raising their right legs for 30 minutes.

Amendments to the penal and criminal procedure codes in early 1983 gave the government increased latitude for action when the conduct of religion disturbed public order. The amendments made it illegal to cause disharmony or ill will on religious grounds between adherents of the same or different faiths or to challenge anything done or any decision made by lawfully appointed religious authorities (the method by which religious officials would be appointed not being specified). An accused was denied recourse to the defense that he acted according to an honest interpretation of his religion. The amendments also made it illegal to allege that any person had ceased to profess a religion or should not be accepted as an adherent of one. As of early 1984, although it appeared that the amendments were intended to curb deteriorating relations within the Muslim community in Peninsular Malaysia, they applied to all religions.

The government has tended to view politicization of groups other than political parties as having a potential impact on public order, apparently in the belief that political positions taken by special interest groups might provoke irresponsible or unbalanced criticism of government practices and policies; this could in turn promote ethnic resentment or other disorder by confusing citizens or hindering the official development effort. Since communist insurgents near the border with Thailand were dealt a sharp blow in the late 1970s, Malaysians have repeatedly been warned that the communists might infiltrate special interest groups (see Communist Insurgency, this ch.). In early 1981 officials charged that a Moscow-based united front organization was also seeking to exert political influence through certain unnamed groups.

Citing these threats as justification, the parliament in 1981 passed amendments to the 1966 Societies Act that severely restricted the freedom of nonpolitical organized groups to engage in political activities (see Recent Political Developments, ch. 4). Before being amended, the law had loosely regulated the activities of all organized groups in the country by requiring that they be registered with the government. In the early 1980s there were an estimated 30,000 such societies, including everything from sports clubs to private welfare organizations to labor unions and professional organizations. The severe enforcement and control measures in the 1981 amendments provoked a storm of criticism, and the amended Societies Act was again modified with new amendments in early 1983. Several key measures remained in effect in early 1984, however, including the right of the Registrar of Societies to enter society's premises without a warrant and to prohibit a society from maintaining links with foreign groups. Decisions of the registrar could be appealed to the minister of home affairs, and ex-detainese under the ISA or convicted criminals were barred from holding office in a society.

Two groups were viewed as potential internal security problems during the late 1970s and early 1980s. The first comprised students studying abroad, some of whom—mostly Malays—have been charged with acting in an "un-Malaysian-like" manner—professing policies that bordered on socialism, Marxism, or Maoism, or having been dangerously influenced by foreign Islamic doctrines. The government has publicly warned that such students could be monitored by the staff of Malaysian embassies abroad and that their conduct would not be tolerated when they returned to Malaysia. As of early 1984 student activism and campus unrest within the nation were not problems; such activity ceased in 1975 when, in the wake of violent student demonstrations the year before, the parliament amended the Universities and University Colleges Act of 1971 to place severe limits on the range of political activity open to students and professors.

The government has also closely monitored the activities of labor unions, believing that public order, worker interests, and the progress of national development would best be served without strikes or worker lockouts. Regulations limiting union activity were tightened in 1980 after a bitter and disruptive dispute during 1978-79 involving the national air carrier, Malaysian Airline System (MAS). In that incident, the government reacted strongly to union activity, declaring MAS workers to be engaged in an illegal strike and arresting several union officials under the ISA. As of early 1984 strikes were still legally permissible but appeared to be declining in number and length as the government increasingly referred labor disputes to compulsory arbitration (see Employment and Labor Relations, ch. 3).

Journalists and the information media in Malaysia have generally conformed to the government's insistence that the functioning of democracy should be characterized not by discordant voices of special interests but harmony and discipline. Broadcasting media were all government controlled, and all major newspapers had close connections with political parties in the National Front coalition. Print media were required to apply annually for permits to publish, and self-censorship ensured that criticism of the government was constructive and restrained. Certain publications judged harmful to national security—usually of foreign origin—at times have been removed from circulation under provisions of the ISA. In late 1981 the government also used the ISA to detain a journalist and a publisher accused of publishing communist propaganda.

Communist Insurgency

Of the three communist party organizations in early 1984, only two, the Communist Party of Malaya (CPM) in Peninsular Malaysia and the North Kalimantan Communist Party in Sarawak, have been active in recent years. The remaining one was a small factional offshoot of the CPM and, like it, operated primarily on both sides of the border with Thailand. Both the CPM and the party in Sarawak were recognized by China, but neither was supplied by or subservient to that nation. Relations among the parties in Peninsular Malaysia have generally been contentious, and there has been no evidence of anything other than the most casual of links between the parties on the peninsula and the party in Sarawak. The CPM was committed to forming an independent state of Malaya that would comprise Peninsular Malaysia and Singapore. The other small party on the peninsula aimed at forming a communist state for all of Malaysia. The

Sarawak party sought to form an independent state on northern Borneo. All three parties were very poorly armed, and members in recent years have had to devote most of their time and attention to basic survival.

Peninsular Malaysia

Communism as an organized force came to what is now Malaysia in the early 1920s, emerging in a pattern that has characterized the party ever since. Early organizing attempts by British and Indonesian branches of the international movement were unsuccessful, but Chinese agents, playing on the strong emotional attachment most Chinese had for the land of their origin and on animosities they felt toward Malays, gained entrance to the Chinese community.

The CPM was founded in April 1930 in Singapore after communist activity had been conducted for several years in various Chinese associations located in cities on the peninsula. The party played a signficant role in labor strikes during the 1930s, but in general it was unable to ally itself with the emerging Malay nationalist movement and remained an overwhelmingly Chinese organization. During World War II, when the CPM organized the nation's principal anti-Japanese resistance movement, it gained some prestige and sympathy, and a few adherents were attracted from among Malays and other ethnic groups. The CPM emerged from the war years a well-organized and substantial force.

In the immediate postwar period, however, the British suppressed the movement, causing divisions to erupt between those in the CPM wishing to follow legal means to overthrow the colonial government and those espousing armed struggle. By 1947 the armed struggle faction, led by Chin Peng, had won out, and after quickly reorganizing the party and recalling former members of the resistance movement to active service, the CPM launched an insurrection in 1948. The insurrection, which came to be known as the Emergency, seriously threatened the stability of the colonial government. When officially declared over in 1960, the Emergency had claimed the lives of an estimated 11,000 persons, 2,500 of whom were civilians (see The Emergency, ch. 1).

Despite the seriousness of the challenge, however, the insurrection had essentially been defeated by the mid-1950s. The British brought in military reinforcements, and subsequent counterinsurgency campaigns, relying on the police Special Branch to infiltrate the CPM and provide intelligence, proved very effective. Critical sources of supply, intelligence, and recruitment for the communists were drastically cut by the government's relocation of ethnic Chinese "squatter settlements" on the edges of the jungle to protected "New Villages." This caused hardship for many but also provided residents immunity from communist extortion, reestablished their confidence in the government, and, by granting the settlements considerable autonomy in government, blunted communist propaganda about British exploitation of the people. The relocation forced members of what the government referred to as the Communist Terror Organization to emerge from their jungle hideouts in search of new sources of food, supplies, intelligence, thereby risking capture or annihilation. The New Villages provided a model for similar "strategic hamlets" latere set up by the United States in the Republic of Vietnam (South Vietnam).

Any Malay support for the communists that had originally existed fell away as the British announced plans to proceed toward decolonization and as Malays began to look to Malay politicians to express nationalist sentiments. In addition, the large majority of Chinese aligned themselves with the anticommunist Malayan Chinese Association, formed in 1949 and loyal to the government. The CPM's arbitrary use of assassination alienated many erstwhile sympathizers. The CPM soon became identified in the minds of most citizens in Peninsular Malaysia as an insurrection by radical Chinese rather than a legitimate political movement. At their strongest, the communists were able to field an estimated 14,000 armed fighters in the party's military arm, the Malayan Races Liberation Army: however, by 1960 the CPM had only some 500 fighters, most of whom had been forced into a remote and inaccessible area of southern Thailand known as the Betong Salient.

During the early and mid-1960s the CPM concentrated on reorganization and rebuilding, rhetorically opposing the formation of Malaysia in 1963 but offering virtually no material resistance. By the late 1960s the party had manged to recover some of its strength, and communist activity once again surfaced in northern Peninsular Malaysia. Some scholars have connected the step-up in communist activity to a speech by Mao Zedong in 1968 calling on all communist parites to intensify combat and expand revolutionary bases. For whatever reason, however, the number of insurgent ambushes, assassinations, and acts of sabotage rose appreciably during the early 1970s, and communist units were reported active in Kedah, Perlis, Perak, Kelantan, and Penang states. The government had allowed its counterinsurgency forces to deteriorate while concentrating on the Indonesian opposition to the formation of Malaysia and was caught by surprise by the obvious growth in the size of communist forces, estimated to number some 3,500 in 1970

The increase in terrorist activity occurred in conjunction with a split of the CPM into three parties. The division developed partly because CPM unit commanders were often geographically separated from the central party leadership and enjoyed considerable autonomy from it. The pressure of government counterinsurgency campaigns and the successful infiltration of government agents into the CPM also bred suspicion and disputes in the leadership itself. In addition, some party members reportedly chafed against the older leadership and against the long, drawn-out nature of Chin Peng's armed struggle strategy, which emphasized the importance of building a base in rural areas. Some party members apparently favored a strategy that focused on mounting terrorist attacks in urban areas. Dissension first became apparent in 1967 when some 20 cadres whom the leadership considered disloyal were assassinated. A more serious example of the internal divisions developing in the CPM came in 1970 when the party central committee, responding to fears that younger recruits could be government agents, issued orders that every CPM member over the age of 12 who had joined the party since 1962 be linquidated.

Although many cadres were killed in response to that order, resistance in two units of the CPM's military arm (by then most often referred to as the Malayan National Liberation Army) prompted the formation of two breakaway communist parties. The first, calling itself the Communist Party of Malaya (Revolutionary Faction) drew followers from the parent CPM's Eighth Regiment, which had been located near Sadao, Thailand, and sometimes operated in northern Kedah. After the parent CPM continued to press for more purges, the second group broke away, calling itself the Communist Party of Malaya (Marxist-Leninist). It was formed by a portion of the parent CPM's Twelfth Regiment, located in the Betong Salient of Thailand and in northern Perak. Both factions adopted the title Malayan People's Liberation Army as the name of their armed wings.

Terrorist activity by all three parties forced a sharp deterioration in the security setting by the mid-1970s. Favorite targets of sabotage and violence were construction crews working on the East-West Highway, which cut through routes the communists had traditionally used to travel south, as well as logging camps north of the highway. Although most violence took place along the Malaysia-Thailand border, communist insurgents of one faction or another were able to infiltrate some student groups in cities on the peninsula, and the Communist Party of Malaya (Marxist-Leninist) faction in particular perpetrated acts of urban terrorism.

The government responded to the new threat by increasing sweeps of the border areas. It also reached an agreement with the Thai government—through the auspices of a joint border committee established in 1965—to coordinate the two nations' counterinsurgency operations. Under that agreement some 400 to 500 Malaysian police were deployed to Thailand in order to strengthen law enforcement in the Betong Salient. In addition to improving the security setting in southern Thailand, those police forces, which were under the command of Thai police, were useful in supplying intelligence to Malaysian forces concerning CPM activity.

The climax of guerrilla activity came in the 1975–76 period after the fall of Sagion (renamed Ho Chi Minh City) in April 1975 encouraged a sharp escalation of communist violence. Most activity centered on the border areas, but in August 1975 guerrillas blew up the National Monument in Kuala Lumpur, which commemorated the government's victory in the Emergency. Other acts of urban terrorism followed. Reacting to the increased aggressiveness in communist tactics, the government in 1975 promulgated new and, some charged, draconian security legislation—the Essential (Security Cases) Regulations 1975, which did away with most legal safeguards for those accused in security cases (see Security Offenses, this ch.). The government also published regulations requiring citizen and community involvement in the counterinsurgency effort, leading the way to the development of citizen patrols in neighborhoods and villages. In rural areas the scheme was intended to isolate jungle guerrillas from any potential support. For the same purpose, logging camps north of the East-West Highway were closed, and protected villages were set up in some jungle areas.

The situation along the border deteriorated further after June 1976, when Malaysian communists in southern Thailand orchestrated demonstrations in the town of Betong, Thailand, to protest the presence of the Malaysian police unit stationed there. These demonstrations followed an incident in which a Malaysian aircraft allegedly crossed into Thai territory during a counterinsurgency operation. The demonstrations provoked the Thai government into expelling the Malaysian police unit and ending the previously enjoyed mutual right of each nation to cross the border in hot pursuit of insurgents to a distance of eight kilometers for a maximum of 72 hours. These measures forced Malaysians to adopt defensive security measures, relying more and more on a series of mobile forts established in embattled areas and intended as a southern barrier to communist penetration.

The situation on the border improved markedly after a coup in late 1976 in Thailand brought in a staunchly anticommunist govenment and led to greatly increased joint Malaysian-Thai counterinsurgency operations. The first of several coordinated military stikes against communist bases in Thailand and northern Peninsular Malaysia began in January 1977. The attacks were supported by the Royal Malaysian Air Force and continued into 1978. Although the communist forces avoided head-on combat and inflicted scores of casualties on Malaysian and Thai forces with jungle booby traps, the campaigns effectively destroyed the guerrillas' stores and camps, scattered their forces, and put the communists on the defensive. The campaigns were followed in the early 1980s by a series of smaller operations that have successfully kept the guerrillas on the run and denied them sources of supply in Malaysia.

As of early 1984 the continuing counterinsurgency measures along the border had reduced the strength of the communist parties to a combined total estimated at between 1,800 and 2,300. According to government figures, some 300 to 350 communist guerrillas moved regularly across the border and conducted terrorist activity in Malaysia. Mobile units of Malaysian police and military forces have continued to be deployed in fortified strongholds in northern Peninsular Malaysia. Some 3,000 army troops were stationed along the East-West Highway between Gerik and Jeli in 61 military posts, each of which was no more than two kilometers apart.

Forces belonging to the CPM, which in June 1982 renamed its military arm the Malayan People's Army, were concentrated in three formations in southern Thailand in the early 1980s (see fig. 10). The total strength of these units was estimated to number between 1,074 and 1,333 in early 1983. Six small forward assault units were located in Kedah, Perak, Kelantan, and Pahang states.

The CPM maintained a radio transmitter in southern Thailand. The station, calling itself the Voice of Malayan Democracy, regularly broadcast propaganda to Malaysia. Several of these messages in the early 1980s were ascribed to CPM front groups that were believed to be little more than paper organizations. These included the Malayan Islamic Brotherhood Party (Persatuan Persuadaraan Islam, commonly known as Paperi) and the Malay

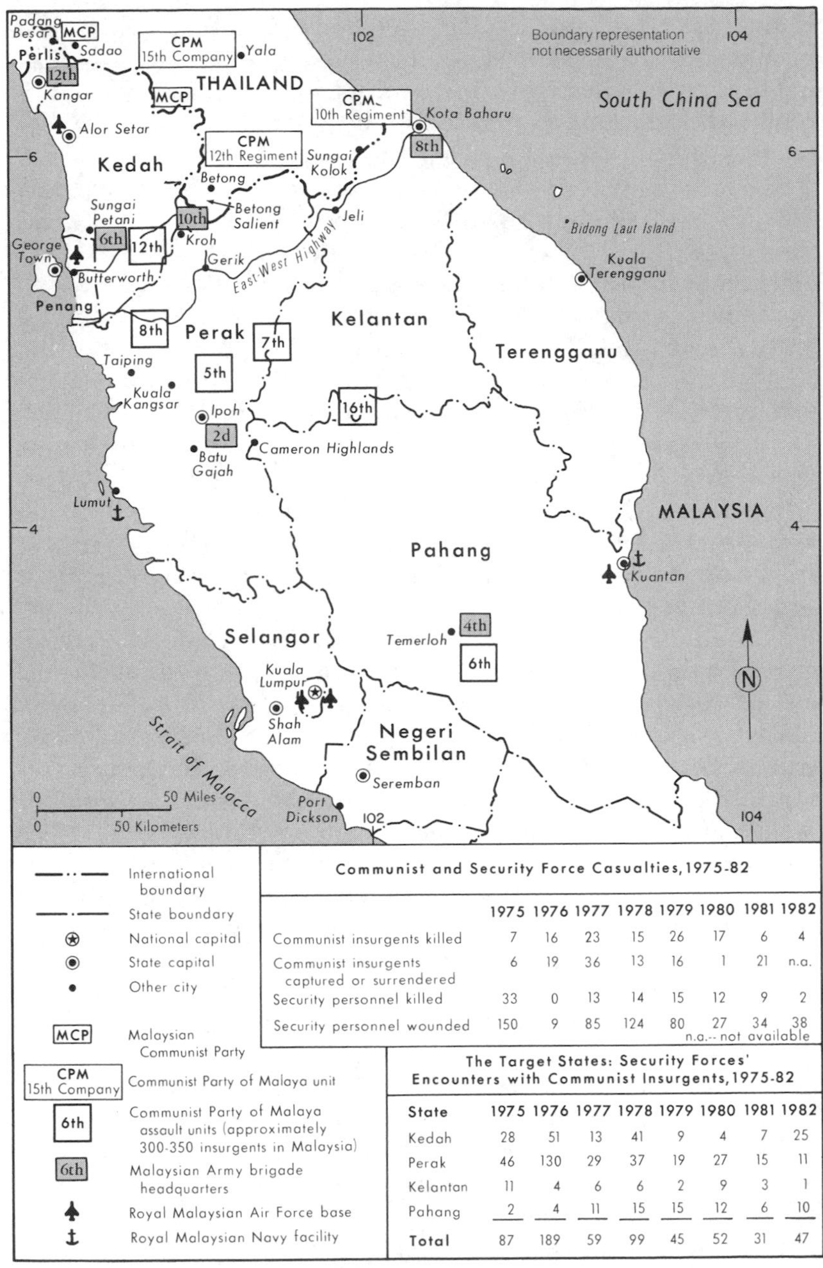

Communist and Security Force Casualties, 1975-82

	1975	1976	1977	1978	1979	1980	1981	1982
Communist insurgents killed	7	16	23	15	26	17	6	4
Communist insurgents captured or surrendered	6	19	36	13	16	1	21	n.a.
Security personnel killed	33	0	13	14	15	12	9	2
Security personnel wounded	150	9	85	124	80	27	34	38

n.a.-- not available

The Target States: Security Forces' Encounters with Communist Insurgents, 1975-82

State	1975	1976	1977	1978	1979	1980	1981	1982
Kedah	28	51	13	41	9	4	7	25
Perak	46	130	29	37	19	27	15	11
Kelantan	11	4	6	6	2	9	3	1
Pahang	2	4	11	15	15	12	6	10
Total	87	189	59	99	45	52	31	47

Source: Based on information from R. Sachithananthan, "Anti-Terrorist Operations in Peninsular Malaysia," *Asian Defense Journal*, Kuala Lumpur, No. 3, March 1983, 21; and "Curbing a Border War," *Asiaweek*, Hong Kong, July 22, 1983, 18.

Figure 10. Communist Insurgency in Peninsular Malaysia and Southern Thailand, 1984

Nationalist Revolutionary Party of Malaya; both of which had been created to attract support from dissident Malays by appealing to issues connected with Islam. Communists have also been reported attempting to recruit members of Peninsular Malaysia's small aboriginal ethnic minority, the Orang Asli (see Glossary).

The CPM's influence in southern Thailand was threatened during the early 1980s by a separatist group of Thai Muslims known as the Patani United Liberation Organization (PULO). In 1981 several hundred Thai Muslim villagers fled into Malaysia, expressing fear of being caught up in violence between Thai security forces, PULO, and the CPM. The coexistence of both PULO and the CPM in the same area has complicated the counterinsurgency effort for both Malaysia and Thailand. Officials in Thailand apparently viewed the CPM as a buffer against PULO, which they considered to present the more dangerous challenge to the Thai government. This attitude has impeded cooperation with Malaysian forces against the CPM, as did the Malaysian government's reluctance to cooperate with Thailand in taking action against a Muslim group such as PULO.

The ethnic compostition of the three communist insurgent groups in the early 1980s was estimated at between 70 and 95 percent Chinese. Most observers agreed that a few insurgents were Malays from Malaysia and an even smaller number were Malaysians of Indian origin. There was disagreement, however, over the role played by Thai Malays in the communist movement. Malaysian security authorities have contended that, in contrast to the Emergency period, a growing proportion of communist insurgents—ethnic Malay and Chinese alike—were of Thai rather than Malaysian origin. This was generally taken as symptomatic of the success of the Malaysian government's counterinsurgency campaigns and its development effort. Thai officials, however, claimed that while Thais occasionally cooperated with the CPM, they were not party members. In the CPM, Malay and Indian membership was concentrated in the Tenth Regiment, which also included some Muslim Chinese. Authorities have expressed puzzlement over the high percentage of female guerrillas in the communist movement during the early 1980s; one government study of three CPM units indicated 45 percent were females.

Government sources in 1983 referred to the Communist Party of Malaya (Revolutionary Faction) as dormant. That group was believed to have some 112 to 121 members and to be located north of Padang Besar, Perlis, on the Thai side of the border. It was relatively isolated from the other parties. The Communist Party of Malaya (Marxist-Leninist) was estimated to number between 602 and 825 and to be centered on the Perak border and in the Betong

Salient. Clashes between the latter group and the CPM were reported in the late 1970s and early 1980s.

In late 1983 it was announced in a broadcast over a clandestine transmitter in Thailand that on December 5 the two factions had joined to form the Malaysian Communist Party, headed by Chang Chen Ying and Huang Chen. The two armed forces were also said to have been merged. The new party expressed its intention to represent communists in Peninsular Malaysia, Sabah, and Sarawak and noted that communists in Singapore must advance their own revolutionary struggle. As of early 1984 this information had not been confirmed by independent observers or other sources.

Sabah and Sarawak

The North Kalimantan Communist Party (NKCP) has been the sole active communist organization in Sarawak since the mid-1960s. No communist group has been identified as operating in Sabah. The NKCP, by its own account, was founded in 1965 after its predecessor, the Sarawak Liberation League, dissolved itself. According to the NKCP, the earlier group had formed in 1954 with help from the CPM. Other sources refer to the NKCP's predecessor by various names, including the Sarawak Communist Organization. During the 1963–66 period of Confrontation, Sarawak communists joined with Indonesian counterparts to protest the formation of Malaysia by conducting guerrilla raids in Sarawak (see External Threats: "Confrontation" and the Philippine Claim to Sabah, ch. 1). After the 1965 coup in Indonesia brought an anticommunist government to power in that nation and an end to Confrontation, however, Indonesian armed forces dealt a severe blow to communist organizations operating in the Sarawak-Indonesian border area.

Communist forces on the border, much debilitated, regrouped under the NKCP structure. Although the NKCP numbered only some 700 during the late 1960s, the Malaysian government committed as many as 10,000 armed forces and police personnel to Sarawak to keep the communists in check. Under pressure and wracked by factional disputes, many guerrillas were killed or wounded. In 1973–74 a leader of the party, Bong Kee Chok, as well as some 550 other guerrillas, surrendered under a general amnesty proclaimed by the government.

Since the mid-1970s the NKCP has been confined to the vast, lightly populated, and remote jungle areas of Sarawak, where the guerrillas have been able to do little damage but have also been able to elude government forces with relative success. As in Peninsular Malaysia, counterinsurgency operations have concentrated on hitting food and ammunition dumps and generally keeping the guerrillas on the run. According to the government, only an estimated 20 communist guerrillas remained in Sarawak's First Division in early 1983. Some 80 to 100 were believed to inhabit areas of the Third, Sixth, and Seventh divisions, which the government has designated as constituting the special Rejang Security Command (RASCOM). Although the government continued to warn of the danger of communist terrorism in Sarawak during the early 1980s, little activity was noted until April 1983, when a 24-hour curfew was imposed on parts of the RASCOM area after the government received reports that guerrillas had come out of the jungles, gathering near the town of Sibu.

The NKCP has adopted as its goal the formation of the independent state of North Kalimantan, which would comprise both Sarawak and Sabah states as well as Brunei. The party considers the incorporation of Sabah and Sarawak into Malaysia to have been an illegal neocolonialist act. In keeping with its self-proclaimed adherence to "Marxism-Leninism-Mao Zedong thought" the NKCP has vowed to accomplish its goal by waging "people's war" in the countryside, building revolutionary bases to encircle the cities, and then seizing political power under the leadership of the proletariat. Little information could be located regarding the internal organization of the NKCP, other than that there was a central committee, which as of 1981 was chaired by Wen Ming Chaun. Front groups, including the North Kalimantan Liberation League, the Sarawak Peasants Association, and the North Kalimantan Iban Brotherhood Party, were believed to be little more than paper organizations. Communism in Sarawak originally drew most support from among Chinese; as of the early 1980s most members of the NKCP were believed to be ethnic Chinese or Indonesians.

Vietnamese Refugees

"Boat people" fleeing Vietnam began landing on the shores of the east coast of Peninsular Malaysia in sufficient numbers in 1978 to alarm local officials and to cause severe dislocations in the economy of the region, already relatively poor compared with the west coast. Public order in the area suffered as the influx of refugees grew. After the national government began sending aid to ease the local burden, residents of the predominantly Malay area expressed resentment that resources they believed would rightly be spent on aiding poor Malaysians like themselves were being diverted to foreigners. Ethnic sensitivities complicated the situation because an estimated 70 percent of the Vietnamese were ethnic Chinese. The refugees were also widely seen as posing potential threats to the national security because they came from a communist nation and possibly included communist subversives. Malaysia did accept for permanent settlement a small number of ethnic Chams, who were Muslims. One of these led the group that attacked the police station in Johore in 1980.

By mid-1979 the number of arrivals had reached as high as 15,000 in one month, and the problem reached crisis proportions. Although many refugees had been turned away from the shore or towed back out to sea, some 70,000 to 80,000 were being held in overcrowded refugee camps, and, despite navy patrols, many more were being found on the beaches each day. National authorities began to state publicly that Malaysia had its own problems and was not obliged to accept refugees. An international outcry ensured when then deputy prime minister Dato' Seri Dr. Mahathir Mohamad, echoing the sentiments of much of the coastal population, was quoted as saying that refugees in the nation would be towed out to sea while the government enacted legislation giving it the power to shoot on sight any refugee who entered the nation's territorial waters. Although Mahathir quickly declared that he had been misinterpreted, that statement and the tough stance adopted by Malaysia and other nations suffering from the refugee flow provoked an international reaction. Under the pressure of world opinion, in late 1979 Vietnam began to enforce a moratorium on departures.

During the early 1980s Malaysia reiterated that it would not accept Vietnamese refugees as legal immigrants, but the nation provided them temporary asylum. Refugees were housed at a camp on Bidong Laut Island, off the coast of Terengganu, pending their resettlement in other countries. Arrivals outnumbered departures, however, and officials feared that a permanent core of refugees might remain in the nation. In the first four months of 1983, for instance, there were some 5,600 new entrants to the camp, but only some 3,400 were accepted by other countries for immigration.

As of early 1984 the refugees presented a variety of public order and internal security problems. The camp at Bidong Laut Island was overcrowded, and social conditions have been exacerbated by the disproportionate number of single young men, many of whom had been in the camp for several months. The presence of unaccompanied children, presumably sent ahead by their families to act as anchors in a resettlement country for the rest to follow, has also been of concern, although fewer minors were sent out of Vietnam after nations accepting immigrants lowered the priority for unaccompanied children. Local officials have also expressed alarm that the presence of refugees has led to the development of a black market, which was accompanied by increased levels of corruption in the area. The national government continued to stress that refugees were possible sources of subversion.

In addition to the Vietnamese refugees, there were an estimated 100,000 refugees from the Philippines living in Sabah in the early 1980s. The overwhelming majority were Muslims who fled violence between the Philippine government and Filipino Muslim insurgents seeking a framework for autonomy in the southern Philippines. Unlike the Vietnamese refugees, the Filipinos shared a common ethnic and religious heritage with Malaysians and have not been seen as a security threat—although their presence has at times put a strain on local resources on Sabah.

The Security Setting and the National Defense Concept

National defense planners have long recognized that the nation's physical setting presents special logistics and patrol problems for military operations. Malaysia's two segments are separated by an approximately 650-kilometer stretch of the South China Sea. The western half of the nation forms a peninsula, one side of which borders the Strait of Malacca—a major international waterway for both commercial and military traffic. The country's extended coastline divides into two separate seaboards in the west and a third in Sabah and Sarawak, requiring a similar division of patrol formations. The extent of territory over which naval and air surveillance must be maintained was greatly expanded in 1979 when the nation extended the boundaries of its claimed territorial waters and in 1980 when the nation established a 200-nautical-mile Exclusive Economic Zone (EEZ—see Glossary) and made formal claims to portions of the Spratly Islands enclosed therein.

Land forces also faced special challenges, largely because many parts of the country remained quite inaccessible. Land transport in Sabah and Sarawak is confined to a sparse road network near the coast; inland much of the territory is still untracked jungle, swamp, and mountain terrain. Although there had been some improvement in the transportation network in Peninsular Malaysia by the early 1980s, many areas there are also impassable jungle, swamps, or mountains. The completion of the East-West Highway in 1982, however, provided an important boost to the limited road network linking the two coasts of the peninsula.

From the end of World War II until the late 1970s, defense readiness was viewed mainly as a function of maintaining internal security and focused on counterinsurgency or guerrilla warfare. Malaysian decisionmakers judged that national security could best be provided for by developing armed forces to support the police in dealing with internal subversion, pursuing friendly relations with neighboring states, and maintaining defense arangements with Australia, Britain, New Zealand, and Singapore. Developing the capacity to provide for independent self-defense against external aggression was considered a matter that could be addressed over the long term. Although the nation had been forced to deal with an external threat during the 1963–66 Confrontation with Indonesia, that campaign, in which British and other Commonwealth of Nations forces played a major role, stayed relatively low-key and had been settled without provoking a lasting change in Malaysia's national defense strategy.

The nation's defense needs were quickly reassessed, however, after Vietnam concluded a peace and friendship treaty with the Soviet Union in November 1978 and then invaded Kampuchea the next month. The resulting threat to Thailand, China's punitive attack on Vietnam in February 1979, and the growing role of the Soviet Union in Southeast Asia greatly alarmed national leaders. The influx of Vietnamese refugees provided a clear example of Malaysia's proximity and accessibility to Indochina and of Malaysia's vulnerability to regional instability. Many remembered that the Japanese invasion of Malaysia had been launched from the northeast coast of Peninsular Malaysia.

Responding to the changed security setting, the government initiated an armed forces modernization and expansion program that focused on rearming and retraining for conventional defense. The deputy defense minister in 1982 stressed, however, that the program represented only a "slight shift in strategy from guerrilla warfare to open warfare" and that counterinsurgency operations remained a top priority in the early 1980s. Special emphasis continued to be placed on the economic development of areas near the Thai border where the armed forces worked to maintain a "Maginot Line" of defense in order to guard the East-West Highway and other development projects.

Beginning in 1983 the armed forces turned to consolidating gains made in the 1979–82 period, focusing available resources on the development of a technologically modern force rather than reinforcing existing personnel strength. Defense planners had to make this trade-off under the pressure of economic constraints that caused the government to cut expenditures in all areas in 1982. The moves toward consolidation also reflected the fact that external challenges to the national security appeared less urgent than previously, instability in Indochina having come to be viewed as more of a medium-term threat than an immediate one.

The only exception to this attitude appeared to center on the protection of potential petroleum-bearing seabed areas underlying the nation's EEZ in the South China Sea. Vietnam, the Philippines, China, and Taiwan all have claims in the same area, which conflict principally in the Spratly Island Group. Since 1980 Vietnam has occupied a fortified position on one of the islands, Amboyna Cay, also claimed by Malaysia. Malaysia itself occupied an atoll in the region, Terumbu Layang Layang, in mid-1983.

Five-Power Defense Arrangement

Realizing that its defense forces were in a formative stage, the newly independent Federation of Malaya signed the Anglo-Malayan Defense Agreement (AMDA) with Britain in 1957. AMDA provided that Britain, while assisting in the development of the federation's forces, would remain the guarantor of the country's defense. In 1959 Australia and New Zealand, although not signatories of the agreeement, formally associated themselves with it. In 1963 Sabah and Sarawak, as well as Singapore, were brought under the provisions of AMDA, which was then retitled the Anglo-Malaysian Defense Agreement.

Malaysia began to speed up the development of its own forces after fiscal retrenchment in Britain in the mid-1960s culminated in the 1967 decision to withdraw its forces "east of Suez" by 1971. When AMDA itself was about to expire in 1971, the Malaysian government, expressing a continued requirement for external defense support, negotiated a five-power defense arrangement to take its place. Although no treaty was signed to formalize the new defense agreement, letters were exchanged spelling out the arrangements. Australia, Britain, and New Zealand were to station forces of modest size, most of them Australian, in Singapore and Malaysia. In the event of an attack on one member, other member countries were to hold immediate consultations on measures to be taken. The continuing indivisibility of Malaysia and Singapore for defense purposes was acknowledged. In 1971 all five members together formed the Integrated Air Defense System to provide for joint air defense of Malaysia and Singapore.

By early 1984 almost all Australian, British, and New Zealand forces deployed to Malaysia under the five-power defense arrangement had been withdrawn in recognition of Malaysia's progress in assuming responsibility for the independent defense of the nation. The only significant military unit remaining was one squadron of 23 Royal Australian Air Force Mirage jets stationed at Butterworth Air Base on the west coast opposite Penang. That squadron was scheduled to be withdrawn in late 1985. As of early

1984 the five-power defense arrangement was still in force, and Malaysia hoped it would remain so for the foreseeable future. Joint air exercises of two or more of the five countries continued to be held regularly as they have since 1971. Naval and ground exercises have been held jointly since 1981.

Foreign Military Relations

The maintenance of good relations with other nations in Southeast Asia was a keystone of national defense policy in the early 1980s, and toward that end Malaysia has vigorously promoted the goals of the Association of Southeast Asian Nations (ASEAN), of which it was a member along with Brunei, Indonesia, the Philippines, Singapore, and Thailand. Under Malaysia's sponsorship, ASEAN has embraced the goal of developing a Zone of Peace, Freedom, and Neutrality in Southeast Asia. ASEAN has no defense aspect, and Malaysian leaders have consistently indicated their determination that it should never develop one.

Military relations with other ASEAN member states were conducted strictly on a bilateral basis or, in the case of Singapore, through the five-power defense arrangement. Malaysia has cooperated closely with Singapore in intelligence matters relating to internal security in both nations. Malaysia has also maintained a naval facility at Woodlands, Singapore, for which it signed a new long-term access agreement in 1983. Members of the Singaporean armed forces were allowed to atend a combat training center in Malaysia, and Singaporean air defense was provided by the Integrated Air Defense System, the operating center of which was located at Butterworth Air Base.

During the early 1980s the nation maintained its closest military relations with Indonesia. The two countries have conducted joint anticommunist military operations on the borders of Sabah and Sarawak since the early 1970s and have cooperated on patrols aimed at preventing infiltration of either country as well as controlling smuggling and piracy, particularly in the Strait of Malacca, which both bordered. Malaysia and Indonesia have regularly held joint naval, land, and air exercises and participated in exchange programs for officer training.

Cooperation between Thailand and Malaysia in dealing with communist insurgents began in 1965 with the establishment of a joint border agreement and reached its peak during the 1977–78 period when the two nations together mounted major counterinsurgency operations along their shared border. According to Malaysian sources, small-scale joint operations have since continued, and with the permission of the Thais some 50 members of the Malaysian police were stationed in Songkhla, Thailand, in the early 1980s to aid in combating communists based near there. The two nations have also conducted joint naval operations since 1979 and joint air operations since 1981. Cooperation has been hampered, however, by long-standing border issues, principally disagreement over how to handle the movement mounted by ethnic Malays in southern Thailand. Thailand would like to obtain Malaysian cooperation in dealing with Thais who allegedly cross into Malaysia to take refuge there, but Malaysia has taken the position that the ethnic Malays in Thailand are not a common enemy and so do not constitute a proper target of joint military operations.

Malaysia has maintained only the most limited of military contacts with another member of ASEAN, the Philippines, owing to the disagreement between the two nations over the status of the Philippines' irredentist claim to Sabah. Malaysia contended that the Philippines has not satisfactorily renounced that claim. The Philippines, on the other hand, has charged that Malaysia has allowed Filipino Muslim insurgents to shelter in Sabah.

Malaysia has cooperated militarily with other nations, for instance joining in exercises in which Brunei, Canada, Japan, and the United States have also participated. A small number of armed forces personnel have pursued advanced military studies in Australia, Britain, India, and the United States. Malaysia has also accepted United States military aid in the form of Foreign Military Sales credits; these totaled approximately US$117 million over the 1972–82 period. The anticommunist Malaysian government has maintained no military relations with China, the Soviet Union, or East European countries. Malaysia committed elements to United Nations peacekeeping forces in the Congo in 1960 and in Namibia in 1983.

The Armed Forces in the National Life

The role of the military in the national life of Malaysia has been apolitical when compared with other developing countries or with many of its neighboring states. In Malaysia the armed forces were under the complete control of a civilian government that was widely accepted as legitimate by the general population, as well as by both the military leadership and rank-and-file personnel. The distinction between civilian and military affairs was sharply drawn and firmly adhered to. Defense forces were not directly involved in politics, and any expansion into nonmilitary roles appeared improbable as of early 1984.

Manpower and Personnel

Armed forces staff requirements have traditionally not presented a significant drain on the nation's work force. Combined strength in all three available pool of personnel of the requisite early 1984. The total available pool of personnel of the requisite age for military service (20–55) was some 5.2 million in the early 1980s, approximately one-half of whom were males. Although the pool from which recruits could be drawn was fairly large, the nation experienced isolated labor shortages during the early 1980s, especially in technical fields; this posed some difficulties for the military in attracting qualified recruits in certain specialties. The problem was complicated by the inability of the armed forces to offer economic incentives comparable to those obtainable in some private sector positions.

The ability to attract qualified recruits was also hampered by the decision to augment existing force levels rapidly, which compelled the services to be less selective than they might have liked. Armed forces strength grew nearly 60 percent from 1979 until mid-1982, when recruiting was frozen as a result of fiscal retrenchment brought about by adverse economic conditions. The rapid expansion in size had other negative effects on readiness. It put a strain on training resources, causing some officers to complain about the quality of their subordinates. The officer corps itself was hard pressed to find sufficient numbers of adequately trained and experienced personnel to fill the increased number of command assignments. Moreover, improvement in logistics and support services did not keep pace with force expanision. Although the recruitment freeze caused a scale-down in the creation of new combat units—especially in the army—many welcomed the opportunity to consolidate their gains and repair deficiencies caused by too rapid promotions or insufficient training

The nation had no compulsory national service laws, and the armed forces were completely staffed by volunteers. There have been no reported difficulties in attracting recruits. The National Security Ordinance, which had not been repealed by the early 1980s, required that all male citizens between the ages of 21 and 28 register for possible induction into one of the three military services, the police, or a civil defense force. It was unclear, however, whether the provisions of the law have been implemented since the Confrontation with Indonesia in the mid-1960s.

Recruitment was conducted on a centralized basis, candidates being selected for military service and then assigned to one of the three separate branches. There was some unsuccessful agitation during the early 1980s for each service to administer its own selection process. As of early 1982 a general freeze on recruitment remained in effect, exceptions being made only for physicians, engineers, and computer and other technical specialist. In 1981 over 90 percent of recruits were Malay males between the ages of 18 and 25, for whom service in the military was a desirable career because of pay and perquisites and because it enabled them to acquire badly needed technical skills.

Most members of the armed forces were Malay, and recruitment patterns perpetuated the ethnic composition. In 1981 some 75 percent of all officers and 85 percent of other ranks were Malay; 16 percent of officers and 6 percent of other ranks were Chinese. The highest percentages of non-Malays were found in technical specialties and in the navy and the air force. In the army most non-Malays served in the special forces or in the Malaysian Rangers, a multiethnic but primarily Malay regiment. As of late 1983 the chief of the defense forces and the three service chiefs and their deputies were Malay. In the army, three out of four division commanders and 11 out of 12 brigade commanders were Malay.

The overrepresentation of Malays in the armed forces does not appear to have been a subject of controversy or a major source of discontent in the military itself or in the society at large. It was generally acknowledged that the preponderance of Malays occurred despite efforts to increase non-Malay participation because very few non-Malays were attracted to military service. The reluctance to pursue a military career was especially noteworthy among the Chinese, who, in general, preferred to take advantage of the opportunities open to them in commercial or technical fields and did not wish to cut their ties with private business (which a career in the military would require), and questioned whether the topmost positions in the armed forces would be open to them. Although such matters were not publicly discussed within the military for security reasons, it did not appear that ethnically based factionalism has existed to any significant degree or that ethnic identity had been a factor in promotions, except perhaps to the very highest level posts, which have always been filled by Malays.

Top military leaders in Malaysia have regularly had strong family ties with the prime minister. For instance, the nation's first prime minister was an uncle of the then defense chief. The defense forces chief in early 1984 was a cousin of former prime minister Datuk Hussein bin Onn. The former prime minister's brother was deputy chief of the army until he was replaced in late 1983 by Major General Hashim Mohamad Ali, Mahathir's brother-in-law. Observers in the foreign press linked the premature retirement of the deputy chief of the army, Lieutenant General Datuk Ja'afar Onn, as well as that of the chief of the army and deputy to the chief of the defense forces, General Tan Sri Zain Hashim, to the constitutional crisis then under way. Speculation was that the two officers were more sympathetic with the position of the sultans in the constitutional crisis than with that of the government.

Women were accepted into the armed forces for service in noncombat positions. There were some 500 women in the army in the early 1980s; this represented well under 1 percent of the total armed forces personnel and far less than the 4 percent quota established for female personnel. Most women entered the army through the Army Reserve Force, a volunteer paramilitary organization. No figures could be located for the number of women serving in the navy and the air force.

Defense Spending and Industry

Armed forces budgets increased sharply after the modernization and expansion program was initiated in 1979 (see table 18, Appendix). Defense expenditures peaked in 1982 at almost M$3.7 billion (for value of the ringgit—see Glossary). In current prices that sum was over 150 percent higher than defense spending in 1978; in real terms defense expenditures had doubled. The 1982 defense budget accounted for 13.2 percent of the total central government expenditures, up from nearly 12 percent in 1978. Military spending as a percentage of the gross national product (GNP—see Glossary) was some 6.3 percent in 1982, the latest year for which figures were available as of early 1984.

Despite the steady growth of the defense budgets over the 1978–82 period, adverse economic conditions in the nation had led to budgetary retrenchment beginning in 1982, causing a number of planned defense projects to be postponed or scrapped altogether. Spending on defense fell 8.8 percent in 1983 and was projected to fall another 9.4 percent in 1984. Funds budgeted for 1984 represented 11.3 percent of total central government expenditures. The effect on the modernization program was uncertain.

The defense budget was divided into two parts development expenditures, which funded capital improvements, and operating expenditures, which covered salary and other routine expenses. Reflecting the emphasis laid on building a technologically modern force, development expenditures in 1982 were almost five times what they had been in 1978; in the 1981–83 period they accounted for 41 to 45 percent of the total armed forces budgets—a remarkably high ratio in any nation. In 1983, however, development expenditures were cut 16 percent and were projected to fall another 30 percent in 1984, bringing the development portion of the defense budget down to 31 percent. Although traditionally the army, by far the largest of the three services, had been allotted the lion's share of development expenditures, during the early 1980s priority was accorded to building up the air force and the navy to balance the capabilities of the three services.

Unlike in other Southeast Asian states, the military in Malaysia played virtually no role in the economic life of the nation. Members of the armed forces were forbidden to engage in private business. That caveat did not extend to retired personnel who have at times entered the business world after leaving active duty, but there was no evidence that they exercised significantly more influence than did their civilian counterparts. The military's institutional participation in public investment bodies was limited to a pension fund and a cooperative for uniformed personnel and civilian defense employees.

Procurement decisions were under the purview of the Supply Division of the civilian Ministry of Defense, which had final say over recommendations from each of the three services. The division was responsible for policymaking and management decisions regarding the provision of equipment and stores, including aircraft, ships, ordnance, electronics, rations, and services. The Defense Research Center supported the efforts of the Supply Division. The center, which was equipped with laboratory testing facilities, inspected equipment and carried out operations research development projects for the armed forces. Since 1980 each service has been responsible for its own routine logistics operations.

The domestic defense industry has largely been neglected, the nation relying mainly on foreign sources for most military equipment. Defense planners have indicated that they have a long-term plan to work toward self-reliance, however. As of early 1984 Malaysia had a small domestic arms production capacity, which was sufficient to meet much of the armed forces requirements for small arms, ordnance, and ammunition. Dockyards at several ports were capable of performing routine maintenance, and new dry-dock facilities at Lumut and dockyards near Singapore could provide full maintenance and repair facilities. During the early 1980s Italian M.B. 339 aircraft were locally assembled, and the air force was capable of performing major overhauls of up to fourth-echelon maintenance.

In mid-1983 a task force was formed to work out the details of setting up domestic production of assault rifles, envisioned to take the form of a joint venture between a government-owned corporation and a foreign arms manufacturer. The decision to proceed toward domestic production was taken for military rather than economic reasons: rifles could undoubtedly be purchased at a cheaper rate on the competitive international market than they could be made locally, but for national security purposes, it was deemed necessary to ensure an uninterrupted source of supply.

The Organization and Structure of the Armed Forces

The defense establishment comprises the civilian Ministry of Defense and the three separate military services. These are the Malaysian Army, the Royal Malaysian Navy, and the Royal Malaysian Air Force.

The modern Malaysian military traces its beginnings to an "experimental company" of 25 young Malays whom the British accepted into service in the colonial army on a provisional basis in 1933, in response to long-standing agitation for a Malay unit by the Malay rulers. The experiment was pronounced a success within a short time, and the unit was officially designated the First Battalion, the Malay Regiment, on January 1, 1935. A second battalion was formed in December 1941, in time to fight alongside the British army in an unsuccessful attempt to hold back the Japanese invasion later in the month. After the Japanese scattered across Peninsular Malaysia; some elements joined the British-supported guerrilla units known as Force 136.

After the war the British authorities recalled surviving members of the Malay battalions and reactivated the Malay Regiment. The outbreak of communist insurgency in 1948 led to the steady growth of the regiment, which by the end of the Emergency in 1960 had eight battlions and had been renamed the Royal Malay Regiment. As the name of the formation implies, entry into the Malay Regiment during the colonial period was restricted to Malays; the continuance of the unit's ethnic identity in the postindependence period is guaranteed in the Constitution.

The first multiethnic military units in the country were formed in 1953 when the threat posed by communist terrorists was at its height, and additional forces were needed. The new units comprised the Federation Regiment and the Federation Armored Car Regiment, renamed the Federation Reconnaissance Corps in 1960 and the Malaysian Reconnaissance Corps in 1963. Theoretically, the new units were to be composed of 50 percent Chinese, 25 percent Malays, and 25 percent Indians and Eurasians. In practice, however, few qualified Chinese responded, even when offered extra incentives to do so, and adherence to the planned ratios proved impossible.

After independence in 1957 the country continued to rely on Britain to provide external security, and British forces continued to be stationed in the nation. At the same time, the armed forces embarked on a long-term program to develop first the capacity to handle threats to public order and eventually to undertake independent self-defense as well. The army dominated the new nation's armed forces. The navy was only a fledgling force, and the air force was not set up until 1958. The new military establishment was closely patterned on the British model, and Britons continued to fill crucial positions in the defense structure until they were gradually replaced by Malaysians. Although a military college had been set up in 1954 to train officer recruits, many senior officers had attended the Royal Military Academy at Sandhurst or the British Army Staff College at Camberley.

When Malaysia was formed in 1963, a new unit known as the Malaysian Rangers was added to the army, increasing the non-Malay element in the armed forces. The rangers were an outgrowth of the Sarawak Rangers, expert jungle fighters created originally in 1862 by Sir James Brooke as an independent force to subdue tribal chieftains; these units were later incorporated into the Sarawak Constabulary (see Police, this ch.). During the years of the Emergency, the British army used ethnic Iban volunteers from Sarawak as jungle trackers to help in locating communist strongholds in Peninsular Malaysia; these units were given the name Sarawak Rangers in honor of the earlier formation. When the Emergency ended, the units returned to Sarawak and were incorporated into the British army as colonial forces available for worldwide service. The Sarawak Rangers were released from British service into the Malaysian Army when Sarawak was incorporated into Malaysia in 1963; at the same time, they were renamed the Malaysian Rangers.

Using British help, the rangers began to expand into a multiethnic force. The first battalion comprised the Iban of the Sarawak Rangers; most of the second battalion was raised in Sabah, formed around a cadre of personnel from the Royal Malay Regiment and the Malaysian Reconnaissance Corps. Subsequent batalions were recruited on a Malaysia-wide basis. Within a few years, the first two battalions of the rangers lost their original territorial and ethnic connotations and assumed a more integrated multiethnic character. Except for a few specialized or technical units, the Malaysian Rangers although often commanded by officiers from the Royal Malay Regiment, remained the sole multiethnic formation of any significance in the armed forces as of the early 1980s.

The armed forces were built up gradually during the 1960s, spurred by the Confrontation with Indonesia and, more important, by the British decision to withdraw its forces from east of the

Suez. Total armed forces strength grew from 33,000 int he mid-1960s to 50,000 in 1971. The withdraw most heavily affected the air force, which in a very short period had to take over air defense of the nation, replace personnel seconded from British forces with Malaysians, and acquire new aircraft to fill the vacuum left by the pullout of the British Royal Air Force. The navy was faced with similar problems and, like the air force, had to increase its strength and inventory. Despite the need to assume an increased responsibility for external defense, the armed forces remained oriented toward filling an internal security role.

The army, highly experienced in guerrilla warfare, continued to be the dominant branch of service. During the 1969 riots, army units were called in to restore order in Kuala Lumpur when available police proved unable to do so. The army's forceful crowd-control techniques—of which the Chinese community bore the brunt—prompted many observers to question the utility of employing the army, which was trained for combat, in a law enforcement role. Thereafter, special police units were set up to provide for such contingencies, although the armed forces continued to be charged with supporting the police when necessary (see Police, this ch.).

The new emphasis on external defense in the wake of the Vietnamese invasion of Kampuchea in 1978 focused the attention of strategic planners on acquiring a conventional defense capability. For the first time, the armed forces conducted extensive training exercises in conventional warfare tactics, and the air force and navy began to be upgraded not only to act as support elements of the ground forces but also to take on external surveillance and defense roles. As of early 1984 the services were in the process of consolidating training and support for the large numbers of recruits brought into the forces during the 1979 to mid-1982 period, while continuing to augment their inventories with modern equipment.

The Ministry of Defense

Command of the armed forces is vested by the Constitution in the supreme head of the federation, also known as the paramount ruler (see The Federal Government, ch. 4). All activities of the defense establishment are carried out under his authority, as ex officio supreme commander of the Malaysian armed forces. The Constitution further specifies that all officers hold the paramount ruler's commission and that he has the prerogative of granting mercy in military offenses triable by court-martial. The power to declare war, however, rests with the parliament. Thus, the armed forces are servants of both the paramount ruler and the people, the latter exercising control through elected representatives in the parliament, which determines the size and composition of the services and appropriations needed to support them.

In practice, control of the armed forces in early 1984 was exercised by the National Security Council (NSC), which was under the Ministry of Home Affairs and had the responsibility for coordinating the country's defense and security efforts. Proceedings of the NSC were not made public; meetings were chaired by the prime minister (who has also held the defense portfolio since 1980) and attended by selected cabinet members. Attending the meetings as representatives for security matters were the chief of the armed forces staff and the inspector general of police. States and districts also had security councils at which the police and army were represented: subjects usually discussed covered social and economic issues believed to have ramifications for internal security, including the problem of squatters in rural and urban areas and matters relating to development projects.

The Ministry of Defense was the headquarters of the defense establishment but was subject to the decisions and directions of the NSC. The ministry was a completely civilian institution. The minister chaired the Armed Forces Council, which was responsible for administrative, command, and disciplinary matters related to the armed forces. Matters relating to their operational use remained the province of the NSC. One member of the Armed Forces Council was appointed by the Conference of Rulers (see The Conference of Rulers, ch. 4). Other members included the chief of the armed forces staff, the secretary general for defense, senior staff officers of each service, and, at times, additional military or civilian members.

Joint planning and coordination of the armed forces was accomplished through the offices of the Chief of the Armed Forces Staff Committee. The committee also was responsible for giving the Ministry of Defense and the NSC professional advice on strategy and operations and on the military implications of defense policy. It included the chief of the armed forces staff as chairman, the three service chiefs of staff, the chiefs of the personnel and supply staffs of the Ministry of Defense, and the chief of staff of the Ministry of Defense. The ministry was divided into six functional divisions that operated on a combined service basis and the army, navy, and air divisions, which administered their own services and acted as command headquarters.

The Ministry of Defense maintained several training institutions for officers of all three services. The Armed Forces Defense

College ran courses on a variety of military subjects for up to 400 officers a year. The Malaysian Armed Forces Staff College prepared officers for command, staff, and managerial positions that were open to field-grade officers. In 1982 the college expanded its syllabus to allow each service to offer courses of interest to its own officers during the second term of the one-year program. The National Institute of Defense Studies was open to officers above the rank of brigadier general. The latter two institutions were located at the Ministry of Defense headquarters in Kuala Lumpur. A plan to relocate them to the site of the Armed Forces Defense College at Rawang, some 30 kilometers distant, fell victim to fiscal retrenchment in mid-1982, but it was uncertain as of early 1984 whether the plan had been scrapped or whether its implementation has simply been postponed.

Army

The Malaysian Army in early 1984 was essentially a light infantry force of about 80,000 strong. Its traditional character was being transformed, however, by the acquisition of armored vehicles. The army had formerly eschewed armor because of its marginal utility in jungle terrain or guerrilla warfare.

The army was organized according to the conventional pattern into 12 infantry brigades under the operational command of four divisional and one corps headquarters (see table 19, Appendix). The infantry brigades were composed of 37 battalions, 26 of which made up the all-Malay Royal Malay Regiment and 11 of which belonged to the multiethnic Malaysian Rangers. Additional formations included three cavalry, four field artillery, one armored personnel carrier, five engineer, and five signals regiments; two antiaircraft batteries; and one special forces (commando) regiment.

Ground forces also included the general services corps, which handled clerical, pay and education, legal, and public relations services; the military police; electrical and mechanical engineers, medical and dental, ordnance, intelligence, and women's corps; and the Army Reserve Force. For administrative convenience, the army was organized into two regional units: Region I, comprising Peninsular Malaysia, and Region II, comprising Sabah and Sarawak.

As of early 1984 army vehicles included light tanks, armored cars, armored scout cars, and armored personnel carries. A large number of armored fighting vehicles and personnel carriers were on order. Arms included 5.5-inch guns, 105mm howitzers, 81mm mortars, 89mm rocket launchers, 120mm recoilless rifles, antitank guided missiles, and antiaircraft guns. The basic infantryman's weapon was the M-16.

The Malaysian special forces regiment was organized in 1965 to conduct commando-style operations on land and sea and by air. It had a virtually independent tactical role in the army and acted as the chief of the Army Reserve Force. In the early 1980s the special forces consisted of a headquarters establishment in Kuala Lumpur and one parachute and one special forces battalion that were billeted in Sungai Udang, Malacca. The special forces ran its own training center.

The army maintained recruit training centers at Port Dickson in Negeri Sembilan and at Kota Kinabalu in Sabah. After basic training at one of these, noncommissioned recruits received further training in units to which they were assigned. Specialist training was available at a variety of schools. Cadet officers of all three services spent their first four months of service undergoing basic training at Port Dickson. Army cadets then entered the Royal Military College at Sungai Besi for either the regular two-year course or, in some cases, a one-year, short-service course. The army maintained the Jungle Warfare School in Johore and offered advanced officer training in technical specialties. As did the other services, the army also sent some personnel overseas for further education.

According to the army leadership, the quality of officers and other personnel turned out by the training centers during the 1979–81 period was adversely affected by the rapid expansion of forces. The problem was complicated by a lack of adequate training facilities in the country. During that period, greatly increased personnel requirements forced the military to be less choosy in selecting recruits than it would have liked. Young officers had to be placed in positions of command before they were sufficiently trained or experienced to handle command responsibilities. Combat proficiency, morale, administration, and discipline were said to have suffered. Recognizing this, the army slowed its own growth in 1981, well before the government-ordered cutback in mid-1982.

The Army Reserve Forces, formerly known as the Territorial Army, formed the nation's second line of defense; it numbered an estimated 35,000 as of mid-1982. Plans to expand the reserves to a number equal to or greater than the regular army by 1990 had to be shelved in 1982 because of economic constraints. Reservists were volunteers who trained on weekends and at annual camps. Most units were raised in rural areas, and training took place in regular army camps in small towns. Since 1979 reserve officer training units have been in place in institutions of higher learning in the nation. Rank structure and military formations were similar to those found in the regular army. The Army Reserve Force was intended to support the regular army and performs functions identical to it. Defense analysts in the early 1980s have noted, however, that before the reserves could provide optimal combat support, there must be considerable improvement in training, the professional standards of reserve officers, and equipment supply and services. In addition to the reserves, there were also small militias known as the Local Defense Corps, organized in some remote villages to provide counterinsurgency support and intelligence.

Navy

The Royal Malaysian Navy (RMN) came into being as a volunteer force to augment British naval forces during World War II. Most of its personnel served aboard ships of the British Royal Navy in India, Ceylon, and East Africa. This volunteer force was demobilized after the war but was reactivated in 1948 as an indigenous force under British command and control. It served in the area as a colonial defense unit until independence in 1957, at which time it was transferred to the new government. The naval force continued to be based at Woodlands, Singapore, however. In 1970 the government began building a base for its navy at Lumut, on the coast of Perak facing the Strait of Malacca; it was scheduled for completion in 1984, when it was to become the Fleet Operations Command Center and the main fleet base. As of early 1984, the RMN headquarters was located in Kuala Lumpur. The navy continued to use the base at Woodlands, to which Singapore had guaranteed it long-term access. Other bases included a modern facility at Kuantan on the east coast of Peninsular Malaysia, which was completed in 1981, and a facility at Labuan Island, Sabah, that was undergoing improvement in the early 1980s. Operational command of naval forces was shared by naval commanders at Woodlands and Labuan Island, who had authority to operate ships out of Peninsular Malaysia and out of Sabah and Sarawak, respectively.

The navy was undergoing expansion in the early 1980s to meet new responsibilities associated with the increase of areas under its control and changes in the regional security setting. In light of this, it was seeking to acquire a force capable of performing both a blue-water role as well as inshore and coastal patrol tasks. Naval operations focused mainly on the Strait of Malacca and the South China Sea. The former is a heavily traveled international waterway, where for many centuries pirates have preyed on unarmed commercial vessels (see Federated and Unfederated States, 1826–1909, ch. 1). In addition to ensuring safe transit through the strait, the navy also devoted its resources to maintaining constant surveillance on Soviet warships using the channel, which averaged three per month in the 1981–82 period. United States naval vessels, which used the strait over twice as frequently during the same period, were not so closely watched. Operations in the South China Sea appeared to center on protecting seabed resources believed to underlie Malaysia's EEZ and, over the longer term, on providing defense against possible threats to national security from the Indochina region. During the late 1970s and early 1980s the navy also devoted some attention to patrolling the seas separating Sabah and the Philippines, where piracy and smuggling have long been problems.

The navy was the smallest of the three services in early 1984, having a personnel strength of approximately 8,700 (see table 20, Appendix). The RMN was attempting to build a balanced fleet: its inventory included two frigates (one of which carried surface-to-air missiles) and eight missile fast attack craft, in addition to conventionally armed fast attack craft, large patrol vessels, minesweepers, landing vessels, and other support craft. On order were two missile frigates and four minehunters. The fleet had no submarines in early 1984, but Malaysia has expressed interest in seeking foreign assistance to provide submarine training for some of its personnel.

After undergoing basic training at Port Dickson, naval officer cadets entered a three-year course at the Singapore base. That program included a year of sea training. Personnel of other ranks attended special schools at various facilities. Most training of officer cadets and other ranks was scheduled to be moved to the Lumut base during the mid-1980s. The navy had a small volunteer reserve force, the Royal Malaysian Naval Volunteer Reserve.

Air Force

The Royal Malaysian Air Force (RMAF) was the youngest of the nation's armed forces. It was created in 1958 with personnel who had been serving with the British Royal Air Force as flight personnel or with the Royal Air Force Regiment (Malaya) in guard and maintenance units. Using a number of seconded personnel from the British air force, the RMAF first performed an air transport role in support of the army. In the late 1960s it began to work toward developing the nucleus of an air defense capability in anticipation of the British pullout in 1971, and during the 1970s the RMAF lent limited air strike support to army counterinsurgency operations. Not until the armed forces modernization and expansion program was inaugurated in 1979, however, did the national defense doctrine embrace the concept of the air force acting in more than a support role for the army. At that time, the RMAF began to be developed along conventional lines, stress being laid on improving air defense and maritime surveillance capability.

The RMAF headquarters was located in Kuala Lumpur in early 1984. Operational control of the air fleet was vested in the commander air headquarters, who was assisted in Sabah and Sarawak by the deputy commander. In early 1984 a new air force facility was under construction at the Subang Airport near Kuala Lumpur. The older Sungai Besi air base, also near Kuala Lumpur, had been in operation since the 1950s and was unsuitable for further expansion. Upon completion, the Subang base was to become the major base for air transport. At that time, the Sungai Besi base was to become the home of the helicopter squadrons, the air operations command headquarters, and the air support division. Fighter aircraft were deployed at the Kuantan, Butterworth, or Alor Setar bases. Other bases were located at Kuching in Sarawak, Labuan Island in Sabah, and Kluang in Johore. Plans to build a major new base at Gong Kedak on the east coast of Kelantan fell victim to budgetary retrenchment in 1982.

The air force had a personnel strength in early 1984 of about 11,000. Most observers agreed that the RMAF attracted relatively more Chinese that the other services, particularly as pilots. The air force's inventory of over 200 aircraft included 16 jet fighters, 12 counterinsurgency aircraft, a large number of transport, reconnaissance, liaison, and training aircraft, and 71 helicopters (see table 21, Appendix). The most advanced aircraft was the F-5E/F Tiger II fighter. The RMAF also had United States-made Sidewinder air-to-air missiles. On order were some 40 A-4 jet fighters and the improved Super Sidewinder air-to-air missle. The air force was organized into 15 squadrons based on type and mission of aircraft involved. Many of the trainer aircraft were capable of performing a dual combat/trainer role. One squadron of Australian Mirage fighter-bombers was based at Butterworth under the combined command of the integrated Air Defense System; they were not used in operations against local insurgents.

Training was the responsibility of the Air Support Command, which also handled logistics. After taking basic training, cadet officers entered a two-year course at the army's Royal Military College. Pilots then took basic flight training on Swiss-made PC-7 trainers at the Flying Training School at Alor Setar. Advanced jet training was offered at Kuantan on Italian-made M.B. 339A airplanes. Both these aircraft were acquired in the early 1980s. Specialist training in a variety of subjects was available at the Air

Technology Institute and at Kuantan, Labuan Island, and other locales. No data were available regarding the size of the Royal Malaysian Air Force Volunteer Reserve in the early 1980s, but the volunteer force, which was open to both men and women, was believed to be quite small.

Ranks and Conditions of Service

Officer grades corresponded to those in the British system with minor deviations, which occured mainly in the RMAF, where grades of company- and field-grade officers corresponded almost completely to those of the Malaysian navy (see fig. 11). Officer insignia in the army and air force featured various combinations of stars and crowns, both of which were based on traditional Malay designs, as well as a crossed kris and sheath. The kris was a traditional Malay dagger having a wary blade that in current times was carried only by Malay royalty and dignitaries on ceremonial occasions.

There were six ranks of noncommissioned personnel in the army and air force and five in the navy. The highest noncommissioned rank was a warrant officer class I, but that was not equivalent to the warrant officer rank in the United States armed forces, there being no warrant officer rank in the Malaysian armed forces.

Most uniforms were essentially the same as those in the British forces. The most distinctive exception belonged to the officers and other ranks of the Royal Malay Regiment, where the normal white ceremonial uniform for noncommissioned personnel was worn with a dark green sarong extending from waist to knee. For officers, the ceremonial dress consisted of a white tunic, black trousers, and a black sash. Ceremonial headdress for all members of the Royal Malay Regiment was a *songkoh,* a traditional Malay cap.

In early 1984 the pay system was the same for all three services and consisted of a base salary as well as certain allowances. Incremental pay increases within grade usually occurred at two-year intervals. Extra emoluments included uniform and, under certain circumstances, housing allowances. Army commandos, navy divers, and air force pilots, among others, were granted additional bonuses. Medical and dental benefits were minimal. The entire compensation schedule has been revised periodically to reflect economic conditions, and in general the armed forces offered compensation equivalent to that in the civil service. This has been less true, however, in comparison with the private sector, especially for technically trained individuals.

The usual retirement period for enlisted ranks was after 21

years of service. For company-grade officers or their navy equivalents, the mandatory retirement age was 45; for major and lieutenant colonel and their equivalents it was 50; and for colonel (or navy captain) and above, 55 years of age. Retirement pay was based on a percentage of base pay depending on the number of years of service. Provisions were made for widows of retirees and widows of uniformed personnel who died while on active duty.

Police

The Royal Malaysian Police (RMP) was the sole institution authorized to carry out police activities; it was under the control of the federal government. The RMP was headed by the inspector general of police, who was responsible to the minister of home affairs for the control and direction of the force. The only other military force in Malaysia besides the three armed forces and the police was the small Johore Military Force, a largely ceremonial palace guard maintained by the sultan of Johore.

Historical Development

From their earliest times, the police in Malaysia have had a marked paramilitary aspect. Fifteenth-century accounts of life on the peninsula describe a feudal society in which the ruler of a particular area was supreme and one of the next most powerful figures was the *temenggong*, who was in charge of the armed forces and the police. The duties of the *temenggong* included arresting criminals, building prisons, and carrying out executions. A police force under his control patrolled city streets at night; control of outlying areas was left to village headmen. Neither the Portuguese nor the Dutch colonial authorities made any significant change in this system.

In the first years of British hegemony the responsibility for enforcing law and order was also left largely to community leaders and, by the mid-nineteenth century, to business guilds in some Chinese and Indian settlements. Paramilitary formations of Sikhs and Punjabis and recruits from the northern portion of British India were sometimes used to keep order in towns. The first modern police force was established in Penang in 1806 and the second in Malacca in 1824. Within a few decades other police forces were organized on a state basis. Five of these were consolidated into the Federated Malay States Police force in 1896. That organization was less an integrated unit, however, than one under centralized British administration. Police forces in the unfederated

OFFICERS

Army	Leftenan Muda	Leftenan	Kaptan	Mejar	Leftenan Kolonel	Kolonel	Brigadiar Jenderal	Mejar Jenderal	Leftenan Jenderal	Jenderal	Field Marshal
UNITED STATES EQUIVALENT	Second Lieutenant	First Lieutenant	Captain	Major	Lieutenant Colonel	Colonel	Brigadier General	Major General	Lieutenant General	General	General of the Army
Navy	Pegawai Muda Laut	Naib Leftenan Muda	Leftenan Laut	Komander Muda	Komander	Kapitan	Komodor	Laksama Muda	Naib Laksama	Laksama	Laksama Tentera Laut
UNITED STATES EQUIVALENT	Ensign	Lieutenant Junior Grade	Lieutenant	Lieutenant Commander	Commander	Captain	Commodore	Rear Admiral	Vice Admiral	Admiral	Fleet Admiral
Air Force	Leftenan Muda Udara	Naib Leftenan Udara	Leftenan Udara	Komander Muda Udara	Komander Udara	Kapitan Udara	Komodor Udara	Naib Marshal Udara	Marshal Udara	Marshal Besar Udara	Marshal Tentera Udara Di-Raja
UNITED STATES EQUIVALENT	Second Lieutenant	First Lieutenant	Captain	Major	Lieutenant Colonel	Colonel	Brigadier General	Major General	Lieutenant General	General	General of the Air Force

Figure 11. Ranks, Insignia, and United States Equivalents for Malaysian Armed Forces, 1984

ENLISTED RANKS

Army	Private	Lance Corporal	Corporal	Sergeant	Staff Sergeant	Warrant Officer Class I
UNITED STATES EQUIVALENT	Basic Private	Private First Class	Corporal	Staff Sergeant	Sergeant First Class	Sergeant Major
Navy		Lance Corporal	Corporal	Sergeant	Staff Sergeant	Warrant Officer Class I
UNITED STATES EQUIVALENT		Seaman	Petty Officer Third Class	Petty Officer First Class	Chief Petty Officer	Master Chief Petty Officer
Air Force	Private	Lance Corporal	Corporal	Sergeant	Staff Sergeant	Warrant Officer Class I
UNITED STATES EQUIVALENT	Basic Airman	Airman First Class	Senior Airman	Technical Sergeant	Master Sergeant	Chief Master Sergeant

NOTE–There is no insignia worn for the rank of private, and there is no navy equivalent.

Figure 11. Continued.

states were generally more autonomous, having a comparatively larger Malay component. There were very few Malays in the officer corps of any of the forces, however, and very few Chinese at all.

During the latter part of the nineteenth century and the early part of the twentieth century, the area that is now called Peninsular Malaysia was characterized by almost constant disorder punctuated by insurrections and rebellions in various states. Many local territorial chiefs employed armed retainers, who often terrorized the countryside. Increased immigration of Chinese and Indians brought new problems, including those associated with urbanization. Criminal activity by Chinese secret societies also complicated the situation. Under these conditions, law enforcement authorities were required to maintain a paramilitary capability to combat banditry and terrorism in outlying areas and to develop an increasingly sophisticated capacity for handling criminal investigations.

Law enforcement in Sabah and Sarawak in traditional times was rudimentary, often dealing only with tax collection. In Sarawak, the first police forces were formed by "White Raja" Sir James Brooke, the first of the white rajas, in the nineteenth century. These later became the Sarawak Constabulary, in which emphasis was placed on paramilitary training and procedures. In the portion of northern Borneo that later became the Malaysian state of Sabah, the British North Borneo Company raised the North Borneo Armed Constabulary in 1882.

When the Japanese occupied the peninsula in 1942, they used the police to persecute the Chinese and to support operations against the largely Chinese anti-Japanese guerrilla forces and their suspected supporters. When the war ended and the British returned to the peninsula in 1945, the police organization was in disarray, and much of the police force was no longer trusted by the public. To deal with these problems, the British merged the forces previously under Japanese control and started retraining and reorganizing the entire force. In Sabah and Sarawak, which were ceded to Britain in 1946, the British dealt with the police in a similar manner. The Sarawak Constabulary was organized into the Regular Police, having responsibility for civil police duties; the Field Force, which patrolled jungle and outlying areas; and the Special Force, created to investigate and combat subversion. A similar police establishment was set up in Sabah.

The police force on the peninsula, renamed the Federation of Malaya Police in 1948, was assigned the primary responsibility for maintaining public order in the face of threats by communist insurgents, the Emergency being viewed as essentially a law and order, rather than a national security, problem. Joint operations with the armed forces were under police control, and combined units were referred to as "security forces." During the first years of the prolonged Emergency period, the size of the police force was increased fourfold, and an auxiliary police of a somewhat greater size was organized. At its peak strength the police, including reserves and auxiliaries, numbered some 163,000. In recognition of the importance of gathering information in counterinsurgency conflicts, the Special Branch of the police was assigned primary responsibility for running the national intelligence system.

During the Emergency the government attempted to transform the police from a virtually all-Malay force into a multiethnic one. For the most part, however, this proved unsuccessful because few Chinese could be induced to join. A small number of Chinese did enter service in the officer corps and in nonuniformed elements, such as the detectives, but only in the Special Branch was the Chinese component of significant size.

As order was reestablished in the nation, the police increasingly turned to performing civil police duties. Some paramilitary units were retained, however, to protect the Malaysia-Thailand border and to staff forts in and around the Cameron Highlands, established to protect the aboriginal Orang Asli from communist terrorism or subversion.

The incorporation of Sabah and Sarawak into Malaysia in 1963 led to the creation of the RMP, in which the constabularies in Sabah and Sarawak were also brought under the control of the federal government. Police from Peninsular Malaysia were soon seconded to Sabah and Sarawak to augment the size of forces there and help them develop standards comparable to those on the peninsula.

As was the case with many other elements in Malaysian society, the 1969 riots had lasting effects on the police. During the riots, army units had to be called in when it became clear that the situation was beyond the control of the police. The magnitude of the problem led the police subsequently to increase the strength of the force's paramilitary units. At the same time, the counterinsurgency responsibilities assigned to the police were cut back to allow them to concentrate more on civil policing, and the army assumed the chief role in conducting operations against guerrillas. The police retained responsibilities, however, for intelligence gathering and for combating underground communist activity, including infiltration, subversion, and sabotage.

As of early 1984 the RMP remained a national force in the sense that it operated under the authority of the federal government. Complete integration had not been attempted, however. Although personnel from Peninsular Malaysia continued to be seconded to the forces in Sabah and Sarawak, personnel from Sabah and Sarawak were not regularly assigned to the peninsula. The organization of the RMP below the state level in Sabah and Sarawak has also not been standardized with that in Peninsular Malaysia.

Organization and Structure

The strength of the RMP was estimated to number some 60,000 in the early 1980s. For security reasons, however, exact figures were rarely made public. There were an additional several thousand volunteers who assisted with security tasks when needed. Although the geographical distribution of police personnel was also not made public, it was generally assumed most were in Peninsular Malaysia.

The headquarters of the RMP was located in Kuala Lumpur. It was organized on a directorate basis to carry out the missions of maintaining law and order, preserving the peace and security, preventing and detecting crime, apprehending offenders, and collecting security intelligence. RMP headquarters consisted of the Office of the Inspector General and four staff departments: Management, Criminal Investigations, Internal Security and Public Order, and Special Branch. The police commissioners of Sabah and Sarawak and the chief police officers of the state-level forces in Peninsular Malaysia were responsible for day-to-day command and administration. The RMP maintained state-level forces in all states except Perlis and Kedah, in which a single joint force operated. A state-level force was also maintained for the Federal Territory of Kuala Lumpur. All of the headquarters of the state-level forces were organized in the same manner, as was the federal headquarters.

Matters relating to the equipping, staffing, and general administration of the RMP were handled by the Management Department. The department was responsible for providing training, personnel, and logistics support for all elements of the force. It also handled public relations and maintained a computer division for record keeping. Virtually all day-to-day civil policing fell under its purview, including matters relating to the Traffic Police. The Management Department also administered the three auxiliary police units in Peninsular Malaysia—the Police Volunteer Reserves, auxiliary police assigned to public institutions, and the Police Reserve—as well as the Border Scouts and Auxiliary Police maintained in both Sabah and Sarawak.

In carrying out responsibility for control and coordination of logistics for the RMP, the Management Department also administered the Marine Police and the Air Police. The former was essentially a coast guard. It was tasked with patrolling the territorial and coastal waters to prevent, detect, and investigate breaches of the law, including piracy and illegal fishing in territorial waters. The Marine Police assisted the navy in maritime search and rescue missions and interception of unauthorized vessels entering Malaysian territorial waters, and in general it policed areas of the country accessible only by water. The Marine Police have contributed to counterinsurgency operations in northern Peninsular Malaysia, supported security forces operating against insurgents in Sarawak, and run antipiracy and antismuggling patrols in the Strait of Malacca and off the coast of Sabah. In early 1984 the Marine Police had nearly 50 patrol boats and several other smaller craft. The far smaller Air Police was used for surveillance, transport, and rescue missions. During the early 1980s it had fewer than five aircraft and operated only in Peninsular Malaysia.

The Criminal Investigations Department (CID), created in 1970, was responsible for detecting and investigating criminal offenses and prosecuting criminals. At both federal and state levels, the CID was organized into functional specialties that dealt with specific kinds of crimes. It also maintained the Malayan Railway Administration at the federal level. Details regarding the operations of the nonuniformed CID were not generally made public.

Command of the paramilitary units of the RMP was vested in the head of the Internal Security and Public Order Department, which handled all matters affecting security and joint military-police operations against communist insurgents in border areas. The department also supported the regular police throughout the nation. The director of the department had authority over the Police Field Force (PFF) and the Federal Reserve Units (FRU); he was also responsible for the formation and training of Area Security Units (ASU) in parts of the nation considered vulnerable to internal security challenges. The director sometimes exercised operations control over the Marine Police.

The PFF was trained and equipped on military lines. It was estimated to number some 19,000 in early 1984 and to be organized into 21 battalions, including two Orang Asli battalions that operated directly under the army. The PFF was trained for jungle warfare, and its units were deployed to undertake field operations against insurgents, to contain and suppress riots, and to support the activities of the regular police. Personnel were recruited among the regular police and usually served a seven-year stint in the unit before transferring back to regular duty. Participation by PFF battalions in counterinsurgency operations occurred when the battalions were assigned to support army brigades—usually for three-month stretches. At other times they performed more conventional public order and policing duties. The PFF was equipped with armored cars and personnel carriers. It had a special commando unit that went by the suboriquet "Vat 69."

The FRU were special, highly mobile formations trained to deal with critical public order situations. They were tasked with suppressing riots and dispersing illegal assemblies, controlling crowds, supporting other police units, and assisting in rescue work during national disasters. The FRU were usually based in major towns.

In 1976 the Internal Security and Public Order Department began to form ASU in parts of the country where extra security precautions were considered necessary. These were highly mobile strike-force units, in which senior officers were regular police personnel and subordinates were locally recruited Extra Police Constables. Each platoon-sized unit was trained and equipped similarly to the PFF. Units went on jungle patrols for up to three days at a time and conducted operations against small guerrilla units in their locales; they were intended to dominate their areas both by denying the guerrillas physical entry and by countering communist propaganda. The ASU were in place only in Peninsular Malaysia, where there were an estimated 89 formations in early 1984, numbering some 3,500 personnel. The Border Scouts in Sabah and Sarawak, estimated to be about 1,200 strong, performed similar tasks.

The Special Branch of the RMP was the nation's principal security intelligence agency. Since the Emergency period, it has been charged with collecting, assessing, and disseminating intelligence on all aspects of the national security. The armed forces also maintained a small intelligence unit, but military intelligence officers were usually seconded to the Special Branch to assist in liaison and coordination between the police and the military. Details of the organization, operations, and strength of the Special Branch were not made public. The Special Branch was believed to comprise units based on functional specialties, the most well-known of which being that assigned to surveillance over the CPM. The Special Branch also focused its attention on other potential security threats, including interethnic relations and religious extremism. The degree to which it concerned itself with matters relating to external security was uncertain. There were believed to be a large number of Chinese personnel in the element of the Special Branch that dealt with the CPM.

Personnel and Training

By law, entry into the RMP was open to members of all ethnic groups. Most observers agreed, however, that the ethnic composition of the police did not reflect that of the general population. Because a career in the police has long been popular with Malay villagers, most of the police in Peninsular Malaysia were Malay. In Sabah and Sarawak most of the police came from ethnic groups native to those states. Indians were present at all levels of the RMP, particularly so at the upper levels. Chinese usually served only in the CID or in elements of the Special Branch.

Entry into the RMP depended on the educational qualifications of the applicant. Candidates who had completed at least the sixth year of primary education could enter as constables, the lowest rank in the RMP. Constables were trained at the Police Training School in Kuala Lumpur, which also offered refresher courses to veteran personnel. Those who held certificates from upper secondary schools could enter either as probationary inspectors or could apply for entry into the Police Academy, established in the mid-1970s. Graduates of the Police Academy entered the force as probationary assistant superintendents. Advanced training was available at the Police College. The Special Branch, PFF, and CID maintained separate schools. Personnel from other nations in the region have regularly attended RMP training institutions, and, conversely, RMP officers have often been sent to police courses in foreign countries. The RMP has run language courses in Thai, Vietnamese, Khmer, Mandarin, Tagalog, and Arabic. Instruction in Islam was also included in the RMP curriculum.

Crime and the Criminal Justice System

Public safety did not appear to be imperiled by any abnormally high incidence of crime, and law enforcement officials and the criminal justice system seemed to be coping adequately with what problems did occur. Although, as in all nations, statistics on criminal activity in Malaysia were flawed in various ways, available infoirmation suggested that rates of crime in the 1970s and early 1980s compared favorably with those in other developing countries and several developed ones as well. Preliminary figures indicated that the rise in the incidence of crime experienced in the 1970s had leveled off by the end of the decade and that the incidence of crime had actually fallen in the 1981–82 period. The fall was attributable to declines in both violent crimes and property offenses. Almost one-half of all violent crime in 1982 continued to take the form of robbery without firearms, and property crimes accounted for almost 90 percent of all criminal offenses.

Geographically, the rate of violent crime was highest in the west coast states of Peninsular Malaysia. Over the 1978–80 period, Perak recorded the highest rate of crime in the nation. In 1981–82, however, the Federal Territory of Kuala Lumpur acquired that dubious distinction, reflecting an increase in robbery, assault, and motor vehicle theft associated with the growing urbanization of the area. The nation experienced a disproportionate increase in crimes by juveniles over the 1978–82 period. The government attributed the rise to a lack of parental control and guidance, presumably associated with disruptions in the traditional social structures, and with high levels of unemployment, especially among school dropouts. Curbing juvenile delinquency and rehabilitating juvenile offenders became a high priority of law enforcement officials.

Malaysia's highest law enforcement priority was reserved for combating narcotics trafficking and drug addiction. In early 1983 the minister of home affairs stated that the nation's drug problem was of "epidemic proportions" and posed a threat to the national security. According to most estimates, during the early 1980s Malaysia had the highest per capita incidence of opium or heroin addiction of any nation in Southeast Asia and a considerably higher proportion than the United States. There were 88,000 registered drug addicts in Malaysia as of mid-1982. Drug trafficking on a major scale was usually confined to ethnic Chinese. Addicts were found among all ethnic groups, however, most being males between the ages of 16 and 30. Evidence also pointed to a growing use of marijuana in the early 1980s.

Penang Island, part of Penang State on the west coast of Peninsular Malaysia, was the principal point for domestic distribution of narcotics. The island was also a major international transhipment center for opium and heroin from the area where Burma, Laos, and Thailand converge—commonly known as the Golden Triangle. Drugs were smuggled in by organized syndicates; most entered the nation by sea from Thailand or Burma, but some were brought into the country overland from Thailand and then taken from Malaysian ports to Penang Island. Law enforcement officials found it impossible to police the rugged coastline of the island and the neighboring mainland or the undeveloped border area between Malaysia and Thailand. Some observers have also claimed that laboratories for refining opium into heroin have at times operated in the Malaysia-Thailand border area. It was known that chemicals necessary to the refining process have been illegally imported into Malaysia and then disappeared, presumably used in-country or shipped to refineries in neighboring states.

The nation has enacted very tough antinarcotics laws and control procedures, but drug abuse continued to rise during the early 1980s. Since 1975 all traffickers have been liable for either life imprisonment or the death sentence; the death sentence has been mandatory for trafficking in more than a minimal amount of controlled substances. Many traffickers have been executed. Malaysians used the local term *dadah* to refer to any illicit drug but most often heroin; campaigns against *dadah* were run regularly in schools and the media. There was even a committee against *dadah* in the NSC.

In early 1983 the government moved to toughen its stand further, shifting emphasis from public health to law enforcement and internal security by transferring responsibility for combating the problem from the Ministry of Welfare Services to the Ministry of Home Affairs. Also in 1983 the government passed several new amendments to existing antinarcotics legislation. These authorized police or customs officials to open correspondence and tap telephones of suspected drug offenders; permitted medical officers to examine, forcibly if necessary, any suspects; and lowered the amount of controlled substance necessary to qualify suspects as traffickers. Other new legislation permitted authorities to take suspected addicts into custody for up to one day for medical tests; that period could be extended to two weeks upon securing an order from a magistrate.

The nation had two other special law enforcement problems. Chinese criminal societies, although far less powerful than in the past, continued to operate in Malaysia. Moreover, in the early 1980s Malaysian authorities had to contend with large-scale smuggling of tin both from Thailand to smelters in Malaysia and from Malaysia to smelters outside the country. Malaysia was the world's largest producer of tin; through smuggling it was possible to circumvent quotas on the tin exports, which were designed to maintain international prices on the commodity.

Security Offenses

Offenses covered under the Internal Security Act (ISA) as amended formed a distinctive category of crime, for which the government employed law enforcement and trial procedures substantially different from those used to deal with ordinary crime. The ISA was passed at the end of the 1948–60 Emergency to replace the Emergency Regulations, which were first promulgated by the British and then became part of the national law at independence. Enactment of the ISA in 1960 ensured that the provisions of the Emergency Regulations would continue to have the force of law after the state of emergency was lifted.

The ISA provides for "preventive detention, the prevention of subversion, the suppression of organized violence against persons and property . . . and for matters incidental thereto." Under it, the minister of home affairs is authorized to detain for renewable two-year periods—or place restrictions on the freedom and movement of—any person "acting in any many prejudicial to the security of Malaysia . . . or to the maintenance of essential services therein or to the economic life thereof." This ISA also authorizes the minister of home affairs to prohibit the wearing of uniforms of military or quasi-military organizations, to prosecute members of proscribed quasi-military organizations, and to prohibit the printing, sale, and distribution of any documents or publications that he considers prejudicial to the national interest, public order, or national security. Under the ISA police can arrest and detain suspects for up to 60 days without charging them with a crime if they have reason to believe the suspect had acted or was about to act in a manner that would require detention under the ISA. The ISA was amended in 1975 to make the death sentence mandatory for possessing firearms, ammunition, and explosives in areas designated "security areas" or for providing such items to others in those areas.

Malaysian courts interpreting the powers delegated under the ISA have held that in case of preventive detention, the burden of proof lies with the detainee, who must, unlike in ordinary criminal cases, prove his innocence. Procedures regulating preventive detention under the ISA were in comformity with constitutional restrictions on preventive detention. These ensured that the detainee could present his case to an advisory board that would review it every two years and make recommendations regarding the disposition of the detainee's case. The recommendations of the advisory board were not binding, however, and the Constitution provided that on the grounds of national security the government could not be required to disclose all its evidence to the advisory board or to the detainee.

In late 1975, in the wake of increased terrorism by communist insurgents, the government used laws enacted in 1969 (when the state of emergency still in effect in early 1984 was first declared) to introduce new procedures for use in handling security cases. The new procedures were issued as the Essential (Security Cases) Regulations 1975, under the Emergency (Essential Powers) Ordinance 1969; the latter was issued by the National Operations Council during the 1969–71 period when the parliament was suspended (see The Kuala Lumpur Riots of May 1969 and Their Aftermath, ch. 1; Recent Political Developments, ch. 4). A legal challenge to the validity of those regulations was appealed in 1978 to Britain, to the Judicial Committee of Her Majesty's Privy Council (see Criminal Procedure, this ch.). The Privy Council ruled that the 1969 ordinance was invalid because executive promulgations during a state of emergency had the force of law only until the parliament could sit once again. In early 1979 the parliament enacted the 1969 ordinance as the Emergency (Essential Powers) Act 1979, thereby revalidating the 1975 regulations.

Providing for the use of extraordinary legal procedures in security cases, the regulations applied ex post facto and to juveniles. They authorized prosecutors to arrest without warrant anyone suspected of security offenses. When brought to trial, an accused and his counsel were entitled only to a copy of the charges against him. Evidence of witnesses could be heard in the absence of the accused and his counsel; witnesses could testify in disguise or anonymously; the government could confine defense cross-examination of witnesses to written form. The accused was denied protection from self-incrimination. Evidence by hearsay, juveniles, accomplices, and in the form of affidavits was admissible. The regulations required the judge to impose the maximum penalties for all offenses.

The lack of specificity of what constituted offenses under the ISA has drawn criticism from both inside and outside the nation, as have the extraordinary procedures enacted in 1975 to bring offenders to trial. The national leadership has consistently defended the need for the ISA and the regulations, however, arguing that without these measures it could not cope with existing threats to national security. The government took the position that detainees were not political prisoners but had taken part in communist, procommunist, or subversive activity, or had been involved in proscribed organizations that were dedicated to the overthrow of the government by force. In early 1983 the minister of home affairs stated that detainees had not been tried because there was insufficient evidence to convict them but could not be released without threatening public order or national security.

Since 1969 an estimated 3,500 persons have been detained for varying periods under the ISA. In mid-July 1981, when Prime Minister Mahathir took office, there were 540 still held. Since then the government has maintained a tough stance on the need for the ISA and has used the legislation; at the same time, it has released many detainees, some of whom had been held for over 10 years. The number of detainees in mid-1983 was estimated to have fallen to around 300. Many of those released since mid-1981 had not been required to confess or recant publicly, as had previously been the case. Some were released conditionally and were still subject to restrictions on their freedom of movement and activity.

Penal Law

Criminal law is primarily defined in the penal code that was written by the British for the Straits Settlements and came into force in 1872. The code was modeled on the Indian Penal Code of 1860 and was gradually applied in other sections of Peninsular Malaysia. In 1948 it was amended to cover all the peninsular states. Other amendments followed, the most important of which was one in 1976 that among other things extended the coverage of the code to include Sabah and Sarawak, raised the age of criminal liability from seven years of age to 12, introduced the principal of extraterritorial jurisdiction for offenses against the state, and provided that maximum fines set by the Penal Code be raised fourfold.

The Penal Code defines categories of offenses as those against the state, the armed forces, public tranquillity, the person, or property. It also details crimes by public servants and offenses relating to giving false evidence, coins and currency, public health, religion, documents and banknotes, breaches of trust, marriage, defamation, and criminal intimidation, insult, or annoyance. The Penal Code lists death, imprisonment, caning, and fines as legally approved punishments. The Criminal Procedure Code establishes that the sentence of death be carried out by hanging and that caning be limited to 24 strokes for adult males and 10 for youthful males. Caning of females, males sentenced to death, and males over the age of 50 was prohibited. Pregnant women could not be sentenced to death.

Under the Penal Code, the death sentence was mandatory for murder and of attempting to murder or injure the head of any Malaysian state. Offenses punishable either by death or by life imprisonment included perjury resulting in the execution of another person, abetting the suicide of persons under the age of 18 or of unsound mind, kidnapping for murder, and certain offenses relating to the armed forces. According to Amnesty International, at least 14 persons were put to death in 1982, most for drug trafficking offenses.

The Penal Code provided that criminal culpability could be

mitigated by several factors, including age, intent, self-defense, accident, mistake, insanity, or actions taken under the physical compulsion of another. Intoxication was not a defense unless it had occurred through no fault of the offender or had rendered the offender insane at the time of the crime; intoxication could be a mitigating factor in proving intent, however. Under the Criminal Procedure Code, if a person found to have committed an offense was acquitted by reason of insanity, that person could be confined to a safe place, including a mental institution. The Penal Code also established that abetment of criminal offenses and criminal conspiracy constitute legally culpable offenses.

In most cases a judge had considerable latitude in passing sentences. For many crimes the Penal Code established both maximum and minimum penalties or maximum penalties alone and left the judge to decide the sentence appropriate to the offender and the seriousness of the offense. With the exception of few crimes, all prison terms were for life or for 10 years or less. Caning, fines, and imprisonment could be adjudged singly or in conjunction with the sentence.

Criminal Procedure

The RMP had primary responsibility for criminal investigation and arrest; police were required to have an arrest warrant except in security cases, when an offender was caught in the act, or when an offense was punishable by three years or more of imprisonment. Police also assisted advocates within the Prosecution and Litigation Division of the Attorney General's Office, who represented the state in prosecuting criminal offenders. The attorney general served as the nation's chief public prosecutor.

Responsibility for investigation and prosecution of criminal corruption offenses was vested in the National Bureau of Investigation (NBI), also under the authority of the attorney general. The NBI was set up in 1973 to replace the Anti-Corruption Agency; its officers were not members of the RMP but had the powers of police officers. The NBI chiefly enforced the Prevention of Corruption Act of 1961 but also investigated and prosecuted cases under the Penal Code, the Customs Act of 1967, and other laws.

Criminal court procedures were based on the British system and were outlined in the Criminal Procedure Code. Under that code, accused individuals were guaranteed a fair trial in one of the established courts having jurisdiction in the area where a crime was committed. An accused had a right to counsel, and an indigent accused was provided counsel at the state's expense in serious cases. Bail was possible except for serious offenses or for offenses under security legislation. In nonsecurity offenses, trial was in open court, although trial could be held in camera at the judge's discretion. An accused could not be retried for the same offense, but in some cases the prosecution could appeal to a higher court.

Criminal and civil cases were adjudicated in Malaysia's court system, the structure of which at the highest levels—the Federal Court and two subordinate high courts—is set forth in the Constitution. An amendment ratified in early 1984 renamed the Federal Court the Supreme Court. The Constitution leaves the organization of lower courts to be set up under federal statute; it also provides for the states to establish courts that exercise jurisdiction over matters relating to religious and customary law when all parties are subject to the same system of religious or customary law.

The Supreme Court is the highest court in the land. It functioned primarily as an appeals court but is mandated original jurisdiction over other matters as well (see Judiciary, ch. 4). The nation's two high courts had final appeals jurisdiction in matters of fact in criminal cases; there was one high court for Peninsular Malaysia, having its principal seat at Kuala Lumpur, and one high court for Sabah and Sarawak, which sat at Kuching. The high courts also had original jurisdiction in all criminal cases outside the jurisdiction of subordinate courts and over all capital cases.

Decision was made by judge alone in all criminal cases in the nation except in Peninsular Malaysia where, in capital cases and cases under the Kidnapping Act of 1961, the judge sat with a jury. Decisions rendered by the two high courts in criminal cases could be appealed only on procedural grounds. Formerly, decisions on criminal cases could be appealed to Britain to the Judicial Committee of Her Majesty's Privy Council; this avenue of appeal was abolished on January 1, 1978, however. Appeal on civil grounds remained technically possible. In early 1984 a constitutional amendment severed that residual link between the Malaysian and British legal establishments.

The subordinate court system differed in Peninsular Malaysia, Sabah, and Sarawak. In Peninsular Malaysia there were three levels of courts that exercised jurisdiction in criminal cases; these included the *penghulu* (village headmen) courts, which were used less to try cases than to facilitate the informal settlement of minor disputes, and magistrate's and sessions courts. Offenders between the ages of 10 and 18, except those accused of offenses punishable by death or life imprisonment, were tried in camera in juvenile courts. Juvenile courts had no jurisdiction in security cases. Decisions of both sessions and magistrate's courts could be appealed to the High Court in Malaya.

In Sabah and Sarawak there were no juvenile courts. Subordinate courts consisted of magistrate's courts divided into three classes according to the limits of their jurisdictions. The magistrate's courts tried less severe criminal cases, the remaining few being tried directly in the high court. Magistrate's courts in Peninsular Malaysia and Sabah and Sarawak heard 94 percent of all criminal cases in the nation in 1981.

In Peninsular Malaysia the states maintained a system of Islamic courts, in which a Muslim judge presided over courts that rendered decisions on Islamic religious law. These courts had jurisdiction only over Muslims and only over offenses punishable with up to six months' imprisonment, a fine of up to M$1,000, or both. Decisions of the religious courts could be appealed to the rulers.

A separate system of courts known as native courts operated under state law in Sabah and Sarawak; these tried cases rising from breaches in customary law, including Islamic religious law, when all parties were subject to the same customary law. In Sarawak appeals from these courts lay to resident's native court and sometimes to the Native Court of Appeal. In Sabah decisions could be appealed to a district officer or to the Native Court of Appeal.

Offenders convicted in either the federal courts or state religious or customary law courts could apply to the ruler or the governor of the state in which the offense occurred for pardons or for mitigation of the sentence. The paramount ruler exercised this power over offenders tried by courts-martial, sentences imposed by Islamic courts in Malacca and Penang states, and decisions of the Islamic and federal courts in the Federal Territiory of Kuala Lumpur.

The Prison System

Traditional policies and concepts regarding prisons and the treatment of prisoners as basically punitive have been modified by the concept that reformation and rehabilitation of prisoners would better serve society's interests. Since 1953 the principles governing the treatment of offenders and the management of penal institutions in the nation have conformed almost entirely with the Standard Minimum Rules for the Treatment of Prisoners prepared by the United Nations. As was the case in many developing nations, however, living conditions in Malaysian prisons were at best spartan, and medical treatment was sometimes inadequate. Amnesty International has charged that offenders detained under security legislation have been subjected to particularly harsh treatment, held in solitary confinement, and physically abused. A delegation of lawyers from France, Japan, and the United States, representing various human rights groups, visited several penal institutions in the nation in August 1982 and publicly confirmed a number of those charges.

The Malaysian Prison Department under the Ministry of Home Affairs administered and operated the prison system. During the early 1980s there were 30 penal institutions, including 18 prisons, five juvenile reformatories, two rehabilitation centers, and five detention camps in the nation. The total of those confined was some 11,000 in 1981. Most penal facilities were conventional walled compounds; some of the juvenile reformatories were open farms where inmates worked the field and acquired agricultural skills. First offenders and well-behaved prisoners were generally separated from recidivists and serious offenders. There were also separate facilities for women. Those detained under security legislation were segregated form other prisoners. According to Amnesty International, detainees were held at the Batu Gajah Special Detention Camp and the Taiping Detention Camp, both in Perak, as well as at a camp in Sibu, Sarawak, and one near Kuching, Sarawak. Amnesty International has also charged that some detainees have been held for months at a time at centers maintained by the RMP Special Branch.

* * *

Information on Malaysian national security must be drawn from a variety of sources, there being no single publication offering a summary of all relevant matters. Stanley Bedlington's *Malaysia and Singapore: The Building of New States,* however, provides an excellent, if dated, introduction to issues that continue to affect Malaysian security. Anthony Short's *The Communist Insurrection in Malaya, 1948–1960* offers a detailed look at the history of communist insurgency in Penisular Malaysia. More current data on communism in Malaysia can be found in Richard Sim's *Malaysia: Containing the Communist Insurgency,* in "Anti-Terrorist Operations in Peninsular Malaysia" by R. Sachithananthan, and in annual issues of the *Yearbook on International Communist Affairs,* edited by Richard Staar. Human rights and social issues are treated in *Report of an Amnesty International Mission to the Federation of Malaysia: 18 November-30 November 1978* and in yearly issues of *Amnesty International Report* and *Country Report on Human Rights Practices*, the latter presented to the United States Congress by the Department of State. The texts of Malaysian security legislation contain valuable reference material: these include the Internal Security Act of 1960 and the Essential (Security Cases) Regulations 1975, which, like all Malaysian legislation, are published in *His Majesty's Government Gazette*.

No single comprehensive study of the Malaysian armed forces could be located. Kin Wah Chin's *The Defence of Malaysia and Singapore* treats the development of security arrangements with Britain, Australia, New Zealand, and Singapore up to 1971 and touches on the development of the Malaysian armed forces as well. Three articles by Harold Crouch—"An Arm's-Length Stance on Business Activities," "A Strict Division," and "Time to Consolidate on a New Front Line"—provide valuable insights into the state of the armed forces as of late 1983. Monthly issues of the *Asian Defense Journal*, published in Kuala Lumpur, focus on current developments in the armed forces and contain articles on historical matters and the security of the Southeast Asian region. Two articles in particular, "The Making of an Air Force" and "The Malaysian Army: An Overview," both by A. Khalid, were helpful in preparing this chapter.

Standard references for data on military matters in various nations include annual issues of the International Institute for Strategic Studies' *The Military Balance* and also *Jane's All the World's Aircraft*, *Jane's Armour and Artillery*, *Jane's Fighting Ships*, *Jane's Infantry Weapons*, and *Jane's Weapon Systems*. Also valuable are *DMS Market Intelligence Report: South America/Australasia; World Armies*, edited by John Keegan; *Combat Fleets of the World*, edited by Jean Labayle Couhat; *Encyclopedia of World Air Power*, edited by Bill Gunston; *Air Forces of the World*, edited by Mark Hewish et al.; and *Air Power*, edited by Anthony Robinson. Information on defense spending and other matters can be found in annual issues of *World Military and Social Expenditures* by Ruth Leger Sivard; *World Armanents and Disarmament: SIPRI Yearbook*, prepared by the Stockholm International Peace Research Institute; and *Foreign Military Sales, Foreign Military Construction Sales, and Military Assistance Facts*, put out by the United States Department of Defense.

Sources of information on the police and the criminal justice system include "The Bayonet and the Truncheon" and "The edited by Tun Mohamed Suffian; and *Singh's Commentary of the* Police and Political Development in Malaysia," both by Zakaria bin Haji Ahmad; *An Introduction to the Constitution of Malaysia, Malaysian Criminal Procedure Code* by Awther Singh. Data on the institutional set-up of the police, the judiciary, and the criminal justice system are available in the yearbooks *Malaysia* and *Information Malaysia*. (For further information and complete citations, *(see Biblography)*.

Appendix

Table

Table 1. Metric Conversion Coefficients

When you know	Multiply by	To find
Millimeters	0.04	inches
Centimeters	0.39	inches
Meters	3.3	feet
Kilometers	0.62	miles
Hectares (10,000 m^2)	2.47	acres
Square kilometers	0.39	square miles
Cubic meters	35.3	cubic feet
Liters	0.26	gallons
Kilograms	2.2	pounds
Metric tons	0.98	long tons
. . . .	1.1	short tons
. . . .	2,204	pounds
Degrees Celsius . . . . (Centigrade)	9 divide by 5 and add 32	degrees Fahrenheit

Table 2. Fertility Rates by Ethnic Group, Peninsular Malaysia, 1970 and 1980

Ethnic Group	Age-Specific Fertility Rate (by age-group)[1]					
	15–19	20–24	25–29	30–34	35–39	40–44
Malay						
1970	75	250	265	226	150	75
1980	41	195	256	211	146	66
Decline (in percentage)	45	22	3	7	3	12
Chinese						
1970	26	199	292	229	140	70
1980	24	159	230	159	66	23
Decline (in percentage)	8	20	21	31	53	67
Indian						
1970	72	279	264	202	117	54
1980	46	210	240	148	55	18
Decline (in percentage)	36	25	9	27	53	67
Total[2]						
1970	57	234	275	224	142	71
1980	36	185	245	185	108	46
Decline (in percentage)	37	21	11	17	24	35

Year	Total Fertility Rate[3]			
	Malay	Chinese	Indian	Total[2]
1970	5.21	4.78	4.94	5.02
1980	4.58	3.31	3.59	4.03
Decline (in percentage)	12	31	27	20

[1]Number of annual live births per 1,000 women in the age-group.

[2]Total does not include other ethnic minority groups.

[3]Number of live births a woman would have if she experienced the current levels of age-specific fertility for her entire reproductive period.

Source: Based on information from Malaysia, Department of Statistics, *1980 Population and Housing Census of Malaysia: General Report of the Population Census*, Kuala Lumpur, 1983, 48.

Table 3. Population of Peninsular Malaysia by State and Ethnic Group, 1980

	Malay		China		Indian		Total[1]	
State	Thousands	Percentage	Thousands	Percentage	Thousands	Percentage	Thousands	Percentag
Johore	877	14	598	16	103	9	1,580	14
Kedah	781	13	199	5	81	7	1,078	10
Kelantan	799	13	45	1	6	1	859	8
Malacca	241	4	170	5	33	3	447	4
Negeri Sembilan	260	4	197	5	93	9	551	5
Pahang	519	8	197	5	50	5	769	7
Penang	303	5	485	13	103	9	901	8
Perak	789	13	710	19	241	22	1,744	16
Perlis	115	2	22	1	4	0	145	1
Selangor	647	11	524	14	248	23	1,426	13
Terengganu	495	8	27	1	3	0	525	5
Federal Territory	305	5	478	13	128	12	920	8
TOTAL[2]	6,132	100	3,651	100	1,093	100	10,945	100

[1]Includes 69,000 persons belonging to other unspecified ethnic groups.
[2]Figures may not add to total because of rounding

Source: Based on information from Malaysia, Department of Statistics, *1980 Population and Housing Census of Malaysia: General Report of the Population Census*, Kuala Lumpur, 1983, 21.

Table 4. Ethnic Composition of Peninsular Malaysia by State, 1980
(in percentage)

State	Malay	Chinese	Indian	Other	Total*
Johore	56	38	6	0	100
Kedah	72	18	8	2	100
Kelantan	93	5	1	1	100
Malacca	54	38	8	1	100
Negeri Sembilan	47	36	17	0	100
Pahang	68	26	7	0	100
Penang	34	54	11	1	100
Perak	45	41	14	0	100
Perlis	80	15	2	3	100
Selangor	45	37	17	0	100
Terengganu	94	5	0	0	100
Federal Territory	33	52	14	1	100
PENINSULAR MALAYSIA	56	33	10	1	100

*Figures may not add to total because of rounding.

Source: Based on information from Malaysia, Department of Statistics, *1980 Population and Housing Census of Malaysia: General Report of the Population Census*, Kuala Lumpur, 1983, 21.

*Table 5. Urban Population and Growth Rates by Ethnic Group, 1970 and 1980**

Area Ethnic Group	Percentage of Population in Urban Areas		Average Annual Growth Rate (1970–80)	
	1970	1980	Urban Areas	Rural Areas
Peninsular Malaysia	29	37	4.7	0.9
Malay	15	25	8.0	1.4
Chinese	48	56	3.2	-0.2
Indian	35	41	3.2	0.5
Sabah	16	21	6.0	3.3
Sarawak	15	18	3.9	2.0
MALAYSIA	27	34	4.7	1.2

*Urban area defined as having 10,000 or more inhabitants.

Source: Based on information from Malaysia, Department of Statistics, *1980 Population and Housing Census of Malaysia: General Report of the Population Census*, Kuala Lumpur, 1983, 16, 21.

Table 6. Structure and Growth of Gross Domestic Product, 1970–83[1]
(in percentage)

Sector	Share of GDP		Average Annual Growth Rate[2]				
	1970	1982	1971–75	1976–80	1981	1982	1983[3]
Agriculture, forestry, and fishing	32.0	24.0	4.8	3.9	4.2	6.3	2.1
Mining and quarrying	6.6	4.2	0.4	8.9	-2.0	6.3	20.1
Manufacturing	13.9	18.3	11.6	13.5	4.9	3.6	7.4
Construction	4.0	5.3	6.6	12.6	15.1	10.8	8.4
Utilities	1.9	2.5	9.8	10.2	9.9	8.6	8.9
Transportation, storage, and communications . . .	4.9	7.7	13.0	9.6	2.3	9.5	10.0
Wholesale and retail trade	13.8	13.8	6.3	8.2	6.9	7.7	5.4
Financial and business services	8.7	8.0	7.2	8.0	7.7	5.5	5.8
Government services	11.5	13.4	10.1	9.0	17.1	3.4	3.1
Other services	2.6	2.8	9.3	6.6	4.2	6.3	6.6
GROSS DOMESTIC PRODUCT[4]	100.0	100.0	7.4	8.5	7.1	5.2	5.6

[1]Gross domestic product (GDP—see Glossary) at 1970 market prices, not deducting imputed bank charges and adding import duties. Current price series were unavailable but would show a larger share for industry and services.
[2]Straight-line estimation starting from year before the period and ending on last year of the period.
[3]Preliminary estimate.
[4]Figures may not add to total because of rounding. Totals under average growth are averages, not sums, and are based on GDP adjusted for import duties and bank charges.

Source: Based on information from Malaysia, *Fourth Malaysia Plan*, 1981–1985, Kuala Lumpur, 1981, 11; and Malaysia, Ministry of Finance, *Economic Report, 1983–84*, 12, Kuala Lumpur, 1983, xiv–xv.

Table 7. Incidence of Poverty in Peninsular Malaysia by Occupation, 1970 and 1980[1]

Occupation	1970				1980			
	Thousands		Percentage		Thousands		Percentage	
	Households	Poor Households	Incidence of Poverty	Share of Poor	Households	Poor Households	Incidence of Poverty	Share of Poor
Rural								
Agriculture								
Rubber smallholders	350.0	226.4	64.7	28.6	425.9	175.9	41.3	26.4
Oil palm smallholders	6.6	2.0	30.3	0.3	24.6	1.9	7.7	0.3
Coconut smallholders	32.0	16.9	52.8	2.1	34.2	13.3	38.9	2.0
Paddy farmers	140.0	123.4	88.1	15.6	151.0	83.2	55.1	12.5
Other agriculture	137.5	126.2	91.8	16.0	172.2	110.5	64.1	16.6
Fishermen	38.4	28.1	73.2	3.5	42.8	19.4	45.3	2.9
Estate workers	148.4	59.4	40.0	7.5	112.5	39.5	35.1	5.9
Total agriculture	852.9	582.4	68.3	73.6	963.2	443.7	46.1	66.6
Other industries	350.5	123.5	35.2	15.6	546.4	124.8	22.8	18.7
Total rural	1,203.4	705.9	58.7[2]	89.2	1,509.6	568.5	37.7[2]	85.3
Urban								
Mining	5.4	1.8	33.3	0.2	5.4	1.8	33.0	0.3
Manufacturing	84.0	19.7	23.5	2.5	182.3	24.4	13.4	3.7
Construction	19.5	5.9	30.2	0.7	34.0	5.9	17.4	0.9
Transportation and utilities	42.4	13.1	30.9	1.7	85.0	16.3	19.2	2.4
Trade and services	251.3	45.4	18.1	5.7	467.7	49.2	10.5	7.4
Total urban	402.6	85.9	21.3[2]	10.8	774.4	97.6	12.6[2]	14.7
TOTAL	1,606.0	791.8	49.3[2]	100.0	2,284.0	666.1	29.2[2]	100.0

[1]Poverty line definition not available but, according to the government, took into account changes in prices and subsidies to the poor.
[2]Average incidence, not sum.

Source: Based on information from Malaysia, *Fourth Malaysia Plan, 1981–1985*, Kuala Lumpur, 1981, 34.

Table 8. Distribution of Per Capita Gross Domestic Product (GDP) by State, 1970 and 1980[1]

Sector	GDP per Capita (in ringgit)[2]		Percentage of GDP per Capita[3]											
			Selangor[4]		Penang		Sabah		Negeri Sembilan		Johore		Perak	
	1970	1980	1970	1980	1970	1980	1970	1980	1970	1980	1970	1980	1970	1980
Agriculture, forestry, and fishing	347	407	68	59	42	33	191	193	127	136	132	135	88	89
Mining and quarrying	75	85	148	70	---	1	6	283	10	14	31	8	318	175
Manufacturing	167	377	316	255	127	226	18	11	128	88	95	106	121	72
Construction	49	83	280	232	107	104	106	113	48	74	48	70	51	65
Utilities	21	42	200	204	136	139	67	53	101	157	79	74	116	103
Transportation, storage, and communications	57	119	194	237	137	159	111	82	117	98	98	77	76	61
Wholesale and retail trade	155	231	260	213	170	204	98	75	41	78	53	75	99	85
Financial and business services	101	151	166	171	107	125	94	81	95	98	81	82	91	94
Government services	132	238	217	169	57	102	97	71	117	106	90	87	69	85
Other services	32	46	226	237	130	145	63	59	74	90	106	78	127	89
ALL SECTORS	915	1,836	184	145	81	128	111	101	98	99	92	94	100	86

Table 8. (Continued).

Sector	Percentage of GDP per Capita[3]													
	Pahang		Malacca		Sarawak		Terengganu		Kedah[5]		Perlis		Kelantan	
	1970	1980	1970	1980	1970	1980	1970	1980	1970	1980	1970	1980	1970	1980
Agriculture, forestry, and fishing	159	137	851	87	83	86	79	100	121	124	n.a.	119	72	69
Mining and quarrying	87	37	6	5	187	265	37	338	12	4	n.a.	4	2	3
Manufacturing	44	37	42	50	46	34	16	23	21	21	n.a.	27	11	12
Construction	96	57	39	62	102	112	24	40	47	24	n.a.	15	56	50
Utilities	42	59	88	120	56	53	21	54	25	39	n.a.	46	25	36
Transportation, storage, and communications	86	53	70	61	65	58	40	26	45	43	n.a.	16	65	59
Wholesale and retail trade	46	44	85	115	71	63	33	38	15	35	n.a.	14	28	32
Financial and business services	96	78	90	97	60	57	88	78	85	81	n.a.	76	90	71
Government services	114	99	119	106	68	71	66	85	56	73	n.a.	112	54	71
Other services	74	61	81	95	47	50	7	38	33	41	n.a.	28	4	28
ALL SECTORS	100	81	75	80	78	75	52	72	62	69	n.a.	60	48	46

---means less than 0.5 percent.
n.a.--not available.
[1]Gross domestic product (GDP--see Glossary) in constant 1970 prices divided by the total population. Except for "All sectors" total, not adjusted to add import duties and subtract imputed bank charges.
[2]For value of the ringgit--see Glossary.
[3]Value from each region divided by population in each region and expressed as a precentage of the national average.
[4]fIncluding the Federal Territory (Kuala Lumpur), which had a regional per capita GDP equivalent to 217 percent of the national average in 1980.
[5]Including value from Perlis in 1970, for which separate data are unavailable.

Source: Based on information from Malaysia, *Fourth Malaysia Plan, 1981–1985*, Kuala Lumpur, 1981, 100–101.

Table 9. Distribution of Selected Consumer Durables by State, 1980

State	Households (in thousands)	Percentage of Total Households Having Each Item: Auto-mobile	Motor-cycle	Refri-gerator	Tele-phone	Air Con-ditioner	Radio	Tele-vision	Electric Fan
Peninsular Malaysia									
Johore	286.4	18	42	29	6	1	76	61	38
Kedah	215.5	12	34	15	4	1	64	36	25
Kelantan	177.5	10	24	11	2	1	65	28	18
Malacca	80.5	19	35	37	8	2	80	63	47
Negeri Sembilan .	105.0	20	42	33	7	1	76	59	42
Pahang	150.0	16	41	19	4	1	72	50	27
Penang	163.7	23	37	40	15	3	75	59	58
Perak	332.1	17	35	27	7	2	71	52	41
Perlis	31.9	12	37	18	3	1	71	38	30
Selangor	266.8	28	36	40	15	5	80	68	51
Terengganu	106.9	10	27	14	3	1	65	34	17
Federal Territory	188.2	30	23	48	21	6	75	67	57
Total Peninsular Malaysia									
1980	2,104.6*	19	35	28	8	2	73	53	38
(1970)	(1,594.9)	(9)	(13)	(10)	(4)	(1)	(48)	(12)	(15)
Sabah	176.3	17	2	24	5	3	58	35	22
Sarawak	223.1	13	13	21	10	2	61	27	22
Malaysia (1980)									
Urban	855.8	31	27	49	19	6	76	67	60
Rural	1,648.2	11	32	16	3	1	68	40	24
Total Malaysia . . .	2,504.0	18	30	27	8	2	71	49	36

*Figures do not add to total because of rounding.

Source: Based on information from Malaysia, Department of Statistics, *1980 Population and Housing Census of Malaysia: General Report of the Population Census*, Kuala Lumpur, 1983, 1949–51.

Table 10. National Budget Expenditures by Sector, 1966–84[1]
(in percentage of total)

Sector	First Malaysia Plan, 1966–67		Second Malaysia Plan, 1971–75		Third Malaysia Plan, 1976–80		Fourth Malaysia Plan, 1981–84[2]	
	Operating	Development	Operating	Development	Operating	Development	Operating	Development
Defense and security	22.2	21.3	25.9	13.5	18.8	15.8	17.6	16.8
Commerce and industry	0.3	6.7	0.9	18.3	1.0	15.6	2.8	15.0
Agriculture and rural development	2.7	27.8	2.5	24.0	2.6	18.3	4.1	13.6
Transportation	2.1	12.5	1.5	18.3	1.0	16.8	2.8	15.1
Communications	4.9	6.6	2.5	3.4	2.1	5.6	n.a.[3]	4.2
Utilities	n.a.	5.3	n.a.	4.2	n.a.	8.5	n.a.	10.0
Education	22.4	7.9	24.1	9.9	19.9	7.8	17.6	9.1
Health	7.6	4.2	7.6	2.4	6.2	1.3	5.3	1.4
Housing	n.a.	4.7	n.a.	2.0	n.a.	5.5	n.a.	9.1
General administration	12.4	2.7	10.2	2.9	8.2	2.9	10.5	1.9
State grants	9.0	n.a.	5.9	n.a.	3.4	n.a.	3.0	n.a.
Other transfers	1.7	n.a.	1.2	n.a.	18.5	n.a.	13.4	n.a.
Public debt service	9.6	n.a.	11.8	n.a.	12.8	n.a.	19.5	n.a.
Pensions	4.2	n.a.	3.7	n.a.	3.5	n.a.	n.a.[4]	n.a.
Other	0.9	0.3	2.2	1.1	2.0	1.9	3.4	3.8
TOTAL	100.0	100.0	100.0	100.0	100.0	100.0	100.0	100.0
(in billions of ringgit)[5]	(9.3)	(3.2)	(18.0)	(7.5)	(44.9)	(21.1)	(69.1)	(41.4)

n.a.--not available and included in the "Other" category of expenditure unless otherwise noted.

[1]Includes net lending through treasury.

[2]The Fourth Malaysia Plan actually spans the 1981–85 period. Data are based on actual spending through 1982, estimated expenditure for 1983, and budgeted expenditure for 1984.

[3]Communications included under "Transportation".

[4]Pensions included under "Other transfers".

[5]For value of the ringgit--see Glossary.

Source: Based on information from Bank Negara Malaysia, *Bank Negara Malaysia: Quarterly Economic Bulletin*, Kuala Lumpur, 16, NOs. 1–2, March-June 1983, 60–64; and Malaysia, Ministry of Finance, *Economic Report, 1983–84*, 12, Kuala Lumpur, 1983, xxviii–xxxix.

Table 11. Consolidated Public Sector Finance, 1976–84 (in percentage of gross national product)

	1976–80	1981	1982[1]	1983[1]	1984[2]
Revenue					
Corporate income tax	4.5	5.1	4.4	5.2	4.4
Personal income tax	2.2	2.0	2.3	2.8	3.0
Petroleum taxes[3]	3.2	6.7	6.6	6.1	5.6
Rubber duties	2.2	0.9	0.2	0.5	0.8
Tin duties	1.3	0.5	0.3	0.1	0.1
Palm oil duties	0.6	0.3	0.1	0.1	0.1
Other duties[4]	3.9	4.2	4.0	4.0	3.8
Other taxes[5]	5.2	4.8	4.9	6.2	6.4
Nontax revenue[6]	2.3	4.4	5.5	3.4	2.7
State revenue[7]	4.7	4.8	5.3	4.5	4.2
Operating surplus of public authorities	1.0	0.5	0.7	0.5	0.4
Total revenue	31.1	34.2	34.3	33.4	31.5
Expenditure					
Operating	26.7	31.8	32.9	33.2	31.5
Development	14.7	25.6	22.2	19.3	13.4
Total expenditure	41.4	57.4	55.1	52.5	44.9
Public sector deficit	-10.3	-23.2	-20.8	-19.1	-13.4
Debt financing					
Net foreign borrowing	2.3	5.8	8.4	9.2	n.a.
Net domestic borrowing	5.9	7.8	10.3	7.1	n.a.
Special receipts[8]	---	0.9	0.3	0.3	n.a.
Change in assets[9]	2.1	8.8	1.9	2.5	n.a.
Total debt financing[10]	10.3	23.2	20.8	19.1	13.4

---means less than 0.5 percent.
n.a.--not available.
[1]Estimated actual.
[2]Budget estimate as of mid-1983.
[3]Royalties, cash payments, and, starting in 1980, export duties.
[4]Import duties and surcharges and small amounts of export duties.
[5]Excise, sales, road, gambling, and other taxes.
[6]Revenue from commercial undertakings, interest, investment, licenses, and other fines and fees.
[7]State revenue is treated as a residual estimate.
[8]Foreign grants and drawings from the International Monetary Fund (IMF—see Glossary).
[9]Drawdown of assets held at the Central Bank of Malaysia.
[10]Figures may not add to total because of rounding.

Source: Based on information from Malaysia, Ministry of Finance, *Economic Report, 1983–84*, 12, Kuala Lumpur, 1983, xii–xiii, xxxii–xliii.

Table 12. Balance of Payments, Selected Years, 1970–83[1] (in billions of ringgit)[2]

	1970	1975	1980	1981	1982	1983
Exports[3]						
Petroleum	0.2	0.9	6.7	6.9	7.7	7.6
Timber	0.9	1.1	4.0	3.6	4.6	4.4
Palm oil	0.3	1.3	2.9	3.1	3.1	2.8
Rubber	1.7	2.0	4.6	3.7	2.7	3.6
Tin	1.0	1.2	2.5	2.1	1.5	1.6
Other agriculture and crude materials	0.3	0.9	1.8	1.8	1.7	2.5
Other processed minerals	0.3	0.5	1.4	1.4	1.4	2.6
Chemicals	---	0.1	0.2	0.2	0.2	0.3
Equipment	0.1	0.6	3.2	3.3	4.3	5.5
Other manufactures	0.1	0.6	0.9	0.9	1.0	1.0
Total exports	5.0	9.4	28.1	27.0	28.1	31.9
Imports[4]						
Food	0.5	0.7	1.2	1.6	1.7	3.0
Consumer durables	0.1	0.2	1.0	1.1	1.2	n.a.
Other consumer goods	0.6	0.9	2.2	2.5	2.6	n.a.
Machinery	0.5	1.0	2.6	3.1	3.5	n.a.
Transportation equipment	0.1	0.2	1.0	0.9	1.5	n.a.
Metal products	0.3	0.5	1.8	1.7	2.1	n.a.
Other capital goods	0.2	1.1	1.8	2.0	2.2	n.a.
Manufacturing materials	1.0	1.9	6.7	7.3	7.9	n.a.
Construction materials	0.1	0.3	0.6	0.8	1.1	n.a.
Petroleum	1.0	0.5	1.9	2.1	1.6	n.a.
Agricultural inputs	0.2	0.3	0.9	0.8	0.7	n.a.
Other intermediate goods	0.3	0.5	1.7	2.4	2.8	n.a.
Total imports	4.0	8.3	23.3	27.0	29.5	31.5
Net services and transfers[5]						
Freight and insurance	0.3	0.6	1.9	2.0	2.2	2.5
Travel and tourism	0.1	0.1	0.5	0.6	0.7	0.5
Investment income	0.4	0.7	2.0	1.8	2.3	3.6
Other services	0.1	0.4	0.8	1.0	1.1	0.2
Transfers	0.2	0.1	0.1	0.1	0.1	0.1
Total net services and transfers	1.0	1.8	5.3	5.5	6.4	6.9
Current account balance	---	-1.1	-0.5	-5.5	-7.8	-6.6
Net capital movements[6]						
Government loans	---	0.9	0.3	2.9	4.4	n.a.
Corporate investment	-0.3	0.8	2.1	2.8	3.1	n.a.
Short-term capital	-0.3	-0.5	-0.9	-1.4	-0.3	-2.3
Overall balance of payments	---	0.2	1.0	-1.2	-0.6	0.1
Net change in Central Bank reserves[7]	-0.1	-0.2	-1.1	0.5	0.6	-0.3

---means less than M$0.05billion.

n.a.--not available.

[1]Data for 1980–82 period were under revision in late 1983; data for 1983 were preliminary estimates.

[2]For value of the ringgit--see Glossary.

[3]Exports are at free on board (f.o.b.) prices. 1970 and 1975 data include reexports of petroleum from Brunei. "Palm oil" includes palm kernel oil except in 1983. "Crude materials" include other minerals as well as agricultural products. Figures do not add to total because of rounding and adjustments to the trade data for balance of payments accounting.

[4]Imports are at f.o.b. prices. Figures do not add to total because of adjustments to the trade data for balance of payments purposes.

Table 12. (Continued).

[5]All are net outflows of resources. "Investment income" include undistributed earnigns from foreign companies. Figures may not add to total because of rounding.

[6]"Government loans" include program and project loans to government and public authorities, changes in assets, and net contributions to internatioanl commodity agreements. Short-term capital includes credits to the national shipping and airline companies, loans of less than a year's duration, and errors and omissions in the balance of payments.

[7]Net of allocations and loans from the International Monetary Fund (see Glossary). Minus sign means an accummulation of reserves.

Source: Based on information from Bank Negera Malaysia, *Bank Negara Malaysia: Quarterly Economic Bulletin*, Kuala Lumpur, 16, Nos. 1–2, March-June 1983, 83–94; and Malaysia, Ministry of Finance, *Economic Report, 1983–84*, 12, Kuala Lumpur, 1983, xvi–xix.

Table 13. Direction of Trade and Financial Flows, Selected Periods, 1970–83
(in percentage)

Country	Exports[1]		Imports[1]		Foreign Debt[2]		Investment[3]
	1970–72 Average	1980–82 Average	1970–72 Average	1980–82 Average	1970–72 Average	1980–82 Average	1978–83 Average
Singapore	22.4	22.3	7.7	13.1	n.a.	n.a.	7.7
Japan	17.9	21.4	19.3	25.1	5.3	11.4	20.4
United States	13.2	13.7	8.1	15.7	24.4	54.8	7.6
Britain	6.8	2.8	13.4	4.7	39.3	3.1	13.3
Netherlands	3.9	6.0	1.3	0.7	9.6	n.a.	n.a.
West Germany	3.0	3.1	4.7	4.7	n.a.	2.9	4.4
France	2.0	1.5	1.5	1.7	n.a.	n.a.	n.a.
Italy	3.1	1.2	1.2	1.1	n.a.	n.a.	n.a.
Australia	2.0	1.7	6.4	5.2	n.a.	n.a.	6.9
Canada	2.1	0.5	1.1	1.2	n.a.	n.a.	n.a.
Sweden	0.4	0.3	1.2	1.0	n.a.	n.a.	n.a.
Thailand	1.1	2.3	3.6	3.4	n.a.	n.a.	1.7
Philippines	1.8	1.4	0.3	1.0	n.a.	n.a.	1.4
Indonesia	0.7	0.4	3.8	0.7	n.a.	n.a.	1.4
South Korea	2.3	3.1	0.3	1.8	n.a.	n.a.	4.3
Taiwan	1.3	2.2	1.9	2.4	n.a.	n.a.	n.a.
Soviet Union	3.1	2.2	0.3	0.2	n.a.	n.a.	n.a.
India	0.6	2.2	0.3	0.7	n.a.	n.a.	n.a.
China	1.3	1.1	4.7	2.3	n.a.	n.a.	n.a.
Saudi Arabia	0.1	0.5	1.6	4.7	n.a.	n.a.	n.a.
Other	10.9	10.1	17.3	8.6	21.4	27.8	30.9
TOTAL	100.0	100.0	100.0	100.0	100.0	100.0	100.0

n.a.--not available.

[1]Data are based on free on board (f.o.b.) prices and for 1982 are preliminary.

[2]Outstanding debt of the federal government in the form of long-term market and project loans. United States data include some dollar-denominated market loans from other sources. The World Bank (see Glossary) and the Asian Development Bank accounted for 14.7 percent and 1.2 percent, respectively, of the total during the 1970–72 period and for 10.8 percent and 7.5 percent, respectively, of the total in the 1980–82 period.

[3]Approved foreign investment through June 1983, which is more than the actual investment.

Table 14. Land Development by State, 1971–80
(in hectares)

State	FELDA[1]	FELCRA[2]	RISDA[3]	Regional Authorities	State Agencies	Private Sector	Total Land Developed
High-income							
Selangor[4]	342	---	---	---	10,189	8,279	18,810
Middleincome							
Johore	81,645	12,782	2,308	16,307	18,735	11,038	142,815
Malacca	2,087	1,621	---	---	---	3,373	7,081
Negeri Sembilan	62,710	6,735	2,807	---	5,567	12,878	90,697
Pahang	164,869	8,143	10,434	18,225	47,033	13,491	262,225
Penang	---	---	---	---	---	---	---
Perak	17,133	9,332	7,252	---	13,530	7,206	54,453
Sabah	1,428	---	---	---	57,815	---	59,243
Sarawak	---	---	---	---	76,654	---	76,654
Low-income							
Kedah	6,879	4,377	1,324	---	10,942	184	23,706
Kelantan	10,693	1,437	7,338	5,663	11,048	279	36,494
Perlis	3,187	---	---	---	---	---	3,187
Terengganu	22,732	6,247	---	15,623	41,492	4,599	90,693
TOTAL	373,705	50,710	31,463	55,848	293,005	61,327	866,058

---means none.
[1]Federal Land Development Authority.
[2]Federal Land Consolidation and Rehabilitation Authority.
[3]Rubber Industry Smallholders' Development Authority.
[4]Including the Federal Territory.

Source: Based on information from Malaysia, *Fourth Malaysia Plan, 1981–85*, Kuala Lumpur, 1981, 110.

Table 15. *Production and Export of Major Primary Commodities, Selected Years, 1969–83*
(in thousands of tons unless otherwise indicated)

Commodity	1969–71 Average		1979–81 Average		1982		1983[1]	
	Production	Exports	Production	Exports	Production	Exports	Production	Exports
Rubber[2]	1,287	1,364	1,560	1,554	1,378	1,516	1,530	1,500
Sawlogs[3]	17,198	8,818	29,143	15,636	32,907	19,277	34,540	20,700
Sawn timber[3]	2,725	1,331	6,152	3,291	6,280	2,943	6,280	3,200
Palm oil	457	432	2,528	2,099	3,511	2,700	3,300	2,813
Palm kernel oil[4]	50	29	270	221	455[1]	333	n.a.	n.a.
Coconut oil[2]	98	40	66	69	70[1]	59	n.a.	n.a.
Copra[5]	24	22	19	35	19[1]	28	n.a	n.a
Rice[6]	1,088	---	1,323	---	1,314[1]	---	n.a	n.a
Tin[7]	74	91	61	69	52	49	39	53
Crude oil[7]	11,672	5,566	99,473	11,136	110,632	87,762	139,284	102,957
Bauxite	1,063	981	669	610	589	420	n.a	n.a
Iron ore	3,558	n.a	418	n.a	340	n.a	n.a	n.a
Canned pineapple and juice	n.a	62	45	46	41	46	n.a	n.a

---means none or less than one-half of unit.

n.a.--not available.

[1]Preliminary.

[2]Production for Sabah and Sarawak estimated from exports.

[3]In thousands of cubic meters.

[4]Production data estimated from raw kernel production.

[5]Production from plantations on Peninsular Malaysia.

[6]Milled rice based on a conversion rate of 65 percent from paddy to rice. Production data are for the crop year (see Glossary) beginning in the previous calendar year.

[7]In thousands of barrels. Exports include partly refined oil and, for 1969–71, include quantites imported from Brunei for reexport.

Source: Based on information from Bank Negara Malaysia, *Bank Negara Malaysia: Quarterly Economic Bulletin*, Kuala Lumpur, 16, Nos. 1–2, March-June 1983, 70–86; and Malaysia, Ministry of Finance, *Economic Report*, *1983–84*, 12, Kuala Lumpur, 1983, xx–xxi.

Table 16. Structure and Growth of Manufacturing, Peninsular Malaysia, 1970–83
(in percentage)

Sector	Structure in 1979[1]	Annual Growth[2] 1970–81 Average	1982	1983
Estate-crop processing	16.1	13.7	27.0	3.0
Food, beverages, and tobacco products	14.0	5.6	-0.2	8.0
Electrical machinery	13.2	10.4	45.8	50.0
Wood products	10.6	8.4	-23.9	5.9
Basic metals and metal products	9.4	9.7	1.5	11.9
Chemicals	8.0	7.4	-13.8	5.9
Textiles and garments	7.3	11.6	-5.0	2.1
Nometallic minerals	5.0	9.6	-0.3	6.0
Paper and paper products	4.5	12.4	-5.2	n.a.
Rubber and leather products	4.3	5.4	-12.9	2.4
Petroleum products	3.6	5.9	32.8	16.2
Transportation equipment	3.5	11.0	-8.7	15.0
Other	0.5	21.4	-0.8	3.5
TOTAL	100.0	10.1	2.0	7.8

n.a.--not available.

[1]Based on a survey of large industrial establishments in Peninsular Malaysia, whose total value added was estimated to be M$6.7 billion (for value of the ringgit--see Glossary).

[2]Based on production index for selected large establishments in Peninsular Malaysia, having weights calculated from the 1968 industrial census. "Other" refers to "pioneer" industries outside of the other sectors listed. The total refers to the average for all manufacturing industries, not to a sum. The 1970–81 average is a straight line estimation from the base year 1970 to the end year 1981.

Source: Based on information from Bank Negara Malaysia, *Bank Negara Malaysia: Quarterly Economic Bulletin*, Kuala Lumpur, 16, Nos. 1-2 (March-June 1983), 72–76; and Malaysia, Ministry of Finance, *Economic Report, 1983–84*, 12, Kuala Lumpur, 1983, xxvi–xxvii.

Table 17. Political Parties in House of Representatives, 1959–82 (number of seats)

Party	Election Year 1959	1964	1969	1974	1978	1982
Ruling coalition parties						
United Malays National Organization	54	59	51	62	70	70
Malayan Chinese Association	17	27	13	19	17	24
People's Movement of Malaysia	---	---	8	5	4	5
Sabah People's Union	---	---	---	---	8	10
Malayan Indian Congress	3	3	2	4	3	4
Sarawak National Party	---	10[1]	9	9	9	6
Sarawak United People's Party	---	3[2]	5	7	6	5
United Conservative Bumiputra Party	---	---	10	8	8	8
Malaysian Front Islamic Council	---	---	---	---	---	0
United Sabah National Organization	---	14[3]	10	16	5	0
Total ruling coalition parties	74	116	108	130	130	132
Opposition parties						
Democratic Action Party	---	---	13	9	16	9
Pan-Malaysia Islamic Party	13	9	12	13	5	5
Other minor parties	14	9	10	2	1	0
Independents	3	1	0	0	2	8
Total opposition parties	30	19	35	24	24	22
TOTAL	104	150[4]	143[5]	154	154	154[6]

---means not in existence at that time.
[1]Total for four parties grouped under Sarawak Alliance.
[2]In opposition at that time.
[3]Total for three parties grouped under Sabah Alliance.
[4]Total includes 15 seats for Singapore, then a member of the federation. Actually, total should be 159; seven seats for Sarawak and two seats for Sabah are unaccounted for in published sources.
[5]Total should be 144; one vacancy at that time due to death.
[6]1983 amendment raised number of seats from 154 to 176.

Table 18. Funds Budgeted for Defense and Internal Security, 1977–84

				Defense[1]				Internal Security[2]	
Year	Total at Current Prices[3]	Ratio of Development to Operating Expenditures	Percentage Change at Current Prices	Percentage Change Adjusted for Inflation	Total as Percentage of Gross National Product	Total as Percentage Total Central Government Expenditures	Total[3]	Ratio of Development to Operating Expenditures	Total
1977 . . .	1,324	27:73	18.3	13.0	4.2	12.5	663	18:82	1,987
1978 . . .	1,406	22:78	6.2	1.1	4.0	11.9	777	23.77	2,183
1979 . . .	1,704	31:69	21.0	17.0	3.9	11.9	843	22:78	2,547
1980 . . .	2,255	36:64	32.3	24.0	4.5	10.7	1,134	36:64	3,389
1981 . . .	3,333	41:59	47.8	34.7	6.1	12.3	1,360	34:66	4,693
1982 . . .	3,695	45:65	9.7	4.7	6.3	13.2	1,446	29:71	5,141
1983[4] . . .	3,368	41:59	-8.8	-12.3	n.a.	11.9	1,472	32:68	4,840
1984[5] . . .	3,051	31:69	-9.4	n.a.	n.a.	11.3	1,403	17:83	4,454

n.a.--not available.
[1]Primarily allotted to armed forces.
[2]Primarily allotted to police.
[3]In millions of ringgit; for value of the ringgit--see Glossary.
[4]Estimated figures.
[5]Projected figures.

Source: Based on information from Malaysia, Ministry of Finance, *Economic Report, 1983–84*, 12, Kuala Lumpur, 1983, 38; Malaysia, Ministry of Finance, *Economic Report 1982–83*, 11, Kuala Lumpur, 1982, 37; and *International Financial Statistics*, 36, No. 10, Washington, October 1983, 282.

Table 19. Order of Battle for Malaysian Army, 1984

	Number	Source
Total strength—80,000		
Organization		
Corps headquarters	1	
Division headquarters	4	
Infantry brigades	12	
Infantry battalions	37	
Cavalry regiments	3	
Field artillery regiments	4	
Armored personnel carrier regiment	1	
Antiaircraft batteries	2	
Engineer regiments	5	
Signals regiments	5	
Special forces (commando) regiment	1	
Equipment		
Scorpion 90 light tanks (diesel)	26	Britain
AML-60 and AML-90 armored cars	140	France
Ferret scout cars	60	Britain
V-150 Commando armored personnel carriers	200	United States
Panhard M3 armored personnel carriers	140	France
Model 56 105mm pack howitzers	92	Italy
5.5-inch guns	12	Britain
81mm mortars	n.a.	-do-
M-20 89mm rocket launchers	5	-do-
120mm recoilless rifles	n.a.	n.a.
SS-11 antitank guided wire missiles	n.a.	France
40mm Bofors L/70 antiaircraft guns	n.a.	Britain
40mm M-1 antiaircraft guns	n.a.	-do-
On order		
Simba armored fighting vehicles	162	Belgium
Stormer armored personnel carriers	20	Britain
Condor armored personnel carriers	459	West Germany

n.a.--not available.

Table 20. Order of Battle for Royal Malaysian Navy, 1984

	Number	Source
Total strength—8,700		
Frigates		
Yarrow class with four Seacat surface-to-air missiles	1	Britain
Type 41	1	-do-
Fast attack craft, missile		
Spica-M class with two or four Exocet surface-to-surface missiles	4	Sweden
Perdana class with four Exocet surface-to-surface missiles	4	France
Fast attack craft, gun		
Jerong class, 254 tons	6	Malaysia
Large patrol craft		
Kedah class	4	Britain
Sabah class	4	-do-
Kris class	14	-do-
Landing ships, tank		
511–1152 class	3	Ex-United States Navy
Minesweepers, coastal		
Ton class	2	Ex-British Royal Navy
Support ships		
Logistic support ship	1	West Germany
Multipurpose support ship	1	South Korea
On order		
Type FS 1500 frigates with four Exocet surface-to-surface missiles	2	West Germany
Lerici-class minehunters	4	Italy

Table 21. Order of Battle for Royal Malaysian Air Force, 1984

	Number	Source
Total strength—11,000		
Organization and equipment		
2 Fighter squadrons		
F-5E Tiger II	12	United States
F-5F Tiger II	4	-do-
2 Counterinsurgency/training squadrons		
Aermacchi M.B. 339A	12	Italy
1 Maritime reconaissance squadrons		
RF-5E	2	United States
PC-130H	3	-do-
3 Transport squadrons		
C-130 Hercules	6	-do-
HS 125	2	Britain
F. 28 Fellowship	2	Netherlands
DHC-4A Caribou	15	Canada
NC-212 Aviocar	4	Indonesia
1 Liaison squadron		
Cessna 402B	12	United States
2 Transport helicopter squadrons		
S-61A Sea King	37	-do-
2 Liaison helicopter squadrons		
Alouette III	24	France
2 Training squadrons		
Pilatus PC-7	44	Switzerland
Bell 47 helicopters	6	United States
Bell UH-1H helicopters	44	-do-
Sidewinder air-to-air missiles	120	-do-
On order		
A-4 Skyhawk	34	-do-
T-A4 Skyhawk	6	-do-
Beechcraft Super King Air transport	1	-do-
Super Sidewinder air-to-air missile	n.a.	-do-

n.a.--not available.

Bibliography

Chapter 1

Allen, G.C., and Audrey G. Donnithorne. *Western Enterprise in Indonesia and Malaya: A Study in Economic Development*. New York: Macmillan, 1957.

Allen, James de V. *The Malayan Union*. (Southeast Asia Studies, No. 10.) New Haven: Yale University Press, 1967.

Ampalavanar, Rajeswary. *The Indian Minority and Political Change in Malaya, 1945–1957*. Kuala Lumpur: Oxford University Press, 1981.

Andaya, Barbara Watson. *Perak, the Abode of Grace: A Study of an Eighteenth-Century Malay State*. Kuala Lumpur: Oxford University Press, 1979.

———. "The Role of the *Anak Raja* in Malay History: A Case Study from Eighteenth-Century Kedah," *Journal of Southeast Asian Studies* [Singapore], 7, No. 2, September 1976, 162–86.

Andaya, Barbara Watson, and Leonard Y. Andaya. *A History of Malaysia*. New York: St. Martin's Press, 1982.

Andaya, Leonard Y. *The Kingdom of Johor, 1641–1728*. Kuala Lumpur: Oxford University Press, 1975.

Barraclough, Simon. "Managing the Challenges of Islamic Revival in Malaysia: A Regime Perspective," *Asian Survey*, 23, No. 8, August 1983, 958–75.

Bass, Jerome R. "Malaysia: Continuity or Change," *Asian Survey*, 10, No. 2, February 1970, 152–60.

Bastin, John, and Robin W. Winks (eds.). *Malaysia: Selected Historical Readings*. Kuala Lumpur: Oxford University Press, 1966.

Bedlington, Stanley S. *Malaysia and Singapore: The Building of New States*. Ithaca: Cornell University Press, 1978.

Bird, Isabella L. *The Golden Chersonese and the Way Thither*. Kuala Lumpur: Oxford University Press, 1967 (reprint.).

Boxer, C.R. *The Portuguese Seaborne Empire, 1415–1825*. London: Hutchinson, 1969.

Burns, P.L., and C.D. Cowan (eds.). *Sir Frank Swettenham's Malayan Journals, 1874–1876*. Kuala Lumpur: Oxford University Press, 1975.

Butcher, John G. *The British in Malaya, 1880–1941: The Social*

History of a European Community in Colonial South-East Asia. Kuala Lumpur: Oxford Unversity Press, 1979.

Carlson, Sevinc. *Malaysia: Search for National Unity and Economic Growth*, 3. (Washington Papers, No. 25.) Beverly Hills: Sage with Center for Strategic and International Studies, Georgetown University, 1975.

Chai, Hon-Chan. *The Development of British Malaya, 1896–1909*. Kuala Lumpur: Oxford University Press, 1964.

Chang, David W. "Current Status of Chinese Minorities in Southeast Asia," *Asian Survey*, 13, No. 6, June 1973, 587–603.

Cheah, Boon Kheng. "Sino-Malay Conflicts in Malaya, 1945–1946: Vendetta and Islamic Resistance," *Journal of Southeast Asian Studies* [Singapore], 12, No. 1, March 1981, 108–17.

Chee, Stephen. "Malaysia and Singapore: The Political Economy of Multiracial Development," *Asian Survey*, 14, No. 2, February 1974, 183–91.

———. "Malaysia and Singapore: Separate Identities, Different Priorities," *Asian Survey*, 13, No. 2, February 1973, 151–61.

Ch'en, Jerome, and Nicholas Tarling. *Studies in the Social History of China and South-East Asia: Essays in Memory of Victor Purcell*. Cambridge: Cambridge University Press, 1970.

Chew, Ernest. "Swettenham and British Residential Rule in West Malaya," *Journal of Southeast Asian Studies* [Singapore], 5, No.2, September 1974, 166–78.

Chin, John A. *The Sarawak Chinese*. Kuala Lumpur: Oxford University Press, 1981.

Cole, Fay-Cooper. *The Peoples of Malaysia*. Princeton: Van Nostrand, 1945.

Courtenay, P.P. "The Plantation in Malaysian Economic Development," *Journal of Southeast Asian Studies* [Singapore], 12, No. 2, September 1981, 329–48.

Drabble, J.H. "Investment in the Rubber Industry in Malaya, c. 1900–1922," *Journal of Southeast Asian Studies* [Singapore], 3, No.2, September 1972, 247–61.

———. "Some Thoughts on the Economic Development of Malaya under British Administration," *Journal of Southeast Asian Studies* [Singapore], 5, No. 2, September 1974, 199–208.

Drummond, Stuart, and David Hawkins. "The Malaysian Elections of 1969: An Analysis of the Campaign and the Results," *Asian Survey*, 10, No. 4, April 1970, 320–35.

Emerson, Rupert. *Malaysia: A Study in Direct and Indirect Rule*

Kuala Lumpur: University of Malaya Press, 1964.

FitzGerald, C.P. *The Third China: The Chinese Communities in Southeast Asia*. Singapore: Moore Books, 1965.

Funston, N.J. "The Origins of Parti Islam Se Malaysia," *Journal of Southeast Asian Studies* [Singapore], 7, No. 1, March 1976, 58–73.

Gullick, John M. *Malaysia: Economic Expansion and National Unity*. Boulder: Westview Press, 1981.

Hall, D.G.E. *A History of South-East Asia*. London: Macmillan, 1964.

Hirth, Friedrich, and W.W. Rockhill (trans.). *Chau Ju-kua: His Work on the Chinese and Arab Trade in the Twelfth and Thirteenth Centuries, Entitled Chu-fan-chi*. New York: Paragon Books, 1966 (reprint.).

Hoffman, J.E. "Early Policies in the Malacca Jurisdiction of the United East India Company: The Malay Peninsula and the Netherlands East Indies Attachment," *Journal of Southeast Asian Studies* [Singapore], 3, No. 1, March 1972, 1–38.

Hughes, Richard. *Far Eastern Economic Review* [Hong Kong], October 6, 1983, 47 (column).

Indorf, Hans H. "Malaysia 1978: Communal Coalitions Continue," *Asian Survey*, 19, No. 2, February 1979, 115–23.

———. "Malaysia 1979: A Preoccupation with Security," *Asian Survey*, 20, No. 2, February 1980, 135–43.

Johnstone, Michael. "The Evolution of Squatter Settlements in Peninsular Malaysian Cities," *Journal of Southeast Asian Studies* [Singapore], 12, No. 2, September 1981, 364–80.

Kennedy, J. *A History of Malaya, A.D. 1400–1959*. London: Macmillan, 1962.

Kessler, Clive S. *Islam and Politics in a Malay State: Kelantan, 1838–1969*. Ithaca: Cornell Univesity Press, 1978.

Khoo, Kay Kim. "Malay Society, 1874–1920s," *Journal of Southeast Asian Studies* [Singapore], 5, No. 2, September 1974, 179–98.

———. "Sino-Malay Relations in Peninsular Malaysia Before 1942," *Journal of Southeast Asian Studies* [Singapore], 12, No. 1, March 1981, 93–107.

———. *The Western Malay States, 1850–1873: The Effects of Commerical Development on Malay Politics*. Kuala Lumpur: Oxford University Press, 1972.

Lamb, Alastair. *Chandi Bukit Batu Pahat: A Report on the Excavation of an Ancient Temple in Kedah*. (Monographs on Southeast Asian Subjects, No. 1.) Singapore: Eastern Universities Press, 1960.

Lebar, Frank M. *Ethnic Groups of Mainland Southeast Asia*. New Haven: Human Relations Area Files Press, 1964.

Lebar, Frank M. (ed.). *Ethnic Groups of Insular Southeast Asia, Vol. I: Indonesia, Andaman Islands, and Madagascar*. New Haven: Human Relations Area Files Press, 1972.

Lee, Kam Hing. "Malaya: New State and Old Elites." Pages 208–57 in Robin Jeffrey (ed.), *Asia: The Winning of Independence*. New York: St. Martin's Press, 1981.

Lee, Yong-Leng. *North Borneo (Sabah): A Study in Settlement Geography*. Singapore: Eastern Universities Press, 1965.

Leong, Stephen. "The Malayan Overseas Chinese and the Sino-Japanese War, 1937–1941," *Journal of Southeast Asian Studies* [Singapore], 10, No. 2, September 1979, 293–320.

Loh, Philip Fook-Seng. *The Malay States, 1877–1985: Political Change and Social Policy*. Singapore: Oxford University Press, 1969.

———. "A Review of the Educational Developments in the Federated Malay States to 1939," *Journal of Southeast Asian Studies* [Singapore], 5, No. 2, September 1974, 225–38.

MacAndrews, Colin. "The Politics of Planning: Malaysia and the New Third Malaysia Plan (1976–1980)," *Asian Survey*, 17, No. 3, March 1977, 293–308.

Mackie, J.A.C. *Konfrontasi: The Indonesia-Malaysia Dispute, 1963–1966*. Kuala Lumpur: Oxford University Press, 1974.

McKie, Ronald. *The Emergence of Malaysia*. Westport, Connecticut: Greenwood Press, 1973.

Mahathir bin Mohamad. *The Malay Dilemma*. Singapore: Asia Pacific Press, 1970.

Matheson, Virginia, "Concepts of Malay Ethos in Indigenous Malay Writings," *Journal of Southeast Asian Studies* [Singapore], 10, No. 2, September 1979, 351–71.

Mauzy, Diane K. "The 1982 General Elections in Malaysia: A Mandate for Change?" *Asian Survey*, 23, No. 4, April 1983, 497–517.

———. "A Vote for Continuity: The 1978 General Elections in Malaysia," *Asian Survey*, 19, No. 3, March 1979, 281–96.

———. "Malaysia in 1981: Continuity and Change," *Asian Survey*, 22, No. 2, February 1982, 212–18.

Miller, Harry. *A Short History of Malaysia*. New York: Praeger, 1965.

Mills, L.A. *British Malaya, 1824–1867. Kuala Lumpur: Oxford University Press, 1966*.

Milne, R.S. "Malaysia and Singapore in 1974," *Asian Survey*, 15, No. 2, February 1975, 168–73.

———. "Malaysia and Singapore, 1975," *Asian Survey*, 16, No. 2, February 1976, 186–92.

Milne, R.S., and K.J. Ratnam. *Malaysia—New States in a New Nation: Political Development of Sarawak and Sabah in Malaysia*. London: Cass, 1974.

Milner, A.C. *Kerajaan: Malay Political Culture on the Eve of Colonial Rule*. (Association for Asian Studies, Monograph No. 40) Tucson: University of Arizona Press, 1982.

Ongkili, James P. "The British and Malayan Nationalism, 1946–1957," *Journal of Southeast Asian Studies* [Singapore], 5, No. 2, September 1974, 255–77.

Pringle, Robert. *Rajas and Rebels: The Ibans of Sarawak under Brooke Rule, 1841–1941*. Ithaca: Cornell University Press, 1970.

Purcell, Victor. *The Memoirs of a Malayan Official*. London: Cassell, 1965.

Rao, Chandriah Appa, et al. *Issues in Contemporary Malaysia*. Kuala Lumpur: Heinemann Educational Books (Asia), 1977.

Ratnam, K.J. *Communalism and the Political Process in Malaya*. Kuala Lumpur: University of Malaya Press, 1965.

Regan, Daniel. "At the Crossroads of Civilizations: The Cultural Orientations of Malaysian Intellectuals," *Journal of Southeast Asian Studies* [Singapore], 11, No. 2, September 1980, 320–34.

Reischauer, Edwin O., and John K. Fairbank. *East Asia: The Great Tradition*. (A History of East Asian Civilization, 1.) Boston: Houghton Mifflin, 1960.

Ricklefs, M.C. *A History of Modern Indonesia: c. 1300 to the Present*. Bloomington: Indiana University Press, 1981.

Robinson, Francis. *Atlas of the Islamic World since 1500*. New York: Facts on File, 1982.

Roff, William R. *The Origins of Malay Nationalism*. (Southeast Asia Studies, No. 2.) New Haven: Yale University Press, 1967.

Rogers, Marvin L. "Malaysia and Singapore: 1971 Developments," *Asian Survey*, 12, No. 2, February 1972, 168–76.

———. "Malaysia/Singapore: Problems and Challenges of the Seventies," *Asian Survey*, 11, No. 2, February 1971, 121–30.

Rudner, Martin. "The Draft Development Plan of the Federation of Malaya, 1950–55," *Journal of Southeast Asian Studies* [Singapore], 3, No. 1, March 1972, 63–96.

Runciman, Steven. *The White Rajas: A History of Sarawak from 1841 to 1946*. Cambridge: Cambridge University Press, 1960.

Ryan, N.J. *The Cultural Heritage of Malaysia*. Singapore:

Longman Malaysia, 1971.

———. *The Making of Modern Malaysia and Singapore*. Kuala Lumpur: Oxford University Press, 1969.

Sadka, Emily. *The Protected Malay States, 1874–1895*. Kuala Lumpur: University of Malaya Press, 1968.

Sandhu, Kernial Singh. *Early Malaysia: Some Observations on the Nature of Indian Contacts with Pre-British Malaya*. Singapore: University Education Press, 1973.

———. *Indians in Malaya: Some Aspects of Their Immigration and Settlement (1786–1957)*. Cambridge: Cambridge University Press, 1969.

Short, Anthony. *The Communist Insurrection in Malaya, 1948–1960*. New York: Crane, Russak, 1975.

Snodgrass, Donald R. *Inequality and Economic Development in Malaysia*. Kuala Lumpur: Oxford University Press, 1980.

Stevenson, Rex. "Cinemas and Censorship in Colonial Malaya," *Journal of Southeast Asian Studies* [Singapore], 5, No. 2, September 1974, 209–24.

Stubbs, Richard. "The United Malays National Organization, the Malayan Chinese Association, and the Early Years of the Malayan Emergency, 1948–1955," *Journal of Southeast Asian Studies* [Singapore], 10, No. 1, March 1971, 77–88.

Tarling, Nicholas. "Borneo and British Intervention in Malaya," *Journal of Southeast Asian Studies* [Singapore], 5, No. 2, September 1974, 159–65.

———. *Sulu and Sabah: A Study of British Policy Towards the Philippines and North Borneo from the Late Eighteenth Century*. Kuala Lumpur: Oxford University Press, 1978.

Tilman, Robert O. "Mustapha's Sabah, 1968–1975: The Tun Steps Down," *Asian Survey*, 16, No. 6, June 1976, 495–509.

Tilman, Robert O., and Jo H. Tilman. "Malaysia and Singapore, 1976: A Year of Challenge, A Year of Change," *Asian Survey*, 17, No. 2, February 1977, 143–54.

Tregonning, K.G. *A History of Modern Sabah, 1881–1963*. Kuala Lumpur: University of Malaya Press, 1965.

———. "Tan Cheng Lock: A Malayan Nationalist," *Journal of Southeast Asian Studies* [Singapore], 10, No. 1., March 1979, 25–76.

———. *Under Chartered Company Rule: North Borneo, 1881–1946*. Singapore: University of Malaya Press, 1958.

Turnbull, C.M. "British Planning for Post-War Malaya," *Journal of Southeast Asian Studies* [Singapore], 5, No. 2, September 1974, 239–54.

Vaughan, J.D. *The Manners and Customs of the Chinese of the*

Straits Settlements. Kuala Lumpur: Oxford University Press, 1971 (reprint.).

von der Mehden, Fred R. "Malaysia in 1980: Signals to Watch," *Asian Survey*, 21, No. 2, February 1981, 245–52.

Von Vorys, Karl. *Democracy Without Consensus: Communalism and Political Stability in Malaysia*. Princeton: Princeton University Press, 1975.

Vreeland, Nena, et al. *Area Handbook for Singapore*. (DA Pam 550–184.) Washington: GPO for Foreign Area Studies, The American University, 1977.

Wang, Gungwu (ed.). *Malaysia: A Survey*. New York: Praeger, 1964.

Winstedt, Richard. *Malaya and Its History*. London: Hutchinson's University Library, 1957.

Wolters, O.W. *Early Indonesian Commerce: A Study of the Origins of Srivijaya*. Ithaca: Cornell University Press, 1967.

———. *The Fall of Srivijaya in Malay History*. Ithaca: Cornell University Press, 1970.

Wong, Lin Ken. "Twentieth-Century Malayan Economic History: A Select Bibliographic Survey," *Journal of Southeast Asian Studies* [Singapore], 10, No. 1, March 1979, 1–24.

Yen, Ching-hwang. "The Confucian Revival Movement in Singapore and Malaya, 1899–1911," *Journal of Southeast Asian Studies* [Singapore], 7, No. 1, March 1976, 33–57.

———. "Early Chinese Clan Organizations in Singapore and Malaya, 1819–1911," *Journal of Southeast Asian Studies* [Singapore], 12, No. 1, March 1981, 62–92.

Yeo, Kim Wah. "The Anti-Federation Movement in Malaya, 1946–48," *Journal of Southeast Asian Studies* [Singapore], 4, No. 1, March 1973, 31–51.

———. "The Grooming of an Elite: Malaya Administrators in the Federated Malay States, 1903–1941," *Journal of Southeast Asian Studies* [Singapore], 11, No. 2, September 1980, 287–319.

———. *The Politics of Decentralization: Colonial Controversy in Malaya, 1920–1929*. Kuala Lumpur: Oxford University Press, 1982.

Yong, C.F., and R.B. McKenna. "The Kuomintang Movement in Malaya and Singapore, 1912–1925," *Journal of Southeast Asian Studies* [Singapore], 12, No. 1, March 1981, 118–32.

Yuen, Choy Leng. "The Japanese Community in Malaya Before the Pacific War: Its Genesis and Growth," *Journal of Southeast Asian Studies* [Singapore], 9, No. 2, September 1978, 163–79.

Chapter 2

Akashi, Yoji. "The Japanese Occupation of Malaya: Interruption or Transformation." Pages 65–90 in Alfred E. McCoy (ed.), *Southeast Asia under Japanese Occupation*. (Southeast Asian Studies, Monograph series, No. 22.) New Haven: Yale University Press, 1980.

Arasaratnam, Sinnappah. *Indians in Malaysia and Singapore*. Kuala Lumpur: Oxford University Press, 1970.

Bedlington, Stanley S. *Malaysia and Singapore: The Building of New States*. Ithaca: Cornell University Press, 1978.

Butcher, John G. *The British in Malaya, 1880–1941: The Social History of a European Community in Colonial South-East Asia*. Kuala Lumpur: Oxford University Press, 1979.

Chai, Hon-Chan. "Education and Nation-Building in Plural Societies: The West Malaysian Experience." (Development Studies Centre, Monograph No. 6.) Canberra: Australian National University, 1977.

Chang, Paul Min-Phang. *Educational Development in a Plural Society*. Kuala Lumpur: Malaya, 1973.

Clammer, John R. *Straits Chinese Society: Studies in the Sociology of the Baba Communities of Malaysia and Singapore*. Singapore: Singapore University Press, 1980.

Courtenay, P.P. *A Geography of Trade and Development in Malaya*. London: Bell and Sons, 1972.

Dodge, Nicolas N. "Population Estimates for the Malay Peninsula in the Nineteenth Century, with Special Reference to the East Coast States," *Population Studies* [London], 34, No. 3, November 1980, 437–75.

Fisk, E.K. "Development in Malaysia." Pages 1–23 in E.K. Fisk and H. Osman-Rani (eds.), *The Political Economy of Malaysia*. Kuala Lumpur: Oxford University Press, 1982.

Goh, Cheng-Teik. *The May Thirteenth Incident and Democracy in Malaysia*. Kuala Lumpur: Oxford University Press, 1971.

Gosling, L.A.P. "Migration and Assimilation of Rural Chinese in Trengganu." Pages 203–21 in John Bastin and R. Roolvink (eds.), *Malayan and Indonesian Studies*. Oxford: Clarendon Press, 1964.

Gullick, John M. *Indigenous Political Systems of Western Malaya*. London: Athlone Press, 1958.

———. *Malaysia: Economic Expansion and National Unity*.

Boulder: Westview Press, 1981.

Heidhues, Mary F. Somers. *Southeast Asia's Chinese Minorities*. Hawthorn, Victoria, Australia: Longman, 1974.

Hirschman, Charles. "Demographic Trends in Peninsular Malaysia, 1947–75," *Population and Development Review*, 6, No. 1, March 1980, 103–25.

———. *Ethnic and Social Stratification in Peninsular Malaysia*. Washington: American Sociological Association, 1975.

———. "Occupational and Industrial Change in Peninsular Malaysia, 1947–1970," *Journal of Southeast Asian Studies*, 13, No. 1, March 1982, 474–90.

———. "Political Independence and Educational Opportunity in Peninsular Malaysia," *Sociology of Education*, 52, No. 2, April 1979, 67–83.

———. "Recent Urbanization Trends in Peninsular Malaysia," *Demography*, 13, No. 4, November 1976, 445–61.

———. "Sociology." Pages 1–58 in John Lent (ed.), *Malaysia Studies: Present Knowledge and Research Trends*. DeKalb: Center for Southeast Asian Studies, Northern Illinois University, 1979.

Hirschman, Charles, and Suan-Pow Yoeh. "Ethnic Patterns of Urbanization in Peninsular Malaysia, 1947–1970," *Southeast Asian Journal of Social Science* [Singapore], 7, Nos. 1–2, 1979, 1–19.

Hodder, B.W. *Man in Malaya*. London: University of London Press, 1968.

Husin Ali, Syed. *Malay Peasant Society and Leadership*. Kuala Lumpur: Oxford University Press, 1975.

———. *The Malays: Their Problems and Future*. Kuala Lumpur: Heinemann Asia, 1981.

Jackson, James. *Planters and Speculators: Chinese and European Agricultural Enterprise in Malaya, 1786–1921*. Kuala Lumpur: University of Malaya Press, 1968.

Jackson, R.N. *Immigrant Labour and the Development of Malaya: 1786–1920*. Kuala Lumpur: Government Printer, 1961.

Jones, Gavin W. "Malay Marriage and Divorce in Peninsular Malaysia: Three Decades of Change," *Population and Development Review*, 7, No. 2, June 1981, 255–78.

———. "Structural Change and Prospects for Urbanization in Asian Countries." (Papers of the East-West Population Institute, No. 88.) Honolulu: East-West Institute, 1983.

———. "Trends in Marriage and Divorce in Peninsular

Malaysia," *Population Studies* [London], 34, No. 2, July 1980, 279–92.

Kadir H. Din. "The Physical Infrastructure." pages 44–65 in E.K. Fisk and H. Osman-Rani (eds.), *The Political Economy of Malaysia*. Kuala Lumpur: Oxford University Press, 1982.

Kessler, Clive S. *Islam and Politics in a Malay State: Kelantan, 1838–1969*. Ithaca: Cornell University Press, 1978.

Khoo, Kay Kim. *The Western Malay States, 1850–1873: The Effects of Commercial Development on Malay Politics*. Kuala Lumpur: Oxford University Press, 1972.

Lamb, Alastair. "Early History." Pages 99–112 in Gungwu Wang (ed.), *Malaysia: A Survey*. New York: Praeger, 1964.

Lee, Yong-Leng. *North Borneo (Sabah): A Study in Settlement Geography*. Singapore: Eastern Universities Press, 1965.

———. *Population and Settlement in Sarawak*. Singapore: Asia-Pacific Press, 1970.

Lim, Chong-Yah. *Economic Development of Modern Malaya*. Kuala Lumpur: Oxford University Press, 1967.

Lim, Teck-Ghee. *Peasants and Their Agricultural Economy, 1874–1941*. Kuala Lumpur: Oxford University Press, 1977.

Loh, Philip Fook-Seng. *Seeds of Separatism: Educational Policy in Malaya, 1874–1940*. Kuala Lumpur: Oxford University Press, 1975.

Mahathir bin Mohamad. *The Malay Dilemma*. Singapore: Asia Pacific Press, 1970.

Malaysia. *Fourth Malaysia Plan, 1981–1985*. Kuala Lumpur: National Printing Department, 1981.

Malaysia. Department of Statistics. *Annual Statistical Bulletin: Malaysia, 1981*. Kuala Lumpur: 1982.

———. *General Report: Population Census of Malaysia*, 1. Kuala Lumpur: 1977.

———. *1957 Population Census of the Federation of Malaya*. (Report No. 14.) Kuala Lumpur: 1960.

———. *1980 Population and Housing Census of Malaysia: General Report of the Population Census*. Kuala Lumpur: 1983.

———. *1980 Population and Housing Census of Malaysia: Preliminary Field Count Summary*. Kuala Lumpur: 1980.

Malaysia. Ministry of Education. *Kajian Keciciran* (Dropout Study.) Kuala Lumpur: Dewan Bahasa dan Dustaka, 1973.

M. Anuar Adnan. "The Extractive Industries." Pages 229-59 in E.K. Fisk and H. Osman-Rani (eds.), *The Political Economy of Malaysia*. Kuala Lumpur: Oxford University Press, 1982.

Milne, R.S. "The Politics of Malaysia's New Economic Policy,"

Pacific Affairs [Vancouver], 49, No. 2, Summer 1976, 235–62.

Milner, A.C. *Kerajaan: Malay Political Culture on the Eve of Colonial Rule*. (Association for Asian Studies, Monograph No. 40.) Tucson: University of Arizona Press, 1982.

Mohamed Suffian bin Hashim, Tun. *An Introduction to the Constitution of Malaysia*. (2d ed.) Kuala Lumpur: Government Printer, 1978.

Nagata, Judith. *Malaysian Mosaic*. Vancouver: University of British Colombia Press, 1979.

———. "Religious Ideology and Social Change: The Islamic Revival in Malaysia," *Pacific Affairs* [Vancouver], 53, Fall 1980, 405–39.

Ness, Gayl. "Economic Development and Goals of Government." Pages 307–22 in Gungwu Wang (ed.), *Malaysia: A Survey*. New York: Praeger, 1964.

Ooi Jin-Bee. *Peninsular Malaysia*. London: Longman, 1976.

Palmore, James A., Robert E. Klein, and Arafinn bin Marzuki. "Class and Family in a Modernizing Society," *American Journal of Sociology*, 76, November 1970, 375–90.

Parkinson, Brien K. "Non-economic Factors in the Economic Retardation of the Rural Malays," *Modern Asian Studies* [Cambridge], 1, No. 2, 1967, 31-46.

Purcell, Victor. *The Chinese in Malaya*. New York: Oxford University Press, 1967 (reprint).

Puthucheary, Mavis. *The Politics of Administration: The Malaysian Experience*. Kuala Lumpur: Oxford University Press, 1978.

Roff, Margaret Clark. *The Politics of Belonging: Political Change in Sabah and Sarawak*. Kuala Lumpur: Oxford University Press, 1974.

Roff, William R. *The Origins of Malay Nationalism*. (Southeast Asia Studies, No. 2.) New Haven: Yale University Press, 1967.

Rudner, Martin. "The Economic, Social, and Political Dimensions of Malaysian Education Policy." Pages 62–91 in Kenneth Orr (ed.), *Appetite for Education in Contemporary Asia Development*. (Studies Center, Monograph No. 10.) Canberra: Australian National University, 1977.

———. "The State and Peasant Innovation in Rural Development: The Case of Malaysian Rubber." Pages 321–331 in David Lim (ed.), *Readings on Malaysian Economic Development*. Kuala Lumpur: Oxford University Press, 1975.

Sandhu, Kernial Singh. *Indians in Malaya: Some Aspects of Their*

Immigration and Settlement (1786–1957). Cambridge: Cambridge University Press, 1969.

Saw, Swee-Hock. "Trends and Differentials in International Migration in Malaya," *Ekonomi Dan Pembangunan* [Banjarmasin, Indonesia], 4, No. 1, 1963, 87–113.

Shamsul, A.B. "The Politics of Poverty Eradication: The Implementation of Development Projects in a Malaysian District," *Pacific Affairs* [Vancouver], 56, No. 3, Fall 1983, 455–76.

Shamsul Bahrin, Tunku. "The Pattern of Indonesian Migration and Settlement in Malaya," *Asian Studies* [Quezon City, Philippines], 5, No. 2, August 1967, 233–57.

Sidhu, Manjit Singh, and Gavin W. Jones. *Population Dynamics in a Plural Society: Peninsular Malaysia*. Kuala Lumpur: University of Malaya Co-operative Bookshop, 1981.

Silcock, T.H. "Communal and Party Structure." Pages 1–28 in T.H. Silcock and E.K. Fisk (eds.), *The Political Economy of Independent Malaya*. Berkeley and Los Angeles: University of California Press, 1963.

Smith, T.E. *Population Growth in Malaya: A Survey of Trends*. London: Royal Institute of International Affairs, 1952.

Snodgrass, Donald R. *Inequality and Economic Development in Malaysia*. Kuala Lumpur: Oxford University Press, 1980.

Stevenson, Rex. *Cultivators and Administrators: British Educational Policy Towards the Malays*. Kuala Lumpur: Oxford University Press, 1975.

Sulong Mohamed. "The Geographical Setting." Pages 24–43 in E.K. Fisk and H. Osman-Rani (eds.), *The Political Economy of Malaysia*. Kuala Lumpur: Oxford University Press, 1982.

Sutlive, Vinson, Jr. *The Ibans of Sarawak*. Arlington Heights, Illinois: AHM, 1978.

Tham, Seong-Chee. *Malays and Modernization: A Sociological Interpretation*. Singapore: Singapore University Press, 1977.

Trocki, Carl A. *Prince of Pirates: The Temenggongs and the Development of Johor and Singapore, 1784–1885*. Singapore: Singapore University Press, 1979.

United Nations. ESCAP (Economic and Social Commission for Asia and the Pacific). *Migration, Urbanization, and Development in Malaysia*, 4, New York: 1982.

Von Elm, Barbara, and Charles Hirschman. "Age at First Marriage in Peninsular Malaysia," *Journal of Marriage and the Family*, 41, No. 4, November 1979, 877–91.

Wang, Gungwu. "Chinese Politics in Malaya." Pages 173–200 in Gungwu Wang (ed.), *Community and Nation: Essays on*

Southeast Asia and the Chinese. Singapore: Heinemann, 1981.

Wolters, O.W. *The Fall of Srivijaya in Malay History*. Ithaca: Cornell University Press, 1970.

———. *History, Culture, and Region in Southeast Asian Perspectives*. Singapore: Institute of Southeast Asian Studies, 1982.

Zakaria, Abdul Aziz. *An Introduction to the Machinery of Government in Malaysia*. Kuala Lumpur: Dewan Buhasa dan Pustaka, 1974.

Chapter 3

Anand, Sudhir. *Inequality and Poverty in Malaysia*. New York: Oxford University Press for the World Bank, 1983.

Asia Pacific Centre. *The Markets of Asia/Pacific: Malaysia*. New York: Facts on File, 1981.

Bacheller, Martin A. (ed.). *The Whole Earth Atlas: New Census Edition*. Maplewood, New Jersey: Hammond, 1983.

Bank Negara Malaysia. *Bank Negara Malaysia: Quarterly Economic Bulletin* [Kuala Lumpur], 16, Nos. 1–2, March-June 1983 (entire issue).

Bautista, Romeo M., et al. *Capital Utilization in Manufacturing in Developing Countries: A Case Study of Colombia, Israel, Malaysia, and Philippines*. New York: Oxford University Press, 1982.

Bowring, Philip, and James Clad. "Seeking a Private Push," *Far Eastern Economic Review* [Hong Kong], December 29, 1983, 50–52.

Bruch, Mathias. "Technological Heterogeneity, Scale Efficiency, and Plant Size: Micro Estimates for the West Malaysian Manufacturing Industry," *Developing Economies* [Tokyo], 21, No. 4, September 1983, 266–77.

Chantrasmi, Mary, and Tham Siew Yean. "Money, Banking, and Monetary Policy." Pages 287–307 in E.K. Fisk and H. Osman-Rani (eds.), *The Political Economy of Malaysia*. Kuala Lumpur: Oxford University Press, 1982.

Chee, Peng Lim, et al. *A Study of Small Entrepreneurs and Entrepreneurial Development Programmes in Malaysia*. Kuala Lumpur: University of Malaya Press, 1979.

Cheong, C.L. "Water in Agriculture in Malaysia." Pages 325–32 in E. Pushparajah and Chin Siew Lock (eds.), *Conference on*

Soil Science and Agricultural Development in Malaysia. Kuala Lumpur: Malaysian Society of Soil Science, 1980.

Chon, Chiseck. "Accelerated Industrialization and Employment Opportunities in Malaysia," *Geoforum*, 13, No. 1, January 1982, 11–18.

Clad, James. "The Debt Burden Builds," *Far Eastern Economic Review* [Hong Kong], November 3, 1983, 71–74.

———. "Shaping the Future," *Far Eastern Economic Review* [Hong Kong], September 29, 1983, 106–108.

———. "Unity in Diversity," *Far Eastern Economic Review* [Hong Kong], October 30, 1983, 68.

Das, K., et al. "Focus: Malaysia '81," *Far Eastern Economic Review* [Hong Kong], August 28, 1981, 38–70.

Dipak Mazumdar. *The Urban Labor Market and Income Distribution: A Study of Malaysia*. New York: Oxford University Press for the World Bank, 1981.

Direction of Trade Statistics Yearbook, 1977. Washington: International Monetary Fund, 1977.

Encik Ismail Alowi. "Growth and Composition of Malaysia's Imports in the Seventies," *Bank Negara Malaysia: Quarterly Economic Bulletin* [Kuala Lumpur], 15, No. 3, September 1982, 44–56.

FAO Production Yearbook, 1981. Rome: Food and Agriculture Organization, 1982.

FAO Trade Yearbook, 1981, 35. Rome: Food and Agriculture Organization, 1982.

Fisk, E.K. "Development in Malaysia." Pages 1–23 in E.K. Fisk and H. Osman-Rani (eds.), The Political Economy of Malaysia. Kuala Lumpur: Oxford University Press, 1982.

Food and Agriculture Organization. *Tropical Forest Resources Assessment Project (in the Framework of the Global Environment Monitoring System—GEMS): Forest Resources of Tropical Asia*. Rome: 1981.

Gullick, John M. *Malaysia: Economic Expansion and National Unity*. Boulder: Westview Press, 1981.

Higgins, Benjamin. "Development Planning." Pages 148–83 in E.K. Fisk and H. Osman-Rani (eds.), *The Political Economy of Malaysia*. Kuala Lumpur: Oxford University Press, 1982.

Hill, Ronald David. *Agriculture in the Malaysian Region*. Budapest: Akadémiai Kiadó, 1982.

Hoffman, Lutz. *Industrial Growth, Employment, and Foreign Investment in Peninsular Malaysia*. Kuala Lumpur: Oxford University Press, 1980.

Horii, Kenzō. *Rice Economy and Land Tenure in West Malaysia:*

A Comparative Study of Eight Villages. (Institute of Developing Economies, Occasional Papers series, No. 18.) Tokyo: Institute of Developing Economies, 1981.

Information Malaysia, 1980/81. (Ed,. Millicent Danker.) Kuala Lumpur: Berita, 1981.

International Financial Statistics Yearbook, 1983. Washington: International Monetary Fund, 1983.

Ismail Salleh. "Public Finance." Pages 308–40 in E.K. Fisk and H. Osman-Rani (eds.), *The Political Economy of Malaysia*. Kuala Lumpur: Oxford University Press, 1982.

Kadir H. Din. "The Physical Infrastructure." Pages 44–65 in E.K. Fisk and H. Osman-Rani (eds.), *The Political Economy of Malaysia*. Kuala Lumpur: Oxford University Press, 1982.

Kusnic, Michael W., and Julie DaVanzo. "Who Are the Poor in Malaysia? Sensitivity to Measurement of Income." Santa Monica: Rand, December 1981.

Leinbach, T.R. "Industrial Strategy in Malaysia: The Role of Export Processing Zones," *GeoJournal* [Wiesbaden], 6, No. 5, 1982, 459–68.

Lim, C.P. "Soil Surey and Agricultural Development in Sarawak." Pages 23–30 in E. Pushparajah and Chin Siew Lock (eds.), *Conference on Soil Science and Agricultural Development in Malaysia*. Kuala Lumpur: Malaysian Society of Soil Science, 1980.

Lim, David. "Malaysian Development Planning," *Pacific Affairs* [Vancouver], 55, No. 4, Winter 1982–83, 613–39.

Lim, Mah Hui. "Capitalism and Industrialization in Malaysia," *Bulletin of Concerned Asian Scholars*, 14, No. 1, January-March 1982, 32–47.

———. *Ownership and Control of the One Hundred Largest Corporations in Malaysia*. Kuala Lumpur: Oxford University Press, 1981.

Loose, Rainer. "Gaining New Territory in West Malaysia," *Quarterly Journal of International Agriculture* [Frankfurt], 22, No. 2, April-June 1983, 179–93.

Malaysia. *Fourth Malaysia Plan, 1981–1985*. Kuala Lumpur: National Printing Department, 1981.

Malaysia. Department of Statistics. *1980 Population and Housing Census of Malaysia: General Report of the Population Census*. Kuala Lumpur: 1983.

———. *Preliminary Figures of External Trade for the Period January to December, 1982*. Kuala Lumpur: 1983.

Malaysia. Ministry of Finance. *Economic Report, 1982–83*, 11. Kuala Lumpur: National Printing Department, 1982.

———. *Economic Report, 1983–84*, 12. Kuala Lumpur: National Printing Department, 1983.

Malaysia. Ministry of Information. Federal Department of Information. *Malaysia, 1979: Official Yearbook*, 19. Kuala Lumpur: 1982.

"Malaysia," *Times* [London], October 3, 1983, 13–17.

"Malaysia: Trade and Investment Survey," *Journal of Commerce*, May 24, 1983, A7-A11.

M. Anuar Adnan. "The Extractive Industries." Pages 229–59 in E.K. Fisk and H. Osman-Rani (eds.), *The Political Economy of Malaysia*. Kuala Lumpur: Oxford University Press, 1982.

Meerman, Jacob. *Public Expenditure in Malaysia: Who Benefits and Why*. New York: Oxford University Press, 1979.

Osborn, James. "Economic Growth with Equity? The Experience of Malaysia," *Contemporary Southeast Asia* [Singapore], 4, September 1982, 153–73.

Osman-Rani, H. "Manufacturing Industries." Pages 260–86 in E.K. Fisk and H. Osman-Rani (eds.), *The Political Economy of Malaysia*. Kuala Lumpur: Oxford University Press, 1982.

Ozay Mehmet. "Malaysian Employment Restructuring Policies: Effectiveness and Prospects under the Fourth Malaysia Plan, 1980–85," *Asian Survey*, 22, No. 10, October 1982, 978–87.

Paramananthan, S. "Soil Surveys in Peninsular Malaysia:Progress and Problems." Pages 3–23 in E. Pushparajah and Chin Siew Lock (eds.), *Conference on Soil Science and Agricultural Development in Malaysia*. Kuala Lumpur: Malaysian Society of Soil Science, 1980.

"Profile: Malaysia," *Asian Finance* [Hong Kong], 9, No. 10, October 15, 1983, 39-70.

Pushparajah, E., and Chin Siew Lock (eds.). *Conference on Soil Science and Agricultural Development in Malaysia*. Kuala Lumpur: Malaysian Society of Soil Science, 1980.

Rafferty, Kevin. "Factories in Paradise," *Institutional Investor* (International Edition), May 1982, 205–16.

Rogers, Marvin L. "Patterns of Change in a Rural Malay Community: Sungai Raya Revisited," *Asian Survey*, 22, No. 8, August 1982, 757–78.

Salleh, M. Zainudin, and Zulkifly Osman. "The Economic Structure." Pages 125–47 in E.K. Fisk and H. Osman-Rani (eds.), *The Political Economy of Malaysia*. Kuala Lumpur: Oxford University Press, 1982.

Segal, Jeffrey. "A Bamboo Umbrella: Malaysian Chinese Business and Politics Unite under Multi-Purpose," *Far Eastern Economic Review* [Hong Kong], September 3, 1982, 93–95.

———. "Foreigners Fade Away," *Far Eastern Economic Review* [Hong Kong], April 2, 1982, 42–43.

———. "A Fragile Prosperity," *Far Eastern Economic Review* [Hong Kong], April 14, 1983, 54–56.

———. "From Awful to Good," *Far Eastern Economic Review* [Hong Kong], April 21, 1983, 52–55.

———. Malaysia Changes Its Tune on Swap-shopping Deals," *Far Eastern Economic Review* [Hong Kong], January 27, 1983, 50–52.

———. "Toughing It Out," *Far Eastern Economic Review* [Hong Kong], October 29, 1982, 76–78.

Sharif, Kamarrudin. "The Demographic Situation." Pages 66–87 in E.K. Fisk and H. Osman-Rani (eds.), *The Political Economy of Malaysia*. Kuala Lumpur: Oxford University Press, 1982.

Sherwell, Christopher. "Malaysia Counts the Cost of Carrian," *Financial Times* [London], October 13, 1983, 22.

———. "Malaysia Treads Rough Road to New Identity," *Financial Times* [London], August 23, 1983, 3.

Siddique, Sharon, and Leo Suryadinata. "Bumiputra and Pribumi: Economic Nationalism (Indiginism) in Malaysia and Indonesia," *Pacific Affairs* [Vancouver], 54, No. 4, Winter 1981–82, 662–87.

Sikes, Jon. "Reversing the National Depletion Policy," *Far Eastern Economic Review* [Hong Kong], August 25, 1983, 51–53.

Smith, Patrick. "Balanced Growth for Now but Overcapacity Looms," *Far Eastern Economic Review* [Hong Kong], March 10, 1983, 47–48.

———. "Malaysia's Great Leap Forward," *Far Eastern Economic Review* [Hong Kong], June 16, 1983, 101–04.

———. "Now for Malaysia (Private) Inc.," *Far Eastern Economic Review* [Hong Kong], September 15, 1983, 69–72.

———. "Using Natural Resources to Forge a Firm Platform," *Far Eastern Economic Review* [Hong Kong], June 23, 1983, 70–72.

Snodgrass, Donald R. *Inequality and Economic Development in Malaysia*. Kuala Lumpur: Oxford University Press, 1980.

Sricharatchanya, Paisal. "The Hot Tin Hunt," *Far Eastern Economic Review* [Hong Kong], August 11, 1983, 48–49.

Sulong Mohamed. "The Geographical Setting." Pages 24–43 in E.K. Fisk and H. Osman-Rani (eds.), *The Political Economy of Malaysia*. Kuala Lumpur: Oxford University Press, 1982.

Sundaram, Jomo Kwame. "The Ascendance of Bureaucrat Capitalists in Malaysia," *Alternatives* [Delhi], 7, No. 4, September 1982, 467–90.

———. "Malaysia's NEP Heightens, Not Soothes, Ethnic Tension," *Asian Wall Street Journal* [Hong Kong], August 15, 1983, 4.

Tan, Loong-Hoe. "Equity and Malaysian State's New Economic Policy," *Asian Pacific Community* [Tokyo], No. 14, Fall 1981, 77–92.

United States. Department of Commerce. International Trade Administration. Office of Country Marketing. *Marketing in Malaysia*. Washington: 1981.

United States. Department of Labor. Bureau of International Labor Affairs. *Country Labor Profile: Malaysia*. Washington: GPO, 1980.

United States. Department of State. *Country Reports on Human Rights Practices for 1982*. (Report submitted to United States Congress, 98th, 1st Session, Senate, Committee on Foreign Relations, and House of Representatives, Committee on Foreign Affairs.) Washington: GPO, February 1983.

Vijayaledchumy, V., and Ooi Sang Kuang. "The Malaysian Economy: Development Planning," *Bank Negara Malaysia: Quarterly Economic Bulletin* [Kuala Lumpur], 12, No. 4, December 1979, 119–26.

von Uexkull, H.R. "Fertilizer Use and Future Trends in Malaysia." Pages 275–88 in E. Pushparajah and Chin Siew Lock (eds.), *Conference on Soil Science and Agricultural Development in Malaysia*. Kuala Lumpur: Malaysian Society of Soil Science, 1980.

Wawn, Brian. *The Economies of the ASEAN Countries: Indonesia, Malaysia, Philippines, Singapore, and Thailand*. New York: St. Martin's Press, 1982.

Wu, John C. "The Mineral Industry of Malaysia." Pages 641–55 in *Minerals Yearbook, Vol. 3: Area Reports*. Washington: GPO, 1981.

Yee, Kew Tan. *The Land and the Agricultural Organisation of Peninsular Malaysia: A Historical Interpretation*. (University of Wales, University College 8of Swansea, Centre for Development Studies, Monographs series, No. 13.) Norwich, England: Geo Abstracts, 1981.

Yuan, Chong Kwong. "Trade and External Relations." Pages 184–204 in E.K. Fisk and H. Osman-Rani (eds.), *The Political Economy of Malaysia*. Kuala Lumpur: Oxford University Press, 1982.

Zakaria bin Haji Ahmad. "The Political Structure." Pages 88–103 in E.K. Fisk and H. Osman-Rani (eds.), *The Political Econ-*

omy of Malaysia. Kuala Lumpur: Oxford University Press, 1982.

Zulkifly Hj. Mustapha. "The Agricultural Sector." pages 205–28 in E.K. Fisk and H. Osman-Rani (eds.), *The Political Economy of Malaysia*. Kuala Lumpur: Oxford University Press, 1982.

(Various issues of the following publications were also used in the preparation of this chapter: *Asian Wall Street Journal* [Hong Kong]; *Asia Yearbook* [Hong Kong]; *Bank Negara Malaysia: Quarterly Economic Bulletin* [Kuala Lumpur]; *Business Asia* [Hong Kong]; *Far East and Australasia* [London]; *Far Eastern Economic Review* [Hong Kong]; *Financial Times* [London]; *International Financial Statistics;* Joint Publications Research Service, *South and East Asia Report* and *Southeast Asia Report;* and *Natural Rubber News*.)

Chapter 4

Amnesty International Report, 1982. London: Amnesty International, 1982.

Asia Yearbook, 1978. (Ed., Hiro Punwani.) Hong Kong: Far Eastern Economic Review, 1978.

Asia Yearbook, 1979. (Ed., Donald Wise.) Hong Kong: Far Eastern Economic Review, 1979.

Asia Yearbook, 1980. (Ed., Donald Wise.) Hong Kong: Far Eastern Economic Review, 1980.

Asia Yearbook, 1981. (Ed., Donald Wise.) Hong Kong: Far Eastern Economic Review, 1981.

Asia Yearbook, 1982. (Ed., Donald Wise.) Hong Kong: Far Eastern Economic Review, 1982.

Asia Yearbook, 1983. (Ed., Donald Wise.) Hong Kong: Far Eastern Economic Review, 1983.

Ayoob, Mohammad (ed.). *The Politics of Islamic Reassertion*. New York: St. Martin's Press, 1981.

Barraclough, Simon. "Managing the Challenges of Islamic Revival in Malaysia: A Regime Perspective," *Asian Survey*, 23, No. 8, August 1983, 958–75.

Bass, Jerry. "Malaysia in 1982: A New Frontier?" *Asian Survey*, 23, No. 2, February 1983, 191–200.

Bedlington, Stanley S. *Malaysia and Singapore: The Building of New States*. Ithaca: Cornell University Press, 1978.

Cheah, Cheng Hye. "Constitution Fight Pits King Against

Mahathir," *Asian Wall Street Journal* [Hong Kong], October 12, 1983, 114.

"Constitutional Amendments: 22 New Constituencies: Appeals to Privy Council Abolished," *Malaysian Digest* [Kuala Lumpur], 14, No. 15, August 15, 1983, 1.

Das, K. "After Hussein, What?" *Far Eastern Economic Review* [Hong Kong], May 8, 1981, 10–11.

———. "The Attraction of Opposites," *Far Eastern Economic Review* [Hong Kong], January 23, 1981, 14.

———. "The Bahasa Backlash," *Far Eastern Economic Review* [Hong Kong], January 22, 1982, 10–11.

———. "A Battle Royal," *Far Eastern Economic Review* [Hong Kong], October 13, 1983, 17–18.

———. "Chinese at the Crossroads," *Far Eastern Economic Review* [Hong Kong], September 3, 1982, 44–47.

———. "A Crisis on Hold: A Ruler Calls for Consultation to End a Constitutional Problem," *Far Eastern Economic Review* [Hong Kong], November 17, 1983, 21–22.

———. "A Difficult Year for the National Front," *Far Eastern Economic Review* [Hong Kong], August 29, 1980, 32–33.

———. "The End of the Affairs," *Far Eastern Economic Review* [Hong Kong], December 29, 1983, 13–15.

———. "Faux Pas in the Party," *Far Eastern Economic Review* [Hong Kong], September 1, 1983, 16.

———. "Grassroots Power," *Far Eastern Economic Review* [Hong Kong], March 21, 1982, 14–15.

———. "The Harun Factor," *Far Eastern Economic Review* [Hong Kong], May 22, 1981, 8–9.

———. "Home for Hari Raya," *Far Eastern Economic Review* [Hong Kong], August 7, 1981, 10–11.

———. "In from the Cold: Anwar and Harun Come Back to UMNO with a Bang," *Far Eastern Economic Review* [Hong Kong], September 17, 1982, 10–11.

———. "Keeping It a Secret," *Far Eastern Economic Review* [Hong Kong], November 3, 1983, 16–17.

———. "The King Holds the Ace," *Far Eastern Economic Review* [Hong Kong], December 1, 1983, 14–17.

———. "Mahathir Picks His Men," *Far Eastern Economic Review* [Hong Kong], July 24, 1981, 8–9.

———. "Mahathir Plays It Tough," *Far Eastern Economic Review* [Hong Kong], December 15, 1983, 14–15.

———. "Mahathir's Date with a Mandate," *Far Eastern Economic Review* [Hong Kong], March 26, 1982, 10–11.

———. "Mahathir's Prize Catch," *Far Eastern Economic Re-*

view [Hong Kong], April 2, 1982, 23–24.

———. "Mahathir's 'Restoration'," *Far Eastern Economic Review* [Hong Kong], June 11, 1982, 38–41.

———. "Mahathir's Soft Shoe Shuffle," *Far Eastern Economic Review* [Hong Kong], May 7, 1982, 10–11.

———. "Mahathir Turns the Tide," *Far Eastern Economic Review* [Hong Kong], April 30, 1982, 17–19.

———. "No Startling Changes," *Far Eastern Economic Review* [Hong Kong], June 16, 1983, 28–29.

———. "The Old Guard Changes," *Far Eastern Economic Review* [Hong Kong], July 3, 1981, 14–16.

———. "The Paper Chase's New Hurdles," *Far Eastern Economic Review* [Hong Kong], March 7, 1980, 21.

———. "Passing on PAS," *Far Eastern Economic Review* [Hong Kong], September 22, 1983, 32–33.

———. "Perils of Polarisation," *Far Eastern Economic Review* [Hong Kong], February 3, 1983, 14–15.

———. "Preaching Moderation," *Far Eastern Economic Review* [Hong Kong], March 3, 1983, 20–22.

———. "Requiem for a Dream," *Far Eastern Economic Review* [Hong Kong], July 16, 1982, 16–17.

———. "A Ruler's Compromise," *Far Eastern Economic Review* [Hong Kong], October 27, 1983, 16–17.

———. "Societies in Shock," *Far Eastern Economic Review* [Hong Kong], October 29, 1982, 12–13.

———. "A Split with the Sultan," *Far Eastern Economic Review* [Hong Kong], October 23, 1981, 8–9.

———. "Straining at the Leash," *Far Eastern Economic Review* [Hong Kong], April 24, 1981, 10–11.

———. "The Sultans Dig In," *Far Eastern Economic Review* [Hong Kong], November 24, 1983, 18–20.

———. "Sultan vs. Politician," *Far Eastern Economic Review* [Hong Kong], May 15, 1981, 12–13.

———. "The Thaw Continues: A New British Programme Should Help Further Iron Out Kinks in Relations with Malaysia," *Far Eastern Economic Review* [Hong Kong], August 4, 1983, 54–55.

———. "Turmoil in the Opposition," *Far Eastern Economic Review* [Hong Kong], December 12, 1980, 14.

———. "Withdrawal from Debate," *Far Eastern Economic Review* [Hong Kong], December 10, 1982, 12–13.

Davies, Derek, and George Lauriat. "Spicing Up Sabah's Recipe," *Far Eastern Economic Review* [Hong Kong], July 18, 1980, 24–35.

The Far East and Australasia, 1983–84. (15th ed.) London: Europa, 1983.

"FM: Guidelines on Principles of Interventionism Vital for Detente," *Malaysian Digest* [Kuala Lumpur], 14, No. 7, April 15, 1983, 8.

Gratton, Reg. "Leading Dissident Muslim Activist Joins UMNO," *Asia Record*, 3, No. 2, May 1982, 6.

———. "Mahathir Calls Early Election, Front Members Jockey for Seats," *Asia Record*, 3, No. 1, April 1982, 6.

Gullick, John M. "Malaysia: The Prospect for the 1980s," (Pt. 2.), *Asian Affairs* [London], 11, June 1980, 144–51.

Indorf, Hans H. "Malaysia in 1977: A Prelude to Premature Parliamentary Elections," *Asian Survey*, 18, No. 2, February 1978, 186–93.

———. "Malaysia 1978: Communal Coalitions Continue," *Asian Survey*, 19, No. 2, February 1979, 115–23.

———. "Malaysia 1979: A Preoccupation with Security," *Asian Survey*, 20, No. 2, February 1980, 135–43.

Information Malaysia, 1980/81. (Ed., Millicent Danker.) Kuala Lumpur: Berita, 1981.

Jenkins, David. "Sultans as Symbols: A Focus for Identity. Traditional Rulers Adjust to Change," *Far Eastern Economic Review* [Hong Kong] June 30, 1983, 26–32.

Joint Publications Research Service—JPRS (Washington).

The following items are from the JPRS series:

Southeast Asia Report.

"Cause of Uncertainty in Malaysia-U.S. Ties Cited," *New Straits Times*, Kuala Lumpur, September 4, 1983. (JPRS 84509, No. 1350, October 11, 1983).

"Chinese Urged to Concentrate Political, Economic Power," *Kin Kwok Daily News*, Selangor, July 23, 1983. (JPRS 84467, No. 1347, October 5, 1983).

"Learning from Japan," *Borneo Post*, Kuching, August 30, 1983. (JPRS 84509, No. 1350, October 11, 1983).

"Learning from Korea," *Sarawak Tribune*, Kuching, August 17, 1983. (JPRS 84509, No. 1350, October 11, 1983).

"Musa Advocates Cautious Absorption of Islamic Values," *Borneo Post*, Kuching, August 19, 1983. (JPRS 84509, No. 1350, October 11, 1983).

Kahin, George (ed.). *Government and Politics of Southeast Asia*.

(3d ed.) Ithaca: Cornell University Press, 1976.

Kulkarni, V.G. "The Chinese Dilemma," *Far Eastern Economic Review* [Hong Kong], April 30, 1982, 20–21.

"Look East Policy Right for Malaysia," *Malaysian Digest* [Kuala Lumpur], 14, No. 10, May 31, 1983, 1–2.

McBeth, John, and K. Das. "A Frontier of Fear and Factions," *Far Eastern Economic Review* [Hong Kong], June 20, 1980, 16–19.

"Mahathir Addresses Nonaligned Summit 8 March," Foreign Broadcast Information Service, *Daily Report: Asia and Pacific*, 4, No. 051 (FBIS-APA-83-051), March 15, 1983, O1–O8.

"Mahathir on Soviet Threat; Dhanabalan Departs," Foreign Broadcast Information Service, *Daily Report: Aisa and Pacific*, 4, No. 072 (FBIS-APA-83-072), April 13, 1983, 01.

Malaysia. Ministry of Foreign Affairs. *Malaysia in Brief, 1983*. *Kuala Lumpur: 1983*.

Malaysia. Ministry of Information. Federal Department of Information. *Malaysia, 1979: Official Yearbook*, 19, Kuala Lumpur: 1982.

"Malaysia Conducting 'Virtual Boycott' of UK," Foreign Broadcast Information Service, *Daily Report: Asia and Pacific*, 4, No. 193 (FBIS-APA-81-193), October 6, 1981, O1–O2.

"Malaysia '81," *Far Eastern Economic Review* [Hong Kong], August 28, 1981, 38–70.

Martin, Bradley K. "Malaysia's Prime Minister Speaks in Japan on His 'Look East' Policy," *Asian Wall Street Journal* [Hong Kong], November 11–12, 1983, 3.

Means, Gordon P. *Malaysian Politics*. New York University Press, 1976.

Milne, R.S., and K.J. Ratnam. *Malaysia—New States in a New Nation: Political Development of Sarawak and Sabah in Malaysia*. London: Cass, 1974.

"Minister Criticizes U.S. Sale of Stockpiled Tin," Foreign Broadcast Information Service, *Daily Report: Asia and Pacific*, 4, No. 043 (FBIS-APA-82-043), March 4, 1982, O2.

Mohammed Suffian bin Hashin, Tun, H.P. Lee, and F.A. Trindade (eds.). *The Constitution of Malaysia: Its Development, 1957–1977*. Kuala Lumpur: Oxford University Press, 1978.

"A Mole and His Masters," *Far Eastern Economic Review* [Hong Kong], July 24, 1981, 9–10.

Morrison, Charles E., and Astri Suhrke. *Strategies of Survival: The Foreign Policy Dilemmas of Smaller Asian States*. New York: St. Martin's Press, 1978.

Nagata, Judith. "Religious Ideology and Social Change: The Islamic Revival in Malaysia," *Pacific Affairs* [Vancouver], 53, No. 3, Fall 1980, 405–39.

Nelson, Daniel. "The British Come Back," *Far Eastern Economic Review* [Hong Kong], March 24, 1983, 34–35.

Pillai, M.G.G. "Malaysia: British Business Must Learn to Hustle," *Times* [London], October 3, 1983, 15.

"PRC Policy Toward Asian Communist Parties Viewed," Foreign Broadcast Information Service, *Daily Report: Asia and Pacific*, 4, No. 212 (FBIS-APA-82-212), November 2, 1982, O1–O2.

Pura, Raphael. "Mahathir Takes Royalty Crisis to Public," *Asian Wall Street Journal* [Hong Kong], November 28, 1983, 1, 3.

———. "Malaysia Constitution Talks Are Fruitless," *Asian Wall Street Journal* [Hong Kong], November 21, 1983, 1.

———. "Malaysia Deadlocked by Royalty Crisis," *Asian Wall Street Journal* [Hong Kong], November 17, 1983, 1, 4.

Purcell, Victor. *The Chinese in Malaya*. New York: Oxford University Press, 1968.

———. *Malaysia*. New York: Walker, 1965.

Roff, William R. (ed.). *Kelantan: Religion, Society, and Politics in a Malay State*. New York: Oxford University Press, 1974.

"Royal Assent Given to Constitutional Amendment Bill," Foreign Broadcast Information Service, *Daily Report: Asia and Pacific*, 4, No. 245 (FBIS-APA-83-245), December 20, 1983, O1–O3.

Segal, Jeffrey. "A Bamboo Umbrella: Malaysian Chinese Business and Politics Unite under Multi-Purpose," *Far Eastern Economic Review* [Hong Kong], September 3, 1982, 93–95.

———. "A Break in the Ranks: The Departure of Lee San Choon May Mean Problems for the MCA," *Far Eastern Economic Review* [Hong Kong], April 7, 1983, 10–11.

———. "A Fragil Prosperity," *Far Eastern Economic Review* [Hong Kong], April 14, 1983, 54–56.

———. "The Third Time Around," *Far Eastern Economic Review* [Hong Kong], March 31, 1983, 14.

Sherwell, Christopher. "Royal Row Threatens Mahathir's Credibility," *Financial Times* [London], December 13, 1983, 4.

Smith, Patrick, and Rodney Tasker. "Look East, Bumiputras," *Far Eastern Economic Review* [Hong Kong], February 12, 1982, 45–46.

"SRV, USSR Blamed for Regional Instability," Foreign Broadcast Information Service, *Daily Report: Asia and Pacific*, 4, No. 073 (FBIS-APA-83-073), April 14, 1983, O1.

Sundaram, Jomo Kwane. "Malaysia's NEP Heightens, Not Soothes, Ethnic Tension," *Asian Wall Street Journal* [Hong Kong], August 15, 1983, 4.

Tilman, Robert O. "Mustapha's Sabah, 1968–1975: The Tun Steps Down," *Asian Survey*, 16, No. 6, June 1976, 495–509.

Tilman, Robert O., and Jo H. Tilman. "Malaysia and Singapore, 1976: A Year of Challenge, A Year of Change," *Asian Survey*, 17, No. 2, February 1977, 143–54.

Tōnan Ajia Chōsakai. *Tōnan Ajia Yōran 1981*.

United States. Congress. 97th, 2d Session. Senate. Committee on Foreign Relations. *U.S. Policies and Programs in Southeast Asia*. Washington: GPO, 1982.

United States. Department of State. Bureau of Public Affairs. *Background Notes: Malaysia*. (Department of State publication, No. 7753.) Washington: GPO, October 1983.

van der Kroef, Justus M. "ASEAN Security and Development: Some Paradoxes and Symbols," (Pt. 2.), *Asian Affairs* [London], 9, June 1978, 143-60.

von der Mehden, Fred R. "Malaysia in 1980: Signals to Watch," *Asian Survey*, 21, No. 2, February 1981, 245–52.

———. "Malaysia in 1981: Continuity and Change," *Asian Survey*, 22, No. 2, February 1982, 212–18.

Von Vorys, K. *Democracy Without Consensus: Communalism and Political Stability in Malaysia*. Princeton: Princeton University Press, 1975.

Wain, Barry. "Singapore Link with Malaysia Grows Stronger," *Asian Wall Street Journal* [Hong Kong], September 12, 1983, 1.

———. "Small Malaysia Pressure Group Helps Promote Social Change," *Asian Wall Street Journal* [Hong Kong], November 18–19, 1983, 1.

———. "Trying to Limit the Role of Malay Hereditary Rulers," *Asian Wall Street Journal* [Hong Kong], September 5, 1983, 8.

Zakaria bin Haji Ahmad. "The Political Structure." Pages 88–103 in E.K. Fisk and H. Osman-Rani (eds.), *The Political Economy of Malaysia*. Kuala Lumpur: Oxford University Press, 1982.

(Various issues of the following publications were also used in the preparation of this chapter: *Asian Recorder* [New Delhi], January 1977–December 1979; Foreign Broadcast Information Service, *Daily Report: Asia and Pacific*, January 1977-January 1984; *Keesing's Contemporary Archives* [London], January 1977-January 1983. *New York Times*, January 1977-December 1983; and *Washington Post,* January 1977-January 1984.)

Chapter 5

Amnesty International. *Report of an Amnesty International Mission to the Federation of Malaysia: 18 November-30 November 1978*. London: 1979.

Amnesty International Report, 1981. London: Amnesty International, 1981.

Amnesty International Report, 1982. London: Amnesty International, 1982.

Amnesty International Report, 1983. London: Amnesty International, 1983.

Asia Yearbook, 1974. (Ed., Hiro Punwani.) Hong Kong: Far Eastern Economic Review, 1974.

Asia Yearbook, 1976. (Ed., Rodney Tasker.) Hong Kong: Far Eastern Economic Review, 1976.

Asia Yearbook, 1978. (Ed., Hiro Punwani.) Hong Kong: Far Eastern Economic Review, 1978.

Asia Yearbook, 1979. (Ed., Donald Wise.) Hong Kong: Far Eastern Economic Review, 1979.

Asia Yearbook, 1980. (Ed., Donald Wise.) Hong Kong: Far Eastern Economic Review, 1980.

Asia Yearbook, 1981. (Ed., Donald Wise.) Hong Kong: Far Eastern Economic Review, 1981.

Asia Yearbook, 1982. (Ed., Donald Wise.) Hong Kong: Far Eastern Economic Review, 1982.

Asia Yearbook, 1983. (Ed., Donald Wise.) Hong Kong: Far Eastern Economic Review, 1983.

Bedlington, Stanley S. *Malaysia and Singapore: The Building of New States*. Ithaca: Cornell University Press, 1978.

Chin, Kin Wah. *The Defence of Malaysia and Singapore: The Transformation of a Security System, 1957–1971*. Cambridge: Cambridge University Press, 1983.

Clementson, J. "Malaysia in the 'Seventies: Communist Resurgence and Government Response," *RUSI Journal* [London], 124, No. 4, December 1979, 50–57.

Combat Fleets of the World, 1982/83. (Ed., Jean Labayle Couhat.) Annapolis: Naval Institute Press, 1982.

Copley, Gregory R. (ed.). *Defense and Foreign Affairs Handbook*. Washington: Copley, 1981.

Crouch, Harold. "An Arm's-Length Stance on Business Activities," *Far Eastern Economic Review* [Hong Kong], October 20, 1983, 50–51.

———. "A Strict Division," *Far Eastern Economic Review* [Hong Kong], October 20, 1983, 46–47.

———. "Time to Consolidate on a New Front Line," *Far Eastern Economic Review* [Hong Kong], October 20, 1983, 47–51.

"Curbing a Border War," *Asiaweek* [Hong Kong], July 22, 1983, 16–26.

Das. K. "Crackdown on Critics," *Far Eastern Economic Review* [Hong Kong], April 17, 1981, 8–9.

———. "A Draconian Defense," *Far Eastern Economic Review* [Hong Kong], July 2, 1982, 17–18.

———. "An Eye on the Imams," *Far Eastern Economic Review* [Hong Kong], January 13, 1983, 9–10.

———. "Fighting a Limited Battle," *Far Eastern Economic Review* [Hong Kong], July 13, 1979, 13–14.

———. "The Jungle War That Refuses to Go Away," *Far Eastern Economic Review* [Hong Kong], March 6, 1981, 26–31.

———. "The Lawyer's Indictment," *Far Eastern Economic Review* [Hong Kong], January 13, 8–9.

———. "Malaysia Shocks the World into Action," *Far Eastern Economic Review* [Hong Kong], June 29, 1979, 10–11.

———. "Operation People's War," *Far Eastern Economic Review* [Hong Kong], April 22, 1977, 10–12.

———. "Perched on a Claim," *Far Eastern Economic Review* [Hong Kong], September 29, 1983, 40–41.

———. "Refugees: Rocking Asean's Boat," *Far Eastern Economic Review* [Hong Kong], June 15, 1979, 21–24.

———. "Starting the Decade with a Bang," *Far Eastern Economic Review* [Hong Kong], January 18, 1980, 30.

———. "Time for the Big Battalions," *Far Eastern Economic Review* [Hong Kong], March 6, 1981, 26–27.

DMS Market Intelligence Report: South America/Australasia. Greenwich, Connecticut: DMS 1982.

"East-West Road Opens New Opportunities on Malaysia's East Coast," *Business Asia* [Hong Kong], October 8, 1982, 323.

"Emergency (Essential Powers) Ordinance 1969. Essential (Security Cases) Regulations 1975," *His Majesty's Government Gazette* [Kuala Lumpur], 19, No. 21, October 9, 1975, 1285–94.

Enloe, Cynthia H. "The Issue Saliency of Military-Ethnic Connection: Some Thoughts on Malaysia," *Comparative Politics*,

10, No. 2, January 1978, 267–85.

Goldrick, J.V.P., and P.D. Jones. "The Far Eastern Navies," *United States Naval Institute Proceedings*, 108, No. 3, March 1982, 60–65.

Government Finance Statistics Yearbook, 6. Washington: International Monetary Fund, 1982.

Gullick, John M. *Malaysia: Economic Expansion and National Unity*. Boulder: Westview Press, 1981.

Gunston, Bill (ed.). *Encyclopedia of World Air Power*. New York: Crescent Books, 1980.

Hewish, Mark, et al. (eds.). *Air Forces of the World*. New York: Simon and Schuster, 1979.

Indorf, Hans H. "Malaysia 1979: A Preoccupation with Security," *Asian Survey*, 20, No. 2, February 1980, 135–43.

Information Malaysia, 1980/81. (Ed., Millicent Danker.) Kuala Lumpur: Berita, 1981.

"Internal Security Act, 1960," *His Majesty's Government Gazette* [Kuala Lumpur], 4, No. 17, July 30, 1960, 111–59.

International Financial Statistics, 36, No. 10, October 1983 (entire issue).

International Financial Statistics Yearbook, 1981. Washington: International Monetary Fund, 1981.

Jane's All the World's Aircraft, 1980–81. (Ed., John W.R. Taylor.) London: Jane's, 1980.

Jane's Armour and Artillery, 1982–83. (Ed., Christopher F, Foss.) London: Jane's, 1982.

Jane's Fighting Ships, 1980–81. (Ed., John E. Moore.) London: Jane's, 1980.

Jane's Infantry Weapons, 1982–83. (Ed., John Weeks.) London: Jane's, 1982.

Jane's Weapon Systems, 1980–81. (Ed., John E. Moore.) London: Jane's, 1980.

Jeshurun, Chandran. *Malaysian Defence Policy: A Study in Parliamentary Attitudes, 1963–1973*. Kuala Lumpur: Penerbit Universiti Malaya, 1980.

Joint Publications Research Service—JPRS (Washington).

The following items are from the JPRS series:

Southeast Asia Report.

"Malaysia Fears Halfway House Becoming Core for Vietnamese Refugees," *Borneo Post*, Kuching, July 15, 1983. (JPRS 84170, No. 1328, August 23, 1983, 83).

"State of CPM Examined," *The Nation Review*, Bangkok, January 18, 1983. (JPRS 82977, No. 1250, March 1, 1983, 45–48).

Jones, P.D., and J.V.P. Goldrick. "The Far Eastern Navies," *United States Naval Institute Proceedings*, 109, No. 3, March 1983, 57–63.

Keegan, John (ed.). *World Armies*. New York: Facts on File, 1979.

Keesing's Contemporary Archives, 1971–1972. London: Keesing's, 1972.

Kessing's Contemporary Archives, 1982. (Ed., Robert Fraser.) London: Keesing's, 1982.

Khalid, A. "The Making of an Air Force," *Asian Defense Journal* [Kuala Lumpur], No. 6, June 1983, 28–35.

———. "The Malaysian Army: An Overview," *Asian Defense Journal* [Kuala Lumpur], No. 3, March 1983, 10–18.

McBeth, John, and K. Das. "A Frontier of Fear and Factions," *Far Eastern Economic Review* [Hong Kong], June 20, 1980, 16–19.

Mackie, J.A.C. *Konfrontasi: The Indoensia-Malaysia Dispute, 1963–1966*. Kuala Lumpur: Oxford University Press, 1974.

Malaysia. *Penal Code*. Kuala Lumpur: Law, 1980.

Malaysia. Department of Statistics. *1980 Population and Housing Census of Malaysia: General Report of the Population Census*. Kuala Lumpur: 1983.

Malaysia. Mininstry of Finance. *Economic Report, 1982–83*, 11. Kuala Lumpur: National Printing Department, 1982.

———. *Economic Report, 1983–84*, 12. Kuala Lumpur: National Printing Department, 1983.

Malaysia. Ministry of Information. Federal Department of Information. *Malaysia, 1979; Official Yearbook*, 19. Kuala Lumpur: 1982.

Mehta, K. "The Army Through Fifty Years—1933 to 1983," *Asian Defense Journal* [Kuala Lumpur], No. 3, March 1983, 29–31.

The Military Balance, 1982–83. London: International Institute for Strategic Studies, 1982.

The Military Balance, 1983–84. London: International Institute for Strategic Studies, 1983.

Mohamed Suffian bin Hashim, Tun (ed.). *An Introduction to the Constitution of Malaysia*. (2d ed.) Kuala Lumpur: Government Printer, 1978.

"Nurturing Islam in a Plural Society," *South* [London], No. 33, July 1983, 22–24.

Robinson, Anthony (ed.). *Air Power*. New York: Ziff-Davis, 1980

Saad, Ibrahim. *Competing Identities in a Plural Society*. (ISEAS Occasional Paper, No. 63.) Singapore: Institute of Southeast Asian Studies, 1980.

Sachithananthan, R. "Anti-Terrorist Operations in Peninsular Malaysia," *Asian Defense Journal* [Kuala Lumpur], No. 3, March 1983, 20–23.

Segal, Jeffrey. "The Third Time Around," *Far Eastern Economic Review* [Hong Kong], March 31, 1983, 14.

Sheridan, L.A., and Harry E. Groves. *The Constitution of Malaysia*. (3d ed.) Singapore: Malayan Law Journal, 1979.

Short, Anthony. *The Communist Insurrection in Malaya, 1948–1960*. New York: Crane, Russak, 1975.

Sim, Richard. *Malaysia: Containing the Communist Insurgency*. London: Institute for the Study of Conflict, 1979.

Singh, Awther. *Singh's Commentary on the Malaysian Criminal Procedure Code*. Singapore: Quins, 1981.

Sivard, Ruth Leger. *World Military and Social Expenditures, 1982*. Leesburg, Virginia: World Priorities, 1982.

Snodgrass, Donald R. *Inequality and Economic Development in Malaysia*. Kuala Lumpur: Oxford University Press, 1980.

"Switching froim Guerrilla Warfare to Conventional Warfare Capabilities," *Asia Research Bulletin* [Singapore], 11, No. 8, January 31, 1982, 885–88.

Tasker, Rodney. "Keeping Islam in Balance," *Far Eastern Economic Review* [Hong Kong], November 28, 1980, 34–36.

Tow, William T. "Asian-Pacific Alliance Systems and Transregional Linkages," *Naval War College Review*, 34, No. 5, September-October, 1981, 32–54.

"Tracking Down Some of the Religious Extremists," *Far Eastern Economic Review* [Hong Kong], August 31, 1979, 59–60.

United States. Arms Control and Disarmament Agency. *World Military Expenditures and Arms Transfers, 1970–1979*. Washington: 1982.

United States. Congress. 90th, 1st Session. House of Representatives. Committee on Foreign Affairs. *Collective Defense Treaties: With Maps, Texts of Treaties, a Chronology, Status of Forces Agreements, and Comparative Chart*. Washington: GPO, 1982.

United States. Congress. 97th, 2d Session. Senate. Committee on Foreign Relations. Subcommittee on East Asian and Pacific Affairs. *Southeast Asian Drug Trade*. Washington: GPO, 1982.

United States. Department of Defense. Security Assistance Agency. *Foreign Military Sales, Foreign Military Construction Sales, and Military Assistance Facts*. Washington: 1981.

———. *Foreign Military Sales, Foreign Military Construction Sales, and Military Assistance Facts*. Washington: 1982.

———. *Security Assistance Programs, FY 1983*. Washington: 1982.

United States. Department of State. *Country Reports on Human Rights Practices for 1981*. (Report submitted to United States Congress, 97th, 2d Session, House of Representatives, Committee on Foreign Affairs, and Senate, Committee on Foreign Relations.) Washington: GPO, February 1982.

———. *Country Reports on Humans Rights Practices for 1982*. (Report submitted to United States Congress, 98th, 1st Session, Senate, Committee on Foreign Relations, and House of Representatives, Committee on Foreign Affiars.) Washington: GPO, February 1983.

Vreeland, Nena, et al. *Area Handbook for Malaysia*. (DA Pam 550–45.) Washington: GPO for Foreign Area Studies, The American University, 1977.

World Armaments and Disarmament: SIPRI Yearbook, 1975. Cambridge: MIT Press for Stockholm International Peace Research Institute, 1975.

World Armaments and Disarmament: SIPRI Yearbook, 1977. Cambridge: MIT Press for Stockholm International Peace Research Institute, 1977.

World Armaments and Disarmament: SIPRI Yearbook, 1978. New York: Crane, Russak for Stockholm International Peace Research Institute, 1978.

World Armaments and Disarmament: SIPRI Yearbook, 1979 London: Taylor and Francis for Stockholm International Peace Research Institute, 1979.

World Armament and Disarmament: SIPRI Yearbook, 1980. London: Taylor and Francis for Stockholm International Peace Research Institute, 1980.

Yearbook on International Communist Affairs, 1980. (Ed., Richard F. Staar.) Stanford: Hoover Institution Press, 1980.

Yearbook on International Communist Affairs, 1981. (Ed., Richard F. Staar.) Stanford: Hoover Institution Press, 1981.

Yearbook on International Communist Affairs, 1982. (Ed., Richard F. Staar.) Stanford: Hoover Institution Press, 1982.

Zakaria bin Haji Ahmad. "The Bayonet and the Truncheon: Army/Police Relations in Malaysia." Pages 193–229 in Dewitt C. Ellinwood and Cynthia H. Enloe (eds.), *Ethnicity and the*

Military in Asia. New Brunswick, New Jersey: Transaction Books, 1981.

———. "The Police and Political Development in Malaysia: Change, Continuity, and Institution-Building of a 'Coercive' Apparatus in a Developing, Ethnically Divided Society." (Ph.D. dissertation.) Department of Political Science, Massachusetts Institute of Technology, 1977.

(Various issues of the following publications were also used in the preparation of this chapter: *Asian Defense Journal* [Kuala Lumpur], January 1978-December 1983; *Asian Survey*, January 1972-December 1983; *Asian Wall Street Journal* [Hong Kong], January 1980-December 1983; *Asia Research Bulletin* [Singapore], January 1980-December 1983; *Asiaweek* [Hong Kong], January 1980-December 1983; *Business Asia* [Hong Kong], January-December 1983; *Far Eastern Economic Review* [Hong Kong], January 1972-January 1983; Foreign Broadcast Information Service, *Daily Report: Asia and Pacific*, January 1978-December 1983; Joint Publications Research Service, *Southeast Asia Report*, January-December 1983; *Malaysia* [Kuala Lumpur], January-December 1983; *New York Times*, January 1981-January 1983; and *Washington Post*, January 1981-January 1983.)

Glossary

adat—Customary law, local or regional custom, customary behavior.

Bahasa Malaysia—Literally, the language of Malaysia; the standard form of Malay known as Bahasa Malaysia is the official national language.

Bumiputra—Literally, sons of the soil; official term for Malays and other indigenous peoples of Malaysia.

crop year—The year beginning July 1; sometimes used in Malaysian agricultural statistics.

dakwah—An Islamic revival movement that has attracted a following especially among highly educated youth.

Exclusive Economic Zone—A wide belt of sea and seabed adjacent to the national boundaries where the state claims exclusive control over the exploitation of fishery, mineral, and other natural resources. The limit of the zone is commonly 200 nautical miles, unless boundary situations with neighboring states require negotiated adjustments.

FELDA—Federal Land Development Authority, a national agency sponsoring resettlement schemes for landless peasants.

fiscal year (FY)—Same as the calendar year.

gambier—A yellowish catechu obtained from a Malaysian woody vine, exported for tanning and dyeing.

gross domestic product (GDP)—The value, in market prices, of all final goods and services for consumption and investment (excluding those intermediate to the production process) produced in an economy during a given period, usually a year. GDP is "gross" because it does not deduct depreciation costs and is "domestic" because it excludes income earned abroad and includes that earned by foreigners in the country.

imam—Islamic prayer leader.

International Monetary Fund (IMF)—Established along with the World Bank (*q.v.*) in 1945, the IMF is a specialized agency affiliated with the United Nations and is responsible for stabilizing international exchange rates and payments. The main business of the IMF is the provision of loans to its members (including industrialized and developing countries) when they experience balance of payments difficulties. These loans frequently carry conditions that require substantial internal economic adjustments by the recipients, most of which are developing countries.

Jawi—Traditional Arabic script of the Malay language.

Kuo-yu or Mandarin—The national Chinese language.

Merdeka—Independence; usually refers to the day of independence of the Federation of Malaya, August 31, 1957.

money supply—The value of cash, demand deposits, and some other forms of deposits at banks that can be converted quickly to cash.

New Economic Policy (NEP)—New government policy announced in the Second Malaysia Plan in 1970. Two major objectives were to eliminate both poverty and the association of ethnicity with economic role.

Orang Asli—Literally, the original peoples; the aboriginal populations of Peninsular Malaysia.

padi—Irrigated rice cultivation.

PAS—Fundamentalist Islamic political group originating in the late 1940s. Known as the Pan-Malayan Party until 1971 when it was renamed the Pan-Malaysia Islamic Party (Parti Islam Sa-Malaysia—PAS). Also known by two other acronyms—PI for Parti Islam and PMPI for Pan-Malaysia Islamic Party.

penghulu—Part-time local official elected or appointed by the state government to serve for five years as principal liaison between district and village.

ringgit (M$)—Basic currency unit, divided into 100 cents. The international exchange value is determined freely in the foreign exchange markets, subject to some intervention by the Central Bank of Malaysia, which sells or buys United States dollars to influence the exchange rate. On average, US$1 was equal to M$2.46 in 1977, M$2.32 in 1978, M$2.19 in 1979, M$2.18 in 1980, M$2.30 in 1981, M$2.34 in 1982, and M$2.32 in 1983.

Rukun Negara—Official state ideology.

Rumi—Malay language script using romanized alphabet.

Shafi'i School—One of the four schools of law of orthodox Islam; the others are the Maliki, the Hanafi, and the Hanbali.

shifting cultivation—Farming characterized by the rotation of fields rather than crops, the use of short cropping periods and long fallow periods, and the maintenance of fertility by allowing natural vegetation to regenerate on fallow land. Clearing of newly or previously cropped land is often accomplished by burning. Also called slash-and-burn, swidden, or land rotation agriculture.

Straits Settlements—Those areas on or around the Malay Peninsula (but also including the island of Labuan off the northern coast of Borneo) that, during the colonial period, were under direct British rule, in contrast to the Malay states. Originally a part of British India, the Straits Settlements were made a crown colony in 1867; they comprised Penang (Province Wellesley [Perai]), Malacca, Singapore, Dindings, and Labuan.

UMNO—United Malays National Organization, the dominant Malay political party.

World Bank—Informal name used to designate a group of three affiliated international institutions: the International Bank for Reconstruction and Development (IBRD); the International Development Association (IDA); and the International Finance Corporation (IFC). The IBRD, established in 1945, has the primary purpose of providing loans to developing countries for productive projects. The IDA, a legally separate loan fund but administered by the staff of the IBRD, was set up in 1960 to furnish credits to the poorest developing countries on much easier terms than those of conventional IBRD loans. The IFC, founded in 1956, supplements the activities of the IBRD through loans and assistance designed specifically to encourage the growth of productive private enterprises in the less developed countries. The president and certain senior officers of the IBRD hold the same positions in the IFC. The three institutions are owned by the governments of the countries that subscribe their capital. To participate in the World Bank group, member states must first belong to the International Monetary Fund (IMF—*q.v.*).

Index

Published Country Studies

(Area Handbook Series)

550–65	Afghanistan	550–151	Honduras
550–98	Albania	550–165	Hungary
550–44	Algeria	550–21	India
550–50	Angola	550–154	Indian Ocean
550–73	Argentina	550–39	Indonesia
550–169	Australia	550–68	Iran
550–176	Austria	550–31	Iraq
550–175	Bangladesh	550–25	Israel
550–170	Belgium	550–182	Italy
550–66	Bolivia	550–69	Ivory Coast
550–20	Brazil	550–177	Jamaica
550–168	Bulgaria	550–30	Japan
550–61	Burma	550–34	Jordan
550–83	Burundi	550–56	Kenya
550–50	Cambodia	550–81	Korea, North
550–177	Cameroon	550–41	Korea, South
550–159	Chad	550–58	Laos
550–77	Chile	550–24	Lebanon
550–60	China	550–38	Liberia
550–63	China, Republic of	550–85	Libya
550–26	Colombia	550–172	Malawi
550–91	Congo	550–45	Malaysia
550–90	Costa Rica	550–161	Mauritania
550–152	Cuba	550–79	Mexico
550–22	Cyprus	550–76	Mongolia
550–158	Czechoslovakia	550–49	Morocco
550–54	Dominican Republic	550–64	Mozambique
550–52	Ecuador	550–35	Nepal, Bhutan and Sikkim
550–43	Egypt	550–88	Nicaragua
550–150	El Salvador	550–157	Nigeria
550–28	Ethiopia	550–94	Oceania
550–167	Finland	550–48	Pakistan
550–155	Germany, East	550–46	Panama
550–173	Germany, Fed. Rep. of	550–156	Paraguay
550–153	Ghana	550–185	Persian Gulf States
550–87	Greece	550–42	Peru
550–78	Guatemala	550–72	Philippines
550–174	Guinea	550–162	Poland
550–82	Guyana	550–181	Portugal
550–164	Haiti	550–160	Romania

550–84 Rwanda
550–51 Saudi Arabia
550–70 Senegal
550–180 Sierra Leone
550–184 Singapore

550–86 Somalia
550–93 South Africa
550–95 Soviet Union
550–179 Spain
550–96 Sri Lanka (Ceylon)

550–27 Sudan
550–47 Syria
550–62 Tanzania
550–53 Thailand
550–178 Trinidad and Tobago

550–89 Tunisia
550–80 Turkey
550–74 Uganda
550–97 Uruguay
550–71 Venezuela

550–57 Vietnam, North
550–55 Vietnam, South
550–183 Yemens, The
550–99 Yugoslavia
550–67 Zaïre

550–75 Zambia
550–171 Zimbabwe

☆U.S. GOVERNMENT PRINTING OFFICE: 1985 -0- 461-018 (10016)